FRIENDSHIP MATTERS

COMMUNICATION AND SOCIAL ORDER

An Aldine de Gruyter Series of Texts and Monographs

Series Editor

David R. Maines, Wayne State University

Advisory Editors

Bruce Gronbeck • Peter K. Manning • William K. Rawlins

FRIENDSHIP MATTERS
Communication, Dialectics, and the Life Course

William K. Rawlins

ALDINE DE GRUYTER

New York

About the Author

William K. Rawlins is Associate Professor of Communication at Purdue University, where he teaches courses in interpersonal and relational communication, communication theory, and qualitative/interpretive research methods. Since receiving his Ph.D. from Temple University, he has published extensively about the unique challenges and dialectical tensions of communicating in friendships.

ALDINE DE GRUYTER
A division of Walter de Gruyter, Inc.
200 Saw Mill River Road
Hawthorne, New York 10532

The paper used in this publication meets the minimum requirements of American National Standard for information Sciences—Permanence of Paper for Printed Library Materials, ANSI Z39.48–1984.

∞

Library of Congress Cataloging-in-Publication Data
Rawlins, William K., 1952–
    Friendship matters : communication, dialectics, and the life course/William K. Rawlins.
       p. cm. — (Communication and social order)
    Includes bibliographical references and index.
    ISBN 0–202–30403–5 (cloth: alk. paper). — ISBN 0–202–30404–3 (pbk.: alk. paper)
    1. Friendship—United States—Sociological aspects.
2. Interpersonal relations.   3. Life cycle, Human.   I. Title.
II. Series.
HM132.5.R38   1992
302.3′4—dc20   91–30676
                                                CIP

Manufactured in the United States of America

10 9 8 7 6 5 4 3 2

To Sandy

Contents

7 Illustrative Analysis: The Communicative Management of Young Adult Friendships

8 Adult Friendships

9 Illustrative Analysis: Circumstances of Adult Friendships

10 Friendships During Later Adulthood

Acknowledgments

I would like to thank several people for their contributions to this work. First, I am grateful to the participants in the studies, whose thoughts and feelings about friendship inform every page of this book, and whose voices give it life. I also appreciate the following students' assistance in securing participants and conducting and transcribing interviews: Liza Chen, Catherine Curtis, Debbie Damsky, Lisa Dillon, Laura Haynes, Andrea Ingrilli, Linda Laitner, Mary Beth Logsdon, Alisha Maes, Pam Malone, Laura Myer, Holly Jean Nachbar, Greg Nixon, Amie North, and Patrick Taylor. Melissa Holl was especially helpful in my work with adolescents, as were Lora Reed, Pam Secklin, and Kathy Werking in my research on later adulthood. Conversing with students—hearing them challenge notions of interpersonal communication and friendship and pose new ways of seeing the world—constantly renews my commitment to teaching.

I appreciate the Purdue University XL Summer Faculty Grant that supported my writing during the summer of 1989, and the diligent preparation of this manuscript by Diana Cable, Beverly Robinson, and Liz Whitworth. Earlier versions of parts of Chapters 1 and 6 have appeared in "A Dialectical Analysis of the Tensions, Functions, and Strategic Challenges of Communication in Young Adult Friendships," in *Communication Yearbook 12*, edited by James A. Anderson and published by Sage Publications, Inc. in 1989. Likewise, parts of Chapter 4 appeared earlier in "Rehearsing the Margins of Adulthood: The Communicative Management of Adolescent Friendships," in *Life-Span Communication: Normative Issues*, edited by Jon F. Nussbaum, and published by Lawrence Erlbaum Associates in 1989. Finally, brief portions of Chapters 4 and 5 appeared in "Adolescents' Interactions with Parents and Friends: Dialectics of Temporal Perspective and Evaluation," by William K. Rawlins and Melissa R. Holl, in the *Journal of Social and Personal Relationships* published by Sage Publications, Inc. in 1988. I thank these publishers for their permission to use this material.

I value the timely sentiments and helpful insights of persons too numerous to mention who have talked with and supported me through-out the writing of this book. In particular, my colleagues at Purdue University's Department of Communication have continually provided spirited, scholarly interaction. Further, I especially thank Ed Shockley, Lainey Jenks, my brothers Rocky, Ron, and Terry, and their families, Jack and Nancy Pollitt, and my Mom and Dad. I am grateful to David Maines for encouraging me from the beginning to write this book, and for listening to, reading, and helping me develop my ideas throughout the project in a spirit of compassionate objectivity. I am deeply thankful to my mentor and dear friend, Art Bochner, for his careful and critical perusal of the entire manuscript, as well as for his many years of inspiration, conversation, and friendship.

Working on this book has significantly shaped our family life over the past three years. I thank my son, Brian, and my daughter, Shelley, for their encouragement, discussion, and lively interest in its progress, as well as for their bright-eyed suggestions of picnics, play, and watching movies together. My wife, Sandy, has contributed generously to this endeavor at all stages—from its initial conception, through gathering and critiquing relevant literature, to commenting on and scrupulously editing multiple drafts. She is an abiding source of energy, expertise, affection, and understanding. We are lifelong friends.

Introduction

Every experience is a two-edged sword. It contributes to the strength of the relationship. But it is also an inherent danger.

Ron, interview participant, age 29

The title of this book, *Friendship Matters*, can be read in various ways. In one sense, it asserts that friendship is regarded as a significant and important aspect of social life in American culture. This sense of friendship raises questions including: How? Why? and For whom does friendship matter? Accordingly, an alternative reading of the two words as a noun phrase implies issues of concern and contention regarding friendship, and much of this book is devoted to scrutinizing these matters as well. The contrasting yet interdependent meanings of these words model the interpenetration of social actions, interpretations, and contexts characterizing the dialectical investigation of friendship presented in the following pages.

As of the late 1970s when I was a graduate student, social scientists had devoted minimal explicit attention to friendship. With a few exceptions, most work addressed friendship in the context of social attraction studies, emphasizing personality variables or residential propinquity. Friendship also appeared as a residual category of social participation in demographic and sociometric studies, contrasting friendships (often implied by the questionnaire choice, "other") with family and work relationships.

Two developments challenged these limiting conceptions and enriched this picture. First, scholars in a variety of disciplines began examining the unique character of friendship. I was particularly stimulated and informed by Robert Paine's (1969) landmark essay, "In Search of Friendship: An Exploratory Analysis in 'Middle Class' Culture," which I find still excites students' curiosity about friendship. Also inspirational to me was Brain's cross-cultural treatise, *Friends and Lovers*

1

(1976), as well as insightful discussions by Douvan and Adelson (1966), Suttles (1970), Kurth (1970), and Hess (1972).

Moreover, various thinkers voiced the need for a more developmental perspective on the emergence, maintenance, and decline of interpersonal relationships (Bochner, 1978, 1984; Knapp, 1978; Baxter, 1984). This view assumes that what brings people together may not be what keeps them together. Static conceptions of relationships say little about what makes friendships "work" or why their continued interaction holds mutual significance for them. Duck and his colleagues (Duck & Gilmour, 1981) emphasized that the dyadic development of relationships also shaped and reflected the constraints and opportunities of different periods in the life course. Even so, few heuristic findings or integrated theory existed regarding the communication involved in forming, maintaining, and dissolving friendships across life.

Since my graduate school days, I have been captivated by the nuances of friendship. Focusing first on young adults, I was struck by the communicative dilemmas posed by the contradictory requirements of their friendships (Rawlins, 1983a,b, 1989). As I studied the case histories of enduring young adult bonds, I became interested in the social predicaments and practices surrounding their formation during adolescence. Consequently, I began investigating adolescent friendships (Rawlins & Holl, 1987, 1988), which, in turn, involved examining the literature on children's friendships. Meanwhile, in conducting courses regarding communication in friendships throughout life, I perceived that the burgeoning research on friendship across diverse disciplines understates its dialectical tensions and the necessity of their ongoing communicative management. As a result, I decided to write a book that would synthesize available work in a way that emphasizes the situated, interactive, and dialectical nature of friendship.

In this book I develop a broad conceptual perspective for tracing and probing the varieties, tensions, and functions of friendship over the life course. I explore how friendships are situated vis-à-vis other personal and social relationships at given points in time, how they are managed communicatively, and how they influence and reflect continually evolving senses of self and social participation. My concern is with the communicative conduct of friendships in light of their changing and persistent forms and functions throughout life. I argue that friendship involves inherent dialectical tensions: (1) as a specific category of relationship within middle-class American culture, (2) in the actual communicative practices occurring between friends, and (3) within and across developmental periods of the life cycle. Consequently, I conceive the formation, maintenance, and dissolution of friendships as presenting continual challenges to communicators. As relationships negotiated within networks of involvements, friendships are ongoing communicative achievements often pursued in the face of incompatible requirements. Emphasizing these notions places communication and a dialectical perspective in a conversation about relational and social life that has been dominated by individualists (psychologists) and social structuralists (sociologists).

My account synthesizes findings from a program of theoretical and empirical research spanning the past 12 years. I have studied conceptual essays and research reports regarding friendship from an array of social disciplines. In addition, I have investigated open-ended, in-depth interviews with over 100 persons, including adolescents, and young, middle-aged, and older adults. Identical interview protocols guided the interactions with all participants within each age group, although each individual's specific concerns and emphases were discussed further as they arose. While all participants were questioned about meanings, expectations, communicative practices, activities, and important events of their friendships, each age group was also asked about issues and social circumstances characterizing their specific stage in the life course.

For the most part, I have intentionally taken the interviewees' words at face value, assuming a hermeneutic stance of recovery and understanding as opposed to suspicion (Ricoeur, 1970). I appreciate the participants' generosity in sharing their thoughts and feelings about friendship and do not typically question their sincerity. Throughout the book, therefore, I minimally alter their words in attempting to display and analyze what Geertz (1976) calls their "experience-near concepts." He elaborates:

> An experience-near concept, is, roughly, one which someone—a patient, a subject, in our case an informant—might himself naturally and effortlessly use to define what he or his fellows see, feel, think, imagine, and so on, and would readily understand when similarly applied by others.
>
> People use experience-near concepts spontaneously, unselfconsciously, as it were colloquially; they do not, except fleetingly and on occasion recognize that there are any "concepts" involved at all. That is what experience-near means—that ideas and the realities they inform are naturally and indissolubly bound up together. (pp. 223–224)

Even so, to protect the privacy and anonymity of my participants, I have used pseudonyms and disguised personal information and locations throughout the book.

Supplementing these interviews, my wife, Sandy, and I assembled an extensive collection of fictional literature, that is, novels, plays, and short stories, written for and about children, adolescents, and adults of all ages, depicting the interactions of friends in diverse circumstances throughout the characters' lives. These works were also examined for their insights about how the benefits, challenges, and communicative practices of friendship change and remain the same across the life course in light of various dialectical tensions and evolving relational configurations.

I want to cultivate conversation and interplay among extant social scientific and humanistic research on friendship, people's verbal descriptions and the actual discourse of friends, fictional representations of friends facing situated exigencies, my experiences and opinions as a person/writer/social investigator, and those of the reader(s) of this book. Accordingly, I have composed the work as a sequence of paired chapters dealing with particular developmental periods of the life cycle. In each initial chapter I delineate ideal–typical social configurations, features, and predicaments of managing friendship during a given developmental era according to available social scientific research. A companion chapter then illustrates and peruses further the difficulties and rewards of friendships during that era using the words of real participants and/or fictional excerpts. Both the research syntheses and the illustrative chapters address and reflect gender-linked patterns of same-sex and cross-sex friendships.

This method of presentation juxtaposes and compares the voices of lived experience and of literary depictions with the abstract, modal trends observed and reported in traditional social scientific analyses of friendship. The illustrative chapters seek to vivify and dramatize rather than verify concepts, and to connect them with actual persons' words and experiences, and imagined individuals' enactments of meaningful episodes. I attempt to portray the various degrees of involvement, enjoyment, choice, risk, ambivalence, ambiguity, practicality, and emotion of friendships in negotiating self-conceptions and human relationships within given yet revisable social matrices.

Chapter 1 presents a dialectical perspective on communication in friendships, highlighting contextual and interactional dialectics shaping friendships across the life course. Chapters 2 and 3 examine children's friendships, analyzing and exemplifying their importance in developing social cognition, learning and practicing systems of justice and fairness, negotiating relationships of equality, managing disagreements, and making the transition from an episodic conception of friendships to one that recognizes the possibility of enduring bonds. Chapters 4 and 5 address the problems and possibilities of friendships as adolescents develop their identities and personal values, learn about intimacy, begin separating from their families of origin, and deal with multiple social contexts and evaluative standards. Chapters 6 and 7 investigate the expanding and contracting significance of friendships during young adulthood as individuals negotiate choices regarding education, livelihood, marriage, children, civic involvement, and recreation. These pursuits display and influence self-conceptions, articulate networks of relationships reflecting emerging values and priorities, and generate constraints patterning the forms and functions of friendships. Chapters 8 and 9 examine and illustrate the practices, dilemmas, and contingent position of friendships for middle-aged adults within the larger social orders of family, work, and community. Chapters 10 and 11 articulate and exemplify the continuities and discontinuities of friendship choices, modes, meanings, and activities during the later adult years. The final chapter takes stock of patterns and themes noted throughout the book and explores their implications for theorizing and practicing friendship.

One important limitation of this book is its concentration on middle-class Americans' experiences of friendship across the life course. Acknowledging their similar focus, Bellah and his colleagues (1985) observe:

> For the past hundred years or so, the middle class, in the modern sense of the term, has so dominated our culture that neither a genuinely upper-class nor a genuinely working-class culture has fully appeared. Everyone in the United States thinks largely in middle-class categories, even when they are inappropriate. (p. viii)

Reflecting and perpetuating this prevailing cultural orientation, most social scientific research on friendship involves primarily middle-class participants. And by conducting a conceptual meta-analysis of scholars' diverse data sets and research reports and describing overall trends, my general account displays modal tendencies, even when actual individuals' voices and specific stories or studies provide counterpoints. Thus, as an overarching chronicle of friendship across the life course, it constitutes a normative one.

The frustrations and delights of friendship emerge during childhood and continue throughout life. Despite their virtues and satisfactions, friendships are often vexing relationships, intermingling each person's expectations, and public and private responsibilities and loyalties in ways difficult to resolve. In attempting to describe such ongoing dialectical challenges, I hope the book facilitates reflection, examination, celebration, and critique of the reader's own assumptions and practices of friendship and the personal circumstances and social worlds that they presuppose and help to shape.

Chapter 1

A Dialectical Perspective on Communication in Friendship

I begin by describing the dialectical perspective informing this analysis of the communication of friends. Then I examine in depth two sets of dialectical principles inherent in the communicative management of friendship. *Contextual* dialectics include the dialectic of the private and the public, and the dialectic of the ideal and the real. *Interactional* dialectics involve the dialectic of the freedom to be independent and the freedom to be dependent, the dialectic of affection and instrumentality, the dialectic of judgment and acceptance, and the dialectic of expressiveness and protectiveness. These principles are employed throughout this book in developing an intelligible frame for understanding the practices and predicaments of communicating in friendships at various moments in the life course.

A Dialectical Perspective

Totality, contradiction, motion, and praxis are basic elements of the dialectical perspective employed here.[1] Analyzed as a totality, communicating in friendships involves the constant interconnection and reciprocal influence of multiple individual, interpersonal, and social factors. Contradictions and dialectical tensions are central features of a dialectical analysis. These antagonistic yet interdependent aspects of communication between friends form the pulse of routine as well as volatile and transitional moments of such dyads. Motion, activity, and change are thus fundamental properties of social life in a dialectical perspective, and the present state of any relationship is considered an incessant achievement. Finally, the concept of praxis describes the human communicator as an ongoing producer and product of his or her

7

choices within an encompassing cultural matrix. In this book individuals are depicted as conscious, active selectors of possible choices from a field that is partially conceived by them, partially negotiated with others, and partially determined by social and natural factors outside of their purview. The choices a person makes throughout life in concrete circumstances simultaneously engender and restrict options.

From this perspective, configurations of contradictions compose and organize friendships through an ongoing process of change across the life course. However, questions arise: What appear to be the principal or secondary contradictions or aspects of contradictions constituting specific friendships? What contradictions are created by the friends' attempts to manage strategically the incompatible requirements of their relationship? What contradictions shape or reflect a friendship's position vis-à-vis other social spheres, such as family and work settings, and larger cultural orders? Such arrangements are clarified by examining how friendships are situated hierarchically and developmentally in social space over time. Studying the synchrony or asynchrony of temporal sequences also provides perspective on the contradictions patterning friendships. Riegel (1976) argues that synchronization is "the most critical issue in dialectical theory" (p. 693). He views asynchronies as responsible for most crises in human development and resultant change. Accordingly, short- and long-term changes in individuals and their relationships must be examined in relation to both rapid and drawn-out life course and cultural developments.

The time grain of these various processes and the extent of their coordination or disorder are key factors in a dialectical analysis. Thus dialectical inquiries are intrinsically historical investigations concerned with the developmental and historical specificity of the process in question (Rossi, 1983). How are human beings consciously acting in this concrete situation and what implications do their actions have for the ongoing constitution of their social worlds in which friendships function as a particular part?

Dialectical Principles Inherent in the
Communicative Management of Friendship

Communicating within friendships involves inherent dialectical features. Two broad analytical classes, contextual and interactional dialectics, are examined next, though in actuality these principles extensively interconnect in the communication of friends.

Contextual Dialectics

Contextual dialectics derive from the place of friendship in the prevailing social order of American culture. They describe cultural conceptions that frame and permeate interaction within specific friendships yet are conceivably subject to revision as a result of significant changes in everyday practices. I will consider the dialectic of the private and the public and the dialectic of the ideal and real, while suggesting their theoretical and practical interdependence.

The Dialectic of the Private and the Public. This principle articulates the tensions produced as experiences and behaviors of friendship transcend private and public realms. The interweaving of these generic, discursive contexts presents significant challenges and opportunities requiring various strategies of communicators.

Within the observable public matrix of American interpersonal relationships, friendship occupies a marginal position. Unlike kin, it is not a certifiable blood relationship. It lacks the religious and legal warrants and the culturally sanctioned procreative function of marriage. And it is generally regarded differently from the possessive and sexual nature of romantic love (Brain, 1976). Nor is friendship objectively defined by economic contracts as are work or professional relationships. Basically, friendship has no clear normative status within publicly constituted hierarchies of role relationships; yet it may compete with, complement, substitute for, or fuse with these other types of social bonds (Hess, 1972). In short, the degree of public recognition of friendship as a category of interpersonal relationship renders it an "institutionalized non-institution" (Paine, 1969, p. 514).

Contrasting with friendship's vagrant position in the public realm is its peculiar moral character as a private bond. Friendship cannot be imposed on people; it is an ongoing human association voluntarily developed and privately negotiated. Consequently, the rights and obligations of friendships can transcend formal, objective, or material institutional requirements and statuses (Paine, 1969). This autonomous quality makes friendship potentially more "pure" than are relationships governed by wider social structures like labor and power, especially if the friends experience those structures as threatening essential human values (Eisenstadt, 1974). Disturbingly, however, sinister, nihilistic, or violent values may also characterize a given friendship's private morality, as, for example, when two friends carry out a suicide pact. Appropriate behavior is determined within the friendship and is upheld principally by each individual's affection for and/or loyalty and commitment to the other. Personal responsibility and trust are the lynchpins of this private order, which may be as evanescent as human caprice or as enduring as human dedication allows.

In its dialectical character, combining public marginality and private morality, friendship weaves in and out of the larger social order like a "double agency," fulfilling both individual and social functions. Sometimes friends wear "feathers" borrowed from other culturally sanctioned roles so that their relationship is viewed publicly as acceptable (Parsons, 1915). For example, this costuming occurs frequently in adult cross-sex friendships in which one or both parties are married to others (Rawlins, 1982). Such a publicly acknowledged cross-sex friendship may threaten the culturally endorsed marriage relationship in others' eyes, whereas defining the bond as a professional one would not. Ironically, although this "disguised" cross-sex friendship might be pursued primarily as a self-serving release from the pressures of an overly constricting marriage, it may function simultaneously to strengthen that socially favored bond.

In contrast, cultivating the private morality and manners of a friendship within, for example, ostensibly political or professional relationships often allows for the special treatment of one's friend or standards of evaluation that differ from public statements. Such arrangements may result in friends as happier clients or constituents, or even more valid appraisals of an individual's performance because of the added concern and insight of one's friend. However, "greasing the wheels" in this fashion can also undermine fair practice and publicly accountable procedures.

Thus the liberating potential of friendship for two individuals might be regarded as its subversive potential from a broader social perspective. Conversely, behaviors that civic-minded people could view as preserving public decorum, friends might perceive as stultifying their freedom of action and expression. Because friendships are constrained but not determined by public roles or institutions, tensions between public and private comportment persist. A given friendship may duplicate culturally encouraged actions but for idiosyncratic reasons. And some partners may conduct themselves in the personalized manner of friends, but clearly for publicly redeemable purposes. The ongoing rhetorical challenge to friends, therefore, is to develop and share private definitions and practices while orchestrating desired social perceptions of their relationship (Paine, 1969).

The dialectic of the private and the public delineates a critical facet of managing friendship. These terms not only reference realms of actual behavior and experience but also comprise interpretive categories used rhetorically by commentators in the service of moral visions (Wells, 1985). Different cultural moments privilege one sphere over the other.

During the reign of an "ideology of intimacy," for example, private and personal relationships like friendship are celebrated for their potential to confirm individuals' self-conceptions (Sennett, 1978). From this ideology, Suttles (1970) argued that a primary basis of friendship was negotiated remissions from public expectations. He observed, "Friendship demands a verifiable self and it cannot be one that complacently complies with public propriety" (p. 107). Still, as Naegele (1958) commented, such an exclusive conception of friendship negates certain readings of the meanings of democracy. Accordingly, in more public-spirited times, Bellah, Madsen, Sullivan, Swidler, and Tipton (1985) have praised civic friendships for facilitating the larger community by serving the social order and derided private relationships for their "therapeutic" cast.

Thus friendship's role as a double agency is categorically vulnerable in American culture. Within a particular dyad, a friend can be criticized or congratulated for asserting a public or private aspect of the relationship in a given situation. Simultaneously, depending on the cultural mood of the day, that same person may be, in contrast, publicly condemned or praised for the same actions. This private/public dialectic interacts with the ideals and realities of communicating in friendship.

The Dialectic of the Ideal and the Real. This dialectic formulates the interplay between the abstract ideals and expectations often associated with friendship and the nettlesome realities or unexpected rewards of actual communication between friends. Indeed, refined and idealized images and forms of friendship develop in the public domain at given historical junctures and are culturally transmitted. Therefore, despite its marginal status vis-à-vis other social roles, people are socialized into normative expectations regarding certain ideal conceptions and practices of friendship (Sampson, 1977; Brown, 1981).

The following characteristics are common to ideal–typical descriptions of friendship as a close dyadic relationship in our culture. First, *friendships are essentially voluntary*. People make and unmake friendships of their own choosing and according to their own standards; outside sources cannot impose friendship on two persons. If individual choice is ruled out, friendship is precluded (Naegele, 1958). Second, related to its voluntary nature, *friendship is a personal relationship* that is privately negotiated between particular individuals. One views a friend as a unique individual and not as a representative of a certain group or class, what Suttles (1970) calls the "person-qua-person" orientation of friendship. Third, *a spirit of equality pervades friendship*. Although friendship may develop between individuals of different status, ability, attractiveness, or age, some facet of the relationship functions as a leveler. Friends tend to emphasize the personal attributes and styles of interaction that make them appear more or less equal to each other. Stressing equality minimizes the risk of exploitation in the relationship (Fiebert & Fiebert, 1969; Kurth, 1970). Next, *mutual involvement characterizes friendships*. The bonds of friendship result from the collaboration of two individuals in constructing a shared social reality. This interpersonal reality evolves out of and furthers mutual acceptance and support, trust and confidence, dependability and assistance, and discussion of thoughts and feelings. Friendships comprise ongoing, mutual achievements (Harre, 1977). Finally, as a voluntary, personal, equal, and mutual relationship, *friendship implies affective ties*. Positive feeling, caring, and concern for the other, the touchstones of companionship, exist between friends. And while friends may feel profound love for each other, the love of friendship is usually distinguished from sexual or romantic loving, with their overtones of possessiveness and exclusivity. Even so, relationships involving these latter forms of loving may also include or aspire to the ideal–typical characteristics of friendship as well (Brain, 1976; Rawlins, 1982).

Of course, the extent to which the above combination of qualities is possible, encouraged, or actually practiced by friends depends on their encompassing social circumstances. For instance, Naegele (1958), maintaining that a dialectical relationship between "norms of personal and impersonal conduct" produces a given epoch's guidelines for both types of interpersonal activity, observes, "Indeed, ideals of impersonal relations are necessary for the elaboration of our kind of ideals of personal relations" (p. 236). If a given era encourages less reserve with relative strangers, heightened strategies for revealing oneself to another may be endorsed to distinguish friends. When people are encouraged to be friendly with everybody, certain practices become necessary for indicating friendship. In contrast, if the norms of impersonal communication promote distance and considerable politeness, more personalized dyads may deviate from rigid stylized expectations without exposing significantly private thoughts and feelings. As mentioned earlier, these practices will receive differential endorsement in terms of a particular cultural epoch's valuations of the public and private spheres, and the appropriate communicative strategies for linking them (Rawlins, 1985).

In addition, Liebow (1967) argues that the public and private realities impinging on the tenuous nature of friendship as a cultural double agency result in its frequent idealization. He states:

> Lacking depth in both past and present, friendship is easily uprooted by the tug of economic or psychological self-interest or by external forces acting against it. The recognition of this weakness, coupled with the

importance of friendship as a source of security and self-esteem, is surely
a principal source of the impulse to romanticize relationships. (pp.
206–207)

In his view, idealized images of friendship derive from, yet serve to
mute, concerns about its sometimes harsh situational realities and
vulnerabilities.

Whether it is championed as a vital, idiosyncratic haven from a
humdrum, bureaucratized social order or simply endorsed as a human-
izing complement to a complacent conventional society, the notion of
friendship retains idealistic overtones. The Western conception of this
bond, Van Vlissingen (1970) maintains, reflects a constant from ancient
Greek thought, "In order for a friendship to last it must be permeated
with ethical concerns" (p. 230). Thus, *as a cultural ideal, friendship appears
to be a categorical repository for the hope of a mutually edifying moral covenant
voluntarily negotiated between people.*

The discursive practices of friendship both manage and regenerate the
tensions between its ideal and real forms. According to Bloch (1971), the
terminology of relationships can pivot between "moral and tactical
meanings." The moral meaning of friendship terms indexes its idealistic
connotations in our cultural system of values. Describing someone as a
friend or speaking in the name of friendship draws on cherished
categorical notions. In contrast, the tactical meaning of friendship labels
uses their moral associations in the interest of transforming social
situations and strategically defining certain types of relationships. As a
result, the specific meanings of these friendship terms derive from how
they are operationalized in given cases.

Actual discourse within and about friendships appears to blend moral
and tactical meanings in constituting a range of relationships that runs
the gamut from private to public in scope and responsibility, and from
idealistic to realistic in primary impulse. Thus the word friend itself has
multiple meanings, including moral ones, and can be employed tacti-
cally to reflect changing social circumstances and various definitions of
self and others. For example, the term may be used to acknowledge
someone who has fulfilled various expectations personally or culturally
associated with friendship, to recognize an affectionate and loyal other,
or to ingratiate oneself to another person. The word may be withdrawn
under contrasting conditions to emphasize social distance (Jacobson,
1976). Maines (1981) states that the unspecified use of the word friend
renders it "a catchall term which is conventionally understood and
recognized as having no fixed referent outside of the situation itself" (p.
172).

However, the prevalence of distinctions between "real friends" versus

"casual acquaintances" and the preoccupations with determining gradations of friendship register the problematic aspects of managing
friendships in the face of such situational definitions and the persistence
of and need for moral meanings of the term. A variety of expressions
and nicknames are typically developed to indicate degrees of intimacy
and the communicative aspects of relationships (Knapp, Ellis, &
Williams, 1980). People reflect cultural values in developing core conceptions of what they variously term "best" or "real" friendship and
then identify and rank other relationships according to their achievement of its defining attributes (Rawlins & Holl, 1987; Rawlins, Leibowitz, & Bochner, 1986). Investigators have shown that these categories are
rather resilient and are preserved by certain strategies. For example, a
person who actually achieves a "best" friendship typically will view it as
continuing even without identifiable rewards or interaction (Allan, 1979;
Rose & Serafica, 1986). Yet, should a best friendship unequivocally end,
persons may decide that it could not really have been a best friendship
in the first place. In both cases, one revises the perceptions of a given
friendship while maintaining the ideals of friendship (Allan, 1979; Rose
& Serafica, 1986).

Consequently, although friendship persists as an enduring cultural
ideal, its purer forms are frequently experienced as elusive personal
realities. There may be great disparity between its cultural connotations
and its meanings deriving from the concrete interaction of particular
friends. This situation occurs, Paine (1969) argues, because "the highest
ideals of friendship are (a) proclaimed as realizable and (b) not protected
institutionally" (p. 521). As a result, aspiring to an ideal friendship
comprises an ongoing challenge for specific individuals across constantly changing personal and social circumstances. To complicate
matters, measures taken to preserve certain prized aspects of friendship
may subvert other cherished values. For example, a person may
strategically breach the code of honesty between friends in order to
protect the other's sensitivity about an issue (Rawlins, 1983b). Paine
(1969) observes, "The ideals of friendship are likely to be spoiled without
such protection. Of course, the fact that the protection is necessary
suggests that the ideals are, in some measure, factitious values" (p. 521).

A dialectical conception maintains that any social formation is revealed through and constituted by the endless interweaving of idealistic
and realistic factors (Ball, 1979). Such a view regards the ideals of
friendship not as "factitious values" in light of concrete limitations but as
guiding principles shaping and shaped by the actual practices of friends.
Communicating within friendship is an active process; it is praxis
occurring between specific people at a given time and place. Friends
may attempt to communicate in ways that conform with the ideals of

their era, but in doing so, they create and encounter real constraints and contradictions. The manner in which they handle these exigencies may revise or ratify the original ideals. Indeed, a culturally patterned set of expectations is associated with friendship. But these patterns are produced and reproduced through a dialectical interplay of ideal conceptions and real constraints across a continuum of private and public discursive realms in the actual communication of a variety of types of friends. Let us examine some dialectical patterns of interaction identified within friendships.

Interactional Dialectics

Perhaps the most ubiquitous concern for communication scholars is codification, the relationships among self's and others' behaviors and the meanings self and others assign to those behaviors. This practice comprises a vital concern in negotiating friendships as well. Friendships are potentially fraught with ambiguity, both in the friends' attempts to interpret each other's words and actions and the significance assigned to their behavior by third parties and/or society at large.

Ambiguity in friendship is often compounded by ambivalence (Brain, 1976; Harré, 1977). The intermittent delights or disruptions of fulfilling or disappointing an array of publicly and/or privately produced ideals and realities within a given friendship can threaten stable interpretations of even the most straightforward actions. An important challenge to friends, therefore, is to behave and to interpret behaviors in a manner that preserves an assumption of benevolent as opposed to malevolent intentions underpinning each other's actions. To perceive good intentions constitutes an "insurance policy" for the relationship when contradictory conditions may result in ostensibly negative behavior by one's friend. Accordingly, communicating within friendship involves a constant interaction between interpretive and behavioral practices to maintain a mutual definition of the relationship as friendship.

In what follows, I consider four dialectical principles that organize, yet compose, ongoing challenges and antagonistic choices in the practical management of communication sustaining friendships. As such, they constitute conceptual and interactional structures informing what ideally/typically occurs in friendships. Though these principles may or may not consciously inform the actual behavior of friends, they are useful as interpretive tools for understanding the communicative predicaments of friendships. They include the dialectic of the freedom to be independent and the freedom to be dependent, the dialectic of affection and instrumentality, the dialectic of judgment and acceptance, and the dialectic of expressiveness and protectiveness.

The Dialectic of the Freedom to be Independent and the Freedom to Be Dependent. As I have stressed, in American culture free choice and voluntary action are definitive qualities of friendship; people remain friends because both individuals choose to do so. The dialectic of the freedom to be independent and the freedom to be dependent conceptualizes the patterns of availability and copresence negotiated in light of this voluntary essence of friendships (Rawlins, 1983a).

Basically, in forming a friendship, each friend grants the other a pair of contradictory prerogatives. The freedom to be independent is the liberty to pursue one's life and individual interests without the friend's interference or help. In contrast, the freedom to be dependent is the privilege of calling on or relying on one's friend in times of need. Both liberties engender choices for self and other. Yet, exercising individual options of independent or dependent behavior also poses de facto contingencies restricting the other's choices. For example, if self innocently plans a vacation at a time when other requests assistance, their options collide. Ironically, the issue may become, who has more freedom to be constrained by the other's choice?

Clearly, in granting each other these freedoms, friends cocreate relational patterns of interaction that may foster or curtail their individual liberties. Of course, each friendship emphasizes different aspects of this dialectic which organize the relationship in particular ways (Rawlins, 1983a). Some pairs value their privilege of depending on each other so much that either person's independent behavior is infrequent and resented. Conversely, other friendships are characterized by a pattern of such mutual independence that dependence is primarily ritually enacted by "touching base" or is actualized only when there is serious need. And, as we shall see, these patterns derive from the friends' overall interpersonal situations and positions in the life course.

Despite typical and predictable practices established in a given friendship, the contradictory nature of these freedoms can make it difficult to know for certain whether a given pattern is affirming or weakening the friendship. A primarily dependent relationship may unwittingly destroy the individuals' capacities for independent action that give friendship its liberating quality. Choosing dependence may become a conscription. Further, independent friends must renew contact to be sure that they are still involved in a friendship. Perhaps one of them has changed careers or fundamental values and views encounters with the other as too limiting and/or undesirable. However, the freedoms are based on mutually contingent choices by both parties that allow for multiple functional arrangements as well as corruptions. Elsewhere, I have detailed possible modes of prohibiting or obligating independent or dependent behavior in friendship as the partners either grant or receive these liberties (Rawlins, 1983a).

To summarize, the ongoing negotiation and enactment of both contradictory freedoms is necessary to preserve friendship though it is difficult to specify their precise functional interrelationship. I term them conjunctive freedoms for two related reasons. First, each freedom is valued in friendship when negotiated in connection with the other. Independence from a friend is appreciated when one retains the option of depending on him or her. Likewise, the privilege of depending on someone is prized when one's autonomy is also preserved. Second, sharing these two freedoms in combination serves to connect friends. Complete independence means no relationship at all, and total dependence constrains both persons by subverting their individual integrity. The ongoing mutual enactment of some composite of these freedoms is essential to maintain a bond of friendship.

The Dialectic of Affection and Instrumentality. This principle formulates the interpenetrated nature of caring for a friend as an end-in-itself and/or as a means-to-an-end. Various communicative quandaries revolve around qualifying one's expressions of need for a friend within the tensions produced by this dialectic.

Few people would question the importance of affection in friendship, and several authors include it as one of the defining characteristics of such bonds (Paine, 1969; Kurth, 1970; Brain, 1976; Rawlins, 1982). Empirical research also attests to its significance across the course of friendships. After surveying a variety of behavioral and attitudinal indices in a longitudinal study of friendship development and maintenance, Hays (1984) concludes, "It may be affection behavior which is primarily responsible for both stimulating the initial formation of a friendship . . . and maintaining that friendship despite environmental constraints and periods of non-interaction" (p. 94). A primary basis for distinguishing between "real friendship" and "casual acquaintance" in Williams's (1959) investigation of suburban friendships involves the extent of "affective involvement" and "norms of affectivity rather than neutrality" (p. 7). Finally, affection figures significantly in Rose and Serafica's (1986) examination of hypothetical and actual strategies for maintaining and ending a variety of friendships and for discriminating "best" and "close" from "casual" ones. Such findings reinforce notions of friendship dating back to Aristotle's friendships of virtue that stress noninstrumental "person-qua-person" caring for one's friend (Suttles, 1970).

Instrumentality, using one's friend to benefit self, receives far less endorsement as an attribute of friendship. In fact, as readily as affection is associated with "true" friendships, instrumentality tends to connote "false" ones. Aristotle argues that utilitarian bonds are inferior and less constant, stating, "Those who are friends for the sake of utility part when the advantage is at an end; for they were lovers not of each other but of profit" (1980, p. 198). From this perspective a primarily useful conception of friends defines friendship in a highly specialized and somewhat tainted way.

In actuality, drawing a sharp boundary between friendships based on affection and on instrumentality comprises a false dichotomy (Paine, 1970). Persons derive utilitarian rewards from friendships regardless of their original purposes for engaging in them. Even Aristotle admits that pleasure and utility could be byproducts of a friendship of virtue. Moreover, Paine (1969) suggests that recognizing a useful relationship as an "instrumental friendship" implies that expressive and emotional factors are also involved. What other considerations operate, then, in preserving or undermining the polar conceptions of friendship as either a true one based on affection or a false one premised on instrumentality, and how do they function in the communicative management of this dialectical pair?

An array of contradictory tensions influences how both affection and instrumentality are manifested and experienced within friendships. Expressions of affection may be spontaneously and generously offered or communicated largely to receive displays of caring and/or instrumental aid in return. Likewise, one may help a friend unselfishly or to obtain increased affection or instrumental gains from him or her. Thus, whether one perceives a spirit of generosity or reciprocity as motivating caring or helpful behaviors affects their interpretation by friends.

Indeed, many authors extol the generous, altruistic impulse in friendship (Paine, 1969; Rake, 1970; Dubois, 1974). One could argue, however, against drawing such a clear line between selfishness and altruism. This view recognizes selflessness as an ideal pursuit but maintains that self-referent agency is an unavoidable reality, even in the best of friendships (Annas, 1977; Wright, 1984). People may derive self-oriented pleasure from their affection for a friend or the opportunity to help him or her. In a sense, selfishness draws individuals toward friends and generosity attracts friends to persons.

Affection or help also may be perceived as voluntary or obligatory. Ironically for the interpretation of behavior by friends, there is a dialectical relationship between these bases for action. Voluntary services or spontaneous displays of affection can make a friend feel obligated to engage in similar behaviors. Consequently, tacit contracts often develop that are experienced as particularly forceful because they are voluntarily undertaken (Kurth, 1970; Wiseman, 1986). Paradoxically, it is important for friends to fulfill voluntarily binding obligations that they have freely developed. If one feels or makes the other feel that his or her concern or aid in a given instance is obligatory, it sours the more edifying interpretations of the gesture. Repeated occurrences render the friendship barely distinguishable from more mundane partnerships.

Underlying this delicate traffic in sentiment and assistance are fears of inadvertent exploitation and/or indebtedness. Accordingly, within friendships, various models of exchange develop, designed to circumvent such risks without exhibiting rigorous or overtly economic practices. Friends take care to recognize that they share a variety of "things," both tangible and intangible (Hays, 1984). Thus friends will strive to maintain approximately equivalent exchange, realizing that the assets of friendship are difficult to specify, especially by outsiders (Paine, 1969; Szwed, 1969). Sometimes an overall pattern of equitable exchange may ameliorate a constant concern with ledgers. La Gaipa (1981a) suggests, "Short-term 'balancing of accounts' is discouraged because of the economic overtones, but long-term imbalance generally leads to the termination of the relationship" (p. 80). Yet whether one is an observer or an actual participant, Paine (1969) argues, economic conceptions of friendship may be inadequate because the nature of the equivalency may vary greatly in specific circumstances.

The dispersal of benefits within the friendship can be recast in terms of mutuality instead of exchange or economics. Paine (1969) asserts that the notion of a bargain takes on a different meaning between friends. He states, "Expressed as a bargain, A, in his concern with his own side of a bargain with B, is, in friendship, also concerned with B's, and vice versa" (p. 512). Such conceptions acknowledge individuals' selfish concerns but view them as necessarily supplemented and fundamentally altered by the mutuality and communality of friendship (Mills & Clark, 1982; Wright, 1984).

Even within mutual friendships, however, dynamic tensions persist among generosity versus reciprocity and spontaneity versus obligation. How friends experience each other's affectionate and instrumental behaviors derives from their ongoing management of both the actualities and symbolic qualities of these contradictory facets of friendship. Szwed (1969) warns, "All that can be known of a partner's motives in a contract is his willingness to continue the alliance. . . . Beyond this fact, individual motivations and goals remain veiled" (p. 108). The meaning and value of particular actions depend on interpretive frames established and maintained between the friends. Optimally, the interplay of routinely benevolent actions and the favorable codification of self's and other's intentions comprises and reflects the self-reinforcing orientation, "The relationship is experienced as a whole and for its own sake" (Peters & Kennedy, 1970, p. 450).

The particular stance that develops is a function of both specific events and the patterns emerging over the course of the relationship. Frequent or poignant communication of disinterested affection can qualify a friend's experience of instrumental obligations. Yuan (1975) found that sufficient affect is necessary within friendship to allow for unquestioned altruism and to "remove the burden of strict reciprocity" (p. 94). Conversely, instrumental acts confirm a friend's affection. La Gaipa (1981a) notes the convincing quality of expressing one's caring through instrumental assistance, "those actions which speak plainer than words" (p. 80).

Indeed, the interweaving of the contradictory dimensions of affection and instrumentality appears to distinguish various types of friends. For example, we found that best friendships were viewed as more intimate as well as more useful than were other friendship types (Rawlins et al., 1986). However, various friends' practices may blend these dimensions to constitute relationships ranging from apparently less caring but highly useful forms to tender bonds studiously avoiding utilitarian exchange. Some friendships begin with patently instrumental purposes and become quite affectionate as well, or instead; opposite trajectories can also occur. Ultimately, the friends determine the actual combination of affection and instrumentality characterizing their relationship and the particular enactment and interpretation of these aspects.

The Dialectic of Judgment and Acceptance. This dialectic articulates the interrelationship between these two interpersonal practices in shaping the communication of friends. Interaction with a friend is widely and duly celebrated for its potential to validate one's self-concept and enhance one's self-esteem (Sullivan, 1953). People are at ease with their friends because they feel liked and accepted by someone familiar with both their strengths and their weaknesses, their charming and their irritating qualities. Yet, as considered in prior sections, this legacy of acceptance masks a variety of antagonistic tendencies and negotiated practices demanding ongoing management in friendships.

Laing (1971) stipulates that all interpersonal messages are implicitly evaluative. Even the most accepting response from another person implies an appraisal of one's self or one's actions as worthy of support. Laing (1971) further indicates that criticizing one's behavior can also be confirming since it communicates that a person is important enough to judge. It is difficult to experience another person's reactions to self as neutral. People tend to perceive positive and/or negative intentions in others' responses to them (Rawlins & Holl, 1988). Of course, individuals often intentionally formulate critical messages as negative feedback designed to curtail another's behaviors. Likewise, people purposefully indicate acceptance or encouragement of another by responding positively.

Evaluation requires criteria. A friend invokes certain standards by communicating either judgmental or accepting messages to another. Because of the nature of friendship, these messages may reflect appraisals of the friend informed by private codes developed within the friendship or by public norms. Comments may regard specific actions, ideas or feelings, the person's comportment as a friend in private or public circumstances, and/or his or her overall worth as a person. Ironically, the sanctioned friend may in turn criticize or accept the appropriateness of these remarks and/or the criteria applied.

Lack of clarity or disagreement about the source of evaluative standards for appraising the behavior of friends, and how or whether the resultant judgments should be communicated, poses continuous quandaries within friendships. For example, one friend may sharply distinguish between public and private contexts in assessing proper behavior, while the other insists that the friendship transcends such arbitrary boundaries. Moreover, some individuals or pairs of friends hold such idealistic expectations of friendship that there is the constant potential for criticism expressed over inevitable shortfalls unless, of course, their ideals preclude the friends from criticizing each other. To complicate matters, guidelines for appropriate behavior between friends change over the course of friendships and across the individuals' life cycles.

How much friends are perceived to care about each other mediates the dialectical relationship between judgment and acceptance (Rawlins & Holl, 1988). Frequently, friends will not criticize one another's failings or lapses because they care enough about each other to "look the other way." Bensman and Lilienfeld (1979) state, "Tolerance, turning a blind eye, is thus a basic requirement of intimacy" (p. 103). In contrast, we have studied adolescents who maintained that criticism could also indicate a person's concern. They felt their friends could easily accept actions that their parents criticized because their friends did not seem to care as much about them as their parents did (Rawlins & Holl, 1988). The boundaries shift between others' responses perceived as judicious and those viewed as judgmental. Perceptions of differential caring temper the experience of judgment and acceptance.

Acceptance remains a vital aspect of communication between friends. But it functions in a dialectical relationship with the friends' judgments. People value a friend's acceptance, especially when they know the other takes their ideas, thoughts, and actions seriously. They also appreciate judgment and criticism from a person who primarily accepts and cares about them. Particular friendships thus develop specific criteria and practices to communicate in light of this dialectical pair.

The Dialectic of Expressiveness and Protectiveness. This final principle delineates the contradictory impulses to be open and expressive and to be strategic and protective of self and/or of another while communicating in friendship (Rawlins, 1983b). Though open and trusting communicative practices often constitute a desired outcome of becoming friends, they are also the primary means for their own achievement. Thus the apt management of this dialectical principle constitutes a reflexive challenge.

Developing and maintaining a friendship conversationally involves revealing personal thoughts and feelings and commenting on the messages and actions of one's friend, in short, expressiveness. Typically, as relationships become more personal, the participants are more relaxed and expressive with each other (Bochner, 1984). However, when friends communicate more openly, they create the necessary conditions for closedness (Rawlins, 1983b). Disclosing private concerns reveals areas of personal vulnerability, and unrestrained comments on the friend's ideas or actions may uncover areas of great sensitivity.

To avoid hurting each other, friends develop protective practices. Each friend tries to curb self-disclosures that render him or her too vulnerable, preserve the other's confidences, and exercise restraint in commenting on touchy issues. Trust develops within friendships to the extent that the dialectic of expressiveness and protectiveness is appropriately managed. That is, self limits self's own vulnerability and strives to protect other's sensitivities while still expressing thoughts and feelings (Rawlins, 1983b).

Establishing and preserving trust comprises a continuous discursive challenge within the contradictory responsibilities of this dialectic. Friends expect and want to trust in the honesty of each other's remarks. However, they also trust their friends not to hurt them by candid comments on personally vulnerable issues about which only a close friend is likely to know. Self might reveal a sensitive concern to other, expecting a restrained reaction. A discreet response would reinforce self's trust in him or her. But what if the friend wants to elicit self's trust in his or her candor and, in honestly addressing the issue, hurts self? Both friend's efforts to enhance trust achieve conflicting results because contradictory assumptions inform their actions. Eventually, friends must negotiate the areas of their discourse in which exercising restraint furthers trust and the topics for which candor affirms it (Rawlins, 1983b).

No universal recommendations can specify what communicative

practices will preserve trust in ongoing friendships. Throughout their relationship, friends continually confront the antagonistic tendencies of unrestrained and expressive versus strategic and protective communication.

Summary of Contextual and Interactional Dialectics

The preceding discussion of contextual and interactional dialectics exaggerates the clarity of the dilemmas and choices facing friends across the life course. These dialectics actually interweave in numerous and sometimes ambiguous ways. For example, the pattern of two friends' mutual independence and/or dependence will shape and reflect the nature and extent of their affection for and/or use of each other. Further, one may utilize a friend for critical appraisals, or like a friend for exercising judiciousness. Finally, the very act of revealing to or concealing from a friend implies an evaluation of the person as able or unable to handle that information.

Particular configurations of enacting these dialectical principles characterize individual friendships and types of friendships in various circumstances throughout life. For example, specific contradictions, such as publicness versus privacy and affection versus instrumentality, may significantly shape a given relationship, while other dialectics comprise secondary oppositions. Moreover, the continuous tensions of managing boundaries between private and public concerns and expressing affection and instrumentality may stimulate some friendships. In contrast, polar aspects of these dialectics may be so pronounced in other friendships that they persist in encapsulated forms as primarily public and instrumental or private and affectionate bonds.

Significantly, then, these dialectical features of managing friendships configure and function differently according to a variety of factors. First, specific individuals will negotiate particular practices within given friendships at various stages in the development of the relationship and in light of each participant's personal attributes and social activities (such as those modally linked with gender). Second, influenced by the foregoing factors, distinct configurations of these dialectical principles develop characterizing certain types and degrees of friendships. Third, particular friendship types enact these contradictions differently at various stages in the friends' life cycles. Finally, the typical patterning of all of these factors will reflect prevailing cultural practices of the moment.

Taken together, these considerations emphasize the contextual and mutable nature of communication within friendships. Throughout this book I will employ this dialectical perspective and these contextual and interactional dialectics as interpretive tools for analyzing the varieties, tensions, and functions of friendship across the life course.

Note

1. For a more extensive consideration of these elements of a dialectical perspective, see Rawlins (1989a).

Chapter 2

Childhood Friendships

The saga of friendship in our lives begins when we are quite young. Some toddlers actively affiliate and seek each other out, while others are ignored, antagonized, or avoided. Yet, from these humble beginnings a child's notions and practices of friendship typically undergo dramatic changes and refinements over the first decade and a half of life. First, in contrast to a surface perception of friends based on their overt features, characteristics, and possessions, children develop a psychological appraisal of friends based on their personal qualities. They realize there may be more to their friends and to themselves than readily meets the eye. Next, from a materialistic, object-centered basis for interaction, later childhood friendships evolve an intersubjective, person-centered core. Thus, talk about shared activities or items is supplemented by discussions of subjective thoughts and feelings; friends are not only physically but psychologically available to each other. Third, during this period self-oriented and one-sided views of incidents between friends shift to mutually derived conceptions of interactions, emphasizing interdependence, shared experiences, and goals. Children learn how to see matters from their friends' and society's perspectives as well as their own (Selman, 1981). Finally, a conception of social relationships as transitory converts into an awareness of their endurance over time and their longer term implications. Friends are not here today and gone tomorrow but deserve special treatment and consideration. As will be seen, these four developments in managing friendships reflect, require, and influence changes in self-conceptions, notions of social bonds, ideas of justice and fairness, ways of handling disagreements, and communicative practices.

This chapter will describe developmental transformations in the nature of friendships throughout childhood and into preadolescence. After noting toddlers' friendship patterns, I will discuss four different modes of conducting friendships characterized by distinctive and broadly age-related configurations of children's perceptions of friends, perspective-taking abilities, interactional practices, and notions of relationship. In doing so, I assume that alterations in the nature of children's friendships reflect a dialectical interaction of cognitive abilities and concrete social experiences. The different modes of friendship demand a certain degree of cognitive, moral, and communicative development, yet engaging in friendships simultaneously presents situations that instantiate, challenge, and extend these very abilities. Consequently, the age-related parameters of the modes described below are overlapping approximations; such changes occur at somewhat different rates for given children based on their specific aptitudes, gender, and experiences. The chapter closes with some general observations regarding gender patterns in children's friendships.

Our Earliest Friendships

From day to day little children may toddle among a fairly intricate social network including parents and other frequently encountered adults, strangers, peers, friends, and possibly siblings. Lewis and his colleagues (1975) observed that young children are mindful of and responsive to this complex collection of people within the first 18 months of life, which in turn necessitates and encourages further cognitive development.

Toddlers must be in close proximity to notice one another and often their voluntary interactions are spawned by shared interest in a specific object or toy (Rubin, 1980). Among groups of children, researchers consider mutual friends those children who approach and initiate interaction with each other (for example, by touching, looking, talking, giving, and/or taking objects) more frequently than with the other children present (Hartup, 1975). For even at this early age friendship involves recognition and selection, though it may be a one-sided or mutual attraction. Rubin (1980, p. 28) remarks, "By the time they are two years old, children seem to have an initial concept of a 'friend,' as a familiar peer from whom one expects particular responses and with whom one engages in a distinctive and enjoyable set of activities."

Momentary Physicalistic Playmates

In his model of children's developmental changes in conceptions of friendship, Selman (1981) describes the friendships spanning roughly ages 3 to 7 as "Momentary Physicalistic Playmates." During this period, a child's friends are drawn from the children who live close by or who are in the same class at day care, kindergarten, or elementary school and therefore are readily available to play with. They are recognized and described according to easily observed physical features (e.g., "pretty," long or curly hair, "my size," "nice smile") or possessions (e.g., candy, a new or "neat" toy, appealing clothes) (Shantz, 1975). Friendship exists while such children are playing together. Thus, Shelley and Pam are friends right now while they are building with Legos, but tomorrow or even later this afternoon, each girl may "make a new friend" riding big wheels or bouncing balls, and their prior friendship vanishes until the next time they play well together. In fact, either girl may be regarded as an intruder by the presently big wheel-riding or ball-bouncing friends.

With a tangibility that can be painful for an adult to witness, one of the key lifelong dramas of sociality—that of inclusion and exclusion—emerges hand-in-hand with the shifting alliances of children's friendships. For as they approach 3 years of age, communication among children demonstrates a rudimentary grasp of fundamental aspects of relating to other people throughout life, "sustained attention, turn-taking, and mutual responsiveness" (Rubin, 1980, p. 17). In his work with preschoolers, Corsaro (1981, p. 224) noticed these skills employed to compose "ongoing peer episodes" and "play groups" whose members considered themselves friends because of their current, shared participation and one of whose primary activities was excluding others who wanted to join them. Of course, few of the children observed seemed to want to play alone so that much of their time was spent trying to be or remain included with others (Corsaro, 1981).

Putallaz and Gottman (1981) describe in detail the complex maneuvering apparent in children's attempts to join an already formed group. A key procedure is "hovering," which describes a child's tentative and carefully managed presence near enough to the other children to get a sense of their shared "frame of reference" without attracting too much attention or appearing to be trying to join them. Once the child understands the nature of the activities the others are doing or the fantasies they are pursuing together, the child will behave similarly, hoping gradually to be perceived or treated as one of them. Howes (1983) also notes the importance of pretending together and fantasy play in structuring friendships at this age.

Given the description so far of young children's friendships, it is perhaps not surprising to note that quarrels and conflicts frequently occur though they are typically not prolonged ones (Gottman & Parkhurst, 1980). Selman (1981) maintains that such fights initiate and reflect realignments among children's friendships and involve "specific fights over specific toys and space . . . rather than personal feelings or interpersonal affection" (p. 250). Once again, behavior together is tied to the moment. Asserting the integral role of quarreling in composing the friendly interaction of her sample of two to five year olds, Green (1933) remarked that the mutual friends in her study were more quarrelsome, but that their degree of quarreling diminished with increasing age. Several authors concur that managing quarrels within children's friendships provides important training for getting along with others (Green, 1933; La Gaipa, 1981b; Rubin, 1980).

When they are 3 or 4 years old, children actually begin using the word "friend" (Mannarino, 1980). Yet when children in this general age group call someone a friend, they are typically commenting on their present enjoyment of engaging in an activity with another child. Meanwhile, they also are separating those who are included from those who are excluded. Consequently, the boundaries drawn through social interaction continuously shift by denoting new friends and demoting others. Gottman (1986) clearly articulates the comprehensive challenges involved in children playing well together at this developmental juncture and thereby remaining friends:

> Coordinated play is an extremely important context for learning how to manage one's emotions. If play is coordinated, it is simply not always possible to get one's own way. Children must learn to inhibit action, to delay getting what they want in the service of the overall adventure, to give and to receive influence, to deal with negative affect such as anger, and to manage positive affect such as joy and excitement in the context of interaction. (pp. 154–155)

During the course of this period, to the extent that children begin to maintain some stable friendships over time, they are more likely to cultivate more sophisticated social skills (Howes, 1983).

Activity and Opportunity

The phrase "Activity and Opportunity" characterizes the friendships of children from roughly 6 to 9 years old. This age span approximately corresponds with Sullivan's (1953) conception of a "juvenile era" in which children need companionship from peers in comprising self-oriented and opportunistic social relationships. By and large, such young friends live close to each other, and are similar in age, sex, size, intelligence level, social class, and degree of physical maturity (Rubin, 1980; Doyle, 1982). In describing their friends, they continue to emphasize clearly observable, physical characteristics (Gamer et al., 1975), although some researchers have found more abstract and affective actions such as support and liking also stressed by friends in this age group (Furman & Bierman, 1983). Above all, they spend considerable time engaging in common activities together—riding bikes, playing sports and games, enacting athletic, military, and domestic fantasies, running and romping (Bigelow & La Gaipa, 1975; Youniss & Volpe, 1978; Doyle, 1982; Furman & Bierman, 1983).

During this age period, children realize that other persons may see the same social actions similarly or differently from them. (I want to say Hi to our teacher in the market; but you do not.) Someone else may describe a shared situation in a contradictory manner because he/she may have different information or motives from self (Shantz, 1975; Selman, 1981). (You have never seen our teacher in the market before; or you do not like her or school.) Even so, self's view of a given situation comprises the "standard" to which the "friend's" actions must comply (Selman, 1981). Consequently, one's friends are expected to do and say the things that self wants, a conception of friendship Selman calls "One-way assistance" (1981). ("If you do not say Hi to Mrs. Collins with me, you are not my friend.") Similarly, Bigelow (1977) labels the second and third grades the "Reward–Cost" developmental stage of friendship as children seem to compare the costs of their efforts on behalf of their friends with the gains they receive from them.

Such dyads organize themselves according to a principle Youniss (1980) terms "symmetrical reciprocity" in which friends give and receive equivalent amounts of whatever they exchange, be it toys and candy or time on a swing. Moreover, such payment in kind is not subject to contemplation; it must be immediately forthcoming and cannot be delayed. Otherwise, the child who is waiting may feel unfairly treated. The understanding and code of friendship for these children is a practical matter (Youniss & Volpe, 1978). One does activities or plays with one's friend when it is convenient, and these interactions are appraised first and foremost as opportunities to enjoy or benefit oneself.

In short, friendships are not particularly sentimental arrangements at this time. They are not based on the personal qualities but on the immediate actions of the individuals involved (Damon, 1977). Basically, if the children are getting along and interacting in a positive manner, they are being friends with each other. When they do not spend time together or behave negatively, they are not friends. Thus, at this point children continue to lack a concept of their "friendship" as an ongoing bond that transcends periods of no contact or disagreement (Smollar & Youniss, 1982).

Despite the episodic and opportunistic qualities characterizing friendship at this juncture, researchers have associated certain developments in social skills with those children who have friends and who exhibit more sophisticated friendship conceptions (Burleson, 1986). Newcomb and Brady (1982) reported that in comparison with nonfriends, both the second- and sixth-grade friends they observed talked more together, exchanged more task-related information, attended more to each other's talk, and issued and obeyed more mutually oriented commands. In short, these authors concluded that the friends were more mutually oriented, socially responsive, and affectively expressive than the mere acquaintances in their study. Foot, Chapman, and Smith (1977) also noted the strong effect of friendship in enhancing the expressiveness of 7 and 8 year olds, stating, "Children laughed, smiled, looked, and talked significantly more with a friend than with a stranger companion" (p. 408).

Sants (1984) argues that advanced levels of friendship conception may reflect children's capacity for compromising and adapting their behaviors to others based on a developing understanding of their distinctive ways of acting and communicating. Sullivan (1965) called this "social accommodation" and viewed it as a function of managing interaction with peers. Observing children in their classrooms and on the playground, Sants (1984) found that those with more advanced conceptions of friendship often attempted control and organizing behaviors, succeeded at control, frequently ignored others but were rarely ignored themselves, and were rarely rejected or victims of aggression. Interestingly, Sants (1984) maintains that degree of friendship conception was especially associated with how these children dealt with companions who were not their friends, suggesting the broader value of friendship understanding for managing interactions at this age.

Equality and Reciprocity

Several significant developmental changes in children's thoughts and actions emerging around their eighth to twelfth years of age are demonstrated in the mode of friendship termed here "Equality and Reciprocity." For one thing, though proximity continues to play a crucial role in mediating friendship selection, throughout this period children increasingly choose their friends based on attitude similarity (Gamer et al., 1975). Such choice becomes important because by 8 or 9 years of age children develop the ability to perceive and describe other persons in terms of psychological dispositions, such as attitudes, personal traits, habits, values, and beliefs that they have regularly observed in the others' actions over time and in diverse situations (Shantz, 1975). Thus, they realize that people can behave according to internal motivations and ongoing psychological traits (Gamer et al., 1975). Accordingly, to pick a friend who shares similar attitudes, habits, and outlooks enhances the possibility of "consensual validation" within friendship, the need that Sullivan (1953) argued preadolescents have for peers to confirm their view of the world and their place in it.

At the same time that 9 and 10 year olds become fairly adept at inferring the psychological dispositions and attitudes of others, they come to understand that other persons can in turn infer the child's own personal traits and motivations. That is, they realize that just as they are able to think about others, their own behaviors and thoughts can become the objects of others' thoughts and evaluations. In short, children develop "self-reflective role-taking" or "reciprocal perspectives" (Shantz, 1975; Selman, 1981). Shantz (1975) remarks that now the child "can figuratively step outside himself and reflect on his own and the other's thinking and the other's thinking about him" (p. 287). (I want to say Hi to our teacher because I like her; but I imagine that you think I want to say Hi to get in good with her.) Such perspective-taking ability is necessary for children to pursue a "two-way" approach to friendship, whereby the friends coordinate and adjust their actions in an attempt to fulfill or reconcile each other's expectations, rather than either friend simply assuming that the other should live up to his/her own standards (Selman, 1981). ("Let's go out that door. We can say Hi to Mrs. Collins, and then we'll be right by the pay phone where you can call your Mom to see if we can stay here longer like you wanted to.")

Friendship begins to involve "a concept of relation" based on reciprocity between similar, equal persons who have selected each other as friends in light of their compatible personalities (Youniss & Volpe, 1978). Youniss and Volpe (1978) describe this important development in friendship practices:

> Friends are not just peers in general, but particular persons who share ideas, feelings, and interests. Two friends are alike and therefore different in similar ways from other peers who are not their friends. . . . At this point, interactions become overt signs of friendship; they are behavioral *acknowledgments* of relationship. (p. 11, original emphasis)

In contrast to the unreflective, "tit for tat," "symmetrical reciprocity" of the prior friendship mode, the relationship now exhibits "cooperative reciprocity," a mutually conceived and enacted, deliberate sharing of assistance and materials that both parties intend as a token of friendship (Youniss, 1980). Moreover, the conventions of the relationship become premised on the similarity and equality of the friends and the importance of helping one's friend when the need arises (Youniss & Volpe,

1978; Damon, 1977). Even so, continuing the friendship is clearly decided by each person's self-interest. In fact, reciprocal trust now emerges as a defining feature of friendship in that each friend assumes that the other will provide help, goods, or kind words when they are needed; and, of course, refusing assistance or hurting self can end the relationship (Damon, 1977). Bigelow (1977) calls the era from 9 to 11 years the Normative Stage due to the procedures and sanctions for sharing within friendship evolving during this period.

Certain ironic attributes and practices of this mode of friendship as a moral sphere become evident at this juncture. As mentioned, friends view each other as equals with reciprocal rights to fair treatment. In fact, Youniss and Volpe (1978) noted in their studies that when one friend was perceived as lacking something or hurting in some way, the other friend viewed it as his/her responsibility to help. The authors concluded, "Inequality was then an occasion for asserting the principle of equality" (1978, p. 11).

Though laudable and functional in terms of children's moral development, this emerging egalitarian ethic within friendship is not without its limitations. Because of the absence of a genuinely mutual orientation, Selman (1981) calls the modus operandi of these dyads "fair weather cooperation." Moreover, Berndt (1982b) asserts the ambivalence that may result from the similarities between friends. On the one hand, one's friend may be viewed as "another self" to identify with and to reinforce self-conceptions. However, the pervasive social comparison associated with such similarity may also stimulate heated competition between friends. Further, citing several studies, Berndt (1986) states, "In contexts, where competitive motivation is aroused, close friends may compete more and share less with each other than do children who are not close friends" (p. 106). He points out, however, that such competition tends to typify the friendships of boys rather than girls, who are more apt to share with their friends, even in competitive situations (Berndt, 1981a, 1986). Interestingly, altruistic behaviors between friends increase from middle childhood to early adolescence and are most likely to occur precisely when they are seen to facilitate equal outcomes between friends (Berndt, 1986). Indeed, the notion of justice between friends arises in childhood and remains a vital yet problematic concern throughout life (Damon, 1977).

Mutuality and Understanding

Sullivan (1953) stipulated that the juvenile era ends and preadolescence begins when children strive for an intimate relationship with a person of their same age and sex, a "chum." He stressed that chumships are especially important for working out with a trusted peer the distinctions between privately held visions and publicly recognized facts regarding virtually any issue the child considers important. The process of developing and receiving this confirmation within friendship Sullivan (1953) called "consensual validation." Obviously, being a real chum to another child requires surpassing a constant preoccupation with one's own interests and becoming truly sensitive to the concerns of one's friend. Thus, Sullivan (1953) viewed the "chum" relationship as critical for enhancing feelings of self-worth and for developing interpersonal sensitivity and genuine altruism. Without these qualities he felt a person could be hampered in forming bona fide intimate relationships with persons of either gender throughout adult life.

Children primarily emphasize personal qualities in selecting and rejecting their closest friends at this age (Austin & Thompson, 1948; Smollar & Youniss, 1982). They want to know, what kind of personality does this potential friend have—nice, mean, fun, sincere? What are his/her preferences and abilities? Whether the friend lives nearby becomes less important than personal characteristics that match with self's and lend themselves to a relationship based on overall equality, acceptance, and mutual respect (Smollar & Youniss, 1982).

More sophisticated conceptions of the friendship itself evolve in light of further developments in perspective-taking abilities. By age 10 or 11 the linear conception of "self-reflective role-taking," whereby one can simply take the other's perspective (I want to say Hi to our teacher because I like her; but I imagine that you think I want to say Hi to get in good with her.) —gives way to "mutual role-taking" (Shantz, 1975). With this latter ability the child realizes that the "other can mutually and simultaneously take the self's view of other into consideration at the same time as the self takes the perspective of other toward the self" (Selman, 1976, p. 172) (I realize that you imagine that I would say that I want to say Hi to our teacher because I like her; *and* I understand that you realize that I would imagine that you think I want to say Hi to get in good with her.) Grasping this potentially infinite spiral of reciprocal perspectives allows both friends to take a third-person view of their relationship (Selman, 1981). (These two friends see this situation differently, but also seem to understand that they do.)

And with this perceptual ability comes the acknowledgment of the mutual composition of human relationships as ongoing interpersonal experiences that transcend either individual. Disagreements are now seen as occurring within the friendship, but the friendship does not end simply because disagreements or separations occur. Close on the heels of mutual role-taking, by approximately age 12 young adolescents acquire the perspective of the "generalized other"; they understand how society in general might view their friendships (Shantz, 1975). (These two people have a stronger friendship than a lot of people, even though they can get jealous of each other from time to time.)

This "moment" comprises a watershed in the dialectical constitution of self and other through friendship. Basically, the young adolescent simultaneously realizes that self and the friend each comprises integrated personalities and that friendships are ongoing and negotiated bonds. Youniss and Volpe (1978) stress that "the concept of the *individual personalities of the relation*" (p. 12, my emphasis), though lacking in young children, is "a pervasive fact for early adolescents." The boundaries and interdependence of self and other are now implicated in the awareness and practice of continuity in relationships.

Best friendships or chums become important and noticeably more stable at this age than in previous grades (Hallinan, 1978/79; Horrocks & Buker, 1951). They are also more complex achievements. Children describe their friendships as egalitarian, same-sex, same-age bonds, characterized by intimacy, prosocial behavior, companionship, similarity, mutual admiration, affection, acceptance, and loyalty (Adler & Furman, 1988). However, they are viewed as quarrelsome, antagonistic, competitive, and exclusive as well (Adler & Furman, 1988). Despite these tensions, Adler and Furman (1988) found loyalty and acceptance, in particular, to distinguish friendships from sibling and parent–child relationships.

The mutuality and intimacy of these friendship are increasingly affirmed through talking together and expressing personal thoughts and feelings. Several researchers have found that such interpersonal exchange does not typify children's friendships until the sixth grade (Bigelow & Gaipa, 1980; Berndt, 1981b; Diaz & Berndt, 1982; Youniss, 1980; Buhrmester & Furman, 1987). Damon (1977) remarks that, "Talking is regarded as important for psychological assistance, secret sharing, and the establishment of mutual understanding" (p. 164). The trust developed in these friendships is the shared conviction that the friends will preserve each other's privacy and keep secrets (Damon, 1977).

Children become possessive about their friends, possibly due to an emerging expectation of permanence and the simultaneous awareness that friendships are difficult to establish and preserve (Bigelow & La Gaipa, 1980; Selman, 1981). Moreover, as Sullivan (1953) contends, chumships often lead to friendship cliques that are exclusive in orientation and evidence strong conformity pressures. Rubin (1980) maintains that such groups assume their greatest significance during preadolescence with their members frequently shifting in the continuous rearrangements of preadolescent cliques and social networks (Fine,

1980). Secrets and gossip function importantly to demarcate group boundaries and to articulate group standards; only persons within the group are told its special secrets and daring stories, and evaluative standards are registered by gossip regarding the clothes, attitudes, or activities of persons outside of the clique (Mettetal, 1983). The group also provides a forum for learning about sex and appropriate aggression, topics that may be improper to discuss with adults (Fine, 1980).

In short, much extant research on children's friendships at this general age bears out Sullivan's (1953) ideas about the prevalence and functional value of chumships. McGuire and Weisz (1982) found that 10 to 12-year-old children with chums exhibited higher levels of altruism and affective perspective-taking skills (i.e., "social sensitivity") than those without friends. And Berndt (1985) observed that with increasing age (across fourth, sixth, and eighth grades) there were greater differences between the altruism demonstrated by friends versus other classmates. Moreover, the friends assumed their friends were striving for equality but their classmates were competing with them. Ultimately, it appears that as children begin to view their friendships as continuing indefinitely, they start to reflect on the consequences of their actions and words for their friends and their friendships. Accordingly, as children enact the friendship mode of mutuality and understanding, they try to limit their aggression toward and competition with each other, acknowledge and deal with violations of expectations within the relationship, and begin to trust each other with the discussion of personal concerns (Berndt, 1986; Sants, 1984; Youniss & Volpe, 1978).

Gender Differences in Children's Friendships

Despite overarching similarities in the developmental transformations of children's modes of friendship, scholars repeatedly have reported gender variations across childhood. Though there is little indication of gender alignments in children's play before the age of 2, certain patterns do emerge in 3- to 4-year-olds' play groups (Rubin, 1980). Such children increasingly choose same-sex playmates and friends and play a lot in pairs, yet also seem concerned about being part of larger groups that form intermittently (Rubin, 1980).

The preference for same-sex friends generally persists during the childhood years with an interest in cross-sex friendships only reappearing in early adolescence (Foot et al., 1980; Sullivan, 1953; Buhrmester & Furman, 1987). Gottman (1986) cites a door-to-door survey finding the rate of cross-sex best friendships decreasing from 36% among 3 to 4 year olds to "nonexistent" among second graders. He also reports sociometric data finding the same-sex preferences among peers at 67% in kindergarten, 68% in first grade, 76% in third grade, and 84% in fourth grade (Gottman, 1986). Cohen et al., (1980) remark that the fifth graders they studied seemed to go to peers of their same gender for intimacy and help. And Hallinan (1979) observed no girls in any of the boys' cliques and no boys in any of the girls' groups in fourth to sixth graders' friendship networks. According to Rubin (1980), by about the sixth grade, "Groups have come to assume major importance and the sex segregation of the groups is almost total" (p. 93).

Summing up the trends described here, Gottman concludes that "Gender is the most potent psychological determinant of friendship choice in middle childhood" (Gottman, 1986, p. 140). In trying to explain the prevalence of same-sex friendships, Rubenstein and Rubin (1984) allude to the well-known preference for similar others in children's friendships, adult encouragement of these choices, and sex-role stereotypes within the peer group that reinforce them.

But how do the friendships of girls compare with those of boys? Fairly consistent tendencies have been described. Basically, starting around age 7, boys tend to play in groups, and girls prefer to play with one other girl (Lever, 1976; Foot et al., 1977; Berndt, 1982a). Thus, while fifth- and sixth-grade boys' friendships were more expansive, allowing other boys to join them, Eder and Hallinan (1978) found those of girls more exclusive, making it rather difficult for other girls to become friends. Even so, McAdams and Losoff (1984) report that girls exhibited higher friendship motivation than boys in both the fourth and sixth grades.

The other frequent finding regarding gender is that girls' friendships are more intimate than those of boys. For example, fourth-grade females shared more secrets than males in Rotenberg's (1986) research. And in their study of fifth and sixth graders Furman and Buhrmester (1985) report that the girls indicated significantly more intimacy, affection, and enhancement of worth than the boys did. And though there were no initial gender differences in the ratings of same-sex friendships across a sample of second, fifth, and eighth graders, the girls exhibited a steady increase in intimate disclosure and a "striking increase during preadolescence in the significance of same-sex friends as intimacy providers" (Buhrmester & Furman, 1987, p. 1111). In contrast, the boys' levels remained fairly constant. By and large, girls are more apt to have a same-sex "chum" and share greater intimacy as opposed to mere sociability (Seiden & Bart, 1975).

We can view these gender differences in the intimacy of children's friendships in various ways. On the one hand, they may signal a lack of experience and consequently limited development of attitudes and skills for managing emotionally involving same-sex friendships that could possibly affect males throughout their lives. At other points in this book we will consider how true or irreversible this observation is. On the other hand, the data may indicate that males experience and define intimacy differently than females. Buhrmester and Furman (1987, pp. 1111–1112) suggest that, "Perhaps preadolescent boys form collaborative friendships in which sensitivity to needs and validation of worth are achieved through actions and deeds, rather than through interpersonal disclosure of personal thoughts and feelings." This possibility exists as well although its ramifications warrant careful scrutiny. Consider that in Adler and Furman's (1988) study, even though the fifth- and sixth-grade boys studied reported less intimacy, affection, and enhancement of worth in their friendships than the girls did, there were no significant differences in the reported importance of or their satisfaction with their relationships with friends. But this issue cannot be resolved here. However, I will continue to examine the gender patterning of friendships throughout life in terms of how it shapes and reflects both males' and females' personal and social circumstances, experiences, abilities, and outlooks. Let us now turn to a chapter that utilizes recollections and fictional depictions to illustrate the problems arising and the pleasures and self-development resulting from childhood friendships.

Chapter 3

Illustrative Analysis: Children's Interaction in Friendships

The preceding chapter sketched four modes of friendship spanning approximately the first 15 years of childhood. The modes, corresponding roughly to several age divisions, were distinguished according to particular configurations of children's perceptions of friends, perspective-taking abilities, interactional practices, and notions of relationship. In describing these modes, I acknowledged that both the age ranges and the features comprising each mode could overlap due to differences in children, their gender, concrete circumstances, and opportunities for and actual participation in friendships. Table 3.1 presents a summary of the four modes.

Table 3.1. Modes of Friendship during Childhood

	Momentary Physicalistic Playmates (Selman, 1981) (roughly ages 3–7)	*Activity and Opportunity (roughly ages 6–9)*	*Equality and Reciprocity (roughly ages 8–12)*	*Mutuality and Understanding (roughly ages 9–14)*
Perception of Friend	Observable, physical features of friends, or possessions	Physical attributes of friends	Psychological traits, attitudes and abilities of a friend	Personality of friend, and self–other relationship
Perspective-Taking Ability	Undifferentiated perspectives (Selman, 1981)	Differentiated perspectives (Selman, 1981)	Reciprocal perspectives (Selman, 1981)	Mutual perspectives, generalized other (Selman, 1981)

Table 3.1.   (cont.)

	Momentary Physicalistic Playmates (Selman, 1981) (roughly ages 3–7)	Activity and Opportunity (roughly ages 6–9)	Equality and Reciprocity (roughly ages 8–12)	Mutuality and Understanding (roughly ages 9–14)
Interactional Practices	Proximate, object-centered interaction; play together; inclusion/ exclusion	Play together; immediate and equivalent exchange; inclusion/ exclusion; competition	Cooperative play; sharing of assistance and materials; competition	Sharing personal thoughts and feelings; increase in altruism and sensitivity
Notion of Relationship	Episodic; friends while playing together	Periodic; friendship exists during intervals of favorable interaction	"Concept of relation," based on reciprocity between similar and equal persons (Smollar & Youniss, 1982)	Mutuality; expectation of permanence of relationship

The present chapter employs excerpts from fictional stories about children's friendships and a young woman's remembrances in attempting to reflect the ups and downs, and the distinctive emotional and communicative textures of the various modes of childhood friendship. I conclude by discussing the dialectical processes of friendship during this period.

Momentary Physicalistic Playmates

Rosa is my friend. She lets me hold her new doll. (Jaynes, 1967)

Because of its episodic character, the lived experience of friendship for children often comprises a continuous process of making, separating from or breaking with, and remaking friends. And for young children, parents or adult supervisors are never far removed from the scene. During the day, homemaking parents typically bring their children along when visiting their own friends, many of whom have become friends because they have similar-aged children and comparable free time (Whyte, 1956). Moreover, children attending school or organized day care are rarely far from adult observation and control. Thus, young children's social lives develop in situations governed by adults, be they parents or teachers (Fine, 1981). Adults are therefore part of the childhood friendship process. They may inhibit or facilitate contact with other children by regulating or commenting upon interaction as it occurs.

The following events depict a young child's successful efforts at making a friend after initial isolation:

> Sarah knew how to turn on the drinking fountain, and how to feed the playground pigeons. But Sarah didn't know how to have a friend. So she played in the sand by herself.
>
> The other children made sand pies together, and played ball together, and came laughing down the slide together. . . .
>
> Then one day, a new child came to the playground.
>
> She was about as tall as Sarah. She had a hat, like Sarah's, and she had a petticoat, but hers was green and Sarah's was blue.
>
> The new girl sat in the sand by herself. She played with a tiny silver pitcher and a tiny red teacup.
>
> Sarah watched. After a while, the new girl's mother called to her, "Ann, it's time to go home now." So Sarah knew the girl's name was Ann.
>
> The next day, Sarah came to the playground again. When Ann saw Sarah swinging, she said, "Mommy, *I* want to swing." She chose the swing next to Sarah. . . .
>
> On the next day, Ann brought a red and yellow dump truck to the sand pile. Sarah picked up her shovel and pail and sat down beside Ann. Sarah and Ann played next to each other, but they didn't talk. . . .
>
> On this day, when Sarah saw Ann with a silver piepan, she said, "May I play with your piepan?" And when Ann saw Sara's bright red scoop, she said, "May I play with your scoop?" Then Sarah and Ann made a pie, together. (Miles, 1958)

At the story's beginning, the narrator tells us that Sarah feels excluded and unable to make friends while the other children are playing together. (However, at Sarah's age, somewhere around 3 to 5 years old, it is unlikely that she would or could reflect on her knowledge of friendship. Rather, she would simply perceive that she was playing alone in contrast to their shared activity.) Then she notices a new girl with similar physical features (height) and clothing (hat and petticoat) who is playing by herself with appealing toys. Evidently (we as third parties might conclude), the other girl observes that Sarah resembles her as well because the next day she decides to swing beside her. The following day, compatible and attractive toys draw the two girls into even closer proximity and parallel play in the sand pile, whereupon object-related talking and sharing toys result in the two girls playing together, in effect, making friends.

Two boys, a year or two older, engage in an analogous befriending episode during school hours in the excerpt below:

> But at music time, David could skip.
> "That is hard," said Ron.
> "It is easy for me," said David. "You hop first, then you skip." He showed Ron how to do it.
> "I can skip, too!" said Ron.
> When Ron put a puzzle together, David did, too.
> Then Ron found a spinner game. "Let's play this game together," he said.
> "This is fun," said David. "Will you play with me when we go outside?"
> "Sure, pal," said Ron.
> Soon they went out to the playground. (Moncure, 1976)

For children in this mode of friendship, coordinating play is being friends (Gottman, 1986). This pair's momentary bond is built around skipping, assembling puzzles, and playing games together. For the time being, its proposed extension to the playground is agreed to and consummated by Ron calling David "pal."

Yet as easily as these friendships can develop, things can go awry. Premised largely on being at the same place at the same time with another child who resembles self in obvious ways, and/or who possesses a toy or privilege that self wants, minor changes in self's location or actions toward the other may disrupt or dissolve the friendship. Still, a brief interlude apart or an equally marginal positive action may be all that is required to give the friendship a fresh "start," as portrayed by John and James:

> James used to be my friend.
> But today he is my enemy.
> James always wants to be the boss.
> James carries the flag.
> James takes all the crayons.
> He grabs the best digging spoon.
> And he throws sand.
> So now James is my enemy. Now he hasn't got me for a friend. . . .
> "Hullo, James."

"Hullo, John."
"I came to tell you that I'm not your friend any more."
"Well then, I'm not *your* friend either."
"We're enemies."
"All right!"
"Good-Bye!"
"Good-Bye!"
"Hey, James!"
"What?"
"Let's roller-skate."
"O.K. Have a pretzel, John."
"Thank you, James." (Udry, 1961)

This example concisely depicts the mercurial quality of this mode of friendship. Even so, in reading it, we must keep in mind that while young children may concoct a list of grievances like John's regarding James, they are much more likely to "end" a friendship instantaneously over given infractions, and then basically forget about them if and when they renew the friendship. Second, the word "enemy" for a child like John does not have the complex and malevolent meanings that begin to develop during adolescence; it simply means, "I don't like you right now." "Enemyship" itself is an involved and sustained relationship.

Children exclude others from friendship groups and dyads in this mode for often fickle and typically concrete reasons. "He's too young." "She's barefooted and we're not." "We're already playing." "You can't do what we're doing" (whether this is actually true or not). And seemingly overnight, gender lines are drawn:

The next morning when Frances went to Albert's house, Albert was playing ball with his friend Harold.
"Can I play?" asked Frances.
"She's not much good," said Harold to Albert,
"And besides, this is a no-girls game."
"Can't I play?" said Frances to Albert.
"Well, it *is* a no-girls game," said Albert. (Hoban, 1969, p. 10)

Frances and Harold had played well together yesterday. Even so, today the boys decide to exclude Frances because she is a girl and "not much good," which they communicate with the characteristic directness of children. And we can imagine any number of boys readily allowed to join the game within minutes of this refusal while Frances watches.

Friends also can be liabilities at various times. They can intrude on a child's thoughts and/or refuse to participate in his/her current fantasies or preferred games. They may desire self's toys or gum or chance to choose an activity. In short, they must be pleased when a child may want self-gratification. To add insult to injury, friends may tattle when they do not get their way, or make up something just out of spite. In either case, adults are pulled into the picture and the child may be corrected, punished, or given a lecture about "learning how to share," which according to adults is supposed to be a good thing although the child probably does not think so. Most of the time, however, when things are going well, it is more fun to be with friends than to have "nothing to do and nobody to play with."

Activity and Opportunity

Willy shouted at Sammy, "If you don't give me that hat, I won't be your best friend." (Cohen, 1973)

In the early to middle elementary school years, young persons typically choose friends of their same age and gender, who share their physical characteristics and who enjoy doing the same activities together. Consequently, even though they do not yet conceive of their friendships as lasting bonds, they may spend hours jointly playing at unpredictable junctures or regularly, day after day. Such play remains contingent on the physical availability of the friend and ranges from sports and games to all manner of pretend adventures and real predicaments that the friends both initiate and handle together. In the following story Paul and Ted decide they will deliver groceries, but they do not have anything in which to transport them:

"A wagon! Where will we get a wagon?" Paul asked when they went out. "We'll make one," Ted answered. "Out of our coasters!"

And they did! They worked hard the rest of the day building a wagon. Paul let Ted help him put the box on. Ted let Paul help him put the wheels on. And together they made a fine strong wagon!

Every day after school they worked together. Sometimes Ted steered the wagon and Paul delivered the groceries. Sometimes Paul steered and Ted delivered the groceries. (Beim & Beim, 1945)

Through working together to build a wagon, the two friends auspiciously convert their shared fantasy of a grocery delivery service into an ongoing activity they can jointly pursue. Yet notice the "symmetrical reciprocity" (Youniss, 1980) organizing their interaction; they promptly match each other's privileges. Ted gets to help install the box, so then Paul gets to assist with the wheels; sometimes Ted steers and Paul delivers, and vice versa. "Taking turns" in this fashion within children's friendships anticipates later notions of "fairness-as-equality" (Damon,

1977). However, at this time the procedure is still primarily self-oriented and opportunistic; it is valued when it facilitates one's desires while maintaining a positive interaction with one's friend.

Sharing fantasies is important for playing together, having fun, and being friends at this age. Uneasy about finding someone who plays pretend like he does, 9-year-old Harold is finally convinced by his mother to invite Frank over:

> The two boys played one make-believe game after another, taking turns being the hero and the villain. By the end of the afternoon, Harold's head was in a whirl. He'd had the best time he'd ever had, but it was hard to believe that big Frank Rugby liked to make believe the same way that he did. . . .
>
> He was glad Frank had said he was coming back the next day. Harold felt good that night. He went outside to catch fireflies and made believe he was guarding a jarful of nuclear atoms that could blow up the world. He and Frank could use it tomorrow to play a new game. (Colman, 1978, p. 68)

Once again, we see the positive relationship of children's turn taking and acting as friends. We should also note that playing games such as heroes and villains requires, and early on probably helps develop, differentiated perspectives (Mead, 1934). For example, for such a game to work, the child playing sheriff must see shooting the robber as good while the child playing the robber must see this shooting as something to avoid. Further, when they trade roles, each child must adopt the appropriate and opposite perspective. Next, this excerpt also depicts Harold's growing realization that someone who appears physically different from himself, "big Frank Rugby," might share similar outlooks. In fact, a more developed awareness of a friend's psychological attributes characterizes the next friendship mode. Finally, though today's play has stimulated Harold's imagination, and he eagerly awaits playing with Frank tomorrow, there are no guarantees that Frank also will see fireflies as nuclear atoms. The boys could bicker.

Quarrels are apt to occur during this period because self's view of a given situation dictates the standard by which the friend's actions are evaluated. Consequently, if self's expectations are not met, problems ensue. Meanwhile, the friend may have contrasting ideas about how to pursue the same activity. Accordingly, even though friends in this mode may know that the other sees matters differently, each is liable to insist on the correctness of his or her own perceptions (Selman, 1981). Moreover, just as friends symmetrically match each other's positive actions and offerings in the reciprocal transactions of this mode, they also tend to escalate exchanges of negative gestures (Youniss, 1980;

Bateson, 1958). And since they do not yet conceive of their friendship as transcending squabbles, when they interact negatively, they are no longer friends (Smollar & Youniss, 1982). Witness later developments between Ted and Paul, the grocery deliverers:

> When they came back Ted started to attach the roller skate wheels to a piece of wood. "That's not the way. Let me do it," Paul said. "I can do it myself!" Ted answered, and he wouldn't let Paul help him.
>
> Paul took the hammer and started to nail the box to the piece of wood. "You're not doing it right," Ted said. "I am too!" Paul answered, and he wouldn't let Ted help him.
>
> "Give me the hammer," Ted said. "I'm going to put the handle on." "No you're not," Paul told him. "I'm going to do it." Paul tried to keep the hammer but Ted pulled it away from him.
>
> "I'm not going to make a coaster with you." Paul pushed Ted. "Who wants to make one with you?" Ted shoved Paul. Paul took his box and piece of wood. Ted took his roller skate. They were so mad at each other they didn't even say good-bye. (Beim & Beim, 1945)

Each friend's conviction that his way of doing the job is "the way" or "right" and his refusal to consider the other's approach results in a dispute that disrupts their shared project and, for the time being, their friendship. The two boys' friendship will resume when they begin again doing some activity together and/or interacting in ways that each boy feels good about. For this renewal to occur between children, typically they separate for an interval that varies according to the severity of their argument. Then one or the other friend must initiate some common play, plan-making, or timely exchange of toys and/or treats. The previous quarrel like the one above over the proper method for attaching roller skates need not ever be mentioned (Youniss & Volpe, 1978).

Equality and Reciprocity

We help one another because we want to. (Berger, 1981, p. 61)

The potential of peer friendship to comprise distinctive, mutually negotiated, moral spheres begins to emerge with the mode of "Equality and Reciprocity." For much of childhood, young persons must adapt themselves to patterns of interaction primarily determined by adults and older siblings. Termed *unilateral constraint* by Piaget (1932) and *unilateral authority* by Sullivan (1953), such interpersonal relations with persons in dominant positions teach children about the lawful and obdurate qualities of social life and the necessity of accepting and adopting societally correct interactive practices in getting along with others (Youniss & Volpe, 1978; Youniss, 1980; Corsaro, 1981). In contrast, friendships and peer interactions involve the collaborative and cooperative development of procedures for interacting between equals who lack the power to impose preferences unilaterally. The reciprocal exchange and perspective-taking necessary for such collaboration tend to enhance children's sensitivity to others, and their capacity for expressing and experiencing affection with an equal (Selman, 1981; Youniss & Volpe, 1978; Youniss, 1980).

These opposing bases for regulating comportment become especially evident when parents or other adults try to specify how two friends should interact. The narrator below is increasingly irritated by her mother's mandate that Crystal's preferences must dictate the two girls' actions while she sleeps over:

> I go ask my mother, "Do I always have to let Crystal choose?"
> "Crystal is your guest," Mother reminds me.
> "I wish Crystal was still just my friend," I tell her. (Gordon, 1978, p. 11)

Apparently, "guests" receive privileged treatment in this home, as in many. But our narrator longs for the equality and reciprocity of friendship. Fuming about the unilateral constraints on their behavior, she has trouble sleeping and informs her friend:

> "I wasn't asleep," I tell her.
> "Why not?" she asks.
> "Because I'm feeling mad."
> Crystal sits up in bed. "What are you mad about?"
> I don't see why *you* always get to choose what to do," I say, "just because you're my guest."
> "Me either," says Crystal, making a funny face. "*First dibs* is more fun."
> "*First dibs* on sleeping in my own bed!" I holler right away.
> Crystal and I switched beds.
> "*First dibs* on the bathroom tomorrow!" hollers Crystal.
> I giggle at Crystal, and she giggles back. (Gordon, 1978, pp. 23–26)

Something mutually edifying transpires here. Our narrator complains to her friend about the inequality (and the irrationality) of their enforced host–guest relationship. Instead of trying to preserve her advantage, Crystal agrees and proposes a procedure that gives both girls equal chances to state preferences. They immediately put the procedure into reciprocal practice and share a chuckle certifying its success.

The laughter and responsiveness of such friends celebrate the functioning of a collaborative relationship between two young people who have recognized and selected each other based on personal traits, respective abilities, and similar attitudes about key concerns. In managing their friendships, they try to be aware of each other's expectations and to help when needs arise:

> This is Oliver. He's very smart. He helps me do papers about rockets, and killer bees, and the history of Central America. . . . When we go places he tells me about things. . . . Sometimes when Oliver's head is filled with numbers, and words, and ideas—he forgets to bring his lunch to school. I let him share mine. (Berger, 1981, pp. 11–19)

Whereas one person in this dyad assists with schoolwork and teaches, the other shares his food when his friend forgets his lunch. Essentially, friendship in this mode involves joint trust in the deliberate and mutual sharing of assistance and materials when the need occurs (Damon, 1977). Friendships are preserved because they fulfill the reciprocal interests of two individuals who regard each other as equals.

In developing these early voluntary and negotiated relationships based on the assurance of reciprocal assistance, children enact a critical feature of friendship with implications that reappear throughout life in different guises. One's friends may need or want self to do things that at times conflict with parental teachings, or less problematically, simply clarify the fact that *their group or friendship comprises a distinguishable moral order* (even between siblings who become friends) from the worlds of family, school, scouts, or any other authoritatively governed social domain. The "conspiratorial" potential of friendship enters the ongoing dramas of social life:

> "I want to stay with you," Polly blurted out. "Do you think it'd be OK? My mother would pay for the food and stuff. It'd only be for two weeks. Until school's over." . . .
> "I'll ask my mother," I said. "I'll soften her up, set the table, scrub the bathtub—all those little things that endear kids to their mothers. Then I'll slip it to her so smoothly she won't know what happened. Call you back."
> "You are a true friend," Polly said with a catch in her voice. (Greene, 1981, pp. 19–20)

Yet sometimes the choices are tougher than simply how to persuade one's parents without revealing the obligations one feels to a friend. Helping the friend may get the child into trouble:

> Tanya is my friend, she thought, and I have to go. It was worth a spanking, even worth not getting earrings, to help a best friend. (Matthis, 1971, p. 23)

In short, a child's dilemmas in managing the expectations of friends versus those of others begin to comprise socially constituted moral choices (Youniss, 1980). Although the distinctions and affinities between broader conceptions of justice and fairness to one's friends may not be especially clear to children (and can be difficult for adults to recognize), Damon (1977) observes that "the roots of justice may be found growing in the soil of early friendships" (p. 139).

Still, parents might not completely understand why their child seems to like a particular friend more than the other kids on the street, or why he or she is so petty, jealous, or competitive with youngsters who are supposed to be friends—or so anxious and expectant about and responsive to their actions. On their part, children may not grasp why their own parents are not friends with their friends' "neat" parents, or why adults who say they are friends with each other sometimes do not act like it. Different worlds of friendship continue to evolve according to the premises and practices available to children and those employed by adults:

> Lilly Etta looked at her mother. Then she spoke quietly, "Aren't you going to help Mrs. Brown? She's your friend."
>
> "Yes. I'm her friend and I been her friend for years." Mrs. Allen touched the neckline of her large-flowered dress and stood still for a moment before she started peeling potatoes again. "But I can't help her. She knows I can't help her." . . .
>
> "When I get big," she whispered, just loud enough for her mother to hear, "I don't want friends that can't help me!" . . .
>
> The lump in Lilly Etta's throat was getting smaller, but she didn't want to talk.
>
> "I got to take care of us first. Louise Brown knows that. That don't mean we're not friends. Friends ain't just to help each other." (Matthis, 1971, pp. 16–19)

Despite her mother's explanation of her interpersonal priorities, it is unlikely that Lilly Etta comprehends the complexities of her mother's predicament in declining to aid her longtime friend. For the 9 year old, refusing to help is simply not being a friend.

Mutuality and Understanding

> One of the best things is to have a best friend. (Stolz, 1980a, p. 3)

Sometime during preadolescence to early adolescence children begin to cultivate close friendships with people who have personalities they admire. They realize that though these relationships require more effort to form, they are able to weather bad periods and negative events and to endure, and that their views of themselves will be greatly influenced by their interactions with their friends. The narrator below reflects on her friend's characteristic manner of treating her that differs from other peers:

> "What are the residuals?" I said. Al frequently uses words I don't understand. One nice thing about her though. She never says, "What! You never heard of residuals!" or anything like that. She doesn't treat me as if I were a total idiot because I don't know the meaning of a word, and I know plenty of people who do that. (Greene, 1981, p. 5)

Reflexively, the communicative practices necessary for establishing and maintaining intimacy tend to appear earlier developmentally in girls' friendships than boys, and they negotiate friendships of mutuality and understanding sooner (Buhrmester & Furman, 1987; Smollar & Youniss, 1982). Friends enacting this mode foster understanding of each other through discussing their personal thoughts and emotions. They are at ease together, feeling comfortable in their mutual expression and recognition of the special qualities of their relationship and of each other as individuals.

In the following extended quotation, Marcia, an actual 21-year-old woman, recalls the early period of her still flourishing friendship with Julia:

> "Are you the new girl?" was the question that began this eleven year friendship. I had just moved from across town and, like most children, I was very apprehensive about going to a new school and having to make new friends. But being approached by Julia was probably the best thing that could have happened to me. We became good friends quickly and before long we were inseparable. Every Friday we would spend the night at each other's house and stay up all night talking about boys and what we wanted to be when we grew up. That whole year we never had one argument or fight.
>
> Then something unexpected happened; her father got transferred down to Athens, Georgia, and she was moving in a couple of weeks. Devastated, we tried to spend every waking minute together that we could. We would play "Charlie's Angels" or 4-square. We even wrote to the Guinness Book of World Records to request that we have the chance to set a record for the longest time to continuously play 4-square.
>
> I can still remember the day she moved like it was yesterday. We tried not to think about this being the last time we'd see each other for a long time as we sat on her patio and ate Kentucky Fried Chicken. It seemed like the end of the world when my parents finally convinced me to say good-bye to Julia and get in the car. But before we said good-bye, we made a promise to faithfully write each other and we made up code names so

that anyone who read our letters wouldn't know our identities, M-10 and J-10. The initials of our first names and our ages (probably the product of watching too many episodes of "Charlie's Angels!"). We both survived the separation and are still faithfully writing and calling each other.

Marcia's recollections indicate several features of friendship in this mode. The two girls' relationship involves considerable mutual affection and enjoyment, as expressed by their inseparability, regular sleepovers, delight in playing games together, and reaction to Julia's impending move. Still, their customary all-night discussions of boys and future aspirations, and their kept promises to write, coupled with secret code names to protect their privacy, even more pointedly reveal a friendship of shared emotional investment and trust extending beyond merely common activities. And though their reportedly perfect yearlong harmony might be partially due to selective memory, the absence of recalled quarrels further suggests the degree of understanding established between the girls.

In short, this friendship was of distinct personal significance for each of these young persons, whose partner was not to be replaced easily, if ever. Of course, the concerns and visions shared by these 10 year olds would probably seem naive and simplistic to adults, and at this age the girls predictably had not encountered many of the choices, shifting priorities, and stresses that accompany ongoing maturation. Even so, at this juncture in their lives they were apparently able to discuss personal issues together and to pursue joint ventures like a marathon 4-square game commemorating their bond. Accordingly, they formed a shared rudimentary basis for a friendship that continues to thrive in their young adulthood, even though they remain apart geographically.

The quotation also articulates a commonplace situation reflecting parents' impact on the circumstances of children's friendships at any age until they leave home. Relocation or moving house is a reasonably frequent occurrence for many Americans. In its wake are two classes of children, "new kids" and those who are left behind, *both* of whom now must deal with the breach and make new friends. Younger children typically are not as deeply affected as older ones due to the nature of their friendships. But close or best friends are decidedly more difficult to exchange as early adolescence progresses (like many adults' friends, which we will discuss later). In the case above it appears that Julia spared Marcia much of the difficulty of being "the new girl."

The next narrative excerpt depicts Polly's contemplation of the challenge posed by her best friend's departure:

She didn't see how she could start making another best friend in the fifth grade, which was where she was going to be this coming fall. Just thinking about the school without Kate in it was depressing. It took *time* to make a best friend. It wasn't that she didn't have other friends at school. She did. It was just—just that she and Kate got along so well they hadn't really needed anybody else. (Stolz, 1980b, pp. 1–2)

Returning to the actual friends considered above, Marcia echoes below these initial concerns attending the move-induced breakup of her exclusive, best friendship with Julia. However, retrospectively, she also discusses that the early drawbacks gave way to positive aspects:

During the year we first became friends we were exclusive in our activities; we only did things with each other. Consequently, I didn't meet very many of the other children at my school. In essence, when Julia moved, we both had to "start over" at building new relationships. I think that both helped and put a strain on the relationship. It helped me to be more independent and not to revolve my whole life around my friends. I was emotionally insecure after Julia moved because I felt I couldn't do anything by myself. That was a good learning experience for me even though I was only eleven years old.

Both quotations imply that despite their advantages, there are also risks associated with overly exclusive bonds; sometimes they inhibit independence and broader affiliations. The passages also illustrate the extent to which involvement with close friends shapes children's identities and self-perceptions.

When self or a best friend moves, it typically takes time, experiences together, and gradually developed mutual trust to forge a new friendship that fulfills the expectations of previous intimacy. And there are always comparisons with the prior, and sometimes still maintained, friendship. Despite her misgivings examined above, the fictional character, Polly makes the effort to get to know a girl named Consuela. Her thoughts, portrayed here, imply the heightened standards and increasing complexity of replacing a friendship of mutuality and understanding during preadolescence:

Polly wasn't sure she and Consuela had become friends. Consuela wasn't a person you told things to that you wouldn't tell to anyone else, the way she and Kate had told each other things. If Consuela went away, it wouldn't be the way it had been when Kate had left. Polly had plenty of friends at school now, always someone to eat with, play games with, gab on the telephone with. She didn't need Consuela the way she'd needed Kate. Just the same, she thought that very slowly they were working their way toward a friendship. She found it all too complicated to discuss, even with Gram. So she was just letting matters take their course. (Stolz, 1980a, pp. 114–115)

Like many children her age, Polly's opportunities for friendship coexist with a variety of daily activities undertaken with several persons. Yet by early adolescence, given friendships develop mutual confidence and dependence in ways not always clearly defined or preplanned, much less articulated verbally to someone else. At this time, the self-conceptions, relational alternatives, and social worlds of children become increasingly complicated and interdependent. Meanwhile, interactions with friends continue to generate as well as help the young person deal with the problems and possibilities of growing up.

A Dialectical View of the Interactional Processes of Children's Friendships

From the beginning children's knowledge and practices of friendship are constituted interpersonally and developed in concrete social circumstances (Youniss, 1978). A young person acquires more realistic conceptions of friendship and his or her social self, and must learn appropriate communicative skills for conducting friendships in concert with peers, and subsequently adults, who do not have to like or accept the child (Youniss, 1980; Rubin, 1980). Throughout childhood, the different moments and modes of friendship shape and reflect various configurations of its dialectical features as a situated interpersonal activity. Accordingly, our discussion of children's friendships will conclude by examining how the dialectical principles of the freedom to be independent and the freedom to be dependent, affection and instrumentality, judgment and acceptance, and expressiveness and protectiveness are enacted during this period. Though I address these principles individually below, they actually interweave in composing the interactions of friends.

The freedoms to be both independent of and dependent on one's friend comprise contradictory tendencies in managing availability within friendships. Conflicts between these two liberties are played out differently throughout childhood friendships because younger children do not comprehend that relationships can still persist despite the friends' separation and are therefore not preoccupied with the bond itself. In contrast, once older children understand the possibility of enduring voluntary attachments, they become quite concerned about being apart from friends. Thus, a developmental trajectory occurs across childhood wherein young friends' original characteristic independence gradually transforms into dependence. Ongoing activity and social experience change the early fleeting friendships composed of independent and self-oriented participants into more dependent and mutual pairs, sometimes jealously regarding each other's autonomous relations.

At any point in childhood, however, friendship remains voluntary; it rests on choosing another and/or being selected oneself. Consequently, self or the other person can dissolve the attachment at any time. This undeniable contingency can always incite tensions regarding excessively independent or dependent actions by friends, even though early childhood friendships typically seem to display detached comportment and later ones greater reliance. However, it is not until early adolescence that children's friendships exhibit the full-blown interactive dynamics derived from ongoing attempts and realized abilities to synthesize these antagonistic freedoms within maintained friendships (Selman, 1981; Rawlins, 1983a).

The dialectic of affection and instrumentality formulates the interrelationship between caring for a friend as an end-in-itself and/or as a means-to-an-end (Rawlins, 1989a). Damon (1977) argues that the seminal issue in friendship is affection or liking, yielding the fundamental quandary of identifying "who likes whom." The challenge for children is learning how to express affection toward, and to earn and experience affection from persons who are not compelled to like them. Initially, minimal distinctions exist between affection and instrumentality as bases for friendship; a child simply considers someone a friend because the person's belongings and/or attributes give self pleasure. Thus, as long as one has things to offer, one is liked; both affection and utility are episodically accomplished.

An opposition between materialistic and psychological foundations of friendship begins to arise as children notice desirable personal qualities of others through interacting with them (Damon, 1977). As this recognition occurs, the object-centered and opportunistic practices of earlier friendships are gradually replaced by reciprocated assistance and proven dependability between particular individuals who consider themselves friends. Meanwhile, other children may not be liked because of the way they repeatedly interact with self, even though they possess pleasing toys or privileges.

The potentially conflicting aspects of affection and intrumentality are synthesized differently later on in early adolescence with the negotiation of ongoing, mutually beneficial friendships. Such friends like each other and understand their personal characteristics as continually revealed through activities together and involved discussions of private concerns. They develop sensitivity to their friend's needs and feel good about helping and sharing. In a sense these friends are both liked and useful because of the personal qualities they exhibit *and* the ongoing services they provide within the interactional parameters of a jointly gratifying relationship. Tensions frequently arise, however, when perceptions of mutuality are correctly or mistakenly undermined, and either friend feels that he or she is being used in the name of friendship.

The dialectic of judgment and acceptance assumes primary significance in friendships during this period because eventually it is within these relationships that young people develop both the practices and the standards they will employ together for making moral choices and treating others fairly in situations out of the purview of adults (Youniss, 1980). It is also within their friendships and social groups that judgments are communicated about the very acceptability of the child outside the home.

Consequently, selecting friends reflexively involves increasingly important judgments—because the standards one employs in choosing one's friends shapes the pool of significant peers with whom further guidelines will be negotiated for appraising self's and others' beliefs and actions. Further, accepting someone as a friend may mean rejecting others. And though males typically are more inclusive than females, judgmental lines are drawn with the joy of acceptance and inclusion constituting the dialectical counterpart of the pain of rejection and exclusion. Further, Rubin (1980) warns that despite the edifying potential of friendships, a dark side abides, "Intimate friendships give rise not only to self-acceptance, trust, and rapport, but also to insecurity, jealousy, and resentment" (p. 11).

Throughout our lives, managing friendships presupposes exercising judgment. Yet in childhood, the judgments involving friends develop from hallmarks of unchecked subjectivity to pioneering efforts at collaboration and shared reflection. The early choices of friends based on surface features and self's preferences are gradually supplemented by evaluations of others' personal and psychological qualities across situations. Even so, similarity in gender, attitudes, abilities, and interests still typify children's friendships; it is not until mid to late adolescence that most young people accept pronounced differences in friends (Smollar & Youniss, 1982). Meanwhile, strict conventions governing friends' conduct give way to perceptions of need and reciprocal rights to fair treatment in evaluating self's and others' actions. Preserving equality also becomes essential in legislating behavior between friends (Youniss, 1980).

In short, judging together as friends supplants solitary assessments. Conducting friendship moves from a model of arbitrary rules and unilateral constraints imposed by one person on the other toward a collaborative development of evaluative standards based on perceived need and the mutual desire to foster equality (Youniss, 1980). An accompanying shift occurs from self-oriented to jointly derived perceptions of others and events (Selman, 1981). The emergence of such private and mutually negotiated moral orders underpins some, yet also may compete with other, peer group standards. Accordingly, reconciling their co-constructed moral visions with those of parents and the larger society becomes an essential project for youths in friendships during adolescence.

Practices reflecting the dialectical interplay of expressiveness and protectiveness progressively characterize friends' communication across this period. For much of early childhood, children are notoriously blunt with peers, including their friends, although they soon realize that playmates will not tolerate unchecked enthusiasm, aggressiveness, or temper tantrums (Gottman, 1986). An important aspect of developing "social accommodation" and adapting one's actions to others in middle childhood, however, includes recognizing and avoiding those actions or statements that hurt friends' feelings or make them feel angry or insecure (Sullivan, 1953). A slow cultivation of tact and sensitivity occurs (Rubin, 1980).

As friendship begins to involve revealing and discussing personal thoughts and feelings, each friend's vulnerability to criticism by the other and risk of embarrassing exposure to persons outside the friendship increase greatly. Especially for girls at this juncture, private revelations, confidence, and mutual trust begin to distinguish close or best friends from other less involved companions. Thus, the definitive customs of dyads as well as cliques begin to involve not merely collectively doing things, but talking together and sharing secrets, gossip, and personal knowledge.

Conversation between friends increasingly complements and sometimes replaces mere activities in comprising the essence of the relationship. As adolescence approaches, the risks and rewards of this discourse multiply in confronting, handling, and/or mismanaging the mutually constituted and reflexive tensions of independence and dependence, affection and instrumentality, judgment and acceptance, and expressiveness and protectiveness. Even so, we may notice young persons evolving and practicing key tenets of a classical conception of friendship at this time (Youniss, 1980). That is, they converse as equals who are sensitive to each other's needs and willing to relinquish personal preferences in the interests of shared and equal benefit. They talk through their differences attempting to understand each other. They care about each other.

But in witnessing the encouraging appearance of such collaboration, we must remember that these ethical sensibilities and feelings of belonging have their counterparts in harsh judgments and hurtful exclusion. And though many of the intersubjectively formed practices necessary for mature friendship are realized by early adolescence, the coming years present manifold challenges to young persons and their friendships that differ in emotional poignancy and social complexity from those of childhood where many were first encountered.

Chapter 4

Adolescent Friendships

By early adolescence young persons typically have developed the rudiments of friendship as a voluntary, mutually accomplished, ongoing personal attachment. Friends are equals deserving sensitivity and fair treatment (Berndt, 1985). They reciprocally help and share with one another and cultivate intimacy by discussing personal concerns (Berndt, 1982a; Bukowski & Kramer, 1986).

Even so, early adolescent friendships remain nested in same-sex friendship cliques, exerting strong conformity pressures that begin to wane only during mid adolescence (Costanzo & Shaw, 1966; Adams & Gullotta, 1983). Possessiveness and jealousy cause problems in exclusive friendships as young people struggle to enact interdependence as a viable synthesis of independent and dependent behaviors by friends (Selman, 1981; Rawlins, 1983a). Further, preferences persist for similar others; accepting a friend's differences is a practice that develops across adolescence (Bukowski, Newcomb, & Hoza, 1987). Finally, as puberty dawns, cross-sex relationships reenter the picture as relational possibilities, confusing and finally surpassing same-sex bonds in intimacy by the end of adolescence (Berndt, 1982a).

The pivotal role of friendship during adolescence is recognized by writers on both subjects (Douvan & Adelson, 1966; Dubois, 1974; Coleman, 1980). This period comprises a watershed for friendship for various reasons. Developmental changes in physiology, cognitive abilities, and personal and social expectations interactively facilitate and complicate the adolescent's aptitude and inclinations for friendship. Moreover, the pursuit of identity, intimacy, and appropriate public comportment combine in adolescent friendships with functional significance over the life-course. Accordingly, this chapter explores some of the developmental tasks, problematics, and socially constituted exigencies involved in the communicative management of friendships during adolescence.

I begin by examining how adolescents achieve their self-definitions communicatively in conjunction with their social networks. Friendships assume dramatic importance in this process. Next, I describe adolescents' ongoing communication with their parents and/or friends, and I detail various aspects of communicating with friends within peer culture. I then discuss gender issues and the significance of cross-sex relationships during this period. The chapter concludes with implications of managing friendships within multiple social systems for being-in-the-world as an adolescent, cultivating communicative competence, and developing evaluative standards for appraising self's and others' behaviors.

Adolescence and Friendship: An Overview

One can demarcate the lower limits of adolescence physiologically with the onset of puberty, while its upper limits vary. It can end fairly abruptly when one assumes the responsibilities of marriage and/or full-time work (Sullivan, 1953; Campbell, 1969). Or it can gradually evolve in the late teens into early adulthood as a person separates from his or her family of origin and begins exploring and testing choices for adult identities, relationships, and career paths (Levinson et al., 1979). A central problematic in analyzing and accomplishing friendships during this period derives from its status as essentially preparatory for adult life. The activities of adolescents are frequently evaluated not as ends-in-themselves but primarily as opportunities to learn and practice behavioral skills or cognitions promoting well-adjusted adulthood. Campbell (1969) observes, "What is now will not be then, and the really important things come not now but later" (p. 843). The temporal perspective of adolescence is skewed toward the future (Campbell, 1969).

Meanwhile, developmental tasks of adolescence like articulating one's identity, sense of values, and communicative practices for managing intimacy might be preempted or robbed of their potential for developing internal resources if conducted according to narrow, adult models for appropriate interaction in a conventionalized, competitive workaday world. Several authors argue after Douvan and Adelson (1966) that "learning friendship" is one of the primary challenges of adolescence that can provide significant emotional, moral, and communicative grounding and skills if pursued for its own inherent value instead of solely as a proto-adult practice (Erikson, 1968; Mitchell, 1976; Youniss & Smollar, 1985).

Cognitive changes reaching fruition during this period affect and reflect such interpersonal bonding. The development of formal operations in adolescence comprises a radical change in one's mental capabilities, which Elkind (1984) terms "thinking in a new key." Formal operations entail a shift from thinking in the present to envisioning a world of possibilities. Thinking about the future, hypothetical reasoning, and testing of conjectures become characteristic modes of thought (Adams & Gullotta, 1983). Increasingly, the adolescent thinks about thoughts and begins to formulate and critically evaluate his/her ideals. Such self-examination in conjunction with social perspective-taking skills already developing in preadolescence are necessary for understanding and articulating the mutual expectations of an interpersonal relationship like friendship (Selman, 1981). Attempts to test these conceptions and ideals in actual relations with other peers occur (La Gaipa, 1979).

Research reveals the implications of these maturing cognitive abilities for conceiving of and practicing friendship. Peevers and Secord (1973) found that by eleventh grade subjects used more differentiated statements to describe friends and nonfriends, showed greater interpersonal involvement with friends, and recognized situational and temporal changes in friends and nonfriends. Kon and Losenkov (1978) also discovered that older adolescents could more precisely distinguish degrees of friendship and differentiate between friends and companions. In short, by mid to late adolescence, sophisticated thinking about friendship is in evidence. Epstein observes, "Older children can consider simultaneously all available information about the self, the friend, the friendship, the implications of friendship for the future, and the demands of the environment in which the friendship will occur" (1983, p. 44).

The aptitude for and openness to friendship play crucial roles in the adolescent pursuits of identity and intimacy. The critical task of adolescence is to develop one's identity (Erikson, 1968; Elkind, 1984; Douvan & Adelson, 1966; Marcia, 1980). According to Douvan and Adelson, "In our society the adolescent period sees the most intense development of friendship. . . . He is about to crystallize an identity, and for this needs others of his generation to act as models, mirrors, helpers, testers, foils" (1966, pp. 178–179). Young people at this stage begin to separate from their families and to develop friendship bonds in a world of peers (Epstein, 1983). Leading to adult autonomy, these friendships provide a crucible for forging "a workable, acceptable identity" (Douvan, 1983, p. 63).

Adolescents need close companions to confide in and talk with about their day-to-day concerns (Mitchell, 1976; Johnson & Aries, 1983; Naegele, 1958). Conflict with parents, fears of rejection from the peer group, anxiety about emerging sexuality, and various pressures at school are often major issues for discussion. Intimacy is a necessity. Conger maintains that

> People need, in adolescence perhaps more than at any other time in their lives, to be able to share strong and often confusing emotions, doubts and dreams with others. . . . This means that acceptance by peers generally, and especially having one or more close friends, may be of crucial importance in a young person's life. (1979, p. 66)

Indeed, the need for acceptance and validation of self and the need for intimacy are closely associated in adolescence (Horrocks & Benimoff, 1966; Kon & Losenkov, 1978; Smollar & Youniss, 1982). The young person trying out different self-conceptions wants to feel the validity of both the process and its products. This highly individualized pursuit requires personal validation by someone who views self independently of historical precedents, as might occur in the family, or societal role requirements, as might occur in school or work (Kelvin, 1977). In the process of explaining themselves to each other over a period of time, adolescent friends help articulate each other's identities. Developing a personalized identity and experiencing intimacy appear to be counterparts that interpenetrate during adolescent friendship (Kon, 1981).

The functional significance of adolescent friendship is closely aligned with its role in the search for selfhood and intimacy. As previously noted, starting in later childhood, peer friendships provide an arena for communication independent of the family and historical precedents of interaction; they are achieved, not ascribed. Accordingly, the adolescent is compelled to develop the communication skills requisite for a voluntaristic relationship characterized by much give and take and interpersonal negotiation (Naegele, 1958; Rawlins, 1983a; Suttles, 1970). Further, this type of relationship involves cooperating with peers regarding crucial personal concerns rather than simply pleasing authority figures (Piaget, 1932; Sullivan, 1953; Youniss, 1980).

However, in adolescence one's identity also derives from participating in a bustling, public order of peer relations. For example, study friends and sports friends might confirm or challenge one's abilities in these "objective" domains with limited exposure to one's feelings about such evaluation. Likewise, one may "hang around" with activity and school friends with varying success in general sociability. These everyday interactions communicate a multifacted social appraisal of the presented self to the extent that a person chooses to participate in them (Berger & Luckman, 1966).

Simultaneously, a person developing more personal, subjective ties in the dyadic realm of closer friendship can discuss and interpret experiences occurring in the public arena with peers and their implications for personal worth. At risk are core conceptions of the self and feelings that may contrast with public views. A trusted, intimate other like a best or close friend is necessary for such dialogue. Developing these private views of self may devalue or threaten the validity of evaluative standards held outside of the friendship. Though such discussions may brace a person for further interaction with peers and/or parents and possibly result in altered behavior toward others, their content should remain confidential. Consequently, adolescent friendships are pursued in an interactive and experiential continuum ranging from peer-oriented, public comportment and appraisal to friend-oriented, private communication and evaluation.

The adolescent's self-conscious efforts at self-definition, friendship formation, and social integration interpenetrate and are permeated with rhetorical and dramatistic qualities. Indeed, Elkind (1967, 1980) maintains that early adolescents in particular are prone to feel constantly "on stage" for two reasons. First, developing formal operations initially makes young persons exceedingly self-aware; they are "preoccupied with themselves and assume that other people share that preoccupation" (Elkind, 1980, p. 435). Accordingly, they construct an "imaginary audience" that is always closely observing their actions in given situations (Elkind, 1980). Second, adolescents are self-centered and develop "personal fables" or narratives celebrating their uniqueness, importance, and destinies (Elkind, 1967, 1980). These two tendencies lead to adolescent concern that other people are discussing them and reviewing their self-presentations.

Such suspicion appears justified. Consider the multiple and interconnected social systems potentially enveloping the family during adolescence—"best" and various close friendships; friendship cliques and peer pecking orders; sexual relationships and dating networks; voluntary, elected, or selected clubs, religious organizations, student councils, newspapers and honor societies; athletic, musical, cheerleading, artistic, and academic competitions; part-time jobs; not to mention "Kings" and "Queens" of proms and homecoming dances, and so on. Others continually appraise the adolescent in each of these areas according to various evaluative criteria, some specific to a given enterprise and others involving complex combinations of rankings in diverse domains. *All of these standards are socially constructed and communicated; many contradict each other.*

The family's criteria for evaluating self mostly reflect particularistic and subjective concerns; basically, they are developed to foster emotional security in a child (Eisenstadt, 1956). As the adolescent's encompassing social nexus unfolds, however, the knowledge and appraisal of intimate friends and romantic partners may outstrip the family's in private matters. Simultaneously, the objective rankings of the young person's public pursuits according to universal achievement criteria eclipse the family's judgments of behavior in those endeavors as well (Eisenstadt, 1956). The normative composition of the adolescent's worlds rapidly becomes much less clearcut. Irreducible to simple, predetermined moral codes with attendant "sanctioning agents" (Campbell 1969, p. 843), standards of behavior emerge through interaction across a variety of circumstances according to objective, subjective, and intersubjective criteria.

The acute self-consciousness and theatrical sensibilities of adolescents seem understandable and functional in this ecology of manifold audiences and appraisals. The attempt to define one's identity involves consciously stylizing oneself in various ways and trying out different versions and images of who one is and/or could become (Campbell, 1969). In this process one also chooses the particular audiences whose opinions will matter. Since one's activities and associates are subject to multiple interpretations and judgments, the adolescent must begin to decide who he/she is "playing to." In short, adolescents are engaged in the reflexive process of consolidating their self-conceptions and identities as well as locating the social systems within which they can be developed and sustained.

Within this field of possibilities, friendships occupy a peculiar niche. Though crucial for adolescent development, they essentially comprise a marginal category of social relationships when viewed through the lens of adult socialization. Because the significance of friendships is difficult to identify precisely, it pales in comparison to (1) athletic endeavors, which "teach life" or institutionalized teamwork, coupled with a competitive ethic; (2) academic and vocational endeavors, which teach appropriate skills and attitudes for occupational achievement; (3) romantic endeavors, which teach ways of expressing and managing sexual urges and may anticipate the reproductive functions and the religious and legal bonds of marriage; and (4) family endeavors, which teach intergenerational continuity and duty to one's kin. Friendships have no clear normative status within this publicly constituted hierarchy of role relationships; yet they may compete with, complement, substitute for, or fuse with these other types of social bonds (Hess, 1972).

Despite its marginal status, friendship functions intriguingly as a "double agency," weaving in and out of the adolescent's various social worlds, concurrently fulfilling goals of personal growth and social integration (Rawlins, 1989b). Ironically, though friendships offer adolescents the opportunity to transcend public and parental appraisals and to negotiate private standards for behavior, statistically the demographic profiles of such friends closely resemble each other as well as their families of origin (Campbell, 1969). Adolescent friends are typically the same age, gender, race, grade in school, and social status (Campbell, 1969; Kandel, 1978b). Moreover, they tend to share fundamental values (Douvan & Adelson, 1966) and similar attitudes toward academic pursuits (Kandel, 1978b, Ball, 1981; Epstein 1983), peer culture (Kandel, 1978b; Berndt, 1982a), and illicit activities like drinking and drug use (Jessor & Jessor, 1975; Kandel, 1978b). Clearly, however, these conclusions are based on research that cannot definitively distinguish between similarities in outlooks preceding friendships and those developing through interaction within them (Kandel, 1978a).

Even so, some important ironies accompany the double agency of adolescent friendships. One involves the idea that adolescent friendships comprise a fundamental nexus for beginning to separate from one's parents and for developing an autonomous identity. In this process, persons who are similar to the adolescent confirm already held attitudes and values and individuals who are different urge change (Epstein, 1983). However, adolescents typically befriend persons who are similar to them in many ways. Thus, the relationships conceivably offering the adolescent a forum for personalized questioning, critique, and value formation frequently reflect similar moral horizons as one's family of origin. The double agency of friendship allows partners to test the limits of inherited worldviews in a privately negotiated realm whose evaluative contours, though permissive, are typically not drastically different from one's family. To the extent they diverge, they facilitate and encourage idiosyncratic options for defining self yet heighten the potential for conflict with other social formations. To the extent they mirror conventional social practices, they limit self or mutually conceived choices and minimize the friction and challenges of contesting standards.

Communicating with Parents and/or Friends

In their classic work on adolescence Douvan and Adelson (1966, p. 129) observe, "It is in the intergenerational dialectic that while the child must stand for freedom, so must the parents stand for control." Because of this dialectic, adolescence presents some of life's most poignant communicative challenges to parents and children. While parents are motivated to emphasize the continuity of life, teenagers are inspirited to rebel and define their individuality (Bloom, 1980).

Meanwhile, both parents and children feel ambivalence about the child's attaining autonomy (Rawlins & Holl, 1988). The adolescent faces the paradoxical task of increasing independence while preserving a caring relationship with his or her parents. Parents, in turn, must balance guidance and interference in monitoring their child's development (Adams & Gullotta, 1983). A favorable experience in separating from one's parents is critical in dealing with interpersonal disjunctions later in life (Bloom, 1980).

Research reveals that maintaining a caring and supportive relationship with one's parents is essential to develop autonomy during adolescence (Youniss & Smollar, 1985; Grotevant & Cooper, 1985). For example, O'Donnell (1976) reported that adolescents' self-esteem more closely correlated with feelings toward parents than toward friends. And Greenburg, Siegel, and Leitch (1983) argued that "the development of ego autonomy and optimal adjustment are promoted by the development of independence in the context of warm relatedness to one's parents" (p. 383).

Moreover, in studying a sample of fourth, seventh, and tenth graders, and undergraduate students (whose average ages were approximately 9, 12, 15, and 19 years, respectively), Hunter and Youniss (1982) identified several related tendencies. First, although reported intimacy with friends was initially lower than with parents in the fourth grade, it exceeded the parent–child levels by tenth grade. Levels of giving and helping ("nurture") also rose with increasing age in the adolescent friendships. However, even with these favorable trends in the assessments of friendships, parent–child relations continued to be valued highly as well. Granted, all age groups considered parents more controlling than friends with the differences not diminishing in later adolescence. Yet, intimacy between parents and children did not correspondingly decline with the increased intimacy of the adolescents' friendships, and the nurture provided by parents was consistently high across age levels. Hunter and Youniss (1982) concluded that parents and friends share some common contributions yet still serve distinct functions in shaping the child's experience throughout adolescence.

But adolescents are active participants in their own social–emotional development and individuation, not merely passive respondents to adult or peer socialization practices. Their choices in conversing with, listening to, and ignoring certain persons have important implications for developing their self-conceptions, conceptions of social relationships, and criteria for assessing both. Whom they select, and why and how adolescents choose to interact with others are therefore seminal concerns.

Accordingly, I present here a conceptual framework for understanding a group of eleventh graders' accounts of managing interaction with their parents and friends that reflects an active view of young persons' communicative and behavioral decisions and also challenges the traditional misconception of adolescent friendships as developing in opposition to relationships with parents (Rawlins & Holl, 1988). These adolescents' descriptions of their interactions with parents and friends suggested dialectical interplay between the two groups' reactions that shaped the ongoing achievement of the young persons' activities and self-perceptions. As a result, they reported choosing different conversational partners according to the nature of the topic, the anticipated type of response, and the degree of caring manifested in the relationship.

Two dialectical principles appeared to inform their decisions about potential interactants, the dialectic of historical perspective and contemporary experience, and the dialectic of judgment and acceptance. Overall, parents were conceived as viewing adolescent concerns from the distance of a historical perspective. The fact that they had already "been through" most of the events and predicaments that might worry these young people recommended their input. Moreover, parents' knowledge of the potential impact of certain courses of action on later life choices was considered "wisdom."

Even so, our participants did not always want the existential distance and measured perspective of their parents. For matters involving seemingly current sensibilities and knowledge of the present stakes of action, they elected to talk with friends. They felt that persons who were currently living through similar quandaries would better understand and resonate their significance. Consequently, they dialectically associated parents with a historical perspective and friends with contemporary experience in choosing people to talk with about their concerns.

The dialectic of judgment and acceptance informed their choices as well. I mentioned earlier the significant desire and need in adolescence for acceptance by others. Our participants were no exception; they greatly valued people who understood and accepted them and resented and avoided people who judged and criticized or otherwise "put them down." They viewed parents as much more likely than their friends to criticize them. Parents had certain expectations for their behavior, and violating them resulted in unfavorable reactions by parents communicating a low evaluation of the adolescent, for example, yelling, badgering with questions, and criticizing. In contrast, our respondents perceived their friends as typically accepting them for who they were and not criticizing them. The dialectical juxtaposition identified in our participants' overall association of judgment and criticism with parents and acceptance with friends corresponds with similar findings by Larson (1983), Youniss and Smollar (1985), and Hunter (1985), even though these investigations utilized different research methods.

However, anticipating judgment from parents and acceptance from friends did not necessarily dictate these adolescents' decisions about conversational partners even if accompanied by a desire for historical perspective from parents or contemporary input from friends. The degree of perceived caring also mediated their perceptions of parents' judgmental tendencies and friends' acceptance. Overall, they felt that their parents cared for them more than their friends did, so their criticisms derived from a genuine concern for the adolescent's well-being. In contrast, friends often accepted or even encouraged actions not in the young person's best interests because they did not care as deeply for the individual as his or her parents. Thus, parental caring might impel the adolescent to risk a critical reaction from them, despite an otherwise apparent credo for achieving and protecting independence from parental scrutiny, "Don't tell parents things you did wrong."

Consequently, none of our participants seemed categorically inclined to speak only to parents or friends about everything. They reflected on the issues at stake, the types of responses they might receive from parents and friends, their temporal perspectives, evaluative stances, and the degree of their caring. Their conversational options, however, were not mutually exclusive, nor did they necessarily pit parents and friends against each other. Functioning as counterparts, both parents and friends complement, correct, and mediate each others' views and standards as alternative voices in the ongoing conversations comprising the adolescent's construction of a social self.

Communicating with Friends within Peer Culture

As mentioned earlier, the peer culture of adolescence potentially transcends the purview of the family. The multiple social systems of the teen years utilize interlaced evaluative criteria ranging from those more subjective and intimate than one's family to those more objective and public. Desiring acceptance by close associates and/or peers in general, adolescents continually face the challenge of developing communicative skills appropriate for managing differing social relationships and exigencies often at odds with each other.

The high school juniors we interviewed noted a tension between popularity and friendship (Rawlins & Holl, 1987). Popularity involves recognition and respect by others, a high profile. Requiring numbers of people, it is a public achievement based on demonstrable qualities and accomplishments or appearances. Students remarked that popularity can accompany success in sports or school, for example, but it frequently involves a fair-weather or opportunistic quality, not necessarily trust or confidence. Popular people are "fun" and impressive to be seen with.

In contrast, friendship involves acknowledgment, acceptance, and selection by a particular individual. Based on personal qualities and another's understanding of one's feelings and thoughts, it is a more private, dyadic achievement. Friends have fun together but also take each other seriously.

Talk with close friends performs critical functions in structuring a sense of self and relationships with others (Rawlins & Holl, 1987). Trusting a friend implies mutually negotiated responsibilities and expectations regarding interaction within and outside of the friendship. Conversation between friends should be accepting and mostly uncritical. Honest feedback describing how the friend and other peers perceive self is desired, if rendered sensitively. A friend must talk prudently with others about self, preserving confidences and refraining from criticism. Violating trust is a poignant act that can subvert an individual's self-image and/or perceptions of how others see him/her; such breaches strongly and negatively affect and frequently end particular friendships, and rearrange friendship networks (Rawlins & Holl, 1987).

The two realms of private communication and public comportment appear to require different styles of relating to others. Strategies fostering popularity may inhibit a particular friendship and vice versa. Popular people are frequently too busy with activities or juggling acquaintances to have the time or commitment for intimate friendships (Horrocks & Benimoff, 1966). Further, popular persons may be selected as friends for the wrong reasons. One male we interviewed advised, "Being popular is when people know you, they're not really, you can consider them sometimes your friends but really they just hang around you because you're known and maybe they'll get known." Having what it takes to be respected by peers in general may not always result in affection by particular individuals (Berndt & Das, 1987). In contrast, peers might reject an overly exclusive pair of friends because of their conspicuous self-sufficiency. When friends are not available to others or appear too close, peers can express resentment in numerous ways.

Adolescents must learn to position themselves in communication systems involving overlapping and contradictory demands (Fine, 1981). Recently, Buhrmester and Furman (1986) observed, "Social competencies develop through experiences in interactions that require these competencies" (p. 44). Clearly, one's communicative abilities are challenged by the attempt to maintain close and/or superficial friendships during adolescence, with their inevitable internal conflicts; problems arising from responsibilities to different friends, romantic partners, and family; and the unclear and shifting boundaries marking the larger social system of peers (Rawlins & Holl, 1987). However, individuals limiting their range of social experiences, for example, to highly conventionalized or sequestered intimate relationships, will similarly constrain their scope of practiced communicative compentencies.

Two genres of communicative competencies become necessary in early adolescence for managing the broad variety of possible relationships. Social competence describes the cognitions and performances requisite for handling everyday public interactions with groups of peers. "Intimacy competence" refers to the cognitions and performances necessary for negotiating close dyadic relationships (La Gaipa, 1979). Consequently, the communicative management of popularity versus close friendships theoretically involves different structural properties, conceptions, and performance skills. Following Sullivan (1953), Buhrmester and Furman (1986) argue that preadolescent peer-group interactions foster adeptness at cooperation, compromise, and competition, suggesting, "Children who master these modes of interaction are likely to be accepted and popular in the peer group" (p. 56). Yet as we have seen, the collaborative framework of developing close friendships encourages "high level perspective-taking skills, modes of empathic support, and altruistic concern for friends' needs" (p. 56). Buhrmester and Furman (1986) acknowledge that people can learn and utilize both sets of skills in either social domain. However, the characteristic exigencies of remaining popular or preserving a friendship would magnify the salience of their associated skills.

The interlaced peer networks and ongoing personal relationships of adolescence constitute a complex and intimidating social environment within which to embrace or avoid the problematics and satisfactions of developing these contradictory yet complementary competencies. Adolescents' enactments of the communicative possibilities of this social environment range from public to private excesses, and include various individually pursued and contextually negotiated combinations.

Excessive Public Comportment

Certain modes of communicative behavior reflect publicly constituted extremes. The characteristic stance involves inordinate other-directedness (Riesman, 1961), rigid adherence to social conventions, and surface engagements with people. Young people exhibiting these modes may differ, however, in their principal audience. One pattern of behavior is designed for positive appraisal by peers. The individual gauges his/her actions, opinions, and morals primarily in terms of their appeal to peers. Such a pattern of avid conformity, "the tyranny of the peer group" (La Gaipa, 1979), is typically associated with early adolescence and tends to dissipate with the approach of young adulthood (Douvan & Adelson, 1966).

A variation of the above pattern includes communicative behavior primarily targeted for adult audiences and approval. Button states:

> Many people who lack close friends seem to act with other people at a functional or organizational level. They often make all their contacts through interests or activities and play a valuable part in organizing the activity, club or association. They may assume—and be trapped in— leadership roles. Many young people of this kind have great social poise, and are seen by teachers or youth workers as having considerable social accomplishment and may be very valuable to the adult as helpers. The person concerned is so often able to relate easily and readily with older and younger people, but is in difficulty in relating warmly to peers. (1979, pp. 194–195)

Though both modes may prove functional in peer group contexts and for public interactions later in life, several authors worry about an exclusive reliance on or cultivation of such communicative practices (Button, 1979; Mitchell, 1976; Erikson, 1968). Douvan and Adelson (1966) argue that this facility may be only "manner-deep," comprising a retreat into extroversion and a "social persona" (p. 208). The deeper questions, anxieties, and problems of adolescent identity development remain unresolved, and the adolescent forms the habit of social presentation as a dubious salve for personal quandaries.

Excessive Private Conduct

Specific modes of communicative behavior suggest privately constituted excesses as well. Such patterns involve extremes of inner-directedness (Riesman, 1961), highly idiosyncratic notions of appropriate actions, and overweening expectations of intimate bonds. Naegele (1958) describes "isolates" who seem to develop an intensifying retreat into their private selves in light of overly idealized conceptions of friendship. He presents a penetrating analysis of this disturbing predicament:

> Higher ideals restrict opportunities and enhance the chance of disappointment. Fewer can come up to one's expectations and these, in not being met, are thought about rather than acted. Thought, in turn, generates a degree of self-consciousness which makes easy encounters with others difficult and leads to a sense of isolation. (Naegele, 1958, pp. 247–248)

Different but also restrictive patterns involve orienting oneself almost exclusively to the confines of one's family, or adopting or cleaving to a sole intimate friend or romantic partner to avoid the potential stresses or challenges to self-conceptions arising from sustained or episodic interchange with others (Douvan & Adelson, 1966).

Clearly, between such public and private extremes runs a gamut of relational alternatives. For many adolescents different types of friendships are negotiated along an experiential continuum ranging from peer-oriented, public domains to specific other-oriented, private interaction. Adolescents distinguish a gradient of friendship types according to their potential for private knowledge and evaluation of self, and public exposure (Rawlins & Holl, 1987). These include best, close, average, and specialized friends—like sports or study friends—as well as "Friends you say Hi to in the halls." Within these diverse friendships different levels of trust allow for various degrees of talk and the nature and amount of shared activities.

Such friendships exist within an encompassing social system of peers and continually respond to external as well as internal demands and evaluations. To a degree, these contravening pressures are realized and handled by "hanging around" with a variety of people and selectively participating in the gradient of friendships just described. "Hanging around" provides the fluidity between friends and other peers enabling the fulfillment and/or subversion of both status systems' expectations at once. One can be with friends while visible and active with peers. However, a strategic consideration is that whom one "hangs out" with constitutes an expression of self open to others' scrutiny and comment. Elkind (1967, p. 1030) emphasizes that adolescents are "more concerned with being the observed than with being the observer." Thus, one may deploy one's friends in light of peer appraisal, for example, studying with someone but avoiding being seen hanging around with him or her. Conversely, whom a person hangs out with may affect whether one is chosen as a friend.

Actively managing such an array of relationships in interpenetrating contexts requires and fosters extensive competencies in communicating, including social and intimate adeptness. Stressing the potential of the adolescent milieu for developing social competence, Campbell argues, "Skill in the casual cordiality that marks the business world and the country club is acquired with relative ease when one's life-space is flooded with age-mates toward each of whom one invests a modest but only modest, degree of positive affect" (1969, p. 842). Even so, the complementary necessity for intimacy competence is strongly endorsed by Erikson:

> Where a youth does not accomplish such intimate relationships with others—and, I would add, with his own inner resources—in late adoles-

cence or early adulthood, he may settle for highly stereotyped interpersonal relations and come to retain a deep *sense of isolation*. If the times favor an impersonal kind of interpersonal pattern, a man [sic] can go far, very far, in life and yet harbor a severe character problem doubly painful because he will never feel really himself, although everyone says he is "somebody." (1968, pp. 135–136)

The comprehensive challenge is to develop skills in both sociability and intimacy. One needs to master conventional social practices and appropriate public demeanor. However, one must also learn how to manage close, personalized relationships and to cultivate inner assets. Such differential competencies—like expressing casual cordiality without being too glib and sincere affection without being too possessive—require a spectrum of involvements for their practice and development. Experience in multiple types of social engagements enables the adolescent to acquire a diversified sense of audiences with their respective expectations and standards of appraisal.

Gender Issues in Adolescent Friendships

The gender-linked tendencies in handling these social processes are both clear and complex. Overall, adolescent female friendships are characterized as "involved" (Fischer, 1981), more exclusive, and intimate than males' (Kon & Losenkov, 1978; Hunter & Youniss, 1982), closer emotionally (Douvan & Adelson, 1966; Youniss & Smollar, 1985), and more inclined toward disclosure and discussion of personally involving topics (Johnson & Aries, 1983; Youniss & Smollar, 1985). Adolescent females prize their close friends for evaluating experiences and aiding in their personal development (Richey & Richey, 1980). However, the characteristic emphasis placed on loyalty, confidence and commitment in these bonds often fosters intense jealousy between friends and rejection of others desiring to join their conversations (Karweit & Hansell, 1983; Douvan & Adelson, 1966; La Gaipa, 1979; Bigelow & La Gaipa, 1980; Feshback & Sones, 1971). And, unfortunately for those females not included, Townsend, McCracken, and Wilton (1988) observed that in early adolescence "not having an intimate friend" may more negatively affect a female's as opposed to a male's self-esteem (p. 432).

In contrast, adolescent male friendships are described as "uninvolved" (Fischer, 1981), more inclusive, and group-related than females' (Kon & Losenkov, 1978), disclosing less, and talking mostly about activity-oriented issues (Johnson & Aries, 1983; Youniss & Smollar,

1985). While they do begin to air mutual concerns by mid to late adolescence, males tend mostly to value their friends' companionship and the enjoyment of doing activities together (Richey & Richey, 1980; Smollar & Youniss, 1982). However, since males typically emphasize activity, achievement, and leadership, closeness can be inhibited or problems can arise due to feelings of competition between friends (Karweit & Hansell, 1983; Douvan & Adelson, 1966; Richey & Richey, 1980).

By and large young women appear to evidence intimacy competence earlier than young men during adolescence (Fischer, 1981; Smollar & Youniss, 1982). However, various authors argue that males' and females' conceptions of close friendship may be more similar than the above data suggest, but a significantly greater percentage of young women are describing close friendships (Youniss & Smollar, 1985). Across a variety of studies and samples, Youniss & Smollar (1985) report a large minority of male respondents indicating a pattern of responses "clearly different from those given by the majority of all the subjects" (p. 127). The superficiality of this sizable minority's depictions skews their male samples.

Thus, both female and male adolescents who do manage close friendships within the circumstances we have considered are likely to confront and address similar socially constituted exigencies with corresponding potential for developing intimacy competence. Johnson and Aries (1983) remark about both males and females, "For all participants, frequent conversations with close, same-sex friends revolve around concerns about self, relationships, and the web of daily activities" (p. 225). Moreover, despite gender differences in content issues reportedly discussed with parents (females talked about friends and family problems, while males discussed future-oriented concerns like careers, college, and their need for money), the adolescents we interviewed reported equivalent conversational topics with friends as well as a common overall pattern characterizing their interactional rationales for talking with friends and/or parents within their multifaceted social milieus (Rawlins & Holl, 1988). Perhaps, the extensive documentation of adolescent females' greater intimacy competence derives from the fact that more females embrace the challenge and consequently learn how to communicate with close friends sooner. In contrast, a considerable number of males practice the "hail-fellow-well-met" and activity-oriented carriage appropriate for routine male role requirements and ultimately useful for the world of work but not for facilitating intimacy.

Growing interest in members of the opposite sex occurs with the onset of puberty. Yet the composition of adolescent peer groups typically inhibits extended social encounters between boys and girls. In a comprehensive naturalistic study of young people ranging from 13 to 19 years old, Montemayor and Van Komen (1985) observed that "the majority of both male and female adolescents at every age except 19 were more frequently observed in same-sex than in mixed sex groups" both within and outside of school (p. 292). Only by late adolescence did the groups outside of school become smaller and involve more cross-sex members; the in-school groups remained same-sex associations.

Within same-sex peer groups considerable discussion, fantasy rehearsals, and learning of "rules" regarding interaction with the opposite sex transpire (Fine, 1981). Moreover, Sullivan (1953) argued that by managing same-sex intimacy with "chums" during early adolescence, young people practice the interpersonal sensitivity and mutual discussion of feelings and needs necessary for viable cross-sex attachments. Throughout this period, close same-sex friendships with similar others are increasingly supplemented by intimate bonds with the opposite sex (Sharabany, Gershoni, & Hoffman, 1981). Sharabany et al. (1981) remarked that this transition to cross-sex bonds began in the seventh grade for girls and in the ninth for boys, involving delicately loosening and easing the exclusivity of same-sex bonds and reflecting a developing tolerance of and ability to understand differences between persons. Accordingly, by the eleventh grade contrasting perceptions of intimacy in same- and cross-sex friendships were reduced (Sharabany et al., 1981).

But the prospects of romantic and sexual involvement complicate the rising importance of cross-sex relationships as sources of friendship and intimacy during adolescence. For one thing, it is often important to establish for the peer audience whether mixed sex friends are "hanging around together," "just friends," dating each other, or boyfriend and girlfriend. Boys and girls gain status in their peer groups by having "girlfriends" and "boyfriends," respectively (Dunphy, 1963). Cross-sex friendship is a less valued social achievement, much more difficult for others to understand, and frequently doubted anyway (Schofield, 1981).

However, even though opposite-sex friendships and romantic attachments are attributed separate significance by their members and the larger society, the precise nature of these relationships is not always clear even to their participants, much less to outsiders. The behavioral and psychological distinctions between an intimate cross-sex friendship and a romantic love relationship are not easily drawn (Werebe, 1987; Youniss & Smollar, 1985). Feelings and actions within close friendship may resemble love in many respects, and sexual intimacy may not involve any real concern for the other, "given the ambivalences and ambiguities" that characterize the adolescent's grasp of the emotional and sexual expression of affection (Werebe, 1987, p. 272). Even so, despite wide variance in their specific criteria for shared activities and feelings, adolescents differentiate cross-sex friendships from romantic relationships with important implications for social prestige and treatment of each other.

Mid to late adolescents do pursue opposite-sex friendships. The seventh to tenth graders participating in Kon and Losenkov's (1978) research reported several cross-sex friends although they numbered from two to four times fewer than same-sex ones, and the girls mentioned almost twice as many opposite-sex friends as the boys. The latter figure is especially interesting given the benefits that boys apparently experience in such dyads. When compared with both of their parents and their best male friend, male high school juniors rated their best female friends as providing them with the most ego support and their best male friends as furnishing the least (Wright & Keple, 1981). Female friends were also accorded significantly higher "general favorability" than the boys' fathers or male friends (Wright & Keple, 1981). And males prefer female friends for the disclosure of personal concerns (Johnson & Aries, 1983). Overall, it appears that young males progressively look to cross-sex relationships for emotional gratification, whereas females can be intimate with members of both sexes (Rawlins, 1982). Even so, girls seem to bring their devoted, and males their less involved, styles of friendship to their cross-sex relationships as girls described more attachment, trust, and loyalty toward boys than the boys admitted toward girls (Sharabany et al., 1981).

The move toward romantic involvement typically changes how boys and girls interact. Both parties often feel heightened pressure to impress the other and to present themselves "in the most favorable light" (Schofield, 1981, p. 72). Dating partners discuss more restricted topics than do friends (Werebe, 1987). Werebe (1987) found cross-sex friends much more likely than dating partners to discuss school and close friends, the family, sexuality, the future in general, professional future, and unemployment. Because of their conspicuous lack of intimate talk despite sexual intimacy, Button (1979) discovered that many adolescents did not consider their sexual partners to be friends.

Steady dating differently affects boys' and girls' other friendships as well. Since girls are accustomed to exclusive bonds, romantic relationships are viewed as competing with friendships (Douvan & Adelson, 1966). Accordingly, girls are wary that their friends will desert them for a concentrated involvement with a boy, a move that often does occur (Button, 1979). Douvan and Adelson (1966) argue that such serious romantic commitments inhibit the more "playful" and freewheeling development of identity transpiring within the more relaxed activities and discursive practices of girls' same-sex friendships.

In contrast, boys tend to preserve their male friendships even when they engage in a steady dating relationship (Button, 1979). Indeed, young males seem to have much to learn about negotiating exclusive relationships. Fischer (1981) comments on the tenuous ability of most males to make the change to ongoing cross-sex intimacy in young adulthood in light of their typically limited same-sex commitment and involvement with specific individuals, "If males do make the transition, it may be that late adolescent females socialize the males for heterosexual relationships on the basis of their practice in intimacy with their girlfriends" (p. 21). Clearly, various entanglements and edifications persist among same- and cross-sex friends and romantic and sexually oriented partners during late adolescence and in the coming years of the life course.

Conclusions and Implications

This chapter reflects a view of adolescent development as praxis. Adolescents do not simply and passively respond to the socialization practices of an already determined social structure. Nor are they precluded from influencing their own moral and cognitive development formulated as a self-contained and invariant sequence of stages. Rather, adolescents participate in an interactive process wherein their capacity for self-consciousness and reflexivity emerges partly as a function of cognitive developments and partly as a function of the various social systems continuously produced and reproduced in their everyday interactions. As adolescents' social horizons broaden and their experiences diversify, the normative composition of social systems becomes less uniform and explicit. Their daily lives involve various interconnected social orders, audiences, and evaluative criteria. In these circumstances the double agency of friendship constitutes an ongoing challenge and fundamental resource for articulating one's identity, communicative competencies, and values. The cognitive ability to conceive of one's self and one's relationships increasingly shapes and reflects one's communicative choices in composing and negotiating one's personhood and involvement with others.

As a double agency, adolescent friendship simultaneously engenders social integration and personal growth for its participants. Friendship is symbolic for adolescents. To peers and parents it indicates choosing and/or being chosen by another person, thus symbolizing social acceptance. At the same time having a close friend represents autonomy from peers and parents. Friends can negotiate their own standards within the

friendship and become less influenced by others' opinions. Nevertheless, most adolescents want acceptance by their parents and peers as
well as their friends, producing several interrelated social spheres for
developing and appraising interactional adeptness. As a result, striving
for intimacy with friends and dating partners, preserving caring relationships with parents, and achieving recognition by peers constitute
ongoing communicative challenges.

As the adolescent simultaneously negotiates intimacy, public action,
and identity, the social construction of self as a responsible being and
the nature and significance of one's relationships are at issue. Accordingly, viewing friendship activities as marginal practices that potentially
distract from or interfere with preparation for more objective adult
pursuits comprises a limited and limiting conception. Rather, managing
friendships can be an opportunity to develop moral and interpersonal
sensibilities shaped by and answering to particular intersubjective
standards, ones that endorse conventional behavior in certain instances
and alternative courses of action in others. Importantly, friendships
require an investment of self in their own production and articulation;
an enactment of reasoned and concerned social interaction is inherent in
their composition (Youniss & Smollar, 1985). Thus, Youniss and Smollar
(1985) observe that within their possibilities for enhancing each individual's sense of personal identity, adolescent close friendships embody
prosocial values and social responsibility. Berndt (1982a) adds that
communication with friends "can serve as a foundation for egalitarian
relationships with colleagues, neighbors, or spouses in adulthood" (p.
1448). In the next chapter I will examine excerpts from interviews with
high school juniors and fictional portrayals of adolescents to illustrate
some of the characteristic tensions and triumphs of adolescent friendships.

Chapter 5

Illustrative Analysis: Quandaries of Adolescent Friendship

Adolescent friendships occur within the interconnected worlds of family, peers, school, and the larger society. The young person's participation in a variety of friendships provides contexts for learning about intimacy, developing one's identity and sense of personal values, gaining autonomy from one's family of origin, and dealing with multiple social orders and systems of evaluation. Friendships both facilitate and complicate these critical tasks of adolescence. The present chapter exemplifies some choices, benefits, and dilemmas of adolescent sociality that further articulate a person's conceptions of self and friendship, using excerpts from adolescents' own accounts and portrayals of typical adolescent predicaments found in literature. I will consider tensions between public and private appraisals of adolescents, benefits and problems of close friendship, issues in cross-sex friendships, and interaction with parents and friends. The chapter closes with a discussion of dialectical features of adolescent friendships.

Popularity and Friendship: Public versus Private Appraisals

The social world of the peer group comprises a proving ground wherein the adolescent's views of self and personal relationships are continually devised and revised (Rawlins & Holl, 1987). In this process peers determine the relevant standards for evaluation. Although school size, type, and scheduling affect the probability of peer interaction (Epstein & Karweit, 1983), beyond these institutional constraints adolescent sociality is a realm of now delicate, now brutal distinctions. Peers are graded by degrees according to those who are known and unknown, admired and disliked, included and excluded. The experience of not being selected can produce "the shock of exclusion," one of Elkind's (1984) three adolescent peer shocks. Conversely, frequently chosen adolescents are considered "popular."

"Popularity" is a somewhat mythical term in adolescence, perhaps akin to "success" in adulthood. Many young people aspire to popularity and parents often encourage this quest. Even so, the adolescents we interviewed did not equate popularity and friendship (Rawlins & Holl, 1987). A primary theme regarding popularity was "people know who you are;" "they know your name." This recognition usually occurs because one excels at something like athletics or scholarship, is attractive, or is involved in many activities or clubs. Well-known people have friends but not necessarily "true" or "real friends." People might be their friends just because they are popular.

The following quotations illustrate prevalent conceptions. One male stated:

> I used to be *very* popular in school. As a matter of fact I was about, I was up in the big, big time. Um, just about, um, me and maybe 2 or 3 other guys were the most popular in our grade. And I, I felt then that I had no really true friends because it was just, it was just a big um, we were just using each other's friendships to be popular, you know, to have people like us, you know, girls and to have um respect from other people. And it really wasn't, I mean as far as their, um, as far as them as a person, I wasn't too concerned about them and they weren't too concerned about me. And you know, I knew a lot of people and a lot of people liked me. They were nice to me; I was nice to them, but there wasn't, you know, there wasn't any really, uh, encouragement. We usually cut each other down. . . . I'm not as popular now. I still am somewhat but, it's just because people know me because I was popular. I do well in school, and in sports. But uh now I have friends that I can, you know, I feel like they care about me. I care about them so, no, I don't think popularity has, I think if anything, it works against true friendships, and not for them.

When asked why popularity "works against true friendships," he observed:

> Because usually when you're popular, you're there because you want to be popular, okay. If you don't want to be popular all you have to do is stop um, making a big scene about yourself, you know. And, um, you know if you're popular and you're, you know, you're trying to be popular; it's usually so that people like you and accept you because you're a great person. You know, you're great in sports, you're great in school, you're good looking. But um, you know, when that's the basis of acceptance, things that you do, the way that you look, the, the, uh way that you, um, in sports, if that's the basis of acceptance, it's usually a surface friendship and it's not really too meaningful. It's not too encouraging and um, it comes and goes, it comes and goes with, uh, the outward things that you do. (age 17)

According to this person, popularity derives from public achievements and evaluations. Doing well in visible and objective domains like sports and academics, or being attractive fosters liking and recognition by lots of peers. But the evaluative standards supporting such acceptance, though widely held, regard primarily external accomplishments or appearances. Consequently, they tend to promote "surface friendships" that are temporary or contingent on the "outward things that you do." Further, the speaker recalls "using each other's friendships to be popular" and experiencing minimal mutual concern, even antagonism, in these relationships. Two females echo these sentiments below:

> I think, being popular is; okay, you might be popular and people are with you when the weather's nice. Like they might go somewhere if you want to go there but you might not feel comfortable around them. Or you might be respected in a lot of ways and people look up to you for that, like being #1 in sports or #1 in um scholarship and people look up to you. But you may not be able to confide in them or they may not be there when you want them to be there. And also, when you're popular and everything, it doesn't mean you trust them and they trust you. It just means that they *think* maybe you're funny or they think you are, they respect that in you. (age 16)
>
> Popularity um, is more or less superficial, I think. I mean, they have friends and their friends, you know, they acknowledge 'em because they want to be acknowledged by someone because they're popular for activities or their dress or their hair style and everything. Whereas if you have friends, say they're your friends for you the person within, not the person that you appear to be to people, you always have those friends. Like when you come back after graduation, they're there whether you have long hair or short, I mean, they're always there for you. (age 17)

These adolescents recognize the continuous intermingling of public and private interactions and evaluations. In contrast to the fair-weather or expedient quality of the popular person's companions, one can depend on friends for mutual trust and affection for "the person within, not the person you appear to be to people." Even so, appearances are crucial in adolescent society; both close and superficial relationships develop in the face of ever-present peer perusal and appraisal. If one's friends are popular or have good reputations, it can enhance an individual's social standing and openings to make other friends. One male commented:

> When I first moved here, I met a bunch of people, and like they were all my friends, and a couple people were not, you know, that good reputations here and others were. And now I mostly hang around with, you know, people of better reputations, and I think that's let me meet a lot more people because of that. (age 16)

However, since adolescents do not always perceive their friends in the same manner as their peers or society at large do, they periodically must decide whose assessments to emphasize. In the following case a female uses personal criteria for judging her friends despite her awareness of public perceptions and the potential consequences:

> I know some of my friends don't have the best reputations, but that doesn't necessarily mean you know, because I hang around with 'em I do some of the things they do. But, you know, I don't always base how I like people on what their, their past reputations were. So, um, you know, if they're nice to me and I feel I can trust them, I'm going to consider them a friend. Not just by their past reputations. But I know that, you know, some of my friends don't have that good reputations. And that I am about to be sort of part of that. (age 16)

Her final remark illustrates a key dilemma poignantly associated with managing friendships during adolescence. Young people realize their personal views of actions, self, and friends may not correspond with those of peers, parents, or the larger society. Yet they face diverging scenarios in either relinquishing *or* adhering to their own perceptions. If they turn their backs on individuals they trust and who treat them kindly to conform with opposing social dictates, they may feel wider acceptance and that they have done "the right thing," especially if the spurned friends' wrongdoings continue. However, should those abandoned friends emerge as respectable persons as originally surmised, the conforming individual may rightfully be ashamed for lacking personal convictions.

On the other hand, when an adolescent remains loyal to friends despite their "past reputations" (as in the case above), she risks becoming "part of that" symbolically or in actuality, with a rather permeable border separating the two possibilities. First, she may acquire a bad reputation like her friends', even if theirs are undeserved or she does not behave wrongly. Moreover, it may be difficult for her to preserve her self-conception as a worthwhile person when numerous others treat her poorly. For example, one girl stated:

> If Judy got a new friend, I'd talk to that person too because I tell me that if Judy likes 'em, I should like them too. But like somebody I don't like. If they, if a new person comes in school and they hang around with somebody I don't like, I automatically don't like that person. (age 15)

Under such conditions, one must increasingly rely on validation from "outcast" associates to confirm one's positive self-image and personal beliefs. The second risk is that the bad reputations are deserved and the adolescent "becomes a part" of the actual notorious behaviors to maintain the affection and support of her deviant friends. Either way, giving in to the larger social group's assessments of potential friends often seems the easiest course of action to protect one's status from the outset.

The ironic pinch of this dynamic is that dyads or small cadres of friends are typically enveloped by larger social units, be they a crowd of ruffians or "druggies," the rest of the guys on the football team, or the girls comprising a given grade's most popular, trend-setting clique. And no matter how badly these others' negative reactions may make friends feel for their beliefs and behaviors, sometimes the friends know they are right and must depend on each other to preserve that certainty. In such cases adolescents may get undesirable reputations because they do what they think is correct, even though their cardinal fault simply involves an unpopular or unfashionable position explicitly denounced by the encompassing social network. Consequently, just as consensual validation and encouragement of patently immoral behaviors occur within the private morality of some adolescent friendships, the same process also enables the shared exploration of worthwhile moral visions and actions deviating from those permitted in larger social contexts. An important challenge for adolescents is to discern which development is occurring in specific situations. For this discovery sincere conversation with trusted others, including friends, family and influential adults, is essential.

Benefits of Close Friendship

One phrase summarizes the value of a close friend for adolescents; he or she is "somebody to talk to." Young people spend considerable time discussing their daily experiences in and out of school and during marathon evening telephone calls. While conversing, they joke and laugh, help each other with problems of all kinds, vent frustrations, and offer mutual encouragement. When we asked high school juniors about the primary benefits of their close friendships, both genders' responses were strikingly similar (Rawlins & Holl, 1987). Here are the comments of several females:

> Someone to talk to, let things out. You know if you are really angry at somebody, you can go and tell them about it and it gets it off your chest. You know. It makes you feel a lot better just to tell somebody. And, you know, like if, if you're unhappy with something they can help you work through your problems, help you work things out. So it's not like you're alone dealing with everything; you have somebody else there to help you through. (age 16)
>
> Someone you can share notes with, um, someone you can talk to when you're really down and they, they understand, you know. And they're like not, when you're upset and they don't want to be pulled down, they

won't, you know, like, "Just go away. I don't want to be depressed too."
They understand. They give you some optimistic viewpoints to help
yourself. They don't, they don't go behind your back and repeat something you said, or you can be open with them. You don't have to watch
what you say or watch what you do. (age 17)

Um, like when you're down about something or you're having a
problem, they help cheer you up. And whenever you just need somebody
to talk to and to just tell your problems to, they're there and they'll listen.
And it's also, they can tell you what they're thinking, what their problems
are, and you can help them. (age 15)

Well, it's somebody you can talk to and tell 'em everything and *you know*
they're not going to tell other people. And like, you know, you might say
something to somebody you think is your friend and they go back and
they tell other people that you said something. Where a close friend is
somebody you can trust and you can trust their opinion. (age 16)

Here are various boys' responses:

When you're down, or when you're sad you can just, usually call them up
and, just talk with them and, kind of let out your emotions and he'll be
there when you need him and uh, to help you face crises in life, etc. And
um, I think that's very beneficial sometimes. Sometimes you have doubts
or sometimes you don't believe in yourself and you need somebody to tell
you, um, "It's not like that" or "You're doing okay; it's not easy." And uh,
and just basically be there when you need him and uh sometimes you're
there when he needs you. Um, he can just call you and you can help him
too. So I think helping each other is probably the most important. (age 16)

You can talk to them and get things off your mind that you wouldn't
even say to your parents a lot of times, like if you're having problems
doing some things at home or in school. (age 16)

You can talk to them. That's, the main, main thing. You can relate to
them. They make you feel good. (age 16)

It to me is just having someone to talk with or yea that's good, just
having someone to talk to, when you need someone to talk to. (age 16)

You can just share, you know, between yourselves. You can keep, you
know, you can talk about things; you can do things together; like you
know it's just between you two. For instance, one of your best friends
you can, you know, you can call them something, *you know* that it's in
confidence, that they won't tell other people. Even though something's
wrong with you, you can tell your problems to them and they can help.
And you can try to, um, help each other out. (age 16)

Close friends are persons to talk to and rely on for help in dealing with
problems. And since many adolescents' concerns involve personal
insecurities or how others see them, their close friends must be
trustworthy and loyal. They cannot reveal private matters to others or
talk behind the friend's back. Such breaches of trust may undermine an
individual's self-image through changing peer perceptions of him or her.

Thus, our adolescent interviewees most frequently dismissed friends for two reasons: being "two-faced" or talking behind their backs, and violating confidences (Rawlins & Holl, 1987).

What do same-sex friends talk about? For both girls and boys conversations first and foremost address the opposite sex, but also problems in school, homework and grades, and "anything and every-thing." Girls tend to relate family problems and boys discuss sports. In *Pentimento* Lillian Hellman's character, Lilly, describes her late adoles-cent discussions with her friend Julia:

> But we also talked like all young people, of possible beaux and husbands and babies, and heredity versus environment, and can romantic love last, mixing stuff like that in speeches made only for the pleasure of girls on the edge of growing up. (1973, p.96)

A 16-year-old girl enthusiastically reported in like fashion:

> We talk about most everything, we talk about guys, we talk about other girls. Sometimes we gossip together. We talk about drugs. We talk about things people say about drugs, you know dare or not to dare. We talk about weddings, getting married; I don't feel I want to get married. And we talk about, we talk about sex and birth control and stuff. I mean we talk, we can talk about things that we wouldn't *dare* talk about with anyone, I mean like guys, and we also talk about things that are just common that we can talk about to anyone. But we just talk about 'em. We'll be together and we'll be talking about 'em.

Both profound and mundane matters are examined in free-wheeling dialogue with a trusted equal. Values are momentarily questioned, confirmed, or reshaped through enacting them in conversations about the present and the future. Mutually created scenarios try out possible identities and relationships that can be planned, rehearsed, or discarded in the duration of a talk.

In such conversations adolescents primarily want acceptance and encouragement, not judgment, from friends. The following girl felt that acceptance was indicative of whether someone understood her or not:

> The way they react to what I say and the things I do. I think a lot of people, they're like, "Oh my gosh, you did that!?" My friends say, "Yeah, that's Shelley 'n' she'd do it," and, you know, and they don't put me down for doing it. "Oh God, I wouldn't do that if I were you." It's, "Did you really do it?" "Yeah." "It figures." You know. Or when I say something, well they just accept me for it. They don't, they don't ask 100 questions about why I did it or how I did it or things like that. I don't have to, I don't have to go through all the interrogation so they can understand why I did it.

They'll just accept the fact cause it's what I want to be. That's what I want to do. (age 16)

On many occasions such acceptance and encouragement express friend-ship, enhance self-esteem, and help a person deal with nagging dispar-ities among personal, familial, and public evaluations of events or actions. For example, one boy recalled when another "stuck by" and supported him as pivotal in sealing their friendship:

I have a friend that plays football with me, a close friend. . . . I got kicked out of a game and I didn't do anything, you know. Well I didn't think I did anything. And everybody else said it was, you know, cause I'm, I'm a hothead and I like hitting people out on the field, and they just, you know were putting me down cause I lost my temper and stuff. But my friend *knew* that I didn't hit him. He goes, "Oh you didn't hit him; it was, you know, I guess if you really looked at you like you're a hothead, it looked like you hit him. But really just like an aggressive, you know, you just do that normal." And just, he knew me better to know that I didn't do it. And everybody else didn't believe me. (age 17)

At a time in life when young people are so vulnerable to others' critical reactions, a friend's confirmation of one's favorable self-conceptions is crucial for personal well-being.

However, despite the paramount importance of acceptance, adoles-cents desire honest yet tactfully rendered reactions from friends in certain circumstances. One male discussed this dialectical relationship between judgment and acceptance in describing his friends:

They can accept me for who I am, okay, and they can, uh, you know, I really am comfortable around people who know me well enough and know problems and my faults but yet can accept that and you know can realize that I'm not the same as they are. Maybe I'm growing at a different rate and in different areas. . . . I try and do the same for them. And if I see a problem, I try, and if I think they should know about and if I think it's going to help the problem at all if I confront them about it, then I do. And I think that people who are my friends should feel free to be able to do the same thing to me. But, um, you know, it's, I got to still be able to feel accepted. (age 17)

The ironic role of friends in shaping each other's self-conceptions and personal values during late adolescence hinges on this dialectic. Friends are usually more accepting because they are not supposed to "put you down." But they are privy to most of each other's activities, and condoning a friend's questionable actions may result in real problems or wasted opportunities. Accordingly, if certain conduct or ideas warrant criticism, this speaker hopes that his friends will care enough and "feel free" to "confront" him. Yet, if they speak too candidly or hurt his feelings, they may be perceived as unworthy friends for violating his expectation of acceptance. Adolescent friends face the ongoing challenges of discerning what is in their individual and mutual best interests. Further, since these concerns may at times conflict, they also must communicate these judgments in ways that maintain their good will toward each other.

Problems among Friends

Internal and external difficulties continually threaten the tranquillity of adolescent friendships. Drawn from peer society, friends assert the private values of the friendship in some contexts yet may reinforce alternative peer appraisals in others (La Gaipa, 1979). When these standards clash, a person may feel hurt, resentful of, or betrayed by the friend who sides with the crowd. Both parties could form new friendships as a result. Because of potentially shifting alliances, the knowledge of self that friends possess may confirm adolescents personally, but render them publicly vulnerable as well. Friends partially authorize, yet also threaten, a person's identity. Accordingly, Coleman (1980, p. 411) reports that "anxiety concerning friendship appears to be at a peak for both boys and girls" from the ages of 14 to 16.

Moreover, a contentious harmony pervades many adolescent friendships of either gender; friends not only help with problems, they also cause them. Girls can be possessive about their close friends and jealous of rivals, as evidenced by the following female's description of what causes the most trouble between friends:

> Jealousy, and it's jealousy with other girls too. Like, if Karen's spending more time with somebody else that I don't really care for or I don't know that well; why is she spending time with *her* instead of me? And we spend, with three of us, Sarah and Karen and me, when we were younger, it used to happen a lot cause if one of, if two of us would get in an argument, it would be like who could get the other one mad, who can get Sarah mad at Karen, or whatever. So it would be two against one. (age 15)

According to another girl, third parties who begrudge yet desire the closeness of two friends will try to instigate problems:

> Other people are jealous because our friendship is stable 'n has taken good roots; and they want in on the situation but, um, they don't believe in more than two friends. There's just no way; so what you have to do is you bump off the other person and get in and establish a friendship with that

person. You can't have more than two friends. . . . I have a friend
named Cindy and she's, I like her because I know Cindy and it's not
because she wears a cheerleading uniform on football games or basketball
games. I like her for Cindy because she acts like I do. And other people
intervene. They'll come to Cindy when I'm not around and they'll say
something like, "Oh Michelle said something about you have fat legs."
And I, I'd never say something like that, but they try to get her against me
and work their way into the situation. (age 17)

Some girls argued that their female friends' possessiveness was less
likely with males:

If I would be with Carol, you know we go to the park, we do this, we have
all this fun. Carol goes back and talks about it. For some reason Sheila will
get mad because Carol was with me and we did this, we did that and, um,
that causes a lot of problems when it seems like I can't have no more
friends. You know your friends can't understand sometimes when you
want to, uh, when you do something with somebody else you know. And
that's the kind of trouble that is mostly with girls. That don't really happen
with boys for some reason. Boys just, you know, they just go with
whoever and they just do it. With girls, it's like a little different cause
jealousy's like a big part for some reason. And so that causes a lot of
problems. (age 16)

Sometimes I find it better to talk to guys. Guys, I think are better best
friends than girls are because guys won't get jealous. You know like Diane
might get jealous because I might hang around somebody else, you know.
Or she doesn't like the girl that I'm hanging around at the time. I mean
we're still good friends but I might be talking with somebody. Diane
doesn't really like that cause like Diane might not get along with that
person. Guys don't get jealous that often that I know of anyways, and
they're just a lot easier to talk to. (age 16)

Of course, cross-sex friendships involve their own predicaments in turn,
which we will examine in the next section.

Although boys do not report or openly express as much jealousy of
their close friends as girls do, such envy may still occur. However, the
problems of male friendships more typically reflect deep-seated competition. For males an egalitarian ethic can transform easily into a competitive one, as when one must prove worthy of friendship. On the bright
side, boys contend to improve themselves and their friends, and to
succeed together as teammates. On the dark side, they compete to
undermine and surpass each other as edification veers toward enmity.
John Knowles' classic novel of adolescent male friendship, *A Separate
Peace*, depicts the resulting ambivalence:

"It's you, pal," Finny said to me at last, "just you and me." He and I
started back across the fields, preceding the others like two seigneurs.

We were the best of friends at that moment.

"You were very good," said Finny good-humoredly, "once I shamed you into it."

"You didn't shame anybody into anything."

"Oh yes I did. I'm good for you that way. You have a tendency to back away from things otherwise."

"I never backed away from anything in my life!" I cried, my indignation at this charge naturally stronger because it was so true. "You're goofy!" (1959, p. 10)

Gene and Phineas ("Finny") are "best of friends" as they stride together in front of the other boys. Still, internal rivalry, prodding, posturing, and resentment accompany their shared ascendance. Later on, Gene perceives them as competing more directly against each other:

> I was more and more certainly becoming the best student in the school; Phineas was without question the best athlete, so in that way we were even. But while he was a very poor student I was a pretty good athlete, and when everything was thrown into the scales they would in the end tilt definitely toward me. The new attacks of studying were his emergency measures to save himself. I redoubled my effort. (Knowles, 1959, p. 47)

Indeed, such rivalries do enhance individuals' performances in important domains like academics and sports, and may invigorate relationships if they remain "friendly." However, when individuals compete relentlessly with increasingly malevolent assumptions or aspirations by either or both of them, friendships experience great difficulty or deception.

Competition for members of the opposite sex disturbs both boys' and girls' friendships, which function curiously in the dating process. As already mentioned, the most frequent topic of talk between boys is girls and between girls is boys. Thus friends risk engaging in heartfelt to ribald discussions of possible dates with persons who subsequently may vie for them as well. And, ironically, if the dating relationship does not work out, they hope to turn to friends for solace. The following male's remarks about his friendships exhibit diverse moments of this trajectory:

> We talk about all kinds of things. We talk about what goes on at our homes and what goes on at school, what goes on in our courses. We talk about our other friends, talk about our enemies. Talk about girls we know; we talk about girls we'd like to know. Talk about all kinds of things.
>
> . . . Girls cause a lot of problems between us because we're always, we're always fighting among ourselves about who goes out with the best looking girl. Or if there's a new girl, we all start chasing after her. It gets in the way of friends. We let the girl decide and eventually one of us gets blown away.
>
> . . . There's certain times when I'm mad and he can tell I'm mad and

he'll talk to me. Not, not joke around, he'll be serious with me. And there's certain times when I really feel sad or something and he can tell and he'll try to raise my spirits. When I broke up with one of my girlfriends, he, he just started telling me about all the girls he's gone with that he broke up with, why he broke up with them and it just, I didn't feel as bad anymore. (age 16)

His friend does transcend the normally joking mode of their interactions to bolster him after a "break up." Yet notice that his friend's reassuring messages contain an implicitly competitive exhibit of "all the girls he's gone out with" where similar problems have occurred. Ambivalence seems inevitable in such arrangements where the contest can seem as important as the comfort.

Dating relationships become more prevalent as adolescence progresses, comprising a source of apprehension throughout the period (Douvan & Adelson, 1966), and finally eclipsing same-sex friendships in intimacy (Berndt, 1982a). An especially sensitive and potentially volatile situation accompanies their emergence when friends, who ostensibly care for each other, mutually contend for another person's affection. Some friendships survive the strife, while others break up forever. In either case, once romantic involvements appear as significant options, people begin making the recurring lifelong decisions regarding the respective roles that friendship and romance will play in conducting specific relationships and in composing their social lives. Early enactments of these quandaries transpire in the cross-sex friendships of late adolescence.

Issues in Cross-Sex Friendships

Friendships between boys and girls are valued for similar reasons as same-sex bonds—they talk together about personal concerns, help each other with problems, and pursue various recreational activities. Still, despite many affinities, adolescents distinguish cross-sex friends from "boyfriends" and "girlfriends" according to differing practices. For example, as I stated in Chapter 4, becoming boyfriends and girlfriends seems to inhibit ways of talking and behaving together, as compared with cross-sex friends. Two boys observed:

With a girlfriend you can't tell them *everything* cause they might get mad about some things. But with, if you have a girl as a friend, you can talk to them more because it's not going to hurt them as much cause they're not attached to you as much as a girlfriend. (age 17)

> If you're with a girlfriend, you got to be careful what you say because they might get mad or, you know, if you want to talk to her. But, if she's just a friend, you know, you can say stuff and you don't really, you don't really mind if they get upset or, you know, if she's just a friend. (age 17)

The following girls agreed:

> With a boyfriend you can get embarrassed (laugh) you know. If you do something wrong, you're embarrassed if he's there or something. But with a just like a guy friend you can act yourself and you can do whatever you want, you know, and you won't feel stupid at all. But like, if you're with your boyfriend you're always trying to impress him, and if you start acting stupid and stuff like that and he's you know looking at you and you feel stupid and everything. (age 16)

> Tom Wilson and I started out as real good, started out as just friends. We started joking around and then we started talking like close friends. And, um, he started liking me and I, I, at first I thought I could, and I told him that. And, you know, we tried it for awhile and it ended up we didn't talk very much for about three weeks cause it was like, well, we really weren't sure what was going on. And we ended up not being really close until he started liking, until he started talking to me again. (age 16)

Once a cross-sex friend starts to "like" the other, and they decide to "go out together" and "get serious," spontaneous talk and actions seem stifled. However, romantic sentiments and the physical expression of affection now reflect the ties of boyfriends and girlfriends. Several persons describe these defining distinctions below. The males assert:

> Having a girl as a friend doesn't involve romantic feelings on either part. And you don't, you know, you don't feel like you own each other. Having a girl as a friend, um, there's no physical relationship. Whereas having a girlfriend there's emotions. You know in America you feel like you own the person a lot of times. Um, you know, the physical relationship gets involved. I'd say that's the main difference. (age 17)

> When you have a girlfriend, it's different cause you do all that lovey dovey stuff and stuff like that. But if you have a girl that's a friend, you know, if you don't, if you don't like have feelings for each other or something, then it's just, just a mutual relationship, just, just see each other as friends, and someone that you go to and talk to about something. (age 16)

> Well, one you give a goodnight kiss to and the other one you don't. One, one you're a lot closer to. The other one you just use as, just another guy friend except she's a girl. (age 16)

The females observe likewise:

> Well, if you have a boyfriend he, you two are more intimate and more romantic and, if you're just friends, you feel like you can talk to each other

more and you wouldn't, you know be trying to get intimate with each other. (age 15)

Ben used to just be a friend but, see it's not much different except that, you know, to put it very basically, you don't kiss your boy *friend*, you do kiss your; I mean it's really purely physical once they become your boyfriend. (age 14)

A boy as a friend is just someone you hang around with and can talk to and stuff, but there's no kissing and hugging. I'd say you should have a friend, a guy should be a friend before he's a boyfriend. (age 15)

Whether or not specific young people are, can, or should be friends before they are romantic partners comprise matters of personal opinion, happenstance, and mutually negotiated relational definitions. However, it does appear that later adolescent cross-sex friendships are often experienced and viewed ambiguously as in this male's comments:

Sometimes certain interests get in the way which may tend to uh, uh, ruin a friendship. Uh, sometimes a male may be interested in a female or vice versa and um, I mean this may lead to something that one person wants and the other person doesn't, and it may finally lead to no friendship at all. But it is possible if you, if you just try and be friends and just look at it that way. And if you start looking at more than that, I guess it can turn out to be different from what you expected, or even after that you can still be friends, or maybe you won't be friends anymore. So it's possible. (age 16)

Research indicates that males feel they are supposed to take the initiative in cross-sex bonds and try to transform "just friendships" into romantic or sexual relationships (Bell, 1981). Cultural expectations of "real men" and concerns about peer status may persuade boys to enact sex-typed scenarios with girl friends who are quite satisfied with the status quo. Selected reflections by the fictional character, 17-year-old Owen Griffith, provide insight into such actions (Le Guin, 1966):

My only real relationship with Mike and Jason, who were the nearest thing I had to friends, was a joking relationship. The point was never to be serious about anything. Except maybe sports scores. One of the main subjects to talk about was sex, either by telling dirty jokes, or by being gross . . . (p. 16)

. . . She was the first person I ever met I could really talk to, and talk with. The more we talked, the more there was to talk about. (p. 35)

. . . And the way she laughed at me when I clowned; she wanted to laugh, she needed to. . . . What I realize now is that she needed me as badly as I needed her.

But I fouled up. Because I got my priorities wrong . . . (p. 40)

The thing is, the way a lot of people talk, and the way a lot of movies and books and advertising and all the various sexual engineers, whether they're scientists or salesmen, tell you the way it is, is all the same. Man

Plus Woman Equals Sex. Nothing else. No unknowns in the equation. Who needs unknowns?

Especially when you haven't had any sex yet at all and so *it* is the unknown, and everybody seems to be telling you that it's the only thing that matters, nothing else counts . . . (p. 45) So I began thinking, what am I doing. I mean I see this girl all the time and spend the day at the beach with her and somebody says, "Hey man, so what happened?" and I say: "She gave me a black rock and I gave her an agate." Hey, yeah? Wow!

See, I began thinking what the others would think, not what I, myself, thought. (p. 46)

. . . I only saw Natalie three or four times in the couple of weeks after that. And when I did it was much less enjoyable. I kept wondering things like whether she had ever had another man friend, and what she planned to do about men in amongst her other plans, and what she thought about me in that particular way, and not daring to ask her any of it. (pp. 53–54)

High school junior girls report that boy friends do start "liking" them and try to convert friendships into dating dyads (Rawlins, 1989c). Unfortunately, if the feelings are not mutual, it often spoils the relationship, presumably because the boy feels he has lost face. One young woman recounts:

I like to stay around boys right and some girls right. And we just have fun together and I guess they notice that. Well this guy named Vance, I, we used to do all this stuff together right, and then he turned out to like me. And um, I, I just said no right. I said I'm going out with someone and plus we're friends you know, what if our relationship falls apart? And I, I didn't really like him. You know, I didn't think he was cute or anything but I couldn't just tell him that, so um I like being around him, it's just fun. But, um, I told him that I was going with someone and he, he gets mad cause I said that. And now we don't, we barely even talk anymore now. (age 16)

Another girl doubts the original friendship of boys who cannot be friends when their attempts to date fail:

If you're a friend with a guy, so to speak, and he decides to like you, so to speak, and he wants to go with you and stuff, but you won't go with him, so he doesn't talk to you anymore. He's never a *friend*; he just decided to be a friend until he got to go with you. (age 15)

Cross-sex relationships during adolescence are inherently ambiguous. Societal expectations, personal values, degrees of emerging sexuality, peer group pressures, and coordinated or clashing assumptions and perceptions all combine in shaping the dynamics of given relationships. Whatever occasions the shift, romantic involvement apparently alters adolescents' cross-sex friendships. And the somewhat apologetic or

defensive description of those dyads remaining "just friends" anticipates the tendencies throughout life to marginalize these bonds and to
view them as precursors, threats, or understudies to more institutionalized or socially endorsed relationships. Thus, adolescents' choices in
conducting these affiliations rehearse and mirror later social patterns.

Interaction with Parents and Friends

In managing their daily affairs adolescents talk with both parents and
friends. The oppositional relationship between parents and peers often
associated with adolescence may arise in specific circumstances but
overall it constitutes the exception rather than the rule. Instead, young
people typically view their parents as informed by extensive life experiences yet inclined to judge and criticize. Meanwhile, they see friends
as sharing and therefore more aware of current situations and likely to
accept their actions and ideas. In given cases, adolescents weigh these
respective tendencies as well as the others' perceived degree of caring in
determining who they will consult about their concerns and whose
opinions they will favor in given situations (Rawlins & Holl, 1988).

One female gave the following reasons for preferring her parents'
advice over her friends':

> My parents because I think they have more wisdom. They can take it into
> I guess perspective a little bit more than my friends could, because my
> friends are usually the age I am or some are older, some are younger but
> not very much. Uh, I think our parents have more say in everything
> because—they, they know, they know what might be the circumstances,
> and I'd, I think I'd go with my mom and dad. (age 16)

For this young woman parents are more credible advisors with additional perspective and "more wisdom" than friends, whose age and
experience mirror her own. Even so, she would discuss certain matters
with friends instead of parents. She remarked:

> Um—talk about, let's see, a new guy in school. Um, mom wouldn't
> understand about that, she might but. Um, I don't know because, I don't
> know. I guess we like to, we like to kid around about a lot of things and
> sometimes mom might take it serious or dad might take it so seriously.
> And we talk to our girlfriends and that about, uh, guys and the crushes
> that we have or things like that. They understand because they, they have
> crushes and that too. They can relate more than I think mom and dad can
> because they, my girlfriends would understand more than my parents.
> Uh—not much else because usually I share everything with mom and dad.

Despite her reliance on her parents' wisdom, she converses with friends about "guys" and "crushes that we have" because they currently share the same experiences, which enables them to "understand" and "relate more." Her parents might take these matters too seriously and respond judgmentally.

Frequently, though, both parents and friends are consulted for their opinions, which may coincide or disagree. Below, two males describe their conscious appraisal and active decision-making regarding contrasting advice by parents and friends:

> I usually follow my, my mother's advice because she's been through most of the things I'm going through. But sometimes I'll follow my friends' advice when it, it sounds more reasonable at the time. I think it over, both sides, whatever comes out, whatever I decide, I decide at that time. (age 16)
>
> It's hard to say. I follow the one that I think sounds best and sometimes my parents give me better advice and sometimes my friends give me better advice. So I couldn't, I, I really don't take advice by who gives it. I take it by what it is. (age 16)

Neither boy describes a blanket preference for parental or peer input but seems to utilize both in making the best decision he can.

A female further highlights the circumstantial quality of following differing recommendations by parents and friends:

> I guess this year in debate. This isn't very important, but I was gonna quit because the team was so unorganized and I was really getting upset about it. And my friend told me, "Go ahead and quit, you know, it won't do anything." And my parents told me to hang on and stay with it. And I took my parents' advice and stayed with it. And I'm glad I did now because things are starting to shape up.
>
> Interviewer: Why did you choose your parents in that situation?
>
> Um, they just told me to hang in for a little while, and I figured I'd follow my friend's advice if things didn't improve. (age 16)

Feeling disgruntled about the debate team, she discussed her concerns with both her parents and her friend. Her parents suggested the tougher course of action, namely to "stay with" an increasingly upsetting situation. In contrast, her friend accepted and encouraged her desire to quit the team, as adolescent friends are expected and apt to do. Interestingly, she followed her parents' suggestions with favorable results, even though she also kept her friend's advice in mind to fall back on and to support a change if "things didn't improve."

Bad grades, details of opposite-sex relationships, and risky issues like drugs and drinking comprise topics that adolescents typically avoid discussing with their parents, much preferring friends. Consider the following girl's choice of friends over parents to discuss an event:

> Alright, um, if it has something to do like say there's a big party somewhere, something happening, you know everybody was getting high or some people was getting drunk and all this other stuff, I wouldn't go back and say that to my mom because she'd be like, like if you discuss something like that with your family, they're really kind of uh, they, they're against it, and they start to yell about it, you know, get all into it. And your friends you can sit there, and you laugh about it, but they just talk about it. Say what you didn't like, say what you liked. But you know, you're not comfortable saying stuff like that to your parents. (age 16)

This young woman would anticipate a strong, negative reaction, even yelling, from her mother if she recounted presumably forbidden behaviors occurring at a party. In contrast, she would expect to "laugh" and "just talk about it" with friends. Importantly, she predicts the opportunity to discuss both what she liked and disliked about the experience with her friends. Her mother's judgmental reaction would undermine the chance for such interactive appraisal.

Discussions regarding low grades often epitomize what adolescents dislike most in conversing with parents, namely, episodes of being criticized. One female's comments typifies their position:

> I don't like talking about grades with my parents because usually, first of all, they're pretty good, and then if they aren't as good then they're, they give you the whole "I'm very disappointed" routine. And I just get sick of that and leave. So I'll talk about you know why I got the grade or something with friends. (age 14)

Grades involve some of the adolescent's most unequivocal evaluations of self from the adult world. Good grades portend admission to college and future success. They are interpreted as clear indicators of prudent use of one's abilities and time. High academic achievement is accorded considerable recognition in the school and local media, and can facilitate popularity. Thus, when parents criticize one's grades, they compound the objectively and socially constituted diminution a young person already feels in performing poorly. Accordingly, this individual turns to her friends to avoid a ritualized rebuke and to discuss the reasons for her grade.

Not surprisingly, if someone comes through when a person needs to talk about a matter like grades that is difficult to broach with parents, it can be a pivotal event in their friendship. A girl recalls:

> I just felt kind of confused because of school, because I know I should have been doing better in school. And I was kind of depressed because of my,

a grade that I got on one test. And one of my friends just came up to me, you know, and she shared with me and she said, well don't worry about it. And she goes, there are other tests that you can do. She goes, and that's just one bad grade; she goes, you can bring it up; you know that now, that now that you have to study in that. And she just gave me all the support and all the comfort that I needed. And I think that really showed me that she cared a lot for me and she was there for me when I needed somebody. And I just, proved to me that she was, you know, we were friends. But I didn't know how good of friends we were and her just caring for me and wanting to talk to me and help me, just showed me that she was, she was a good friend, a close friend. (age 16)

Clearly, the persons trusted by adolescents to confide in and talk with are critical contributors to their developing identities and their progressively consequential and life-shaping decision-making. Pursuing autonomy in adolescence comprises one of the first experiences of organizing and prioritizing one's system of interpersonal relationships. Adolescents desire varying degrees of freedom and privilege different people's views regarding specific concerns. The deployment of conversation and/or silence defines self and others' positions in one's personal network. Selectively interacting with others is an attempt to regulate how much one is regulated and to choose the evaluative voices one will hear. Accordingly, adolescents seek and avoid the conversational input of parents and friends at various junctures to enhance their own autonomy and self-perceptions.

Dialectical Features of Adolescent Friendships

The dialectical tensions of friendship become especially poignant during adolescence. Young people experience the social realities of their developing identities as both strategically managed and uncontrollable blends of public conventions and outward appearances on the one hand, and private convictions and inward actualities on the other. While interacting daily and pursuing the goals and expectations of self, family, school, and peers, adolescents negotiate various types of friendships across a continuum of personal and social domains. Since the tension between private knowledge and public exposure of self is a fundamental concern, they are preoccupied with trust and confidence in their "true" or close friendships, which mediates their selection of friends and their distinctions among them. Within the blurred boundaries and the cross-cutting demands of adolescent social systems, changing friendships undermine and challenge, yet also foster the young person's emerging conceptions of self and relationships.

The dialectical interplay of independence and dependence poses recurring strains for adolescent friends. Young people rely greatly on their friends for individuating themselves from their families and peers and for developing their identities. In many circumstances, their dependence on friends coevolves with their increasing independence from others. And though males may tend to stress activities and females to emphasize verbal exchanges, adolescents' identities become enmeshed in the close relationships mediating their public and familial performances. The young person who lacks someone with whom to accomplish privately examined self definitions may habitually look to prescribed conventions and public responses for the ongoing achievement and recognition of self.

However, too much dependence can overburden friendships (Douvan & Adelson, 1966). It often results in possessiveness and jealousy hindering the freedom associated with friendship. Consequently, one person, who may have developed autonomy and self-confidence partly through interacting with a specific friend, may reject the other because of his or her perceived overdependence. Such breaches are especially painful during adolescence because of the intertwined nature of achieving one's budding identity through friendship. Notably in close female bonds, "To lose the friend . . . is to lose part of the self" (Douvan & Adelson, 1966, p. 189).

Contradictions among affective and instrumental motives further incite the potentially feisty interdependence of adolescent friends. Young people wonder why others like or dislike them, particularly when they question their own attractiveness. Are they liked for the person they feel themselves to be inside? Or are they liked for ulterior reasons—because they are smart, athletic, popular, of high status, have their driver's license, appeal to the opposite sex, have permissive parents, or make the other feel more important or accomplished because of their own perceived shortcomings? Everyone knows that friendships provide a variety of benefits and serve crucial personal and social functions, but no one wants to feel used. If friends suspect the other's motives in liking them, whether justly or unjustly, feelings are hurt, trust diminishes, and careful negotiations are necessary to preserve or restore the relationship.

The developments of puberty and sexual urges further complicate feelings of affection. Actual participants as well as third parties may second-guess and interpret dubiously the caring experienced in same- and cross-sex friendships, viewing friendly feelings as possibly veiling sexual interests. Moreover, how either same- or cross-sex friends are treated once dating begins is a significant concern. Are they used to gain a dating target's attention? Are they included on dates or does another crowd take over? Do possible dates preempt all plans made by friends? Do friends continuously compete for other persons? Over time, cultur-ally endorsed gender differences, and ideologies and practices of heterosexuality, homosexuality, and romantic love transform the con-tours of the entire social arena (Thorne, 1986). Meanwhile, Douvan and Adelson (1966, p. 174) observe:

> The peer relations of adolescence are part of the preparation for adult love and friendship: by loving and being loved, by making friends and being befriended, the child learns something of the vicissitudes of affection.

Indeed, expressing and experiencing affection as an end in itself and/or as instrumental in achieving other goals comprise puzzling and inter-penetrated aspects of friendship. These enigmas acquire amplified complexity during adolescence that persists into adulthood.

The dialectic of judgment versus acceptance comprehends the pivotal moral dilemmas generated and managed among friends, peers and families during adolescence. In their dealings with ethical issues and behavioral choices, young friends rehearse and foreshadow the distinc-tive moral alternatives of adult friendships. First, an individual's self-appraisal and self-concept are closely tied to friends' and peers' reactions. And though one's friends also use peer standards in evaluat-ing self, closer friendships can provide a buffer from the critical scrutiny of less benign others. Thus, one's choices of friends comprise significant judgments in their own right, often involving trial and error. Dubois (1974) remarks, "Empirically, the evidence seems to stress the frequency of this paradoxical conflict between the value placed on friendship in youth and the immature capacity to appraise the other" (p. 26). Inaccu-rate views of self combine with equally misguided impressions of others to foster a process of experimenting with and replacing friends (Epstein, 1983).

Within established bonds cross-pressures exist between expectations that friends will accept and confirm each other's actions and evaluate honestly their likely consequences for self, other, the friendship or affected parties. The friends must reconcile private moral visions with the outlooks of their families and the larger society. Each decision to endorse or challenge a friend's behavior reflects selective standards of evaluation. And whether the judged person experiences these criteria as appropriate, too idiosyncratic or too conventional, in addressing their legitimacy, the moral conversation of adolescent friendship transpires. Practicing this "judging-with" friends in a spirit of compassionate objectivity instructs young people in the collaborative development of ethical principles as opposed to the unquestioning acceptance of unilaterally imposed world views (Beiner, 1983; Youniss, 1980).

Yet, despite the risks and advantages involved in friends devising private, alternative moral frameworks together, young people continue to be judged by the standards of encompassing social orders as well. Presaging the unforgiving eye of public gaze in adulthood, adolescents learn that they are judged by the company they keep and their objective achievements; there are both societal and intimate constructions of self. Thus, the private qualities of specific friendships may be compared with their likelihood of causing public embarrassment and constrained opportunities. The verdicts reached, and their means of justification and communication to friends and others, anticipate modes of managing quandaries in friendships later in life.

Above all, friendships provide "somebody to talk to" during adolescence. But this benefit presents ongoing challenges to friends due to the dialectical necessity for both expressive and protective communication in their interconnected social worlds. Close friends tend to discuss their personal feelings, and evaluations of each other and diverse people and events. Even so, mutual expressiveness renders each person vulnerable to the other's critical judgments of the revealed thoughts and feelings, and to the possibility of damaging disclosures outside of the dyad. If friends protect each other's vulnerabilities by withholding caustic commentaries and preserving confidences, trust develops.

However, when one considers the simultaneous expectations for honest judgment from friends, the shifting alliances occurring among even close friends, and the emotional predicaments and impulses of adolescents, the opportunities for violating trust are legion. Accordingly, the adept communicative management of close friendship learned in these circumstances involves developing tolerance of a friend's differences regarding touchy issues, sensitivity to the nuances often distinguishing appropriate from inappropriate matters for critical comment within and/or outside of the friendship, and the ability to distance oneself from feelings when communicating in certain situations. In short, friends learn how to co-construct, recognize, and respect discretionary boundaries between each other as well as their friendship and other people.

Adolescence is a period to idealize friendships while beginning to understand the realities of their contingent existence. Adolescents are privileged to have the time, the "tractable selves," the receptivity to inner feelings, and minimal distractions from the demands of adulthood (Douvan & Adelson, 1966). Yet they are also hampered by their limited experience in dealing with the increasingly demanding events and choices shaping their worlds. Consequently, some important friendships end over divergent interpretations of dilemmas exhibiting magnified salience simply because they are encountered for the first time. Further, intimate friends often feel mutual ambivalence. Their shared activities can produce some of the funniest and enlivening yet also painful and regretful moments of growing up. They bask in the glow of each other's achievements and social successes while sometimes feeling envy and chagrin. Meanwhile, the practices they have developed for deep involvement and opportunistic detachment will both play a role in articulating the place for their friendships in young adulthood.

Chapter 6

Young Adult Friendships

Young adulthood, generally encompassing the late teen years to the early thirties, comprises a pivotal stage for exploring the roles that friendships will play in adult life, constrained by the demands of work, love relationships, and/or family. Friends may provide crucial input regarding one's self-conceptions, career options, mate selection, community involvement, and recreational activities. During this period patterns of friendship vary much more than in earlier life due to the ramifications of gender-linked differences and the range of opportunities associated with socioeconomic status (Brown, 1981). Here, I will primarily discuss modal patterns enacted by middle-class males and females, whose life choices produce characteristic contingencies directly affecting the forms and functions of their friendships.

This chapter describes some praxic features of these young adult friendships—how communicative and behavioral choices made inside and outside such dyads shape and reflect each person's sense of self, values, and social nexus. First, I examine the college years as a vital time for forming and enjoying friendships. Then I compare the interactional dialectics and overall stances typifying same-sex friendships of young women and men, followed by their respective orientations toward cross-sex friendships. The chapter ends with a consideration of the relationships among friendship, work, and marriage in young adulthood.

Further Schooling and Young Adult Friendship

For young people who attend college, these years typically correspond to what Levinson and his colleagues (1979) term the Early Adult Transition period, spanning ages 17 to 22 in their model of male adult development. Beyond mere education for future employment, this is a time for investigating with others various career and lifestyle alternatives in conjunction with one's personal relationships, values, and preferred modes of relaxation. These pursuits occur while mental and physical faculties are nearing peak capacities and transpire in a setting where one is individuated from one's family yet surrounded by peers experiencing similar intellectual and social challenges, self-doubts, and sheer excitement about what their adult lives may hold for them. It is an auspicious period for forming both deep and zestful friendships—a potential window of availability, vitality, and hearty, shared concern for personal essences.

Even so, the transition to college often involves an emotionally trying adjustment period during which, "the college freshman is forced not only to build a new social support system but also to renegotiate relations with family and friends back home" (Shaver, Furman, & Buhrmester, 1985, p. 194). Selectively transcending one's adolescent friendships is a double-edged process anticipating the abrupt revision of friendship networks Americans repeatedly face in relocating throughout their adult lives. Such sifting may also recall imposed splits with friends from childhood. The positive and negative features of preserving adolescent friends sharply contrast. Favorably, such friends mutually anchor and affirm each other's identity during unstable and threatening times like the move to college. They provide continuity in the experience of self and others (Peters & Kennedy, 1970). Since these friendships were developed while dealing with fundamental decisions and life issues for the first time, the partners persist as important conversational recreators of and symbolic links with such unrepeatable moments. Finally, they may set the standards for what is meant by "real friendship" for the rest of one's interpersonal endeavors. Weiss and Lowenthal (1975) found, for example, that the qualities connected with real friends did not change across the life stages of high school, newlywed, middle-aged, and preretirement for their participants. They concluded that "the functions of real friendships may be established at an early age and maintained throughout life" (p. 58).

In contrast, the stability fostered by one's previous friends may actually prevent necessary and appropriate changes in one's actions and attitudes (Tokuno, 1986). Living up or down to prior identities may inhibit adaptation to the requirements of emerging adult scenarios and impede the mature judgment facilitated by other persons who understand and share the likely consequences of current decisions. Even so, certain adolescent friendships are maintained despite enforced separations as individuals remain both historically and currently salient to each other. Still, the realities of limited time and energy force one to relinquish many former friendships and develop new ones in functionally managing the move to college (Peters & Kennedy, 1970). Hays, citing his prior research, states that "the most adaptive social networks for first term university students were those which were most permeable" (1988, p. 405).

Handling new living conditions and educational settings, while developing new relationships and reconciling them with "abandoned" family, friends, and romantic partners, comprise sweeping practical and emotional challenges, often disrupting the previous social arrangements (Shaver et al., 1985). Studying college freshmen across their initial year at school, Shaver et al. observed, "Old friendships and love affairs tended to whither, many new relationships failed to last, and organizational ties were broken faster than they were replaced" (1985, p. 202). Meanwhile, most students readily found cliques of casual friends to affiliate with but did not feel as popular among them as with their high school acquaintances (Shaver et al., 1985).

As a result, many college freshmen report feeling lonely, and 40% of the students in one study viewed leaving their family and prior friends as the principal reason (Cutrona, 1982). Though harder to develop than casual ties, Shaver et al. (1985) found that the increasing network satisfaction associated with new friendships over the first year in college gradually surpassed that attributed to family, old friendships, or romances (Shaver et al., 1985). Moreover, Cutrona (1982) noted that infrequent contact and dissatisfaction with college friends were more closely related to loneliness than contact or satisfaction with either family or dating partners. Students in her study who felt less lonely by spring attributed their relief to slowly building new satisfying friendships, even though many of them were not yet pleased with their "love life" (Cutrona, 1982). By comparison, persons who were still lonely at the year's end most frequently asserted that romantic involvement was the sole path to reduced loneliness (Cutrona, 1982). Consequently, Cutrona (1982) suggests that friendship may be more important than romance in alleviating loneliness at this point in students' lives.

Survey research documents the bittersweet irony that, despite their greater opportunities to make friends than any other age group, more adolescents and young adults express loneliness than at any other stage. In fact, Rubenstein et al. (1979) found reported loneliness to decrease across the life course. Several developments during young adulthood attenuate perceived loneliness. First, young men and women begin to temper their idealized expectations of close associates. A person is more prone to conflict and disappointment with friends from whom one expects too much. Accordingly, due to actual difficulties in forming and keeping friendships in light of excessive demands, or to perceiving existing ones as unsatisfactory despite their positive features, persons with unrealistic expectations tend to be lonelier (Shaver et al., 1985).

Accompanying their more appropriate expectations of friends, young adults become more selective in choosing them. These combined tendencies reduce the disparity between perceptions of ideal and real friends (Weiss & Lowenthal, 1975).

Gender, Moral Visions, and Interactional Dialectics within Same-Sex Friendships

There are many moments in life when friendship simultaneously fulfills emotional and utilitarian needs for both males and females. This coincidence occurs frequently when friendship points beyond itself and eases or personalizes the tasks of politics, business, child-rearing, or schoolwork. In contrast, the projects of honing one's adult practices of intimacy, commitment, and concern in ongoing relationships—while also conversationally refining one's self-conceptions, values, and ideas about career options and marriage partners—comprise emotional work and shared judgment for which caring friendships are uniquely suited. The typical time for these inherently relational tasks is young adulthood.

However, presumably reflecting cultural training and repeated patterns of social and personal interaction, young adult females and males tend to exhibit genderized perceptions of time, differing formulations of their identities, and dissimilar moral visions that interrelate in conducting their friendships. Accordingly, these incongruities are played out in gender-linked standards for evaluating friendships and are contextually magnified in stereotypical career trajectories and responsibilities in marriage and raising children.

Interviewing college juniors and seniors of both genders, Maines and Hardesty (1987) noted that both have comparable plans for the future, including education, marriage, children, and work. But how they expect to coordinate their participation in these spheres clearly diverges (Maines & Hardesty, 1987). Males function in a "linear temporal world" in which "They project a future whose practical end point is defined almost exclusively toward career accomplishment" (Maines & Hardesty, 1987, p. 108). By comparison, females describe "contingent temporal worlds" wherein their careers may occur subject to family responsibilities. For these women life choices unfold in configurations that they must manage simultaneously, whereas the men's options compose a relatively discrete sequence (Maines & Hardesty, 1987). As a result, the present is meaningful for females as an encompassing, though historically disciplined and temporally contingent, "zone of being." In contrast, for males it embodies a stepwise, yet curiously timeless, "zone of potential" tilting toward additional future accomplishments (Maines & Hardesty, 1987; Cottle, 1976).

Research on identity development reveals similar themes. Males typically define themselves by demonstrating competence at objectively rated, competitive tasks and deciding on a career pursuit. Such identity work seems to come before males' psychological availability for intimacy (Hodgson & Fischer, 1979). By comparison, a woman learns who she is through relating to others and identifying the person "with whom she will share her life" (Hodgson & Fischer, 1979, p. 39). Thus, for females, developing intimacy anticipates or complements cultivating self-identity (Hodgson & Fischer, 1979).

These gender-related images of time and identity coalesce in Gilligan's (1982) work on the moral development of men and women. Gilligan (1982) qualifies the "different voice" she identified in women's words as thematic and not necessarily tied to gender. She argues that "the differences arise in a social context where factors of social status and power combine with reproductive biology to shape the experience of males and females and the relations between the sexes" (Gilligan, 1982, p. 2).

She views most males as enacting a moral vision of individual rights, wherein individuals are primary and essentially separate from one another. Life involves a series of relationships, readily replaceable if they violate formal rules or fail to fulfill logical conditions (Gilligan, 1982). In contrast, most females enact a moral vision of mutual obligations and responsibilities, wherein relationships are primary and individuals are viewed as essentially connected with one another. Life involves a web of affiliations that are preserved even if it requires changing rules insensitive to given situations (Gilligan, 1982). She summarizes:

> Thus in the transition from adolescence to adulthood, the dilemma itself is the same for both sexes, a conflict between integrity and care. But approached from different perspectives, this dilemma generates the recognition of opposite truths. These different perspectives are reflected in two different moral ideologies, since separation is justified by an ethic of rights while attachment is supported by an ethic of care. (Gilligan, 1982, p. 164)

As ideal-types constructed from extant research, female and male friendships of this age group exhibit distinctive patterns of enacting their interactional dialectics consistent with the contrasting moral ideologies described by Gilligan. Overall, in managing the contradictory requirements of independence and dependence in friendship, young adults maintain friendships because of volition, not obligation (Shulman, 1975). Moreover, they report more contact with friends than at any other adult stage except for the elderly (Williams, 1958; Verbrugge, 1983).

Yet, although Caldwell and Peplau (1982) identified no gender differences in quantitative indicators, such as the number of intimate, good, or casual friends or the amount of time spent with friends, young men and women evidently experience their similar ostensive management of the dialectic of independence and dependence differently. Wright (1982, 1985) found that women typically associate the satisfactions of friendship with greater interdependence, whereas men do not. As compared with males, female roommates describe more intimacy in their friendships and a higher probability of associating after graduation (Hill & Stull, 1981). Therefore, despite some quantitative similarities, men and women report qualitatively different interactions and activities with friends, implying greater interconnection of lives and mutual dependence in women's friendships than in men's (Caldwell & Peplau, 1982; Aries & Johnson, 1983; Williams, 1985).

More dramatic distinctions are demonstrated in males' and females' management of the dialectic of affection and instrumentality. Women's friendships appear charged by ongoing tensions between the interwoven demands of caring and utility. Research reveals not only emotional sharing (Caldwell & Peplau, 1982), affective generosity (Fox, Gibbs, & Auerbach, 1985), and greater positive affect (Ginsberg & Gottman, 1986), and intimacy (Fischer & Narus, 1981) than men's bonds as characterizing female friendships, but also high expectations for assistance (Margolies, 1985) and "getting as well as giving" (Davidson & Packard, 1981, p. 506). How female friends manage these contradictory aspects in particular contexts can compose relationships ranging from uplifting and functional to emotionally draining and burdensome (Margolies, 1985). Considerable psychological flux and transformational potential derive from these antagonistic tendencies in women's friendships.

In contrast, male friendships are typically encapsulated by their instrumental emphasis. Consistently, males report doing things, shared activities, and instrumentality as fundamental properties of their friendships (Caldwell & Peplau, 1982; Fox et al., 1985). Men also exhibit less intimacy and affection in their friendships than women do (Williams, 1985; Fischer & Narus, 1981; Hays, 1984; Ginsberg & Gottman, 1986), what Fox et al. (1985) term a "lack of emotional involvement in friendship" (p. 499). With instrumentality clearly dominating this dialectical pair, the interaction of male friendships evidences a static quality and a limited range of feelings. Consequently, men are typically more able to form instrumental same-sex friendships without resentment, whereas women have trouble doing so because of their ready tendency to personalize relationships with other females through self-disclosing and expressing affection (Margolies, 1985; Hays, 1985).

The differences in female versus male enactments of the dialectic of judgment and acceptance reflect prior divergences. For females a highly energized dialectical relationship between these two practices also persists because women seem to care more and be more involved with their friends (Fischer, 1981). For example, following their scrutiny of college roommates' conversations, Ginsberg and Gottman conclude that

> *men apparently do not view intense negative affect as an opportunity for closeness, whereas women do.* . . . both men and women express negative affect only to the friends they feel closest to. However, women are far more capable of handling negative affect than men. (1986, pp. 290 and 291, original emphasis)

Wright (1982) indicates that women tend to identify and confront problematic practices and sources of discord in their friendships. Moreover, they are likely to withdraw gradually from the relationship if they cannot resolve the issue. Fox et al. (1985) also remark on the fragility of women's friendships resulting from this propensity for addressing disturbing issues. Wright (1982) notes, however, that women who elect to accept their friends and not to confront areas of disagreement try to preserve the friendship, presumably because of their affection for the friend.

A weak opposition between these evaluative tendencies typifies men's friendships; unconcerned acceptance resulting from less involvement prevails. While males do not criticize their friends much, neither do they communicate robust acceptance. Typically, they sidestep problematic facets and emphasize the more serene areas of their friendships (Wright, 1982). Echoing this finding, Fox et al. (1985) depict men as "reluctant to confront friends about bothersome attitudes or behaviors" (p. 493). This apparent tendency to accept friends' foibles can be interpreted positively, but these practices seem to derive more from a superficial judgment of the friend's value and minimal caring. In contrast to women, Wright (1982) observes the nearly even chances that "a man who decides against confronting such strain will eventually terminate the friendship without ever bringing up the troublesome issue" (p. 14).

The patterns of expressiveness and protectiveness identified in women's and men's friendships have been extensively documented and closely parallel those of judgment and acceptance. Female friendships manifest considerable expressiveness; male friendships exhibit much more protectiveness. As considered above, women tend to confront their friends even at the risk of severing the bond, whereas men are inclined to skirt threatening issues. In addition, women share more emotional concerns, personal feelings and values, and support for the other (Davidson & Packard, 1981; Caldwell & Peplau, 1982; Tokuno, 1983; Aries & Johnson, 1983; Williams, 1985). And women are more likely to express directly their appreciation of friends, whereas men reveal feelings indirectly or through their actions (Helgeson, Shaver, & Dyer, 1987). Moreover, men limit their vulnerability by revealing less about themselves to their friends, avoiding the discussion of feelings or personal issues and focusing more on activities and objective issues such as sports or politics (Davidson & Packard, 1981; Davidson & Duberman, 1982; Tokuno, 1983; Aries & Johnson, 1983).

Indeed, a degree of concern, affection, or involvement appears necessary to animate the contradictions of judgment and acceptance and expressiveness and protectiveness. A given relationship may be too superficial for these antagonistic tendencies to shape its practices significantly. Yet, virtually every interaction within a more interdependent bond may bristle with critical versus accepting overtones and expressive versus protective dilemmas. And the potential for two friends' practices to transform their relationship from one type to another always exists. By pointing out these modal patterns, however, I do not deny that specific male friends may interact in ways I have linked with females above, or that certain women friends' comportment may resemble the male ideal-type (Wright, 1982).

Cross-Sex Friendships in Young Adulthood

Despite recurring gender differences in communicative practices and apparent intimacy in friendships, by the mid-twenties concern and affection for the other person grow in importance in the same-sex friendships of both sexes (Rose & Serifica, 1986; Tesch & Martin, 1983). Ironically, the affective nature of friendship heightens as its competition with romantic and work relationships grows. Young adults' diverse affiliations place rising demands on their time and emotional energy, even while fulfilling a variety of needs.

Cross-sex friendships often face the added exigencies of being perceived within and outside of the dyad as unconsciously or deceptively rehearsing, enacting, or obstructing romantic involvement and the normative adult path to selecting a spouse (Rawlins, 1982). As a result, the partners must rhetorically manage internal and external perceptions of the dyad as comprising "more than friendship" (Brain, 1976; Rawlins,

1982). These bonds also violate the "homosocial norm," which describes a tendency in our culture "for the seeking, enjoyment, and/or preference for the company of the same sex" (Rose, 1985, p. 63).

The contrasts evident in male and female same-sex friendships extend to their orientations to cross-sex relationships. Typically, males sharply distinguish between same-sex and opposite-sex relationships but view their associations with women rather uniformly. Same-sex bonds are sources of friendship, though many of these relationships are not particularly close or involving. Cross-sex bonds offer more disclosure, intimacy, and emotional involvement, which many males have difficulty interpreting as something other than precursors to romance. Males, experiencing limited intimacy with other males, may therefore look to females as potentially loyal, caring and supportive partners. But, informed by the socially conditioned alternatives of either friendship or romance, they often enact their cross-sex friendships as incipient love affairs.

By comparison, females do not differentiate so markedly between same-sex and opposite-sex relationships but do make distinctions among their male partners. They are able to form close relationships with females and males. And they clearly distinguish between males they consider friends and those they regard romantically. Employing a novel sample for investigating cross-sex relationships, Banta and Heatherington (1963) studied engaged couples and a male and female friend of each partner. They found the engaged male's female friend was similar to his fiance but there was little similarity between the female's male friend and her fiance. The authors conclude that roles are more differentiated in engagement and friendship with a member of the opposite sex for females than males.

Moreover, males and females tend to derive unmatched benefits from their cross-sex friendships. Researchers have found that males confide more in their best female than their best male friends (Komarovsky, 1974; Olstad, 1975; Hacker, 1981). And though undergraduate males mentioned more male best friends than female ones in Olstad's (1975) study, they reported spending more time with their best female friends and consulting them more about significant decisions. Finally, young men describe giving less, knowing the other person and being known better, feeling closer (Buhrke & Fuqua, 1987), and obtaining greater acceptance and intimacy in their cross-sex versus same-sex supportive relationships and friendships (Rose, 1985).

In contrast, women receive more acceptance and intimacy from their female than their male friends; only companionship, an activity-oriented pursuit, increases with males (Rose, 1985). Females declare knowing the other and being known better by same-sex others (Buhrke & Fuqua, 1987). They indicate feeling happy more frequently in close same-sex bonds, as opposed to males' prevailing happiness in cross-sex intimacy (Helgeson, Shaver, & Dyer, 1987, p. 227). And both men and women are more apt to search for females instead of males in times of stress (Buhrke & Fuqua, 1987). Finally, though men reported feeling that their same- and cross-sex friendships served similar functions, Rose observed, "Women's expectations for friendship do not seem to be fulfilled to the same extent by men friends as by women friends" (1985, p. 72). Taken together, the research findings comparing males' and females' same- and cross-sex friendships support Komarovsky's (1976) contention that men have greater emotional dependence than women on their cross-sex relationships. Chodorow (1976), in turn, argues that exclusive relationships with men are insufficient for women, who also need bonds with women.

Even so, while achieving limited closeness with other men, males' undifferentiated view of women may overly constrict their behavioral options and undermine their emotionally rewarding cross-sex friendships. The stereotypical male outlook includes several tendencies that potentially subvert cross-sex friendship. First, males are more apt than females to view both men's and women's behaviors in a more sexualized manner (Abbey, 1982). Abbey remarks, "Males do seem to perceive friendliness from females as seduction, but this appears to be merely one manifestation of a broader male sexual orientation" (1982, p. 830). Second, many males acknowledge their sexual motivations for forming cross-sex friendships, which women recognize, rendering them suspicious and reluctant to form friendships with males (Rose, 1985). On their part, most females describe platonic motives (Rose, 1985). Third, males often perceive a responsibility to take initiative and assert masculine sexuality (Pleck, 1975).

However, it should be noted that attracting a romantic partner is a crucial pursuit during young adulthood for both genders. One study reports that both genders view males more positively than females as "first-initiators" of heterosexual relationships, and both sexes prefer indirect initiations; in addition, males indicate more willingness to take the lead (Green & Sandos, 1983). Further, being friends prior to romantic involvement: (1) avoids much of the "brinkmanship" of sexual game-playing and strategically withheld commitments, (2) presents less risk to either party's self-esteem, and (3) better facilitates a more positively toned and gradual break-up, as well as a return to friendship in the event the love relationship does not work out (Rawlins, 1982; Metts, Cupach, & Bejlovec, 1989). When viewed in this way, cross-sex friendship makes considerable sense as a precursor to romance.

It is primarily men who find it difficult to develop cross-sex relationships free from romantic involvement. Rubin, Peplau, and Hill (1980) assert that men believe more in a "romantic ideology" and therefore "may be more ready to fall in love quickly with a wider range of partners while women tend to be more deliberate and discriminating about entering into a romantic relationship" (p. 824). Women seem better able to manage their feelings cognitively and are "less likely to be swept off their feet into a deep love relationship" (Rubin et al., 1980, p. 832). Yet, when women do develop romantic attachments to men, they are more liable to withdraw from their same-sex friendships than men are to facilitate exclusive commitment (Rose & Serafica, 1986). Distinctive relational aptitudes and inclinations persist.

A Commentary on Gender Disparities in Young Adult Friendships

The widely recognized differences in males' and females' participation in friendships come into sharper focus in view of their observed commonalities during young adulthood. While still unmarried and sharing the student lifestyle, both genders experience optimal circumstances for friendship formation, minimally confined "by sex-linked differences in status and role responsibilities" (Caldwell & Peplau, 1982, p. 730). Under such conditions it is not surprising that they report a similar number of and amount of time spent with friends, and the same preference for a select group of close friends over a larger collection of casual ones (Caldwell & Peplau, 1982). Both genders value intimate friendships, with the perceived quality of relationships surpassing their quantity in alleviating loneliness (Caldwell & Peplau, 1982; Shaver et al., 1985). Finally, in Rose's (1985) research men and women cited similar features involved in the formation and maintenance of their same-sex friendships, as well as functions served by them.

As in adolescence, the incongruities typically associated with young adult men's and women's friendships are much less evident in their closer and more enduring bonds (Wright, 1982). While women are frequently seen to disclose more to their friends than men do, McAdams (1985) found no significant differences when intimacy motivation was examined. In other words, males who were highly motivated to be close with their friends revealed as much to them as similarly inclined females. Likewise, Ginsberg and Gottman (1986) did not observe gaps in disclosure between comparably close male and female pairs of friends. Finally, in a study of same-sex best friendships, Ashton (1980) reported no difference in the males' and females' self-disclosure, emphasis on communicative ability, or intimacy.

Yet, it may be, as Helgeson, Shaver, and Dyer (1987) argue, that we should not treat intimacy and self-disclosure as equivalent concepts though they are clearly related. Rather, intimacy involves "appreciation, affection or warmth," while experiencing or developing this mutual regard often facilitates or reflects personal self-disclosure (Helgeson et al., 1987, p. 223). The special information revealed in a caring relational context often directly relates to or displays these fond feelings (Helgeson et al., 1987). So if a person does not feel (or has difficulty admitting) affection or heartfelt concern for another, either it is unlikely that he or she will reveal sensitive private matters, or such self-disclosures will not be experienced as creating intimacy in the richer relational sense of the word. Conversely, positive feelings of intimacy may develop between two persons in light of their well-disposed actions toward each other, yet without extensive self-disclosure. And persons may withhold certain comments to preserve their privacy or to protect the other's feelings (Rawlins, 1983b).

When self-disclosure and intimacy are strongly associated as in the studies of close friendship mentioned above, the conceptual distinction between them is a relatively moot point. However, when they are not linked, some quandaries emerge in attempting to appraise and compare the closeness and overall worth of the typically reported same-sex friendships of men and women. For example, Caldwell and Peplau (1982, p. 731) noted a provocative "discrepancy between subjective reports of intimacy in friendship and objective measures of intimate interactions." Though both men and women were describing best friends, defined abstractly by them in terms of heightened communication, disclosure, and confidence, in actuality, the women emphasized "emotional sharing and talking" privately with a single best friend, while the men stressed "activities and doing things together" with a group of friends (Caldwell & Peplau, 1982, p. 721). Consequently, the authors suggest that males and females may employ separate standards for evaluating the intimacy of their friendships, and what constitutes closeness for men may not suffice for women (Caldwell & Peplau, 1982).

The previously described gender variations in conceptions of time, identity, and moral outlooks are apparent in the evaluative standards that males and females characteristically use to appraise the disclosure, shared activities and affection occurring in their friendships. Women rate communicative exchanges with men lower than their interactions with female friends because they are accustomed to more intimate and personal discussions than men typically pursue and therefore experience unmet expectations. On their part, men may actually perceive themselves as spontaneous and trusting conversants though they seldom share issues that offer emotional insight or render them vulnerable (Davidson & Duberman, 1982). Further, many men think their feelings are best revealed through their actions and that too much revelation is "unmanly" (Williams, 1985). For these reasons men often must learn from women what it means to talk about their feelings in a manner that women perceive as "opening up" and facilitating closeness. Women, in turn, accommodate to male friends in realizing that doing things together comprises a cardinal expression of friendship for them (Helgeson et al., 1987).

Thus, shared activities are coded distinctly by males and females. For men joint endeavors exhibit mutual liking, though they often include individualized displays of competence, competition, and the accomplishment of instrumental goals, all of which men highly value. For women, common activities are not enough to secure relational involvement; they appreciate indications of mutual and intrinsic concern, even while getting something done. Sustained surface engagements, though entertaining, are unfulfilling.

The twist is that instrumentality and competitively based teamwork are rewarded in the working world (Fox et al., 1985). These tendencies directly facilitate the public achievements and market value of a person so central to a man's sense of self, or a woman's who buys into that ethic. Conversely, expressive skills and values primarily lend themselves to the caring communication so necessary for sustaining relationships in private life. It can be difficult to relinquish this relational stance in the work setting. As Margolies remarks, "Asking a woman to completely separate her personal life from her work is like asking a man to separate his feelings about himself from his achievements" (1985, p. 202).

Finally, females and males view affection in friendship differently. Women appear to use similar criteria for evaluating the closeness of their relationships with both genders, and male friends are often not rated as caring or as close as female ones. Moreover, the sexual potential of relationships does not significantly confound females' views of friendship. In comparison, men seem to employ separate standards in assessing the emotional closeness of their friendships with men and women (Buhrke & Fuqua, 1987; Bukowski, Nappi, & Hoza, 1987). Basically, they seem to play down the caring exhibited in their male friendships while strongly emphasizing the affection displayed by their female friends (Bukowski, Nappi, & Hoza, 1987).

There are a few possible reasons for these inconsistent assessments. First, as implied above by female appraisals of male disclosure, since men usually do not communicate affection as directly or sensitively as women do, females' baseline expressions receive higher marks from men (Buhrke & Fuqua, 1987). Second, males confuse female friendliness with sexual attraction, view it differently, and rate it more positively than "mere" friendship with other males (Abbey, 1982). Third and relatedly, males are more homophobic than females; they are more likely to fear being or being labeled homosexual (Morin & Garfinkle, 1978; Lewis, 1978). Such apprehension may lead to repressing feelings of affection for other men and emphasizing the sexual nature of the caring experienced with women (Rangell, 1963). Taken together, these double standards seem to reflect and reproduce traditional sex-role expectations within friendships (Rawlins, 1982).

Some important questions emerge. First, are the modal attachments of male and female friendships equally viable and intense with the genders merely differing in their practices for expressing their commitment (Hays, 1985)? Or are there essential differences in the potential experiences and benefits of the styles of friendship commonly documented by gender alignments in research results? If the latter is the case, can we argue that one form of friendship is preferable over the other in identifiable ways? Does their value change in different personal and social contexts? Why are they persistently associated with the respective genders?

I initially raised related questions in Chapter 2, mentioning then that answers would emerge in considering various moments in the life course. So without definitively answering them all here, studies regarding friendships in young adulthood indicate that friendships involving females are repeatedly evaluated more favorably. When compared with females' responses throughout their freshman year of college, males were less satisfied with their dating partners and friends and less positively portrayed both their old and new closest friends (Shaver et al., 1985). In a sample of same-sex friendships, split into two age groups of 21 to 34, and 35 to 55 years of age, the younger unmarried men's friendships exhibited the lowest rating of overall quality, while the older women's same-sex friendships manifested the highest (Sapadin, 1988). Likewise, using a broadly based index of intimacy, Fischer and Narus (1981) found that female friendships scored the highest and male ones the lowest, with cross-sex bonds in between.

Finally, Wheeler, Reis, and Nezlek (1983) report results from a study of college students' descriptions of their social interactions over a two week period that directly address the relative merits of men's and women's relationships. Their overall conclusions are telling:

> for both males and females, more interaction with females was related to less loneliness. . . . for both males and females and for both male and female partners, disclosure, intimacy, pleasantness, and satisfaction were related to less loneliness. The implication is that both sexes need the same qualities in their interactions to avoid loneliness but that females are more adept at providing them. (1983, p. 947)

Additionally, they observed that males experienced less closeness with their same-sex best friend and their other friends than females did (Wheeler et al., 1983). Trenchantly, the authors remarked that it was unimportant how much time either males or females spent interacting with males; exchanges had to be meaningful to help dispel loneliness. And meaningfulness was more likely with females. Perhaps both genders appreciate the emotional involvement, conversationally demonstrated caring, and interdependence frequently associated with friendships involving females. I will continue to address these matters throughout the book.

I have examined gender-linked patterns in managing young adult friendships abstracted from empirical research. The actual configurations of these practices within specific friendships and their functional or dysfunctional implications derive from and contribute to the bond's place within the two individuals' emerging networks of social relationships, which typically include work affiliations and marriage as young adulthood progresses.

Work and Young Adult Friendship

The career choice has comprehensive impact on young adults' friendships, values, and self-conceptions. Almost imperceptible in their omnipresence, the demands of a serious commitment to work redefine an individual's world view and practical management of everyday living. Henry (1971, pp. 127, 131) observes:

> Man [sic] at work *is* at work—working through on a daily basis, his views of himself, the tasks set by his work environment, his hopes for future relationships and rewards. . . . The world of work takes our time, molds our daily interactions, structures our beliefs and values.

Initially, friendships with co-workers are less common than in later life for single young adults, possibly reflecting their attempts to preserve previously existing and more encompassing relationships (Stueve & Gerson, 1977; Verbrugge, 1979). However, having already commenced rearranging their friendship networks and realizing the limited time for independent bonds, married young adults are more likely to mention co-worker friends (Stueve & Gerson, 1977; Verbrugge, 1979). Other factors influence the likelihood of friendship at work. Fine (1986) cites the physical setting, specific type of job, and organizational culture as either facilitating or subverting employees' autonomy and/or willingness to engage coworkers. Further, most organizational norms limit friendships to people with equal status, except for mentoring (Kurth, 1970; Fine, 1986). The ideologies of certain types of work also affect friendship possibilities. For example, Parker (1964) discovered that people in service professions evidenced a much greater probability of close friends in similar or related work than business executives did. Finally, individuals so deeply involved with their work that they have few contacts outside of it tend to become friends with co-workers (Parker, 1964; Verbrugge, 1979).

Though developed under the rubric of friendship, work affiliations range from patently "friendly relations" to more involved bonds transcending the work setting (Kurth, 1970). The former may compose a "friendly career" in which friendships are primarily cultivated and strategically employed to further one's job advancement (Maines, 1981). Friendship networks premised on members' status and instrumental capabilities (Bensman & Lilienfeld, 1979; Fine, 1986) often replace friendship networks based on a blend of caring, utility, and personal characteristics predating work preoccupations. These new networks persist only to the extent that they are successfully used (Bensman & Lilienfeld, 1979). The shifting sands of promotion and demotion render some friends expendable. Further, the considerable job mobility of young people early in their careers sponsors frequent changes in residences and revisions in their friendships, engendering "expectations of transitoriness" in their interpersonal affiliations (Williams, 1959, p. 9).

Involvement with a work friend risks the complexities of personal versus professional appraisals and obligations, and activates the contradictions of private versus public enactments of the relationship, and idealized versus realized blends of affection and instrumentality and judgment and acceptance. Suppose one friend has access to resources or information that could help the other but is restricted by corporate policy. This person may feel respected professionally if not asked by the friend to compromise public rules but may also be insulted personally, especially if it would provide an important opportunity to be of service. Even so, too frequent or extensive requests may also be offensive (Bensman & Lilienfeld, 1979). Both one's influence at work and the friendship's definition are tested by how and whether demands are made and the nature and interpretation of the privileged friend's response. Not asking a friend may suggest limited openness between the friends, and refusal to accept constraints on the friend's freedom to help could be seen as lacking trust in his or her good intentions (Bensman & Lilienfeld, 1979).

Moreover, how will other employees view the assisting friend? Perceived favoritism could damage both friends' credibility in the organization (Davis & Todd, 1982). Davis and Todd (1982) remark, "A person valuing loyalty over appearance may favor friends and punish enemies within the organization. A person valuing fairness and impartiality above all may be evenhanded to the point of coldness in dealing with friends within the organizations" (p. 85). But what if the two persons in this quotation are parties to the same friendship? How are such predicaments realistically managed in light of contradictory public and private interpretations of the ideal friend or professional? Eisenstadt (1974, p. 142) synoptically observes:

> It is because of this emphasis on pure symbolic relations—which at the same time cannot escape the problems of struggle over power and resources—that these relationships are potentially both very brittle and heavily laden emotionally. Only when they shade off into mere "acquaintance" can these tensions disappear, to erupt once again if either party tries to transform the relationship into one of more "basic" or "real" friendship.

The prevailing practices associated with less close male friendships conform well with the uncertain friendship ethic of the working world. To the extent that a person is accustomed to friendships emphasizing independence, instrumentality, withheld personal judgments, token acceptance, and carefully measured expressiveness, managing work relationships is easier. In fact, these friendships function to cement the sense of self and personal values accompanying a thorough commitment to the values of an organization (Whyte, 1956).

In contrast, to the degree that a person behaves in the manner connected with female friendships stressing interdependence, a vital interpenetration of affection and instrumentality, caring criticisms and heartfelt acceptance, and extensive confidence and candor, the glib "hail-fellow-well-met" style of working world friendships may seem alien and/or unethical. For many women adjusting to these practices may prove difficult and ultimately situational if they attempt to form their customary brand of friendships with female and/or male colleagues (Margolies, 1985).

Frequently, both men and women become more adept at "the structured use of personal associates" (Field, 1984). Careful distinctions are made between relationships of "convenience" and "commitment" to correspond with the progressively segmented quality of adult life (Feld, 1984). Snyder and Smith's (1986) synthesis of self-monitoring research reports that high self-monitors tend to develop situation-specific, activity-oriented, instrumental friendships allowing them to exhibit multiple identities across various contexts; and their close friends are higher self-monitors than are their casual friends. By comparison, low self-monitors negotiate personal disposition-oriented, affective and emotional friendships that permit them to enact a consistent, principled self across contexts; and their close friends are lower self-monitors than are their acquaintances (Snyder & Smith, 1986).

Snyder and Smith (1986) may be identifying people with clear yet different evaluative standards for selecting and appraising close friendships. High self-monitors are sensitive to public appearances and objective expectations for excellence in specific activities, whereas low self-monitors are more concerned with private dictates and subjective codes regarding adherence to personal standards, regardless of the setting. Interestingly, Snyder and Smith (1986) found no reliable gender differences, implying that self-monitoring research may tap underlying "orientations to friendship" (p. 66) missed by other studies. The criteria people use for choosing and judging their friends may transcend typical gender-role associations and increasingly reflect the involvements, values, and requirements of their entire nexus of personal and social activity.

Marriage and Young Adult Friendship

A friend's marriage sponsors the most sweeping changes in singles' friendship practices (Brown, 1981). Accordingly, there is ambivalent interplay among friendship, courtship, and marriage. Friends aid in mate selection and are frequently involved in a couple's original meeting (Ryder, Kafka, & Olson, 1971). However, when a friend is perceived as too involved with someone, efforts at sabotaging the courtship often occur, including highlighting the prospective mate's faults and siding with the friend in quarrels (Ryder et al., 1971). Yet when a marital commitment is announced, friends shift from criticism to acceptance; instead of expressing misgivings, they practice self-restraint to protect the engaged friend's images of self and the prospective mate (Mayer, 1957).

Later courtship and early marriage strikingly constrict friendship networks. Each spouse's contact with peripheral friends disappears and gradually diminishes with close friends (Milardo, Johnson, & Huston, 1983). Following marriage, both males and females confide less in all of their friends (Booth & Hess, 1974). Cross-sex friendships markedly decrease in number and in perceived intimacy (Rose, 1985). Within the marriage, problems develop regarding the blending of spouses' individual friendship networks, concerns about acceptance by the partner's friend and each spouse's freedom to see his or her own friends (Dickson-Markman & Markman, 1988; Ryder et al., 1971). To deal with conflicts generated by opposing choices of individual friends, married pairs often develop "couple friendship" (Ryder et al., 1971; Hess, 1972) or "joint acquaintanceship" (Bott, 1971). But these practices thoroughly constrain the identity-building possibilities of self-chosen dyadic friendships in the interests of marital stability (Askham, 1976). Often the husband exerts more influence in initiating friendships and deciding on those most preferred by the couple (Babchuk & Bates, 1963). Fischer and Oliker argue:

> The higher pay, social status, and friendship incentives in men's work may encourage wives to regard husbands' friends as more instrumental to their own social status. Perhaps more importantly, these unequal resources give husbands more power and privilege to select a couple's joint friends. (1983, p. 129)

Later on, wives more independently choose friends, though the requirements of housework and children limit their own availability and assortment of others for friendship (Babchuk & Bates, 1963; Fischer & Oliker, 1983).

As time passes, married partners repeatedly face the desire for and challenge of selecting and maintaining both couple and individual friendships that can survive both spouses' scrutiny and fit into increasingly restricted schedules. The condition of having too many friends before and during early marriage gives way to concerns about lacking friends as a couple and for each spouse (Dickson-Markman & Markman, 1988). Though these difficulties diminish over time in childless couples, they return to early marriage levels with the birth of a child (Dickson-Markman & Markman, 1988). Young adults enter a period, termed the "life cycle crunch," when the demands of children, work, and money are high and family income and free time are wanting (Wilensky, 1961). During this stage, children foster encounters with neighboring parents, but curb opportunities for wider-ranging social activities (Stueve & Gerson, 1977).

Conclusion

Middle-class young adulthood begins with considerable time for friends and multiple options for ways of life and identity consolidation. As the period unfolds, the typical middle-class American encounters important developmental tasks that include entering the adult world of work, developing personal relationships of varying degrees of intimacy and commitment, and integrating one's identity (Tokuno, 1986). Critical incidents in any of these processes have ramifications throughout the others.

The various moral visions and values discussed and enacted within friendships acquire increasing significance as individuals make choices profoundly shaping their adult lives. Though young adults highly prize personal authenticity and relationships break up early on due to charges of "phoniness" (La Gaipa, 1987), the social contexts of friendship change. Young people gradually realize that consistent action with and loyalty to one's friends no longer comprise the sole or fundamental demonstrations of one's character. To their credit, intimate friendships teach the ethical strength of adhering to commitments (Erikson, 1963), but expanding commitments include comprehensive enterprises like work and marriage that may jeopardize an individual's ability to be steadfast with friends. As a result, perceptions of individuals' authenticity and caliber of character must transcend personal and dyadic enactments to include how their daily lives integrate the social consequences and requirements of their diverse choices.

Time and energy are finite. Individual and negotiated decisions regarding marriage, children, career, civic involvement, and leisure reflect and influence self-conceptions and begin to articulate networks or series of human relationships within which one's values and priorities are continuously enacted. Simultaneously, these pursuits also generate constraints typically patterning the forms and functions of one's friendships at any juncture, owing to their contingent status and extensive reliance on voluntary effort for continued existence. Thus, moral visions and friendship practices thrive that transcend gender but persistently align themselves with gender divisions. Whether consciously or not, normative roles and codes enacted in the workplace and associated by both sexes with marriage and raising children can reinforce these disparities.

Accordingly, continuing attachments depend on how the friends interact within their relationship, and how the dyad articulates with each party's larger network of commitments and involvements. During young adulthood, most friendships end due to external factors and not because of trouble between friends (Rose, 1984). Rose (1984) found the primary causes of friendships' dissolutions to include physical separation, new friends supplanting old ones, interference from dating or marriage relationships, as well as growing to dislike the friend's personal attributes.

Consequently, the ways in which friendships are managed, the bases for distinctions among friends, and the overall significance of friendship in a given adult's existential milieu are strongly indicative of his or her self-defining values. Discriminating among people in developing friendships and managing dialectical contingencies produce modes of interaction that shape and are shaped by certain modes of being a person. Individuals' self-conceptions and conceptions of personal relationships are continually devised and revised as they negotiate friendships within various social systems exhibiting diverse public and private exigencies and evaluative standards (Rawlins, 1989a).

There is great potential for resentment among friends when the talk about values and choices so commonplace throughout this period—and so important in appraising the public and private meanings and implications of one's decisions—gives way to actually living out value-laden choices that contradict one's statements. Work settings may embody values that compete with the ideals of close friends as well as separate them in time and place. Marriage may introduce the couple as the unit of friendship (Hess, 1972), with compatibility no longer a question of two but two pairs of people getting along. Consequently, as the obligations of adulthood expand, the issue usually becomes not whether one continues to care about a friend but whether one's adult nexus allows the person to remain an active part of one's life. And in living out this question, a lot can go awry in coordinating schedules as well as sentiments.

Ironically, the praxic functions of friendships at this stage involve helping each other make decisions regarding self, marriage, and career, which ultimately constrict the opportunities for involvement with friends. Studying these friendships reveals the seams of the multiple social systems in which we live. Young adult life becomes increasingly compartmentalized and friendships are conditional (Lopata, 1981). A dialectical perspective emphasizes that these exigencies affecting friendship in given cases are not abstract trends, but the ongoing products of active human choices.

Chapter 7

Illustrative Analysis: The Communicative Management of Young Adult Friendships

The present chapter examines case studies of three pairs of young adult friends—two women, two men, and a woman and a man, all from middle class backgrounds, living in an urban area of the northeastern United States. The following descriptions are based on two open-ended interviews independently conducted with each friend using a standardized schedule of questions. After comparing these accounts to cross-validate their individual views of important qualities and events in the friendship, I talked with both friends together in a dyadic interview. Except where indicated, I have drawn on their candor and insights expressed during their separate interviews to illustrate the communicative management of various dialectical tensions in maintaining three actual friendships across young adulthood. At selected points fictional excerpts exemplify further specific predicaments. I close with a summary of the outlooks and practices apparent in these young adult friendships.

Darlene and Lana

Darlene is 26, married, and college-educated. She teaches high school English. Lana is 26, divorced, and engaged to be remarried. She has completed a year and a half of graduate study in guidance counseling and teaches English in a junior high school. They have known each other for 13 years and have been close friends for 12. They live 10 miles apart.

Darlene and Lana met during their freshman year in high school. Each woman reported that her initial impression was that the other possessed tremendous self-confidence. In fact, Lana initially thought Darlene was too outspoken and disliked her for this reason. Since they had several classes together, they began talking to each other, discovering (as many adolescent friends do) that both were more sensitive and insecure than their public behavior portrayed. Some of this knowledge was also obtained by playing practical jokes on each other involving a boy they both liked and witnessing the hurt and anguish they had unintentionally caused.

Becoming closer friends was inhibited for a time because they had attended different junior high schools and therefore belonged to separate cliques at the high school. During their junior and senior years they thoroughly transcended these groups, participating in many activities together, talking on the phone often, and double-dating. Throughout high school, Darlene remained the more confident of the two girls. She remembered this high school phase of their friendship as "basically fun, each trying to outdo the other, laughing a lot." Lana in turn saw it as "superficial, we didn't share feelings." With high school drawing to a close, however, she noted, "We double-dated to proms and got really friendly." And consistent with conceptions linking female intimacy and identity, she remarked, "As my confidence in our relationship grew, my confidence in myself grew."

Their college years were significant for the friendship. From the outset Darlene insisted that they room together, with the transition to college affecting them differently as individuals, while deepening their mutual disclosure and knowledge of each other. Darlene recalled:

> I don't think it was really until we hit college that our relationship started to, we began to talk to each other about feelings. They were very closely guarded until we were in college. And even in college we were very, the first two years, we were very, um, careful. I think we were afraid that one or the other would be hurt. I don't know why. I don't know whether we were afraid that when we finally did tell all of the flaws that we would be rejected, but we were very careful about it.

Lana noted other changes:

> By college the tables had turned. Even though Darlene appeared to be the most confident, she really wasn't. It was a front to mask insecurities. I didn't have those basic insecurities; I was just shy. That first year at college was a rough year; we lived together. I found out a lot of things about her that I didn't know—she was self-centered. . . . I became the leader or more dominant in college; she fell back into my spot. She depended upon me—it made me feel good but also made me feel resentful. I knew she had potential.

As freshman roommates, a major fight occurred between them over a senior man who had been dating Lana and then asked Darlene out. The argument concerned whether Darlene had flirted with him, thereby encouraging his request for a date. Both women intimated they had never fully resolved this quarrel.

In their sophomore and junior years at college, Darlene and Lana shared an apartment with a different third woman each year. Darlene did not get along well with either. This was a period when Darlene felt very insecure and needed to count on Lana:

> I needed the commitment of someone more as a friend than a lover type relationship. I needed to know if she would stick by me even at my worst, whereas I never doubted that with Kurt [her boyfriend]. With her with things the way they were, I did doubt if she cared. And when I discovered that she really did, that's when I felt committed to her.

Lana had similar recollections:

> Darlene went through a bad period in her own life and didn't have self confidence or self esteem. I felt she needed me; I was in an upsurge of my personality. I was happy; Darlene had a lot of self doubts. Darlene was insecure at college; I had loads of friends, she only had Kurt. Her only contacts with other people came from me or Kurt. I decided that I was not going to move out even though the intensity of the relationship was such that it was a strain on me. That's when I made my commitment to remain friends with her. It was important to me to sustain our relationship.

The fact that Lana responded to this need and worked through the roommate difficulties as well as other personal problems with Darlene did bring the women closer together. The two friends lived in an apartment by themselves during their senior year and got along beautifully.

Soon after college Darlene married Kurt. Although they talked on the telephone, for a couple of years she and Lana saw each other only occasionally. The two women accounted similarly for this suspension of their friendship. And though Lana, as a "swinging single," somehow seems blamed in their descriptions for this lapse, one also senses the effects of Darlene's new priorities following marriage. Darlene stated, "Lana saw Matt [her boyfriend] a lot more than when we were living together. I saw her rarely for a year or two. Off and on. Also I had just been married and she didn't know what to do with a newly married couple." Lana related:

> When Darlene got married, the relationship changed again because I was single and working and running around, and she was married. We didn't see each other much. Darlene was really into her marriage and her crystal and her this and her that. I couldn't identify with that so we still talked to each other on the phone and saw each other occasionally, but not very much. That lasted for about three years. I still feel guilty about not helping

her decorate her house. Our relationship was on "hold." We still spoke, cared for each other, but there was no real communication.

Though Lana was dating other men at first, later on she became involved with Matt. When Lana married him, she and Darlene and their respective spouses began interacting more frequently; in Lana's words, "Then I got married, then we got friendly again."

A little over a year prior to the interviews Lana had severe marital problems culminating in divorce. Throughout this period she relied on Darlene. Despite the fact that they had seen each other significantly less since college, Darlene made herself completely available for Lana:

> After she became married and it was unpleasant, that was another time when we really began—that was when we had to share our feelings about marriage and marital feelings and emotions that we'd experienced then. . . . The failure of the marriage bonded us together in a different way. I lied to get out of school and help her move out of her apartment while he was at work. When she left Matt, she came here and stayed with us for a while until she got up the gumption to tell her parents. I lent her my house when we went on vacation. . . . I think besides the relationship in college that took us so far, the divorce was a turning point. I think that she realized that I would do anything she asked me, no matter what, and I realized too that I would.

Lana also asserted the significance of Darlene's dialogue and assistance in this time of isolation and need:

> When I really realized that I had a friendship that was something to treasure and something to nurture was when I was going through my divorce. . . . I guess that's the time when we really, really got close because when my marriage went bad, I had her there to talk to and I really thank God for that. So then I turned around again and became dependent on her. She took me back even though I had been wrapped up in myself. . . . Divorce strengthened our friendship quite a bit. She was always there to listen, the only one who always invited me over and took any interest in how I was doing or feeling at that time. Before that, I wasn't too sure if Darlene would do anything for me if I were in a bad situation because I had never really been in a bad situation where I needed to rely on a friend. She came through for me and in my mind it cemented our relationship forever.

Despite the mutual affirmation of the friendship occurring throughout Lana's divorce, this bond never seems permanently placid. Lana's independence again received unfavorable reviews within the friendship. She observed, "Last summer was a devil-may-care ego-centered growth period for me. I sometimes hurt Darlene without intending to." Darlene agreed:

When she starts dating someone new, she usually becomes so totally involved with them that I don't hear from her. And that, she did that with Matt and then she did it with her, not that I expect her to be with me everyday, but she did it with Dan [her new fiance] for a while. Now that has died down. But she, it's almost as if she cuts everyone else off for this other person.

Shortly after Lana's divorce, the women had an angry exchange over Darlene's behavior with one of Lana's dates. Both the objective similarities and their differing interpretations in separately recounting this event suggest its ongoing salience in the emotional history of their friendship. Darlene began:

Right immediately after she was divorced . . . we all went to Mosaro's [a restaurant] one night. And he was very pleasant company and I enjoyed him thoroughly and we had a very good time. And she was furious. She perceived that as this game, some kind of a flirtation, that it wasn't and became very incensed and angry with me over that. And I think she was more sensitive to that then because she was so insecure, than she ordinarily would have been. I don't think she would have minded at all.

Lana presented her side:

Here I was coming off a divorce and she was openly flirting with him. And it really hurt me; it really, really hurt me. And I was angry about it. And she swears she didn't do it; but I know Darlene and I know she did it. You know, I just know she did.

Darlene continued:

She was furious at me because she thought it was deliberate. She was wildly angry. To the point that I had had hand surgery and she came over that night and came and screamed at me when I was sick. I was throwing up and that didn't seem to matter. For which I might add, I have since reminded her that that was about the crudest thing anybody could ever do was to yell at a woman with a busted arm and forty stitches. I have not let that slide.

Finally, we have Lana's closing observations on this event:

I finally went over and told her that I was furious about it. And she was furious at me cause she had just had an operation. And I didn't care. I screamed and yelled at her anyway. And I just wanted to get it straightened out; we couldn't even talk. It was like there was a barrier. And I said Darlene, we have got to talk about this. I said I'm sorry that you just had an operation but I've got to talk about it. So I said, I told her exactly what

I thought. I said I feel like you openly flirted with him. And I said he admits that he openly flirted with you. And he said that you certainly didn't do anything to discourage him. And I said. So she told me that he was a liar. And I thought, Bullshit! And I thought, Oh hell with it. . . . It still sort of pisses me off that she never admitted it.

However, in keeping with this dyad's rhythmic returns to depending on each other for conversation, compassion, and support, Lana currently discusses and listens to Darlene's concerns about being pregnant:

We're swinging back. I'm getting married and I'm doing well. But Darlene's having a baby, for her it's a scary time. So she talks with me a lot about that, things she couldn't say to Kurt because she would be afraid that it would hurt him to know that she's not too sure that she even wanted to have the baby. I try to reassure her; I'm sure she'll deal with it. She's handled everything else in her life. Right now she needs that reinforcement from me. She knows I'd love to have a baby; she really wishes it were me.

A friendship of considerable breadth and depth, this dyad exhibits several themes and predicaments associated with close female friendships spanning adolescence and young adulthood. Both women spoke of the importance of their shared experiences, the fact that throughout their friendship "a lot of water had passed under the dam." They felt very close to each other and prided themselves in their ability to depend on each other.

But reconciling their individual needs for independence and dependence within the friendship continually posed problems as each woman developed other attachments. As noted by Gilligan (1982), they pursue this friendship within a network of involvements. They want intimacy with each other as well as with the men in their lives, and their self-confidence continually reflects their simultaneous management of both relationships. Consequently, certain scenarios repeatedly characterize their friendship. Perceived or actual competition for men makes them insecure as individuals and undermines their closeness and mutual trust. When no competition exists and each woman is happy with her male partner, or when one is experiencing problems and needs to depend on the other, their relationship prospers, and the affection and support within the friendship enhances their individual self-esteem. Yet when either woman is feeling good about herself and doing well romantically, she may desire independence from the friendship. Thus, contingent on who is flourishing and the reasons for it, either woman may resent or welcome the other's dependence or independence. Although Darlene was satisfied with her marriage, she seemed to envy Lana's freedom to meet other men and her independence from their friendship. And when Lana was not romantically involved yet able to depend on her friend, she was jealous of Darlene's security in her marriage.

Overall, when either woman was too dependent or too independent, problems could occur between the friends. However, when either person really needed the other, both women always came through in ways that further cemented the relationship. Their mutual attributions of insecurity and vulnerability recognize their need for dependence and caring but also their ability to hurt each other. Ironically, the strength of a friendship is most clearly revealed when one friend calls on another and he or she responds. But a person is also most vulnerable and his or her autonomy most threatened when compelled to depend on a friend (Rawlins, 1983a). Nonetheless, the actual patterns of independence and dependence in Darlene's and Lana's friendship reflect an overarching ethic of interpersonal connection and interdependence that remains essential to their conception of their bond as well as their respective self-images (Gilligan, 1982).

But how do they communicate in sustaining this crucible of caring and confrontation? Basically, they have negotiated ways of talking that limit and protect each other's vulnerabilities while still expressing significant thoughts and feelings (Rawlins, 1983b). Though the potential for hurting and angering one another persists because of each woman's extensive familiarity with the other's insecurities and pet peeves, and the range of personally crucial topics they discuss, they understand the intentions behind most actions or comments and give each other the benefit of the doubt. As Darlene put it:

> At this point, after having lived together for four years, we know each other so well that anything that one or the other does that irritates us or angers us, we know them so well that we know the motives for it, and so we just write it off. So there's nothing that makes us so mad or so upset or so displeased that we don't know, "Well she did it because of this," or "I did it because of that."

Lana's penetrating understanding of Darlene is both a precondition and an outcome of intensive interaction between the friends:

> She's too strong, and people, I think people feel threatened by that; at least I know I did. And I think if you don't get to the interior of the person, of her, I think she does come across as being, "Well I am right and you are wrong. And what I think is right." And, you know, they don't really know the feelings and the anguish a lot of times that she goes through to be the person she is.

Both women's inclination to view the other positively rests on their track record of joint assistance, talking and laughing together, listening uncritically to each other's revelations, and preserving confidences. Lana describes their mutually accepting conversation:

> She knows I'll listen to whatever she has to say, you know, anything, any fears, or anything she'll go, you know, she'll say something and she'll go, "Isn't that horrible?" And I just always laugh because when I say something to her that other people might be shocked at or something like that about a feeling I have or something, I'll say, "Isn't that terrible?" We both always just say, "No, that's how we feel and there's a rational reason for it."

Likewise, Darlene observes:

> I might say to her, um, "It bothers me that Kurt goes to Trimper's [a local pub] on Thursday nights." And she would say, "Why?" And I would say, tell her, "Because I wonder, you know, with him up there on Thursday nights and the young girls and so on and so forth." Whereas with someone else I don't know if I would say that. I think that they might think, "Oh there's trouble in the marriage—gonna be a divorce." Or, you know, "What's the matter with her? She wants her husband around all the time." But with Lana, I could say it and explain it and she would understand my feelings. . . . No matter what I tell her that I've done or that happened, there's no condemnation. It's total acceptance. And I'm the same with her.

But such acceptance and mutual understanding are ongoing conversational achievements. They are not givens. Even in this friendship of deep affection and a history of commitment, their interaction involves strategic and rhetorical considerations. Though they depend on each other's honest opinions and reactions, they also recognize sensitivities, protect privacy, and avoid unduly angering or hurting the other woman. In contrast, the narrator and Maggie in Alice Adams's (1979) short story, "What Should I Have Done?" seem not to have developed such protective practices derived from jointly expressing both positive and negative emotions. The narrator observes that, "We were friends mainly on the basis of shared or similar humor: we made each other laugh for hours, sitting in the smoking room or out on the drafty steps of our dormitory. We made elaborate fantasies together" (p. 223). After college, Maggie's long-term secret lover, unaware that the narrator knows of his affair with her, remarks at a party that he wishes she could introduce Maggie to a man because she should marry. Recognizing too late the necessity of protecting her friend from this patronizing and callous comment, she lets it slip:

Over the phone a couple days later I say to Maggie: "It was really strange, meeting him, and of course his not knowing I knew who he was. And then his wishing you would marry—"

In a tight, judicious voice she says, "Well, I guess at least partly he does wish that."

After that some terrible drift began, and at last Maggie and I were not seeing each other. Our lives diverged, and I think that she also regretted telling me so much; we all know how that works. (Adams, 1979, pp. 228–229)

In contrast, Darlene and Lana recalled numerous instances when their desire to express misgivings or hurtful information was tempered by concern for the other's feelings, and when their voiced acceptance veiled deep-seated reservations and criticisms. They cautiously chose their moments for commenting and exercised great care in broaching subjects such as family members, relationships with men, husbands, details of their sex lives, and personal appearance.

In general, criticism is tactfully rendered, as explained by Lana:

Sometimes there are some things that I have to be careful about what I say. I have to be careful the way I phrase it, because—although she's gotten better, she takes criticism very hard. And I do too. And um I think we're both aware of that in each other and I think that's why if we do have a comment to make that's maybe not what the other one wants to hear, we're very careful about saying it.

Maintaining the assumption of benevolence in a friendship through accepting a friend's actions is often threatened by the contradictory requirement of honestly judging them. Darlene and Lana manage this dialectic of judgment and acceptance by employing courtesy and care in expressing criticisms. Judgments about most sensitive issues are avoided or developed gradually and indirectly by "talking around the issue;" still Darlene relates how an important subject may warrant explicit though discreet appraisal:

I feel obliged once in a while when I think she's doing something I don't approve of to tell her. But not in the sense that, "You shouldn't do that. What the hell's the matter with you?" But, you know, to say, "It worries me." That's how I usually approach it. If she's doing something that I'm not too keen on, I'll say it worries me that, and as I told her with this relationship she has with Dan now, when she first started to see him and got so serious, I said to her, "It worries me that you are becoming so involved with him so quickly. I wonder if you are emotionally over the first one enough to know what you really want." That's how I usually approach something that I wonder about.

Through employing the sensitive and respectful communicative practices described above, the two women have negotiated in their relationship the ability and privilege of directly confronting each other's violations of mutual expectations that result in hurt or anger. As Darlene puts it:

> We have finally reached the point where we can fight. And I think that's one of the things that's so individualistic about it, about our relationship. There are few people that you can feel very comfortable with to say, "You did this and it really made me mad." Because you're afraid of offending them or that they will become angry with you. Whereas with Lana and I, we now have reached a point where we can do that, and say, "That hurt my feelings," or "That made me angry when you didn't show up or you didn't come or whatever."

Lana describes their typical mutually recognized procedures:

> I almost always know and I think she does too that whatever we said or did was not quite right, and it didn't sit well with the other person. So then we sort of back off for a little bit, and then one or the other, it's not always me and it's not always her, will come forward and say, "What are you mad about? Did I say something to offend you?" Um, you know, "Why haven't you called me? Are you angry with me?" And then that's when, usually when the confrontation takes place. It's almost an unwritten agreement; it's that person's responsibility to come forth and say, "Yes," not say, "No, you didn't do anything." It's that person's responsibility to say, "Yeah, you really made me mad when you said that." And it's just like an unwritten agreement between us that, you know, that's when you say it. You know when that other person knows that there's something wrong. And it's serious enough to break down communications between the two of us. Then somebody has to take the first step, and the other person has to take the second step, and then we can go on and work that problem out.

Some of their angriest exchanges have related to inappropriate behaviors or comments concerning touchy issues.

Any portrayal of this friendship would be incomplete without emphasizing this pair's great enjoyment of each other and the role of humor in their bond. Both women stated enthusiastically:

> We can laugh about—just about anything that might seem terrible, we can find some humor in. And I think that a lot of times that really saves us because we could sit around and, you know, bemoan our fate from here till doomsday. And it wouldn't do any good. (Lana).
>
> We laugh a lot. If she's really down, she can call me and we can end up laughing about it. And if I'm really down I can call her. And we end up laughing—the other day about her divorce—hysterical. And I think that's part of it, that no matter what happens, no matter how bad one or the other is feeling, we kind of share it and yet laugh about how, no matter how bad it is. (Darlene)

When I talked to these women together, their ability to laugh together was readily apparent. Further, they mentioned and demonstrated how their humor often involved mean talk about others and "vicious" nicknames for former friends and acquaintances. I got the impression that these practices reinforced the exclusive boundaries of their friendship, while enacting for each other (and me) the risks of incurring either woman's disfavor. Brain (1976) argues that joking expresses the "element of strain and fragility in all friendships;" it can allow "love to persist without shame and may also betray a latent sentiment of aggression which is not always absent from loving relationships" (p. 3). Given the restraint so often necessary to protect vulnerabilities in this friendship, it is not surprising to see their "hysterical" laughter about such guarded matters as Lana's divorce.

The rich emotional texture of Darlene and Lana's interaction reflected persistent grappling with the contradictory requirements of independence and dependence, expressiveness and protectiveness, and judgment and acceptance in maintaining their friendship. Preserving trust, understanding intentions, and assuming benevolence, their actions together are contextualized by a history of hurting yet depending on each other, shared talk and laughter, and mutual affection. In Lana's words:

> I could share anything with Darlene and I'd, and I know that she would never be judgmental. She just, she'd accept me no matter what I did. I think if I murdered somebody, she would say, "Well, you know, I understand why you did it and you're still my friend. I still love you." And I feel the same way about her. There's a lot of things, you know, that get on my nerves. You know, and I think, "Goddamn her." And you know sometimes when I get angry with her or I don't like something she's said, and there's times even too when I'm jealous of her. But it never makes me not want to be friends with her because there's too many other good things in our relationship to ever give it up.

Ron and Doug

Ron and Doug are both 29 years old and single. Ron is a college graduate who teaches high school social studies. Doug left college after 2 years and works as a maintenance man. They have known each other and been close friends for approximately 15 years. They live two miles from each other.

When Ron was 14, he moved to a new junior high school and met Doug. They soon discovered their homes were in close proximity and began walking to school together. Though neither friend recalled any particularly significant events characterizing the early development of their friendship ("Things clicked." "It seemed so natural."), they did emphasize the importance of their common interests, especially discussing books. While similar pastimes and enjoyment of ideas "cemented the relationship more rapidly and deeply . . . than a lot of school relationships" according to Ron, the two boys' differences both rounded out each other and fostered latent competition. Ron recalled:

> Doug was in some ways a very self-assured person and especially in the areas where I was less self-assured. It's probably why we were friends. We complement each other; what is lacking in one is present in the other. Any time you see somebody who's better in an area where you'd like to be good at, there's envy and a little bit of jealousy.

He described one event during their high school years that intriguingly reflects some of this dyad's dynamics:

> Doug is more honest than I am in terms of recognizing something verbally. I remember once playing basketball in the driveway, you know three or four guys and you're playing a game. And we were playing this game. It was one of those games—on the surface it's a game, but somehow or other it takes on more meaning. I remember once during the game we were fighting for the ball, and we were just wrestling for the ball; it was no fight or anything like that. And afterwards Doug said, "Well, we finally had it out." And I said, "What do you mean?"—But I knew. He said it. I thought it. But he said it. And that didn't endanger our friendship or anything like that, but I valued it because, you know, he's smart. He wasn't afraid not to cover things up with politeness. It was a minor turning point, but it helps you appreciate a person.

For Doug, meeting Ron affected his high school years in at least two important ways. First, their shared interest in books and ideas moved him toward academic rather than technical study. He observed, "High school was like a turning point because rather than go for manual things, I went for the liberal arts and all, and for the college, academic courses. Whereas if I hadn't met him, I'd probably have gone for a skill, vocational stuff." Second, Doug met all of the girls he knew through Ron.

Although they began college the same year, Doug remarked that he and Ron did not spend much time together at the university:

> In college there were other friends. I hung around with other people and yet I missed Ron and stuff like that. I wished he could have gotten into what we were into, but he wasn't interested, or maybe he wanted to but

we never asked. In college we didn't hang around that much together. Phil and my personalities were a little closer. He was what I needed at the time, and so I started hanging around with him. What you need at the time is what you go for.

In Doug's mind, a memorable incident occurred one night when Ron would not compromise his values and drink with Doug and his friends:

> I don't offer him a beer because he doesn't drink. One time when we were going to college, all of us were getting bombed, right, drunk. And he refused to drink. And for some reason that night it bothered me that he wasn't drinking. That was the most depressing time of my life—going to college. I was ready to kill him that night 'cause he wouldn't drink. I was instigating a lot of things so he would take a swing at me, so I could pulverize him. Back then he was a little too narrow-minded in that respect. What the hell, one drink, and to be sociable or something like that. But he wouldn't do it. I admire him for sticking to his principles, but at the same time I get ticked off at him at him for not joining in or whatever. But then I accept that too.

After 2 years Doug quit school, a decision causing significant disagreement between the two friends as Ron maintained that Doug should have finished college. Even so, he recognized that the choice reflected Doug's autonomy in deciding his future. Therefore, like Ron's refusal to drink, the action embodied the self-reliance both friends respect. Ron stated:

> Doug's decision to quit school I thought was wrong at the time. It didn't affect the friendship in the sense that I can point to any kind of turning point because of that argument. But what any argument like that does is it points out the person's, the values on each side and the amount of independence and integrity on each side. So in that sense every argument is a positive thing because it defines the person.

Retaining his interest in reading and ideas but tired of formal academics, Doug returned to mechanical endeavors.

Upon leaving college Doug resumed a long-standing practice within the friendship of phoning Ron frequently for advice, discussion, and solace concerning personal matters, career options, and relationships with women. According to Doug, "For a while there I was calling him everyday. I trusted him and considered him more mature—somebody that could handle a situation much better than I. I would call him and just talk things over." However, Ron remembered that sometimes his insistent advice and Doug's reluctance to follow it proved aggravating to both men:

He was trying to think if he should go back to school and take straight electronics courses at the university or take this correspondence course. Well, I really tried to convince him that the correspondence course was a waste. And the more I tried to convince him, the more attractive it seemed to him. He did not take it in the end, but that put somewhat of a strain on us because it got to the point where I was being frustrated, saying, "Look, you're going to be throwing your money away. This is a very expensive course." I think it was running $1500.00 or something for the course. I just knew that he wouldn't finish it and that it would be a waste. And I couldn't get that across to him. I think that led to a, "Will you get off my back and let me make up my own mind?" situation. As it is, I did ease off and he did make up his mind. —Did he do the right thing? I don't know. But that was a bit of a strain.

After Ron graduated from college and began teaching high school, the friends did not see each other for over a year. Sometime after they renewed contact, Doug tried to enlist Ron's aid in persuading a woman to travel with him:

One time I wanted a girl to go to Europe with me. I tried to convince her and here he is sitting in this chair siding with her. He was wiser; he accepted her the way she was. He knew she wasn't going to go no matter what I said or did, even though she and I had known each other for eight years. In fact, I met her through him.

Like when she left, I blew up at him. I was totally ticked off. . . . I was hoping she would go and he wasn't trying to help me convince her, you know. That's what it amounted to, the traitor. I considered ending, not having anything to do with him then. I don't need an asshole like that around me. . . . I took it pretty hard. I considered ending the friendship there. It really irritated me because he was sticking by his principles, and I finally realized that and I gave in. I compromised because I felt it was stupid to end the friendship—because of all the good things that are involved in the friendship.

Since his preferred female partner refused, Doug invited Ron and his girlfriend, Barbara, to go on the trip with him 2 years before our interviews. After returning from the trip, Doug met a woman, Sumi, with whom he began a sporadic pattern of dating and cohabitation up to the time of the interviews. The intensity of that relationship and Ron's ongoing involvement with Barbara have prevented the friends from spending much time together. Nevertheless, Doug continues with diminished frequency to rely on Ron for opinions and guidance.

Despite their common interests in Zen Buddhism, books, and analytical discussion, Ron and Doug were different in many ways. Doug considered himself to be the learner and follower while Ron was the teacher and leader in the friendship. Whereas Ron was academically inclined, cerebral, and only theoretically interested in karate, Doug was technically adept, very emotional, and physically engaged in karate. Both men spoke of their mutual respect as an outcome of their different strengths. Doug counted on Ron's ability to sort out emotional problems for him; Ron admired and utilized Doug's ability to repair any mechanical or electrical item. Both enjoyed their intellectual and philosophical conversations.

Even so, the complementary nature of this friendship also fostered envy and ambiguous competition. The friends begrudged each other's talents in various domains. Yet when common interests stimulated contention between them, contrasting abilities and concern for the friend's feelings inhibited earnest competition. Meanwhile, both men wanted their special skills acknowledged. Ron described the overall tone of competition in their friendship:

> I don't think it's a matter of competition in the sense of beating the other one out, of gamesmanship. It's more a matter of competing for mutual admiration. I'm sure that each of us wants to gain greater status in the eyes of each other, but not at the expense of each other, like I gain by Doug being put down. No, I think we want to be appreciated by each other. But I can't think of any competition where one comes out a winner and the other comes out a loser.

Doug echoed these sentiments, observing:

> It's a passive competition; it's not aggressive. It's not "Starsky and Hutch" type. I don't like that "stud" type attitude and neither does he. It's more low-key, passive, and that's the extent of it. There's competition and yet Ron's the type that would forfeit if he thought it would be good experience for me.

The friends still compete for recognition by the other though their abilities do not match. Ron and Doug independently provided similar examples:

> *Ron:*
> It would be the areas we were both interested in that we would both want to be seen as competent in those areas. Since I value an area and he values an area, it would be nice to have a little bit of envy of each other's skill in that area. For example, a sport I like to watch mainly because I never had enough coordination to ever do it was gymnastics. I frankly envy Doug's ability in gymnastics and I would like to be in a position where if I did something in gymnastics, he would appreciate that and say, "Yeah, that's good!" Because it's an area we have in common, I want that status. That's the only kind of competition I can think of.
> *Doug:*
> He's got curvature of the spine, he's not as flexible as I am. I'm good at sports. The karate, he wasn't able to do that. He would have loved to; he

did whatever he could, the intellectual aspects. Whereas I did the physical—and the intellectual—but not as deeply as he did. So I'd say he competes with me too. I'm not absolutely sure, but it just works out that way. Maybe it's just me competing with him and it turns into a competition.

In differing degrees and forms and at one time or another, competition for the attention of the opposite sex seems to occur in many friendships. Doug and Ron's friendship was no exception, although it too reflected their complementary qualities, shared practices, and distinctive orientations toward contests. Ron recollected:

We went out with some of the same girls and whatnot, but I don't think we ever competed for them. At least I never thought of it that way. Perhaps we did, maybe I just don't care to admit it. Though we were friends, we had different appeal to the same girl. I mean she saw one thing in me and she saw one thing in Doug. And she liked the things she saw in me, and she liked the things she saw in Doug. And it wasn't like I had more of it or he had more of it, it was just different aspects of our personalities. I don't think we were competing there.

Doug viewed it somewhat differently:

If there's a girl in here and he and I are here, he'll be the outgoing one, and he'll shoot the shit—wittiness and all that. I wish I could do that. But I don't compete on that level. So, it bothers me and yet I want the girl and he wants the girl, and he usually gets her. Yet if he thought the girl, personality-wise, was more my type, then he'd give up right there. Usually the girl'll like him though, like his personality. . . . But things have changed in the past year or two since he met Barbara.

Even in this potentially highly charged domain, the friends recognize their dissimilar attractiveness to women (Both men mentioned women who suggested the two men should "merge" and become one person.), and have negotiated a tempered style of competing for them. Note as well Doug's comment implying that Ron's close relationship with Barbara has curtailed even their low-key vying for women.

All in all, I was struck by how these men handled incipient competition in their friendship. Clearly, they tried to achieve objective recognition and to impress each other. Moreover, their practices did not eliminate or obscure their unmatched capabilities or the resulting envy and resentment. In fact, I surmise that if their talents were more comparable, they would probably compete much more intensely if it were not for another restraining factor. That is, they both seemed to care genuinely about the other's feelings and did not want to use their friend's ego as a springboard for their own self-glorification. In this respect they admirably exemplified the somewhat paradoxical notion in our culture of "friendly competition."

But such reining in of emotions and self-serving desires does not occur without recurring tensions in most friendships. One way to express simultaneously solidarity and antagonism (generated in this case by contrasting skills), is through joking and humor (Brain, 1976). Doug and Ron kidded each other a great deal. Their humorous comments, though typically good-natured, could also address significant issues, vulnerabilities, and differences between the men. At one point in their dyadic interview, the following exchange emerged as they discussed literary characters with whom they identified. Doug said, "Ron can't get into workin' on cars or talkin' to people about cars—cause he's an asshole." Ron immediately quipped, "Doug hasn't had an academic thought since he got out of college." The two friends laughed and continued recalling books and characters they both admired.

Similarly, James Carroll's *Prince of Peace* (1984) depicts the complementary friendship between Frank Durkin (the narrator) and Michael Maguire. Frank esteems Michael to the point of emulating his personal comportment and conversational style in his absence. When Michael returns from Korea a war hero, the two friends initially use humor in a manner resembling Doug and Ron to express and control their conflicting emotions in their first encounter:

> The closer Michael came the taller he seemed. He wore his nervousness quite loosely, as a given of the moment, as if awkwardness between us was the most natural thing in the world. He was the first to speak. "Welcome home," he said when he grasped my hand.
>
> I had to smile; the son of a bitch welcoming *me* home! "Thanks," I said feebly.
>
> "It must have been rough," he said. I realized what he was doing, turning all the shit they'd just been giving him on its ear by giving it to me. He was dodging the embarrassment of our reunion by making a joke on the leering Monsignor Riordan. Michael was proposing an improvisation. I caught it instantly, as if this was Birdland.
>
> "It wasn't that bad." I said. "You do what you have to do. . . ." (p. 77)
>
> "Did you miss me?" he asked somewhat mockingly, as if to deflect the banality of my welcome the way he had the others.
>
> But I met him head on. "Hell yes I missed you. What do you think?"
>
> "I think you're a turd," he said.
>
> "Who's a turd?" I punched his shoulder. It was rock hard, and he cocked his fist to punch me back. . . . (p. 78)
>
> He looked away, as if our needling had run its course and he wasn't sure where that left us. . . . (p. 79)
>
> To my horror I found myself using the line he'd used on me in our shtick for the monsignor. "It must have been rough, Mike."
>
> "Where the fuck have you been, Durk? I've been home on leave for weeks."

> I had to look away, I was so ashamed. I'd been afraid to face him for fear of what he'd think of me. Yet I hadn't thought of him. It had never occurred to me that Sergeant Michael Maguire, D.S.C., Silver Star, could stand in need of me. "Mike, I'm sorry." I found his eyes. "I should have come sooner. I was afraid to. You're a fucking war hero, you know. I'm a chump, a saphead." (p. 81)

In addition to depicting how friends employ humor in such circumstances, this passage also poignantly reflects the contradictory demands of independence and dependence, and of judgment and acceptance. Frank views Mike as strong and independent; he cannot imagine that this war hero would actually need him. His delay in welcoming Mike home also stems from his perceived inferiority to him; perhaps his friend would clearly recognize the disparity between them and no longer accept him. In attributing this autonomy and judgmental orientation to his friend, Frank deprives Mike of the chance to depend on him. As a result, Frank hurts his friend by conveying delinquent and minimal acceptance or caring at a vulnerable and needful moment. Frank is a "turd" because he failed to come through as Mike's best friend, not because he is neither as clever nor as heroic.

Ron and Doug must continually manage these dialectical tensions as well. By and large, in reconciling their respective freedoms to be independent and to be dependent in this friendship, these men conform to an ethic of individual rights that fosters a self-defining pattern of separation (Gilligan, 1982). The ideology of rights specifies that individuals are free to exercise their rights as long as they do not interfere with the rights of others (Gilligan, 1982). Both men endorsed this viewpoint in their friendship. Doug observed:

> There's no obligation. He doesn't impose on my relationships, and I don't impose on his. If he got married, we'd see each other and talk to each other, but the relationship would be different in that I'd respect his right to focus all his attention on the marriage. And I think he does that with me.

Likewise, Ron stated:

> If I needed help, I wouldn't want to make things terribly inconvenient for him, but then again that would depend on how desperate I was. If there was something that he had a strong bias on, went against his sense of honor and I knew that, then I wouldn't ask him to do something like that, because you're putting him in a situation where he's betraying his own values. Nobody has that kind of privilege.

In actually conducting their friendship, however, the friends did not adhere to this doctrine of rights because of their positive concern for each other. When the activity of caring transcends one's preoccupation with individual rights, a person feels responsible for another's well-being and recognizes differences in needs (Gilligan, 1982).

Consequently, Ron and Doug enacted an asymmetrical pattern of interdependence. Though avoiding dependence and undue attachment was integral to this friendship, Doug tended to depend on Ron much more than the reverse; Ron was considerably more self-sufficient. However, problems arose when Ron violated Doug's freedom to depend on him and tried to exert too much influence on his life (Rawlins, 1983a). As described earlier in the correspondence course decision, Ron, in turn, became irritated when Doug did not follow his advice. There were also occasions when Doug inhibited and even resented Ron's requests for help because he took Ron's autonomy for granted. And Doug recalled two major fights that had occurred because Ron asserted his independence and integrity by "sticking to his principles" and refusing to join or assist his friend.

Ron cogently summed up the ideology of individual rights supplemented by joint caring that shaped the practices of this friendship and helped to prevent problems:

> As long as we keep to the basic understanding, which is mutual regard, mutual respect and an acknowledgment of mutual concern, and yet a healthy knowledge of mutual independence. As long as these things exist I don't think there's any real problems in the friendship. Should a situation arise when those things are in danger, then the friendship is in danger. If I refuse to acknowledge Doug's independence and he refuses to acknowledge mine, that might produce a heavy strain, and it might cause a break. It hasn't as yet.

Throughout the interviews I noticed how the men's shared orientation toward their friendship revealed a developing capacity for caring and intimacy, but also the increasing time constraints arising from their work schedules and serious romantic involvements with women. In some ways their stance reflected a transitional period in their lives that had already altered other friendships. According to Doug:

> One of his best friends, Paul, is going to Yale Law School. Ron and he got along well. But now there's been a gulf between them. He's married and got a kid. His wife is strange. She's very jealous of us, protective of him. She's very jealous of his friends. She's been bad mouthing Ron quite a bit and now I think Paul is believing it quite a bit. He's not very understanding of Ron. He's turning very materialistic, the Yale bullshit, "We must choose our friends very discreetly." I don't like that attitude because they were very close at one time and it's a shame.

To a degree, Doug and Ron also discussed their separation as a necessary and seemingly inevitable feature of their friendship. Its meaning and management in the future remain to be seen.

The friends' differing patterns of expressing and protecting personal thoughts and feelings, and various dilemmas of communicating judgment and acceptance interacted with the tensions of negotiating independence and dependence in this friendship. Predictably, Ron was more tight-lipped, protecting his vulnerabilities, rendering him less susceptible to personal judgment by Doug, and thereby reinforcing his independence. Both men remarked:

Ron:
    I don't think he expects it from me that I'm going to say, "Doug, I've got this terrible problem, listen. " No, when I have a problem and I'm in Doug's company, his company is a diversion from that problem and I feel better. It's getting away from my problem, not bringing it to him. Now he may be different. In fact, Doug is more inclined to tell me what's bothering him than I am to tell him what's bothering me. But when it comes down to it, it is what each of us feels comfortable doing.

Doug:
    The thing is Ron doesn't need me as much as I need him. When he's depressed, he works it out for himself. He'll talk about it some, but rarely do you ever get to inside Ron. Or I haven't; I'm too busy talking. But I think he likes it that way. That way he doesn't have to open up.

In many ways Ron resembled the modal inexpressive male observed in countless studies. He disliked pity and "would not cry in front of Doug," although he occasionally voiced anger or disappointment in himself. And Doug stated consummate trust in Ron's ability to preserve confidences. Doug, in contrast, was far more emotional and disclosive. Despite these opposing tendencies, both men described extensive mutual understanding, respect, and sensitivity to the other's feelings. They knew when not to "push" an issue.

Because they have shared many common interests and experiences, they also tolerated each other's foibles and irritating qualities. Avoiding judgmental reactions to actions and ideas, mutual acceptance was a root concern in the friendship quite consistent with preserving each other's autonomy and forming the backdrop for their many discussions. Even so, supported by this tradition of joint acceptance, these friends spent a lot of time mutually developing judgments about intellectual concerns and periodically judging each other.

Intellectual discussion was a primary pastime in this friendship from its beginning; there was endless talk about books, ideas, philosophy, and alternatives to traditional American sports. Notably, these conversations seemed less personal and feeling-centered than Darlene and

Lana's, for example. In fact, these men prided themselves in being analytical and solving various problems through detached discussion. Informed judgments in these interactions depended on knowing the topic well, defending one's opinions, and providing a variety of examples or applications of one's conclusions.

However, their conversations could subtly or abruptly shift from *judging together* to *judging each other* when matters such as career concerns and decisions, and women and personal relationships required attention. For example, both friends wanted to "approve of" the other's dating partner. Obviously, these interactions were more emotional and touchy. Informed judgments in these talks depended on knowing and considering the friend's feelings and past experiences, being sincere, and presenting various options in a respectful manner.

Using these practices Doug and Ron seemed able to alternate and blend the modes of judging together and judging each other and preserve the joint assumption of benevolence in their friendship:

> *Ron:*
> I value his judgment on certain things; on certain things I don't value his judgment at all. In fact, if Doug said something I'd be inclined to take the opposite view. Nevertheless, you know, I know that he's sincere. I know that he cares. And that's an important thing.
>
> *Doug:*
> I don't put him on a pedestal, but I respect his judgment. And that's why I may discuss things, personal things with him, because I can take his comments. I know he's sincerely thinking of me.

The friends independently described their practice of evaluating girl-friends, a matter of ongoing salience and potentially high risk. Ron described his approach:

> If he's involved in a relationship that I feel is unhealthy for him, well I may feel it's unhealthy for him but I don't really have all that much right to come out and tell him so. I don't know what good he's getting out of it. He's the one that has to be the judge of whether the pros outweigh the cons.
>
> So I have to couch it carefully, and do it in such a way that I make it clear that it is his welfare that I am concerned with, and still he's got to make up his own mind. It's more telling him what I see as the options, you know, and if he thinks that way maybe to choose one of these options if it fits with what he wants.

Doug expressed similar perceptions of the process:

> It would bug me if, not jealousy-wise, but it would bug me if, if I didn't approve of the girl he was dating. And I think it bugs him if I'm going out

with a girl that he feels is taking advantage of me or that I'm going to get hurt. As a friend, he's trying to protect me.

. . . Just talking to him and listening to him talk, he comes up with alternatives. Ron will give you a broad range. And it ends up you eventually find the solution for yourself, using what he's, his output.

Interestingly, whereas Darlene and Lana primarily risked hurting the other's *feelings* through criticism, with Doug and Ron the primary risk was that they would experience criticism as undermining their *autonomy*. Acknowledging this potential infringement of rights, Ron judged Doug with compassionate objectivity and in a manner honoring his independence. A result was their ongoing attachment according to Doug:

That's why I stick to him. The judgment is not overbearing, his judgment. So he lets me live my life. He'll put his two cents in which I appreciate because I ask him to anyway but then I live my life the way I want to. Whereas I think other people try to control and they get upset if you don't take their advice. Whereas he doesn't. He's very accepting.

Ron agreed:

Doug can do things that I don't like. I do things that he doesn't like. But as long as we both accept that each of us has the right to do things the other doesn't like, then the friendship continues.

Carol and Brent

Carol is female, 24, single, and a college graduate who teaches history, civics, and French in a high school. Brent is male, 26, engaged, a college graduate who majored in history and political science, and a naval officer. They knew each other in second grade but then lost touch for many years. Reintroduced during Carol's freshman year in college (Brent's junior year), they have been close friends for 7 years. Brent is stationed 79 miles from Carol.

Carol and Brent became close when they were double-dating a brother and sister, Eddie and Denise, who could not go out alone. Brent would pick up Carol on the way and take her home afterward. They began discussing personal issues and feelings relating to their respective partners and came to regard each other as confidants. Carol described the process of getting to know Brent:

Both of us were experiencing similar frustrations with the other partner and we would end up talking about it. Basically, it wound up that he and

I had a closer relationship between us than either one of us had with the other person. So that's probably why it started off; we became closer very, very quickly. . . . I included Brent as part of the things of my first year at college that were very important to me. The circumstances of our friendship greatly enhanced our becoming closer.

Brent remembered similarly this distinctive initial phase of their friendship:

We'd always compare notes at the end of the evening, you know, "What'd he say? What did she say?" things like that. And then with that as a common basis, we used to double a lot, go out, discovered common interests. Just found that it was, I discovered she was someone that I could talk to who would understand things, how I felt about things. I was someone that she could talk to. . . . It was the kind of situation that established some very good basis right at the beginning. It allowed a growth that might not have been possible if I met Carol casually at some other time at a bar or school.

This double-dating arrangement persisted throughout Carol's freshman year. By her sophomore year she felt "very close" as a friend to Brent and "a certain obligation to him." Early in the semester Carol stopped seeing Eddie, and Brent and Denise broke up soon afterward. Carol and Brent remained close, enjoying various topics of conversation and sharing recreational interests with the same group of people. Yet Carol mentioned that she and Brent were also deeply hurt by their breaks-ups and they depended on each other to sort things out emotionally. Brent recalled this period as when he realized he had "a special relationship" with Carol, characterized by mutual trust and honest though sympathetic discussions of differing opinions.

According to Carol, Brent's "recovery period" after dating Denise simultaneously enhanced their mutual attachment and strained its platonic definition because Brent "made me feel as though a romantic relationship coming from him was beginning to occur." She continued, "And that's when our relationship was at its worst, because I was trying to second-guess everything he did." Soon after, Carol began steadily dating someone else who never understood but still "permitted" her friendship with Brent. Upon graduating, Brent joined the Navy and frequently was on extended cruises, which Carol maintained prevented things from becoming "uncomfortable." She remarked:

We both started to see different people; he was away; he was on cruise more. So we were apart and I think we weren't as suspicious of each other. I'm certain he had his own suspicions although we really didn't talk about it. And things just mellowed out.

During the summer of Carol's sophomore year, Brent's mother died suddenly and tragically in an accident. Brent recollected:

> When my mother died, it was the first time Carol had been away by herself, and she'd been on vacation for a while. Carol got her cousin to drive her back the same day and she saw me and told me—not that she had to—"I'll be around and down at your house, if you need anything, just tell me." . . . She was there through the wake and the funeral, not always physically with me, but I always knew that if there was anything that I needed, I knew I could call her and tell her about it. Or if I needed to talk to somebody, I could talk to her.

Likewise, Carol recalled:

> I was away on vacation. My mother called and I came home just that day. And I hate wakes and I stayed the entire time, was with him the whole time. . . . And yet I wasn't even thinking, "Am I spending too much time with him? Am I being too much of a comforter? Is he going to seek more than just solace from me?" I wasn't thinking that; I was thinking about the loss of his mom.

The two friends' mutual admiration is clearly evident in their discussions of the pivotal significance of this unfortunate event for their friendship:

> *Brent:*
> I think that was when Carol really showed the breadth of her commitment. I think she would have a problem finding a like example in my case, but that for me showed the depth of the commitment very graphically.
> *Carol:*
> Right after his mother's death I recognized that I definitely felt a firm commitment to be his friend and to be with him and support him as he had always done for me.

For the rest of Carol's college years the two friends wrote to each other fairly frequently and spent time together during Brent's leaves. Brent appreciated the caring expressed by Carol's continued letters and reciprocated by writing and sending gifts from his different ports of call. Both friends felt the effort invested in writing each other during their extended separations greatly strengthened their friendship.

Whenever Brent was home on leave, the two friends spent a lot of time together talking, doing activities, and going to movies and social gatherings. Moreover, Brent wanted every woman he was seriously dating to meet Carol. Once, when he returned from cruise with a Brazilian woman whom he was contemplating marrying, Carol was especially considerate. According to Brent, "Carol had studied for a whole week to try to speak Portuguese—she cared enough for me to make that much effort to make somebody that I cared about feel at home." Though this relationship eventually did not work out, when Brent later announced his engagement to another woman 5 months prior to our interviews, both friends indicated how the prospect of his marriage called again for a clarification in their own minds of their feelings of close friendship.

Carol and Brent seemed to be very close friends. Both remarked on the other's tremendous capacity for support and acceptance. There was also continual competition between the two friends occurring in a spirit of mutual improvement. Each wanted the other to be the best student, thinker, arguer, swimmer, or tennis player that he or she could. Both friends seemed highly expressive with each other as well, while sensitive to and protective of individual privacy and feelings. Further, their overall patterns of independence made them deeply value their moments of strong dependence.

Even so, because of their closeness and mutual confidence, their respect for each other's opinions, and Carol's desire for more autonomy regarding her social life, a warm (though sometimes testy) tension between judgment and acceptance persisted in this friendship. Both friends celebrated the acceptance they felt from each other:

> *Carol:*
> He's seen me at various points in my young life and he has still remained close with me and accepting. I remember one time I saw him and I get horrible allergies and my eyes puff out and I'm really gross to look at. And I would say how this is so disgusting and he would still be, he would say, "Eh, so what?" And so that total acceptance of me, at all points of my being, my high points and my low points. That's what makes it special; he just accepts it all.
>
> *Brent:*
> Her and I are our two biggest supporters. She's always very supportive. You know, every person has an emotional need to have somebody tell you, "Yeah, you're great. If that's what you want to do, I feel that you can go ahead and you can do it. And no matter what you set your mind to do, you can do it." And Carol and I do that to both of us. Like if there's something I want to do, she'd be the first to say, "Yes, I feel you can do it." Or she would honestly tell me, "Well I think that's beyond your capabilities to do."

Brent's final remarks show Carol's heartfelt acceptance and sincere appraisals. Accepting someone also means judging him or her as worthy of regard, and caring a lot makes one protective of the other's feelings. Accordingly, one may give a friend a hearty vote of confidence for some undertakings, while stating a firm note of concern about others. Brent expressed judgments of the men Carol was seeing, sometimes irritating her by what she felt were patronizing and unsolicited comments. She said that her partners felt scrutinized and judged as well. Carol often resented Brent's judgment of her beaux:

> When I felt that Brent's opinion of who I dated or what I did was far too paternal, he was acting as my brother and not as my friend. . . . I know that I was dating someone in my junior year that he didn't care for. He grew to like him but at one point didn't care for him basically because he didn't like the way he treated me. And I did recognize that, but I didn't want to hear it. It never really threatened our friendship I must admit, but he was often there with an opinion I didn't want to hear and with a face I didn't want to see.

Carol drew an interesting contrast between Brent acting as a brother and as a friend:

> When Brent's my brother, he acts as though he's doing, he's looking out for me and sometimes I'd rather make my own mistakes. That's when he's brother. He's friend when I make my own mistakes and instead of saying, "I told you so," he says, "Okay, so pick yourself up and go on."

Reminiscent of adolescents' distinctions between parental judgment and friends' acceptance, the key issue for Carol was respect for her autonomy. However, like parents and siblings, when friends care, it is often difficult for them to stand back and watch people do things they might regret.

Despite arguments about their personal lives, Carol and Brent have consistently acted and communicated in ways that engendered a joint and robust assumption of benevolence between them. Regarding their arguments over Carol's dates, she described a mutually developed narrative of good will:

> What they've done is really become chapters. That's all, and how they're resolved, and why they are so important is that what eventually comes out of them is not necessarily what is said but the sentiment behind it, that there's concern and that there is care and the ultimate objective is the greatest welfare for either one of us.

Brent echoed, "I think there are times when she disagrees with what I do. But she'll be more concerned that I don't get hurt than it will make her angry because it's something she doesn't like." Both friends understood that if either believed the other was doing something wrong or misguided, they would "speak up" and say what they thought. Even if they disagreed or might be hurt, they wanted to hear the other's viewpoint on important matters.

As edifying as this joint practice sounds, Carol felt that its centrality in their lives would diminish with Brent's marriage. She remarked:

> There isn't much that I couldn't say to Brent. Some things that I feel are better left unsaid would be his private business. And because right now his business, or he is now becoming more and more private because he's getting married, there will be less things that we can say to each other.

Recognizing the importance for Brent of his decision to get engaged, and the likelihood that his marriage would and should take precedence over their friendship made her reluctant to question this hasty commitment:

> When he got engaged, he got engaged very, very quickly, and I eventually did tell him that the fact that he got engaged so fast caused a great deal of confusion and anxiety to me, because I really didn't know whether he went into, stepped into marriage or the idea of getting married with a level head. And initially I didn't see the point in saying anything. I would ask a couple leading questions and just leave it at that. That was all.

Despite her early reservations, Carol became convinced that his fiance did love him and "since the girl accepted me," she decided that "what he needed was support" because "many of his friends look at this marriage with apprehension." Thus, she backed his decision fully and planned to attend the wedding even though it would occur far from her home.

Resembling many close cross-sex friendships in young adulthood, a prominent theme for Brent and Carol was whether or not to transform their friendship into a romantic relationship. Talking with me, both persons described ongoing attempts to make sense of their feelings for each other, interactive dynamics between them, and third parties' constant commentaries on their relationship. Ironically, for all the candor and confidence they demonstrated within their friendship, they had never discussed in any depth the possibility of becoming lovers until our interviews.

Carol was particularly eloquent about the emotional quandaries and internal dialogue she experienced:

> There were some points where I was very clear on how I stood with Brent, and I said "I want Brent as a friend." But because I admired him so, and because I loved him very much, I also said, "Am I letting something pass by?" I mean is that magic or chemistry so important, and here is such a fantastic person? Probably when he told me about Judy [his fiancee] was absolutely the point that I was most clear how I stood about him. That was February of this year. I said ready or not, this is how I must stand and I accept that.
>   When we needed each other, and we both responded to that need, I think anyone would say, "This person really does come through. More

than anybody, more than the people I look to for romance. Do I really just want to be friends with Brent?"

. . . I never dated well. And Brent, no matter what, I never fell without a net, and Brent always provided that. And so there'd be various points where Brent would say, "Look, I don't think he, he has missed, passed up a great opportunity. He never really got to appreciate you. You're too good for him." And those are the points when you really start—I have had romance without love; Brent is love without romance in that we show affection, we have physical, spiritual, emotional affection, but romance is—I hate to reduce it to a kiss on the cheek versus a kiss on the lips—It's more than that. It's difficult to say.

Because she cares deeply for Brent, Carol acknowledges the frequent difficulty of choosing friendship over romance with him. She reflects on the emotional deficits and pain encountered in her romantic involvements and Brent's unfailing support and affection. Even so, she distinguishes between the two types of attachments to Brent, and his engagement makes the choice of friendship lucid in her mind.

In contrast, Brent's account of the sentimental aspects of their friendship is much less developed than Carol's:

I guess we were too close. Maybe that was something to do with it. We were so close friendship-wise that we could never separate it, we could never separate out the romantic aspect of it, you know. I guess romantic implies a closeness that I guess we always felt as friends. You know, except for the physical closeness. And I guess that's why it didn't, it never clicked.

Brent also explains the feelings occurring in the friendship as somewhat muddled. But he seems to be describing his own inability to "separate out" feelings of romance from feelings of friendship in this cross-sex bond, a commonly reported tendency of males in the research literature. For Carol the two sentiments are quite different. However, behaviorally, Brent notes that the "physical closeness" he associates with romantic love was not present. This assertion also contrasts with Carol's observation that they displayed affection physically, among other ways. Apparently, it was not the kind of physical intimacy Brent had in mind.

Both friends mentioned Brent's indirect attempts to convert their friendship into a romance, in his words, "something more." In examining their accounts, it appears that Brent tried tacitly to redefine their bond in order to avoid straining or spoiling the friendship in the event of rejection:

I can't say that the idea has not crossed my—my mind that at times in the relationship that it might, something more might develop as a result of it. Because as I said before, I think that before you can really get involved romantically, you have to be friends. I think there has to be that common sharing like uh, and I guess that's the reason people felt that way, that our relationship was sort of a stage. Because we were such good friends and everyone assumed that it would take the one step further. And, uh, I really couldn't explain why it didn't. I thought about that sometimes, but I really couldn't sit down and explain why it never did.

I'm the type of person that looks for indicators. Now I think I'm pretty perceptive as far as, you know—well I can't say that because there's been cases where I've been massively mistaken—but well, I'll go on my own judgment most of the times when you can tell somebody is more interested or wants to carry something to a further extent. I believe it was sort of mutual that way. Carol and I both felt the same way, and since we both felt the same way, neither one of us would take the first step.

Brent perceived Carol as waiting like him for "indicators," and since neither person took the initiative, no romance developed. In contrast, while Carol noticed his tacit maneuvers, she recalls trying to handle them in a way that protected his feelings and preserved the friendship:

I can only tell you by things that he's alluded to rather than by things he has said how he might feel at different points of our relationship. Because Brent was always careful with our friendship.

He was careful in what he said and what he did with our friendship. I believe that there were points when he looked upon me as a "possible." And he was careful what he did so as not to frighten me. And so I did make assumptions. You know I didn't come right out and say, "Do you love me as someone to be, as someone that you could marry?" Because he would say that, but not in such a serious tone that it was ominous, "You know if I spend time with you it's going to be very painful for me."

. . . He never mentioned it. I think primarily because he would have done so at a great risk. If he had turned to me and offered something beyond a very good, fond friendship, I think it would have been the end of our friendship. And so he never voiced anything that he thought was risky. But it was very obvious in the things that he did and said and the presents that he used to bring me that I had to be very careful and make my position quite clear how I stood.

However, in addition to negotiating and clarifying the nature of bond to each other, they faced the continual challenge of justifying it to third parties:

Carol:

Teasing constant, innuendoes prevalent. Members of the family, "When are you two going to wise up and do something about your friendship?" I was teased, not criticized, teased and questioned, "Are you leading him on?" What is it with you two?" Questioned as to what's really going on, "Why don't you, you've got a fantastic person in your life. Why don't you snatch him?"

Brent:
   A lot of people told us that our relationship is very strange, and
"strange" is in quotes, cause—you know the standard question is,
"There's got to be something going on between the two of you," That's
what the common perception is. It's always in the back of people's minds,
"Why aren't you two going out?"

Besides being a tiresome conversational topic raised by others, both
Carol and Brent experienced considerable social pressure to convert
their friendship into a more typical romantic involvement. Perhaps such
pervasive injunctions sometimes led Brent to regard their mutually
fulfilling friendship as only a "stage" and feel it incumbent on him to
"take the one step further" he mentions above.

   Now that Brent is engaged, the friendship is doubly "deviant"—not
only a close friendship that could challenge the primacy of his upcoming
marriage, but also a friendship between a man and a woman. Though
the essence of their bond has not altered, its position in Brent's
interpersonal world has. Accordingly, Carol observes:

In his marriage, though he says nothing will change, nothing will change,
I know for a fact something will have to change, and the risk is our
closeness will be sacrificed to a slight degree. And I certainly will not be
able to spend as much time with him, although he said, "I don't see any
reason why not." I would. He's a married man and that does make a
difference, "She will always be there; she will always be my friend; she will
always love me right or wrong, but—her influence in my life will be on the
shelf after Judy."

Conclusion

   Taken together, these three dyads illustrate many key features of
young adult close friendships. As longtime friends, they all exhibited
joint expectations for sympathetic ears, support, heartfelt discussion,
guidance, and help in times of need. They similarly celebrated their
common interests and activities, shared fun, and the laughter and
joking that made their friendships joyful. In granting these qualities,
however, they also mentioned strains arising from competition and the
thin line separating admiration from envy and jealousy. Tensions arose
in communicatively managing the contradictory and interrelated demands of independence and dependence, judgment and acceptance,
and expressiveness and protectiveness.

   In these regards, the identifiable differences between males and
females in the relationships were primarily matters of emphasis and
configurations of relational content rather than of fundamental at-

tributes. As others have noted, in close friendships like these where caring emerges as a central activity, the differences statistically associated with male and female same-sex friendships may be attenuated. As essentially expressive and compassionate friendships developed apart from the worlds of work, community or politics and with seemingly minimal hidden agendas, I believe these pairs escaped or encountered in greatly diminished forms the opposing motives of affection and instrumentality that clash in various adult contexts. Their spoken histories simply did not include them.

Of course, these friendships did have friction, and their affection for each other included mutual reliance for both emotional and practical assistance. But the intrinsic impulse shaping these bonds was a basic concern for each other's well-being. They spent considerable time monitoring and discussing each other's self-conceptions, personal relationships, and important decisions defining the future. Their mutual trust and regard for each other as someone to talk to and be there to help resembled the expectations of close friendship established during adolescence. It is readily apparent, however, that the circumstances for their enactment and the issues at stake change considerably during young adulthood.

All of these persons, concerned about the friend's feelings and potential, frequently consulted about various matters, and convinced of the ultimate possibility of marriage, mentioned a tendency and desire to "approve of" their partners' romances. In communicating these judgments, however, they walked the border between welcome guidance and resented interference. Accordingly, they often waited until their opinions were requested. But even when input was solicited, they faced the contradictory expectations in friendship to accept and heartily support the other's choices and to judge and honestly question them. Caring for the friend and respecting his or her values and integrity only made the dilemma tougher in some cases.

Typically, a history of reliable advice and of accepting and encouraging the friend during happy and sad periods and with easy and difficult decisions built up an assumption of benevolence, allowing hurtful truths to be perceived as well-intentioned. But overall, these friends expressed their *caring* by being *careful* about the nature of the issues they addressed and their manner of criticizing each other. Such a comprehensive basis for judging in friendship is the very reason why friends must often refrain from judgmental reactions. Evaluating the other too stridently or frequently can suggest superiority in an otherwise egalitarian relationship, unduly constrain a friend's perceived options, and jeopardize independence and self-confidence. Mutual judgment is a seminal feature of friendship if pursued judiciously, out of clear concern for the other, and with the shared conviction that he or she is free not to take the friend's advice.

Prior to marriage, the conversation of close friends tends to examine and thereby mediate each party's other affiliations, including romantic, family, and work relationships. Friendship composes a privileged inner circle, looking out and monitoring each other's possibilities. The serious romantic involvement or marriage of either or both friends increasingly curtails this privilege and responsibility. In effect, one's interpersonal "center of gravity" shifts at this time with one's close friends changing from co-monitors to the monitored. Except for primarily females who often maintain dual intimacies with a friend and a spouse, the marriage becomes the sensitive inner circle, preserving secrets from others and appraising each other's activities and involvements. Typically, one answers to one's spouse before one's friends, who are now third parties.

So begins the frequently more marginal career of friendship throughout adulthood. Time for friends is contingent on each person's diverse engagements and responsibilities. Meanwhile, suspended friends feel mutual ambivalence as the cherished qualities of friendships grate against reduced opportunities for sharing them. In this milieu the commitments of friendship depend more than ever on unspoken agreements and obligations, because neither friend wants to make a promise that circumstances will render hollow.

Ironically, preserving friendships continually requires managing silence and separation. When friends exercise their freedom to be independent, time apart can be interpreted either as asserting the friends' faith in their bond or beginning a possible breach that may ultimately dissolve the friendship. During a period of separation, there is really no way of telling exactly which is the case, except by renewing contact (Rawlins, 1983a).

Consequently, friendships undergo various acknowledged and unrecognized trials that enhance mutual commitment or encourage a terminal drifting apart. They may arise from tangible problems and exigencies of everyday life, periods of self-doubt, or quarrels spawned by other attachments. Waiting in the wings, lapsed or dormant friendships may be reactivated and restored to center stage as practical and emotional resources. At this point the unspoken in friendship, its shared image, may excuse former neglect. And when a friend calls, we learn something about ourselves. What are we capable of doing? How far will we go for our friend? Because of the complexity of adult life, it becomes more difficult to maintain the assumptions and activities of benevolence. Even so, certain friendships reflect and sustain a valued history of such shared practices.

Chapter 8

Adult Friendships

People disagree on the precise criteria or boundaries announcing the transition from young to mature adulthood. Even so, in providing some broad age-related parameters for this chapter, I view adult friendships as spanning Neugarten's (1968) time periods of maturity (from around 30 to 40 years old) and middle age (from 40 to around 65 years old), with later adulthood and old age approaching thereafter.

Like other periods of life, adulthood involves an ongoing configuring of self with others through communicating in diverse roles and relationships. As the adult years unfold, numerous choices regarding marital, parental, family, work, and community roles and performance define one's day-to-day possibilities and responsibilities while also restricting one's options for alternative life paths. Deciding to marry, have children, and pursue a specific career, for example, result in obligations, benefits, challenges, and frustrations that differ markedly from those of single or married persons without children and in other occupations. Further, many decisions emerging within the specific "life structure" (Levinson et al., 1979) fashioned by these earlier adult choices produce consequences affecting individuals profoundly (like children, spouse, close friends, partners, and employees) and a range of others to various degrees (like kin, in-laws, co-workers, and acquaintances). Consequently, one's continuing life choices during most of adulthood are not simple functions of age or linear development. Instead, they compose an increasingly complex array of contingencies produced by previous selections in conjunction with one's social environment (Atchley, 1982).

However, in recognizing individual praxis, we must also acknowledge how little control many individuals have over their field of concrete options. To a great extent, each person's opportunities and obstacles are socially and culturally patterned according to gender, socioeconomic status (including educational and occupational advantages and disadvantages), marital status, as well as age (Pearlin, 1980). And the significance of one's age interacts with the other factors. Giele (1980) observes how those with privileged educations and better jobs experience changes occurring across adult life more favorably than those lacking such chances. Further, Neugarten (1968, p. 146) argues that the major events punctuating an "orderly and sequential" adulthood (for example, marriage, the arrival and departure of children, occupational promotions, and retirement) are understood through superimposing social and cultural "time clocks" onto biological ones. Thus, one's chronological age is not inherently meaningful, though it does readily represent "events that occur with the passage of time" (Neugarten et al. 1964, p. 197) that must be interpreted further in terms of specific contextual features.

In examining the forms and functions of friendships across the broad expanse of middle to later adulthood, I will employ Hess's (1972) conception that once configurations of personal and social roles begin to diversify during adulthood:

> the number and type of friendships open to an individual at particular stages of his [sic] life depend less upon explicit age criteria for the friendship role itself than upon the *other* roles that he plays. As his total cluster of roles changes over is lifetime, so do his friendship relations undergo change. (Hess, 1972, p. 361)

Studying friendships throughout adulthood involves deciphering their fit and ramifications within the friends' overall arrangements of roles and relationships, which are not strictly tied to age. Accordingly, this chapter will not present a comprehensive chronological series of adult developmental stages as its central focus; other depictions are available (Sheehy, 1974; Levinson et al., 1979). Instead, it is organized thematically around modal patterns and communicative exigencies of the social domains of work, marriage, parenthood, kinship, and neighborhood as they affect and reflect friendship processes, while mindful of various broad trends, contingencies, and changes which transpire over time (Basseches, 1984). Further, I will primarily discuss middle-class male and female patterns and practices of managing friendships across these interpenetrated realms.

One final matter is important in analyzing the friendships of adulthood. As dialectical totalities composed of multiple contradictory processes, adults' existential milieus constantly interweave stability and flux. In Pearlin's (1980, p. 174) words, "Adulthood is not a quiescent stretch interspersed with occasional change; it is a time in which change is continuous, interspersed with occasional quiescent interludes." Basseches (1984, p. 312) notes basic accord among authors on adult development regarding this "fundamental dialectical idea." Adults cultivate reasonably stable configurations of relationships of self with others, termed "life structures" by Levinson et al. (1979). However, inevitable periods of flux, questioning, and critical reflection trigger and reveal changes within oneself and in relations with one's spouse, family, friends, work associates, and/or the larger society. Consequently, individuals find themselves facing or avoiding the requirements of negotiating alternative internal and external arrangements. Viewed in this way, the daily events of adulthood continually present both incipient and undeniable practical and emotional challenges.

Farrell and Rosenberg (1981) suggest that adults typically experience their social nexus as blending worthwhile and confirming aspects with irritating, demeaning, and limiting ones. These features are taken for granted much of the time although events may coalesce to accentuate a person's awareness of them. Farrell and Rosenberg argue, "In this sense, adult development can be seen as an episodic heightening and diminishing of self-consciousness" (1981, p. 46). When consciously dissatisfied, a person may struggle to comprehend or change his or her self, situation or both (Farrell & Rosenberg, 1981). Such activity may include constructive, energetic engagement or detrimental, yet equally vigorous alienation, or some combination of these stances. During stable phases when disturbing issues are less salient, adults may adjust favorably to their circumstances or become unconsciously resigned, "an alienation that is not even aware of itself" (Farrell & Rosenberg, 1981, p. 46).

People continually face the urges and demands for change and adaptation as well as for stability and integrity in managing the internal, interpersonal, and public stresses and pleasures of adult life (Giele, 1980; Fiske, 1980). Living a full life, accomplishing and maintaining personal integrity and self-respect while getting along with others, and perceiving some meaningful continuity in one's existence are important goals throughout adulthood (Giele, 1980; Fiske, 1980). The ongoing achievement or subversion of these aims takes place in one's private and public relationships. How adult friendships figure in this process is the principal concern below.

Work Life and Adult Friendships

In considering work as the paramount organizing principle for middle class adult life, two types of work emerge: home making and money making. However, as cultural critics note, the requirements, rewards, punishments, and symbols of money making work dominate and saturate the public and private moments of middle class existence

(Henry, 1971). For Americans in the work force, positively meeting the challenges of one's occupation favorably defines self; shirking them or failing threatens viable personhood. Our cultural image of "making something of oneself" is, for the most part, making money.

Even so, most people making money also like a home to return to, which necessitates home making work. Married and cohabiting couples, to varying degrees of shared and individual consciousness, arrange their work lives in different ways. Some modes include (1) both partners work full time to make money or develop their talents in ways to eventually produce income, with housework evenly divided or mutually paid for; (2) both partners work full time for or toward eventual income, with housework unevenly divided; (3) one person does money making while the other does home making work full time; and (4), resembling (3), only the homemaker also does part-time money-making work. A couple may shift from one mode to another as their family's internal and external circumstances change.

However, the gender alignments of these modes tend to skew in certain directions, especially when a couple has children. In the dual career couple (#2), the female frequently does the most home making work, which now includes taking care of children. Gilbert reports, "Fathers provide on the average about a third of the child care when mothers are employed full-time" (1988, p. 80). In mode (#3) she typically manages the home and raises children full time, and in (#4) also supplements the family income. My point here is to recognize that someone has to accomplish both types of work on an ongoing basis, though women have tended to embrace primary responsibilities for home making work (Oliker, 1989). I also want to stress that references to "work" or "occupation" in describing the middle class usually refer to those activities, which, in addition to other possible benefits, generate the income necessary for appropriate life-styles, thereby ignoring the labor of home making (Lopata, 1971; Bellah et al., 1985). In the words of a midlife, middle-class male I spoke with, "I never apologize for having to work. Work makes it all possible." The ramifications of this pervasive and privileged though narrowly conceived world of work for adult friendships is the subject of this section.

It is difficult to overstate the centrality of money-making work in composing the lives of middle-class Americans. The nature of one's work shapes adult self-images and values. According to Gould:

> When we attach ourselves to particular work, we are likely to stay with it because, if we are successful, it confirms our status as adults. In return for this gift of adultness, we tend to accept the explicit and implicit value system of the particular organization or career, becoming narrower in

relation to our full potential while becoming deeper in relation to a specific real-life complacency. The work becomes us, not just our activity of choice. (1980, p. 228)

Work articulates one's sense of time, including the general contours and rhythms of one's waking hours, weekly and yearly calendars. Even one's biological age is experienced differently in various jobs. Many sales jobs and management positions expect considerable achievement and advancement by the early thirties; meanwhile, persons in occupations requiring extensive formal education beyond college, like professors, lawyers, and physicians, are typically just getting established at this age (Levinson et al., 1979). Moreover, how and with whom persons spend their time at work determines their place in society in two senses: first, with regard to their income and status (Levinson et al., 1979); and second, in terms of the multiple geographic relocations associated with upward mobility in their careers (Bellah et al., 1985). The recurring enterprise of making new friends and relinquishing old ones is a basic repercussion of pursuing occupational success, reconstructing interrelated senses of identity, and social connection for both adults and children (Maines, 1978).

For employed men and women, the workplace constitutes a primary pool and setting for making friends of varying degrees of closeness. People in similar jobs often share physical proximity, overlapping work schedules, common interests and projects, and allied values, which, taken together, can facilitate routine contact and friendship formation. Further, the culture and traditions of an organization may enhance its affiliative climate by permitting or encouraging joking relations, convivial break times, and light-hearted lunches, and by sponsoring ceremonies and activities outside of work, such as picnics, seasonal parties, and company sports teams (Fine, 1986).

Even so, several matters complicate the likelihood and nature of work friendships. First, people's overall attitudes toward their jobs say much about whether they will form friendships with fellow workers (Parker, 1964). Parker (1964, p. 217) found that people who considered their work "a central life interest," identified with it positively, and would choose to do it "even without financial necessity" were significantly more likely to report between two-thirds and all of their six closest friends as doing identical or associated work. Parker concluded, "If work experiences are not valued, friendships are less likely to arise there" (1964, p. 217). Indeed, if people are involved in, dedicated to, and derive personal esteem and/or social prestige from their occupation, working with others and talking shop afterward are likely to combine self-expression and emotional catharsis with instrumental accomplishment. Such relationships may become close friendships.

But other factors further mediate professional attachments. The inherent goals of the actual work or the employing organization may affect how relationships are developed or experienced. For example, the people described above may be strongly committed to jobs embodying inherently self-serving, divisive, and/or highly competitive aims or values. As a result, the time they spend together doing or discussing work ultimately serves an overarching agenda antithetical to close or real friendship. The more they agree on certain objectives or strategies, the more likely they are to be wary of one another. By comparison, other occupations may intrinsically strive for more edifying and/or encompassing goals not directly or simply reduced to dollars or profit. Accomplishment here includes the workers' contributions to the development and well-being of others and a shared social and/or natural environment. The inherently humane and collective values mutually enacted in doing and discussing such work may serve to draw individuals closer together as friends.

Such distinctions in the activities and moral visions of occupations and organizations are seldom so clearcut. Specific organizational cultures and subcultures may develop reward structures encouraging ethics of cooperation that subdue a rigidly competitive orientation among their workers. Likewise, people involved in seemingly primarily altruistic, aesthetic, or service-oriented pursuits may be organized or rewarded in ways that promote competition, greed, and material gain. To a degree, a culture encouraging genuine cooperation and concern for others among its members engenders and reflects friendship practices that a culture thriving on its participants' competition ultimately limits. But these tentative generalizations mask further ironies and tensions involved in the situated and ongoing achievement of friendships in work settings.

The duration and overlap of the time people spend working is a critical concern for developing friendships. If persons do little else but work, most of their socializing is likely to occur there or be associated with it. However, regular and extended interactions are contingent on both parties' work schedules and the amount of solitary or uninterrupted labor required by their jobs (Fine, 1986). Meeting at breaks or during and after work also depends on the degree of autonomy in one's job and ability to control one's own schedule. Thus, positions in the organizational hierarchy also pattern work affiliations. Co-workers who are relative equals and prime candidates for friendship are frequently accessible but also in direct competition for recognition, resources, and opportunities for advancement. By comparison, two parties' unequal status and power in an organization can normatively constrain a mutually negotiated friendship and strongly affect other company members' perceptions of it. Frequent or extended private conversations may be encouraged or discouraged by the schedules, norms, and physical and hierarchical arrangements of a workplace. And the sociability and "occupational community" associated with certain jobs may be voluntary and incidental to the work itself or fairly essential for competent performance in the organization (Parker, 1964).

Thus, several structural contingencies affect the possibility of two persons meeting on the job and becoming friends. Among other matters, these include (1) their attitudes toward and the nature of their occupation, (2) the amount of mutual competition versus cooperation or independence associated with their jobs, (3) the extent of freedom versus constraint in their daily interaction patterns, (4) their degree of equality versus inequality within the organization's hierarchy, and (5) their overall regularity and amount of time spent together during and after work.

Assuming some initial mutual interest, attraction, and/or liking, various relational scenarios emerge from different combinations of these elements. When relative equals do not primarily see themselves as competitors, compulsory time together on the job may involve "friendly relations" that could lead to friendship depending partly on the nature of their work, enjoyment of each other, degree of mutual assistance, and other time commitments (Kurth, 1970). People in professions requiring shared knowledge and cooperation in the specialized and collective handling of work-related challenges and problems often negotiate the relationship of "colleagues," a term ideally connoting mutual respect and good will, notably informed by the objective standards and conventions of the field involved (Lepp, 1966). Positive affiliations with colleagues resemble friendships and may develop into them over time, though collegiality does not require the voluntary interaction, person-qua-person orientation or depth of mutual concern of friendship. In light of their experiences in working together and observing each other's actions, personal qualities, and values, colleagues may also become close friends, indifferent work associates, or bitter enemies, thereby exceeding, affirming, or barely meeting the minimal requirements of professional collegiality.

Though its pervasiveness and intensity varies by organizational culture and the individuals' personal inclinations, most equals at work must compete with one another, especially earlier in their careers when they are "on the make" (Wilensky, 1968). If their schedules permit only occasional contact, they may maintain the simultaneous distance and "friendliness" characterizing the appropriate demeanor of cordial American business practice. But if compelled to interact frequently and/or for long periods, they may further personalize their encounters, enact "friendly relations," and become acquaintances, or even friends (Kurth, 1970; Paine, 1969). Burt (1983) found that as income and education increased and age decreased, individuals were more likely to report co-worker friends, but these were the most ambiguous relationships he studied. By comparison, Wilensky (1968) found high-seniority colleagues to report more stable friendships at work than the "lightly-held attachments" of the young. Equal status in the older group probably reflects more shared work experiences, acceptance of diminishing upward horizons, and common ground than active competition, whereas equal status among the young implies and incites competition. If competing equals can control their contact, its nature and extent will depend on their joint affinity, emphasis on comparative performance, perceptions of potential career impact, and other time constraints.

Since a spirit of equality pervades friendship, the inequality and unilateral control of one person over another dictated by organizational authority structures typically inhibits truly mutual friendships. Yet friendships are privately negotiated, and a superior and subordinate may become friends if they like each other, some common interests or facets of their relationship function as levelers, and they are able to separate suitably their professional and personal relationships. In such cases it is usually the superior's privilege to initiate the friendship outside or as part of work and to monitor how much it intrudes on "getting the job done." Because subordinates have much to gain by befriending a superior, they may be seen as apple-polishing, seeking favors, social climbing, or otherwise patently attempting to further their own careers through such affiliations.

For their part, senior work associates have few career-related incentives encouraging friendships with juniors. They acquire minimal status or upwardly influential connections; attributions of favoritism, compromised administrative "muscle," or conflicts of interest may tarnish perceptions of their decisions involving particular others; and they may be suspected of taking undue advantage of close subordinates, especially in cross-sex relationships (Fine, 1986). The type of arrangement advocated by Levinson et al. (1979) in these circumstances is a mentor relationship, which openly acknowledges structural inequality and the junior person's career development as its primary aim. Though intrinsically gratifying in many cases, and ultimately rewarding to both participants if the protege thrives in the organization and reflects well on his or her mentor, most mentor relationships are too fundamentally shaped by inequality and extrinsic considerations to be considered friendships. When capably, caringly and mutually negotiated, and if the junior is able to succeed and stand alone, however, the mentorship may eventually be renegotiated as a friendship (Levinson et al., 1979).

Functions and Forms of Work-Based Friendships

Lincoln and Miller (1979) highlight the difference between *instrumental ties* developed through carrying out formal work roles and *primary ties* emerging informally through ongoing interaction that may facilitate or undermine formal organizational objectives. Because friendship is based on voluntary and mutual personal choice, these authors expected friendship networks to transcend status differences and reflect similar personal characteristics unrelated to work standing. However, they found that the patterning of friendships closely resembled formal organizational hierarchies with high status individuals in central positions. The authors decided that organizational life constrains the "freedom of individuals to withdraw from one set of ties and position themselves in another" (Lincoln & Miller, 1979, p. 196). Individual desires for similar others minimally shape networks on the job. The authors conclude:

> Friendship networks in organizations are not merely sets of linked friends. They are systems for making decisions, mobilizing resources, concealing or transmitting information, and performing other functions closely allied with work behavior and interaction. If they acquire structures resembling those of work contact networks, perhaps we should not be surprised. (Lincoln & Miller, 1979, pp. 196–197)

Friendships at work are part of institutional participation and personal career-building, serving important purposes for both organizations and individuals. Work friends enhance a person's commitment to the organization, and supervisors' friendships with subordinates reinforce values supporting the organization's authority structure even as they allow for "friendly" criticism (Corwin et al., 1960). Fine further observes:

> Friendship relationships help to control people in organizations by providing a personal motivation to accept the world as it is, rather than disassociate oneself through alienation. Likewise, friendship paves the way for the smooth organization of promotions and changes within an organization. (1986, p. 201)

Fine's last comment reveals the simultaneous individual benefits of organizationally useful work friendships. Friends help in finding jobs and opportunities for promotions, provide support and third party influence on important decisions, and convey warnings about policy changes and "rumblings upstairs." When relocating, work friends may be preserved due to the structure of organizations, professions, and career paths. There are clear advantages for those who cultivate friendly relations with numerous professional associates (Reisman, 1981).

Despite variations across organizations, dominant American middle class values and practices instigate both competition and cordiality among co-workers on and off the job. May (1967) persuasively describes the contradictory pressures shaping most middle class adults' interpersonal endeavors associated with work life:

> On the one hand, they experience the pressure of a social system that is highly professional, bureaucratic, and competitive—energized throughout by the rewards of promotion. On the other hand they experience the pressure of a social style, predicated on friendliness as its ideal. Whereas the social structure is impersonal, increasingly hierarchical, and competitive, the social style is personal, equalitarian, and helpful. The resultant moral conflicts between system and style are immense. (pp. 161–162)

Americans behave in a friendly manner toward their work associates, many of whom they will likely compete with, professionally evaluate, or decide the future of at other points in time (May, 1967). Depending on the extent of their friendship, such moments may force a person to choose between loyalty to the organization, abstract standards, and/or professional advancement, and loyalty to a friend. One may also have to arbitrate two friends' career gains. Poignant incidents, including actual or perceived betrayals by self or others, can force individuals to question the validity or prospect of friendships with co-workers or in general (May, 1967).

Working adults' less familiar affiliations are typically considered "acquaintances." All things considered, for many adults becoming and remaining acquaintances with work associates seems a prudent choice to avoid obligations, revelation to potential competitors, and personal involvement in work decisions (Williams, 1959; Allan, 1979; Gouldner & Strong, 1987). Robert Paine (1969, p. 515) characterizes acquaintanceship as follows: (1) it is an ongoing relationship without confidence or intimacy; (2) acquaintances deviate little from members of conventional society in their mutual comportment, giving the relationship a superficial quality; (3) acquaintances interact only because the social situation requires them to; (4) acquaintances may portray a "front of congeniality which may be either mandatory or a sensible precaution;" (5) the interaction of acquaintances changes minimally when other persons join them; and (6), as a result of (5), acquaintanceships can be mediated by other relationships and comprise the basis for social networks. The desirability of acquaintanceship for regulating the distance between self and others while fulfilling work-related social demands is readily apparent. Ambiguities occur, however, because acquaintanceship may either comprise an ongoing basis for association with others or a stage in forming a friendship (Paine, 1969). After a while if one person feels "held at arm's length" by another, the presumably neutral attempt to maintain decorum at work may communicate rejection of him or her, undermining effective work relations.

Thus in managing personal tendencies and social cross-pressures to become friends and to compete, two generic modes of friendship develop in the workplace. One type has been variously called, "work contacts" (Granovetter, 1974), "work-based friendships" (Laumann, 1973), and "working friends" (Gouldner & Strong, 1987). By and large, these are friendships developed in and largely restricted to the work context. Pleasant and satisfying despite their limitations, they are highly segmented attachments that may be "situationally emphasized or de-emphasized" (Jacobson, 1976, p. 156). Basically, they are *agentic* relationships (Bakan, 1966), begun rationally and/or conveniently, based on joint activities and projects, characterized by fairly explicit individual rights and "tit for tat" reciprocity, limited in emotional investment, and maintained for as long as their benefits to self exceed their costs. If these persons withdraw or disappear when "push comes to shove," work situations alter, and/or jobs are tight, they are reclassified as "no friends," or "fair weather friends," just as peripheral persons who help during such moments may now be called "friends" (Jacobson, 1976).

Some people develop friendships that transcend the workplace. This type has been termed "social friends" (Granovetter, 1974), "close friendships" (Laumann, 1973), and "talking friends" (Gouldner & Strong, 1987). These bonds encompass more of the friends' lives, meeting needs for intimacy, shared discussion and fun, and personal integration extending beyond mere work roles. Basically, these are *communal* relationships (Bakan, 1966), begun of convenience, utility, and/or personal attraction, based on wide-ranging conversation and joint activities, characterized by diffuse, mutual responsibilities and obligations, deepened by emotional attachment and empathy, and maintained through shared commitment and personal loyalty. These friendships enrich both work and private life, though they require extensive time and effort and may place individuals in awkward situations reconciling professional and personal allegiances and schedules.

Wright (1989) remarks on males' modal tendency to form agentic friendships and the prevalent female inclination to form communal ones. During adulthood these modes of friendship seem to be shaped significantly by social circumstances. From childhood, males are socialized to compete and avoid vulnerability (Lewis, 1978). Though this training inhibits close friendships throughout life for many males, it facilitates agentic friendships at work, and males seem quite adept at separating friendship and caring from professional decisions (Gilligan, 1982; Madden, 1987). In contrast, from childhood females practice and sustain communal friendships, which remain distinct possibilities on the job. Working women are often pulled between the ethics and mutual concern of communal friendships and the organizational appropriateness, efficiency, and/or self-service of agentic ones. Whether one friendship mode dominates or both types persist depends on how career committed the woman or man is, the nature of specific relationships, and the extent to which the occupation, organizational culture, and position in the hierarchy require agentic friendships and networks of indifferent acquaintances. Some women are able to maintain their communal friendships and supportive webs at work; others find it increasingly difficult to be close friends with either male or female work associates (Gouldner & Strong, 1987). In the working world, however, one's mode of friendship often becomes more a matter of occupational stance and organizational situation than of gender.

At their roots, key tensions framing work friendships throughout adults' lives pivot on the degree to which the bonds are based on affection, with caring an edifying end-in-itself, and their emphasis on instrumentality, with caring a potentially alienating means-to-an-end. Blending these needs in a mutually satisfactory manner is difficult, because robust friendships take time—and time, as some people say, is money.

Marriage, Parenting, and Adults' Friendships

Many contemporary middle-class spouses aspire to the ideals of couple companionate marriage (Acker, Barry, & Esseveld, 1981; Oliker, 1989). Embodied in this image of marriage as the partners' foremost attachment in life—self-sufficient, strongly united, and able to meet all of each other's material and emotional needs—is "an ideal of best friendship between the spouses" (Oliker, 1989, p. 33). Pursuing this model can promote marital stability as well as shared and supportive views of life's ups and downs, giving meaning to social existence and combating alienation (Berger & Kellner, 1964). For many people the idea, if not the actual behaviors, of friendship with one's spouse constitutes an essential condition of adult adjustment. When actually practiced, the positive feelings and interactional features of friendship are likely to enhance the well-being of the couple and indirectly their children (Gottman, 1982). Gottman states, "The positive, relationship-enhancing aspects of marriage, which I am calling 'friendship,' build the attachment and the affective bond that make couples willing to go through the difficult processes of relationship repair" (1982, p. 119). However, despite widespread cultural endorsement and the inherent appeal of spouses seeing and treating each other as friends, available evidence suggests that mutually enacted realities of marriage and parenthood in stereotypically organizing and managing the business of daily life limit the joint attainment of this ideal for many people.

To understand these disparities between images and actualities, we can compare research findings on marital friendship with the ideal-typical characteristics of close friendship described in Chapter 1. That is, throughout adulthood to what extent do marriages exhibit (1) voluntary ongoing attachment, (2) a "person-qua-person" orientation (Suttles, 1970), (3) equality, (4) mutual trust, support, help, and discussion, and (5) nonsexual affection and caring? First, marriages are not essentially voluntary like friendships, but are legally and often religiously sanctioned bonds. Haley (1963, p. 119) describes the dilemma potentially facing spouses as, "Now that they are married are they staying together because they wish to or because they must?" By emphasizing their desire and choice to do things for and with each other, spouses act as friends in some instances and "keep romance alive" in others. Conversely, by acting toward one another expressly out of obligation and respect for the institution of marriage, spouses may surrender much of the flavor of friendship (or romance) in their bond. However, the permanent commitment associated with marriage is also one of its most redeeming attributes, distinguishing it from voluntary and more provisional bonds like friendship or love affairs (Swidler, 1980; Oliker, 1989).

Friends validate and care about us for who we are aside from what we have or our status in society, what Suttles (1970) calls a "person-qua-person" orientation. Friends remain friends to the extent that they edify and positively confirm each other as individuals. In contrast, a demeaning offshoot of the institutional preservation of marriage is that spouses can interact as occupants of social roles instead of individuals with personal qualities and needs. Regarding and treating another in comprehensive terms (with their accompanying attitudes and communicative patterns) resembling, "the wife," "Mommy," "meal ticket," "hubby," or "the bacon bringer" contradicts the ongoing personalized sensitivity to each other's feelings associated with friendship. Such actions in marriages may be more common than we care to recognize; but few friends would consider or long tolerate comparable conduct.

Perhaps a tendency within marriage to reduce persons to role-based images of "husbands" and "wives" and "dads" and "moms" would not be as disturbing and inconsistent with friendship if these role-pairs were not so thoroughly laced with inequality and asymmetry of emotional input (Bernard, 1981; Acker et al, 1981). Yet in "traditional" marriages the husband's world and associated needs typically take precedence, while embracing the seemingly ceaseless pressures for achievement, economic advancement, and "success." Even in dual career couples, lopsided divisions of housework, child care, entertainment responsibilities, and personal nurturance often persist (Fischer & Oliker, 1983; Gilbert, 1988). And women raising children tend to lack their husbands' time and opportunities for making friends outside the neighborhood (Harry, 1976; Fischer & Oliker, 1983; Gerstel, 1988). The egalitarian ethics of intimate friendship seem difficult to achieve and sustain in such relationships.

Research also suggests that spouses' interdependence differs from that of close friends (Oliker, 1989). Though mutual trust and dependability in difficult situations anchor all viable marriages and close friendships, asymmetries occur in the degree and quality of joint discussion, conversational support, and understanding of routine trials and tribulations in the marital context. Bernard (1981) reports that women more frequently than men provide a "mental hygiene" function within marriage. And Oliker (1989, p. 21) convincingly observes, "Six decades of empirical research on marriage document women's greater dissatisfaction with many companionate elements of marriage, as well as consensus among husbands and wives on women's greater self-sacrificing marital 'adjustment.'" Marital mutuality seems frequently tenuous at best; but as Gottman observes, "Symmetry in emotional responsiveness probably relates to whether or not husbands and wives are friends" (1982, p. 119).

Finally, sexually expressed affection and, for many, having children together, are significant expectations of marriage. They comprise especially gratifying features of the ideologies of romantic loving and family life fulfilled with spouses. However, they are not definitive attributes of friendship. A drawback of romantic loving is that it tends to be possessive and exclusive, jealously desiring to seal the loved one off from the attentions of others (Brain, 1976). Further, viewing another principally as a sexual partner can objectify him or her and interfere with the "person-qua-person" orientation of friendship.

Ordinarily, these dissimilarities between friendship and romantic love are less salient when friends and lovers are different people. But when individuals are culturally encouraged and personally inclined to combine the two relational types in marriage, it becomes necessary for spouses to negotiate and sensitively communicate their periodic needs for each other as a friend, as a lover, and as combinations of the two. Continually accomplishing these aims to both partners' satisfaction is not easy, especially considering males' modal tendencies to blur the distinction between cross-sex friendship and romance and females' modal inclinations to discriminate clearly between them. Ironically, in some respects husbands and wives may enact the gender-linked patterns we have previously noted within cross-sex friendships. That is, husbands need and rate their wives more highly as friends than vice versa, while weakening the likelihood of fulfilling friendships for their wives because they inadequately confirm their personhood. Further, given the other asymmetries in marriage noted above, sex itself can become a political issue and an arena for consolidating or combating dominance, which always undermines the possibility of friendship (Hutter, 1978). By definition and for both positive and negative reasons, the presence and importance of sexually expressed affection can complicate the ongoing achievement of mutually valued close friendship within marriage.

Despite varying degrees and durations of actual friendship practices between spouses, the "social unity" (Gerstel, 1988) associated with the couple companionate ideal also promotes joint friendships with other couples as a normative corollary. As a result, either spouse's solitary pursuit of friendships can be stymied. Babchuk (1965) states that about half of his sample of husbands and wives did not report one "primary friend" pursued independently of their spouse. The prevailing pattern is for husbands (and wives in dual career couples) to recruit their friends through work; wives assume the tasks of maintaining these relationships as well as managing contact with neighbors and relatives (Babchuk & Bates, 1963; Fischer & Oliker, 1983; Gerstel, 1988). Even so, couples exhibit diverse overall styles of making and keeping friends. These range from a preference for a few close attachments to an extensive network of relatively uninvolved acquaintances. Further, spouses do not always share the same regard for either or both persons in the other couple. Negotiating a mutually agreeable pattern of befriending other couples as well as individuals is another crucial facet of spouses' united experiences of friendship (Newman & Newman, 1975).

Though couple friendships can be derided for their potential superficiality and competitive overtones, they can also effectively serve various private and public functions for married partners. Unlike the nagging irritations, anxieties, and humdrum activities of everyday life, time spent with other couple friends can be relaxing and fun (Larson & Bradney, 1988). Many people use planned gatherings with personal friends as designated junctures to "back off" from the intensity of their occupations, entertain and reward themselves with meals, concerts, and other outings, or share vacations. Getting together with couple friends from bygone days reminds the spouses of continuities in their identities and values as individuals and as couple (Bott, 1971), though they may equally signal regretted changes. When children are included, couple friendships provide a positive context for them to meet or renew friendships with other children, and an opportunity to see their parents relaxed, sociable, sharing the fruits of their labors, laughing, and generating good will.

Couple engagements are not merely privatized retreats. Many couple-oriented activities and involvements bridge private and public spheres, integrating the married partners into wider society. Gatherings of couples constitute personal though not necessarily intimate contexts for developing, extending, and facilitating gratifying work-related relationships. Couple-based friendships may open outward in other ways, embracing shared political convictions or recreational and educational enterprises benefiting their children and other members of the larger community. When married couples share a vital group of friends, both dyadic and social integration result (Wilensky, 1968; Farrell & Rosenberg, 1981). During these intervals the marital conversation expands to include multiple well-meaning voices. Though some of the interactions are routinized and almost perfunctory, others are deeply meaningful or simply worthwhile, generating utilitarian and sympathetic insights that facilitate personal, marital, familial, community, and occupational well-being.

Beneficial as they may be when things go well and needs are met, the tasks of coordinating these multiple relationships and linking the spheres of marriage, family, friendship, and career typically fall on the wife (Gerstel, 1988). Bernard (1972) developed the concept of "her" and "his" marriage based on differences between expectations and actualities, between what one receives compared with what one gives to the relationship, and between appearances and essences. Overall, these same dynamics also appear to characterize and limit the friendships of spouses. Except in clearly equitable arrangements or when marital partners devote continual conscious attention to their collective worlds, "her" and "his" conceptions of friendship within marriage probably also persist. Paralleling research on cross-sex and female same-sex friendships considered in Chapter 6, women's expectations for friendship are not always completely satisfied by their husbands or their couple friendships. Typically they also need at least one close female friend to talk with privately and confide in (Gerstel, 1988; Gouldner & Strong, 1987; Oliker, 1989).

Moreover, in her in-depth case studies of 21 women, mostly married mothers over 30 from middle- and working-class backgrounds, Oliker

(1989) found that despite some overlaps, women obtained different things from their marriages and friendships with other women. Being and staying married was accorded high status and viewed as an economic imperative. Further, they valued access to a man's perspective on the world, mutual fidelity, shared history, and "the authenticity constituted by living out daily life alongside another person" (Oliker, 1989, p. 52). Consistent with our discussion above, Oliker summarizes these women's conceptions of the distinctive qualities of marital intimacy and close friendship with other women:

> The intimacy of marriage was born of sharing and daily cooperation in the context of physical intimacy and permanent commitment. The intimacy of friendship was made of mutual self disclosure and empathetic understanding in the context of voluntary support and contingent commitment. (1989, p. 53).

By comparison, men are more likely to consider their wives as their sole confidante and best friend, especially in traditional marriages (Spanier & Thompson, 1984; Gerstel, 1988; Oliker, 1989). Depending on his wife to fulfill his needs for intimate friendship and to coordinate their other social contacts, the husband may resent her attention to her own friendships outside of the marriage. When a woman raises children, the conjugal friendship throughout much of mature adulthood is constrained by the practical exigencies of the husband's time spent away and necessitated by the emotional demands of consolidating his career (Gouldner & Strong, 1987). Much of the other shared substance of these friendships derives from mutually experiencing their joint commitment to the joys and frustrations of raising children (though typically not to the bulk of the actual labor involved).

At the point in his career when a man may become freer from the pressures of work or less committed to achievement, his wife may also become less encumbered by their now older and more autonomous children (Farrell & Rosenberg, 1981). Farrell and Rosenberg report, "Close to 50 percent of the women in this country return to work during this period" (1981, p. 124). Problems may now arise or increase in marriages when a wife seeks to express her instrumental capabilities and explore more "mastery" at work or elsewhere; meanwhile, her husband strives to express increased caring and pursue more interpersonal connection and love (Fiske, 1980; Gould, 1980). At such junctures the degrees of mutual dependence, responsiveness, encouragement and edification available in the conjugal friendship will be tested and possibly renegotiated. Will he care enough about her as a friend to accept and foster her freedom to be independent? Will she continue to grant him the freedom to depend on her? How will they manage this potential shift from asymmetrical to symmetrical emotional demands and personal possibilities? Like virtually all interpersonal issues in adulthood, the answer depends partly on their involvement in other relationships outside of their marriage.

Kin, Neighbors, and Friends

Most adults' "life structures" (Levinson et al., 1979) include regular contact with kin and neighbors, though its frequency, duration, and intensity vary considerably among couples and individuals. Commentators argue that kinship no longer serves the integrative function it once did, despite the blood bond linking relatives (Rieger-Shlonsky, 1969). The middle-class pursuit of upward mobility moves people farther from their parents and scatters siblings around the nation (Bellah et al., 1985). As a result, the "friendship values" of affection-based voluntary interdependence may now be essential to ongoing interaction among kin (Paine, 1969). Brain states:

> In open societies such as our own, where kinship is organized multilaterally (not just down the male or female line), the number of possible kin is immense, and choice, outside the elementary family, determines the persons one treats as kin. There would even be a case for maintaining that all kin relations within our kinship group are based on friendship and personal choice. One chooses this or that uncle, this or that cousin, even this or that brother or sister to be friendly with. (1976, p. 8)

Moreover, considerable overlap exists in the benefits derived from friends and relatives (Rieger-Shlonsky, 1969). As a result, friends may compensate for the absence of kin in times of need and during seasonal celebrations when family cannot be near. Likewise, kin may supply the moral support and camaraderie of friendship in lonely periods when friends are not available. Culturally, we seem to recognize a reciprocity between the values of kinship and friendship by borrowing terminology from one relational type to honor members of the other. Spouses acknowledge special, though unrelated, old friends by having their children call him "Uncle Ed" and her "Aunt Mel." Specific relatives may be proudly and affectionately singled out as, for example, "Not only my brother, but one of my best friends."

Shulman (1975) found that personal networks including friends, neighbors, and relatives were sustained by regular visits, joint assistance and exchange of personal property, and mutual enjoyment (though obligation and need were mentioned more frequently with kin than friends and neighbors). Following Freud, some authors argue that persons organize themselves around a limited "fund of intimacy" and that investing emotional attention in various relationships reduces their resources for others (Hutter, 1978; Farrell & Rosenberg, 1981). Yet Babchuk (1965) found no relation between couples' frequency of visiting relatives and visiting friends. In fact, Booth (1972) found that the men and women reporting extensive contact with kin also described abundant interpersonal connections of other types as well. Within limits, expanding one's circle of caring may enhance rather than deplete interpersonal resources during adulthood.

Though friendships and kin relations overlap and complement each other in numerous ways, they are conceived differently in our culture. Despite Brain's point about choosing among one's relatives, "blood is thicker than mud," and persons usually feel obligated to assist and observe family rituals with their kin (Bott, 1971). In contrast, selecting each other for shared activities demonstrates the voluntary hallmark of friendship's consensual foundation (Bott, 1971). Moreover, in Shulman's (1975) research identifying three degrees of intimacy in personal relationship clusters, kin comprise the majority of those people ranked closest; friends are mentioned in all three ranks, though mainly in the latter two. Neighbors are named least of all.

Despite their reported closeness and enduring commitment, many kinship relations are ambivalent. Although relatives share history, common loyalties, and backgrounds, there are also "skeletons in the closet," lingering resentments from bygone wounds, and smoldering competition and jealousy, especially among siblings (Gouldner & Strong, 1987). Further, different aged siblings often experience difficulty overcoming hierarchical themes and role-based interactions with each other; their dialogue may easily become strained or stilted. Whereas relations with kin promote continuity of self's identity, it may be an undesirable one, inflexibly grounded in past images or events a person wants to transcend. Kin mutually avoid frequent contact for such reasons, but may become friends if they use their shared history and knowledge as bases for sensitivity to each other's feelings and actions in the present. And married couples maintain reasonably close connections with their parents, feeling shared pride in the spouses' professional and personal achievements (Bott, 1955), and love for their children/grandchildren.

Studies identify structural features and interpersonal resources and outputs distinguishing kin, neighbors, and friends. On a structural level, kin typically engage in minimal face-to-face interaction due to physical separation, neighbors unpredictably move in and out of the local area, and friends may exhibit either tendency (Litwak & Szelenyi, 1969). Accordingly, maintaining vital relationships with relatives involves ongoing communication and mutual assistance despite enforced separation, and neighboring relationships must be established fairly quickly while mindful of their potential turnover (Litwak & Szelenyi, 1969). In sustaining friendships, people must handle reduced face-to-face encounters with past friends as well as potentially mobile current partners. Litwak and Szelenyi (1969) observe that in lacking the permanence of kinship ties and the frequent contact of neighbors, free-standing friendships exhibit the flimsiest structural connections. Since the primary tie that binds such friendships is mutual affection, friends must learn "how to deal with the most idiosyncratic aspects of life" (Litwak & Szelenyi, 1969, p. 466).

Scholars note suburban housewives' particular difficulty in making new friends among their neighbors. Likely neighborhood friends overlap on age, education, work schedules, career aspirations, and young children; and nearby women matched in these essential ways may be scarce (Lopata, 1971; Acker et al., 1981; Oliker, 1989). Moreover, other women's (perhaps understandable) jealous tendencies to protect already established friendships and reservations about a new person's possible stay in the neighborhood may further impede a woman's development of new friends close to home (Margolies, 1985). Meanwhile, constrained social options outside the vicinity, as well as the convenience, personal and practical utility of neighboring relations highly recommend them (Lopata, 1971).

Interestingly, research participants clearly agree on the resources and provisions of kin and neighbors, but are least consistent about friends (Rieger-Shlonsky, 1969). Presuming their commitment, kin are seen as motivated, involved, positively concerned, and interested in self's undertakings (Rieger-Shlonsky, 1969; Verbrugge, 1979). They are viewed instrumentally and expected to "help in major crises and in rites of passage" (Rieger-Shlonsky, 1969; Verbrugge, 1979, p. 1289). People characterize neighbors as possessing "good manners" and reliably displaying civility (Rieger-Shlonsky, 1969). They expect them to socialize and to assist with minor or particularly urgent tasks (Rieger-Shlonsky, 1969; Verbrugge, 1979).

In contrast, friendship spans a variety of contexts and is perceived quite ambiguously (Burt, 1983; Rieger-Shlonsky, 1969). Even so, research participants conceive the primary resources of friendship as commonality, personal resemblance, and capacity for empathy (Rieger-Shlonsky, 1969). When compared with relatives and neighbors, friends are more likely to provide "understanding," and "psychological and moral support" (Rieger-Shlonsky, 1969, p. 359), and to help with problems not requiring instant attention (Verbrugge, 1979).

Ongoing interaction with one's spouse, family, co-workers, neighbors, and friends shapes and reflects the responsibilities, rewards, and overall emotional texture of a typical adult's daily life. Although a variety of events can transform this interpersonal configuration during middle adulthood, one of the more commonplace and disruptive occurrences for married people is divorce. Considering the role of adult friendships in this often comprehensive reorganization of a person's interpersonal nexus provides further perspective on the nature and functions of friendship in relation to other midlife relationships.

Divorce and Friendship

Although all divorces involve the termination of a marriage, their specific interpersonal circumstances vary according to the former spouses' ages, "the duration of the marriage, the number and ages of the children, and the manner of divorcing" (Miller, 1971, pp. 63–64). A divorce's social impact also depends on the density of the separating persons' interpersonal networks (Bott, 1971). Divorces reverberate significantly throughout high-density networks, in which the persons know many of each other's associates, who in turn know each other. But when spouses "move in separate circles," sharing few friends and acquaintances, divorces produce much less social reorganization (Miller, 1971; Hobfoll & Stokes, 1988). Further, divorces transpire over time with married partners experiencing problems, deciding to separate, accomplishing the divorce, and managing the aftermath (Miller, 1971). The roles of friends change for males and females during these different phases of the process.

When women face marital difficulties, Oliker (1989) reports that their friends do considerable "marriage work," attempting to facilitate marital adjustment. Their efforts include listening empathetically, stressing family responsibilities (especially when children are affected), fostering understanding of the husband's perspective, and "advocating accommodation in marital problem solving" (Oliker, 1989, p. 111). Basically, close women friends try to diffuse anger and frustration and persuade the person to stay in the marriage unless the situation is intolerable (Oliker, 1989). However, once a woman decides to divorce, her close friends will support her wholeheartedly. Spanier and Thompson (1984) also observe that male and female friends disapprove of divorce when they perceive a basically harmonious marriage, but when circumstances became chronically negative, they endorse a split. Among Oliker's interviewees, "Marriage work was prescribed until divorce work became unavoidable" (1989, p. 148).

Both men and women dread facing and telling their friends and acquaintances of an impending or final divorce (Gerstel, 1987). Anxious about friends' evaluations, separating spouses engage in efforts resembling public relations within their networks, strategically "managing information" to create desired impressions of self, the spouse, and the nature of their marriage "to ease and legitimate" their divorce in others' eyes (Gerstel, 1987, p. 117) Ironically, Spanier and Thompson observe that, compared with both persons' families, "Friends are the least judgmental" (1984, p. 81). Understandably, one's relatives object because a divorce questions the sanctity of marital and familial bonds; "The investment, commitments, and values involved in family relationships make it more likely that family members would disapprove and intervene in dissolving marriages than friends" (Spanier & Thompson, 1984, p. 82). In contrast, the expectations between friends of loyalty, acceptance, and encouragement of a friend's strong convictions and self-image probably foster less judgmental reactions. Further, Goode (1956) argues that close friends may have more intimate knowledge than most relatives of the troubles warranting the divorce. Family members who are also close friends of either or both spouses may find their commitments, loyalties, and sentiments torn in disparate directions. Does one advise or react as kin, insisting on family values and commitment through tough times? Or does one speak as a friend, acknowledging and encouraging either or both parties' individuality and personal desires? Can a person express ambivalence without unduly hurting or alienating a loved one at such a sensitive moment?

Not surprisingly, divorcing couples divide their friends, with jointly held friends especially susceptible (Gerstel, 1987; Spanier & Thompson, 1984). Deciding who gets which friends and why resembles sorting through shared belongings and involves the sometimes painful process of recalling when and how the friendships were formed or who brought them into the marriage (Gerstel, 1987). A couple's friends may have to side with one or the other spouse, depending on the bitterness of the divorce. Ex-spouses may "put pressure on friends to take sides" in assigning blame (Gerstel, 1987, p. 176). Thus, friends are sometimes compelled to act as evaluators, invoking personal and social standards as well as codes developed within their friendship. Is the divorce a good or bad thing? For whom? Who was right and who was wrong? Why? Where does this leave us as friends? Acceptance of, loyalty to, and honesty with either or both partners become exceedingly problematic under these conditions. As a result, these qualities of friendship may be staunchly upheld or situationally redefined and realigned.

Spanier and Thompson depict the interpersonal predicaments of managing the aftermath of a divorce: "Social and emotional ambiguity abounds. There are few norms to guide the actions of family and friends, and the newly single person has needs and preferences that are much different than when he or she was part of a couple" (1984, p. 167). Recently divorced persons may feel lonely for interrelated reasons. First, they have separated from their former spouses, begun living alone or as single parents, and experienced a personal need or social pressure to begin dating. Second, their accustomed interpersonal networks may have fallen apart or started rearranging themselves in unexpected, disconfirming, irritating, and upsetting ways (Wallerstein & Kelly, 1980). Although friends initially may devote extra effort and attention to divorced persons, over time they may back off due to significant changes in the circumstances of the friendship (Spanier & Thompson, 1984). Previous, coupled friends begin excluding the divorced individual because they perceive him or her as a threat to their own relationship, have sided with the ex-spouse, or unreflectively convene couples as the adult unit of friendship (Hess, 1972; Gerstel, 1987). Old friends may view both male and female divorced persons as sexually available; accordingly, they either avoid or make passes at them, thereby tapering off or compromising the original friendship (Gerstel, 1987).

These are consequential shifts in social patterns and practices. Spanier and Thompson (1984) report that 70% of their sample of men and women described diminished contact after divorce with the friends they once shared with their ex-spouse. Reflecting the apparent male privilege of selecting couple friends, the authors observe, "The more friends women shared with their husbands during marriage, the more likely they were to wish they had more friends after separation" (Spanier & Thompson, 1984, p. 169). Even so, males were more apt than females to lack three persons whom they considered close (Spanier & Thompson, 1984). In Gerstel's (1988) research, over 90% of the men and women said they had at least one person to discuss personal concerns with; but despite an equivalent overall pool of potential confidants, women conversed with their friends about personal matters significantly more often than men did. Gender variations in talking with friends seem to persist during the period following divorce.

Predictably, women and men want to make additional friends following divorce (Spanier & Thompson, 1984). However, Gerstel (1988) argues that women are more likely to face custody of children, reduced income, and constrained opportunities for forming friendships. As a result, they tend to strengthen and deepen their old friendships through talking on the phone and spending time together in their homes (Gerstel, 1988). In contrast, while men have the options of privately and publicly cultivating both old and new friendships, they tend to pursue new ones in public and community contexts (Gerstel, 1988). Gerstel (1988) describes men's desire for "instant networks," which are useful for passing the time, staying active, promoting sociability, and meeting instrumental goals such as winning at sports, performing music and pursuing politics. She notes positively:

> Because these groups fill time, help people cope with their loneliness without requiring disclosure of their feelings, and link them into the wider community, many of the men in our sample found them an effective form of social integration. (Gerstel, 1988, p. 357)

Over time, divorced men's interpersonal networks included more new friends and fewer old ones or kin (Gerstel, 1988).

Unfortunately and understandably, neither women's nor men's friendship experiences are entirely favorable during this period. However, their differences deserve attention. Whereas women associate the desire for new friends with distress, men link distress with the activity of making new friends—the more friends they acquire since separating, the greater their anxiety (Spanier & Thompson, 1984). In Spanier and Thompson's study, "The more new friends a man made, the more likely he was to have had thought about suicide, felt lonely, and have had a hard time accepting that the marriage was over" (1984, p. 184). This finding is especially curious and disturbing, given males' tendencies to seek out new networks of active instrumental friends instead of intensifying their older ones. All in all, with couple friendships dropping off following divorce, gender-linked social opportunities and constraints seem to magnify the benefits and debits of the styles of friendship associated with each gender throughout life.

According to Spanier and Thompson's (1984) research, both family and friends are important sources of support during the aftermath of a divorce. In their study, women received overall more moral, financial, and service support (such as babysitting, errands, and repair work) than men, and the average person's family of origin and co-workers were much more supportive than were in-laws. Women's friends were most frequently mentioned as providing moral support, with men's friends slightly less so than their own mothers. For both men and women, friends offered the most support through assistance and favors. Parents helped more financially than anyone else (Spanier & Thompson, 1984). Accordingly, many people and particularly women regard the period following divorce as a profound test of and tribute to their friends' and families' devotion (Gerstel 1988). Since friends are not obligated in the same normative ways as immediate kin, divorced individuals view their extensive moral and practical support as expressing true friendship (Gerstel, 1988).

Gender Patterns in Adult Same- and Cross-Sex Friendships

Close friendship has deep significance for adult men and women, who both describe mutual dependence, acceptance, confidence, and trust as ideals of friendship (Weiss & Lowenthal, 1973; Fox et al., 1985; Sapadin, 1988). Men and women averaging 50 years old in one sample similarly reported that their close same-sex friends lived nearby and were seen often; and they both discussed an equivalent "program" of topics with their close friends, including a person's "daily web of activities and concerns," "a sense of continuity of one's identity with the past," and "one's relationship to the outside world" (Aries & Johnson, 1983, p. 1193). Further, different friends serve varied functions for both genders across adulthood (Weiss & Lowenthal, 1973).

Despite these resemblances, women's and men's friendships throughout the adult years persistently exhibit the distinctive modal patterns apparent earlier in life. Once again, talking together emerges as a fundamental purpose and practice of women friends. Although addressing the same basic list of topics as men, women talk more often about their intimate concerns as well as routine matters and mutual endeavors, delving deeper than men into personal and family issues (Aries & Johnson, 1983). Several studies find that frequent and extended phone conversations play a critical role for women friends in working through both sensitive and mundane worries as they arise, entertaining each other, or simply staying in touch (Aries & Johnson, 1983; Gouldner & Strong, 1987; Gerstel, 1988). Mutually confirming talk is so important that Johnson and Aries (1983; p. 354) call it "the substance" and "the central feature of women's friendship," and Gouldner and Strong (1987) interchange the terms "close friendship" and "talking friendship" in speaking of women's intimate same-sex bonds.

Men's adult friendships continue to display common interests, shared activities, and sociability as their primary attributes. Male dyads are often geared toward accomplishing things and having something to show for their time spent together—practical problems solved, the house painted or deck completed, wildlife netted, cars washed or tuned, tennis, basketball, poker, or music played, and so on. Shared talk may arise during these pursuits but it is usually not the principal focus. In

Aries and Johnson's (1983) study sports was the sole topic that males reported discussing in greater frequency and depth.

Complementing the instrumental cast of many male relationships, men emphasize independence in their friendships, whereas women strive for interdependence. Fox and her colleagues (1985) report that men in their thirties through fifties describe friendship as involving other persons' needs for their instrumental assistance and want to avoid too much dependency among friends. Accordingly, they try to maintain autonomy and do not like to seek help from others. Developing a loose network of friends limits their obligations to particular individuals (Booth, 1972). As Tognoli observes, "Men thereby create 'freedom' in their relationships with others by maintaining a minimal commitment" (1980, p. 277). Even so, this diligently protected liberty also seals them off from others (Farrell & Rosenberg, 1981).

In contrast, women view their friends' needs as opportunities to give to and care for another. Fox et al. (1985, p. 496) state, "For midlife women, need seems to be an overwhelming expressive condition: the need to talk, the need for comfort, the need to share." Moreover, meeting these needs occurs in a spirit of communal altruism rather than individual exchange or matched reciprocity (Fox et. al., 1985). Overall, demonstrating affection and achieving intimacy with friends appear more important to women than to men during adulthood (Weiss & Lowenthal, 1973; Goldman et al., 1981; McAdams, 1985).

Adult cross-sex friendships seem to be primarily middle-class phenomena (Rubin, 1975). Such friends are typically of similar social status, with people from white-collar occupations and some college education outnumbering blue-collar workers with little college attendance (Booth & Hess, 1974; Rubin, 1985). Like all friendships, "opportunities for prolonged and private interaction" greatly aid in developing opposite-sex bonds (Booth & Hess, 1974, p. 39). Thus, entering the white-collar work force and having cross-sex colleagues are of pivotal importance, though women may still be systematically excluded from influential and recreational male activities in organizations (Lincoln & Miller, 1979; Fine, 1986). When possible and encouraged, participation in sexually mixed groups expands the chances for cross-sex friendships (Lopata, 1975).

Unmarried adults are much more likely to have cross-sex friends; marriage reduces overall interaction as well as the expression of affection between such friends (Booth & Hess, 1974). While both spouses' cross-sex activities dwindle after marriage, women's interaction with opposite-sex friends is particularly likely to decrease (Booth & Hess, 1974). Even so, according to Booth and Hess (1974), women mentioning male friends have probably met them through their husbands; "Women who report that they share friends with their husbands are four times as likely to report cross-sex friends as females who do not share friends with their mates" (p. 42). Booth and Hess conclude that

> The cross-sex friendship patterns reported by females are more likely to show the effects of structural opportunities and normative constraints than those of males. The female who is most likely to report male friends is employed, is married to a husband with a white-collar occupation, and belongs to professional and voluntary associations. A rather large proportion of these friendships with males was initiated by her husband. . . . In contrast, structural opportunities and normative constraints seem to have few effects upon cross-sex relationships reported by males. (1974, p. 46)

Indeed, some kind of male prerogative seems to be functioning (Rawlins, 1982). Males have more chances to make friends outside of marriage (Bell, 1975), preserve the stereotypical privilege of initiating their own cross-sex friendships (Chafetz, 1974), and report more cross-sex friendships than women (Booth & Hess, 1974; Booth, 1972). Further, as in other periods in life, cross-sex friendships seem to benefit men more than women. Although males and females appreciate the opportunity to see professional and personal issues from a member of the other gender's perspective (Sapadin, 1988), Pleck (1975) states that women friends provide a refuge from the competitive pressures of men's interactions with each other. Studying adults, Sapadin (1988) reveals that men rated their cross-sex friendships as more enjoyable and nurturing than their same-sex ones, though similar in perceived intimacy. Men also felt that mutual nurturance characterized the bonds. In contrast, women rated their same-sex friendships as more intimate, enjoyable, nurturant, and higher in overall quality than their cross-sex ones. Further, they "felt much more nurtured by their women friends, in both personal and career areas" than by males (Sapadin, 1988, p. 401).

Friendship Across the Adult Years: Constraints and Opportunities

Two modes of friendship surface repeatedly in analyzing adult friendships: communal friendships, premised on an ethic of care and characterized by emotionally supportive and personally involving communication; and agentic friendships, premised on an ethic of rights and typified by socially facilitative and activity-oriented communication. That the former style is modally linked with females and the latter with males in adulthood derives from early learning and repeated practice in the skills and outlooks associated with each style since childhood, coupled with the concrete social settings and configurations of relationships and roles within which adults live their lives (Fischer & Oliker, 1983). A given female friendship will not necessarily exhibit primarily communal attributes or a male friendship agentic ones. Depending on the social circumstances of their earlier lives and the networks or series of relationships they participate in as adults, women or men may develop friendships of either style as well as bonds combining their attributes.

However, as we have observed throughout this chapter in examining the various areas of adult social life, available evidence suggests that men and women do not experience equal opportunities for cultivating friendships of either mode. Rather, culturally prescribed and personally selected roles enacted by women and men in managing the interpenetrated domains of work, marriage, family, neighborhood, and community life constrain and shape their numbers and forms of friendships. Though the specific role clusters and priorities posed by one's career progress and stage in the family life cycle vary in time from person to person, social researchers have identified some broad, normative, age-related patterns of friendships across adulthood for men and women.

The thirties is a period of "career consolidation" for many adults (Vaillant, 1977; Basseches, 1984). The opportunities for and selection of friends at this time shape and reflect one's occupational sphere. Persons, typically women, who concentrate on housework and raising children, have limited pools for choosing friends in their immediate vicinity, though the ones formed are likely to be communal in nature (Oliker, 1989). Some women are particularly interested in friends who can stimulate them with imaginative conversation and activities (Goldman et al., 1981). Still, the circumstances and demands of this period tangibly restrict their friendships (Williams, 1958) and, overall, "during early marriage and parenthood, women's friendships shrink relative to men's" (Fischer & Oliker, 1983, p. 130).

Men and women who work outside the home have expanded chances for making friends, though these friendships are usually closely tied to their jobs. Occupation-related friendships of similar status are twice as likely as other kinds for men during this period (Jackson, 1977). In general, with marriage and parenthood men begin moving away from the friendships of their youth (both literally and figuratively) and develop work and neighborhood friends (Stueve & Gerson,1977). These latter friends are seen frequently though they tend to be short-lived and not especially close (Jackson, Fischer, & Jones, 1977). By comparison, childhood and kin friends are emotionally closer and more lasting, but reside far away and are not seen often (Jackson et al., 1977). Overall, men spend more time with their less close friends than their intimate ones; in Verbrugge's words, "the longer friends have known each other, the less contact they have" (1983, p. 82). Once a man marries, the percentage of his best friends made at work does not vary until retirement (Stueve & Gerson, 1977).

With the encompassing family and work life responsibilities associated with midlife, men spend sharply diminished time with friends, and married couples are less involved in social activities (Larson & Bradney, 1988; Gould, 1972). Most entertaining occurs at home and centers around the family and routine patterns of relating with neighbors and kin (Stueve & Gerson, 1977; Shulman, 1975). While uniquely gratifying and consistent with the pervasive "identification of self with family" (Gould, 1972, p. 530) demonstrated by adults during this period, Larson and Bradney (1988) report that parents as well as children view family interaction as clearly bounded in its potential for unabashed enjoyment. By and large, both parties have (or recall having) more fun with their friends. Even though men mention more nonkin associates than women during this period, they tend not to be close ones. Linked with marriage, parenthood, and advancing age, Stueve and Gerson (1977) report a striking drop in the percentage of men seeing best friends at least weekly. For men 21 to 34 years old, 73% of the single men, 59% of the married men, and 45% of the married fathers were able to have such contact. Only 36% of the middle-aged fathers (35–49 years old) in their sample described regular interaction with best friends. Farrell and Rosenberg remark, "The midlife male generally exhibits a narrowed focus, family and work being the defining elements in his life" (1981, p. 202).

On their part, women tend to experience a resurgence in friendships when freed from primary parenting responsibilities. Perhaps reflecting the norms of childbearing and women returning to work and/or community involvement at the time, Williams (1958) found women's friendships to increase noticeably after their thirties. And Fischer and Oliker observed in their sample of 1050 adults, aged 18 years and over and living in California, that "After the early childbearing years, women gained nonkin associates, while men lost them" (1983, p. 130). Basically, midlife finds women branching out and enriching their friendships and men routinizing or retreating from their friendships with other men (Farrell & Rosenberg, 1981; Verbrugge, 1983). The conspicuous absence of references to close friends in Levinson et al.'s (1979) case studies of midlife males is well known:

A man may have a wide social network in which he has amicable, "friendly" relationships with many men and perhaps a few women. In general, however, most men do not have an intimate male friend of the kind they recall fondly from boyhood or youth. Many men have had casual dating relationships with women, or perhaps a few complex love-sex relationships, but most men have not had an intimate, non-sexual friendship with a woman. (1979, p. 335)

Fischer and Oliker (1983) argue that since most men's friends are made at work to serve career interests, when careers stabilize at midlife, the making and maintaining of these friendships depends on their intrinsic features. However, midlife men describe minimal regular contact with friends outside of work; and whereas *81%* of the unmarried men (averaging about 25 years old) in one sample report "often or sometimes" having intimate discussions with their friends, only *48%* of the married men (averaging about 41 years old) with a first child in high school confirm similar conversations (Farrell & Rosenberg, 1981, p. 195). Male friendship groups at this time are "dominated by issues of status, acquisition, and mutual use," and preserved through ritualized and superficial interaction or expediency (Farrell & Rosenberg, 1981, p. 202). Ironically and unfortunately, at the point in their lives when many middle-class men have intensifying existential needs for close friendship, they are poorly practiced at caringly disclosive relationships with other men. As a result, by their mid-forties many males may drift toward insulating themselves from others, despite a convivial public persona (Gould, 1972; Farrell & Rosenberg, 1981).

Research regarding friendship during the later years of mature adulthood is virtually nonexistent. Even so, judging from available findings, the friendship of spouses may flourish at this time if or as they replace role-related perceptions of each other with a deep appreciation of each other's independence, companionship, and their shared life experiences. Released from parenting responsibilities, reconciled with career positions, and hopefully still in good health, both genders mainly associate friends "with pleasant or happy social events," though not necessarily with assistance and resources in troubled times (Gamer et al., 1975, p. 343). Gatherings of couple friendships in travel, religious, recreational sports and card-playing groups shape social calendars. Moreover, work settings persist as sources of friendships for women and men at least until retirement. Yet, the older men are, the less likely they are to describe their longer lasting friends as close (Stueve & Gerson, 1977). In contrast to a younger man's "old" friends, these friendships were probably made in adult situations inhibiting the cultivation of extensive intimacy between men.

Having surveyed broad tendencies of friendship among key social domains across the adult years as depicted in the research literature, I now turn to open-ended interviews with a sample of adults. In doing so, I hope to go beyond the abstractions of modal descriptions and view more closely individuals' actual benefits and predicaments of negotiating friendships in concrete circumstances of mature adulthood.

Chapter 9

Illustrative Analysis: Circumstances of Adult Friendships

The present chapter examines communicative features, experiences, and contexts of adult friendships as described in depth interviews with 30 middle-class women and men living in the midwestern United States. I will discuss these individuals' configurations of social and personal friendships, their inclinations to talk and judge with their close friends, and the significance they attributed to being there for friends. I then analyze turning points in these adults' friendships, focusing on dilemmas of friendships with co-workers and the value of friends during tragedies. A consideration of dialectical themes and functions of adult friendships closes the chapter.

Configurations of Social and Personal Friendships

These 30 interviewees ranged in age from 28 to 64 years old. Seven of the 15 women were married for the first and three for the second time; three were divorced and two were widowed. Their occupations included three secretaries, two secondary school teachers, two administrative assistants, two homemakers, two residence hall directors, one floral designer, one housekeeper, one part-time waitress, and one guidance counselor. All had children, with a mean distribution of 2.4 per woman. Eleven of the men were married, one was divorced, and three were single. Their occupations included three university professors, three business executives, two college counselors, one army officer, one assistant manager, one administrative assistant, one industrial arts instructor, one salesman, one building contractor, and one graphic designer. Of the men who were or had been married, all but one had children, with a mean distribution of 2.6 per man.

These women and men described common as well as distinctive social circumstances and relational practices in characterizing their various friendships. Overall, they distinguished among three generic gradations of friends: (1) numerous role-related acquaintances, (2) an array of moderately involved and primarily activity-oriented "social friends," and (3) a select handful of close friends. A positive disposition toward the other person was a general feature of all of these relationships, and changing interactions or circumstances could result in individuals gradually or suddenly shifting from one level of involvement to another. For all of the employed respondents, excepting those mentioning spouses and friends made while growing up, the work setting was the principal source of their current closest friends.

Both genders spoke extensively about surface friendships in societal realms, implying considerable differentiation in degrees of trust, revelation, and common interests among them. They mentioned "workplace acquaintances," "casual friends," "closer acquaintances," and "neighbors" whom they saw frequently, enjoyed and "exchanged pleasantries" with at work or around the neighborhood and community, but in whom they did not confide. A closer class of friends were "work friends" or "business friends who I see on a social basis." Brain (1976) stresses how business often relies on and may cultivate good faith between individuals, which, coupled with mutual benefit, equitable and satisfactory return, and generosity, can produce a situation where "the values of friendship may override the values of the commercial exchange" (p. 146). In such cases business-oriented reciprocity paves the way for personal pleasures, alliances, and good will, as well as social integration. Men and women who engaged in work less explicitly mediated by monetary exchange spoke similarly of closer co-workers, that is, "colleagues," with whom they shared projects and solved professional problems.

James, a married, 36-year-old university professor and father of three describes the pivotal role his work plays in constituting a field of acquaintances and potential friends:

> I have a lot of acquaintances, a lot of people I call friends that I only see once in a while and I frankly don't think of much except when we're together, you know. Most of those are professional. Most of those are people I come in contact with through work that I consider friends that aren't really sharing kinds of friends. I have very, very few that I would consider true friends. That I would really sit down and tell them what's bothering me, or what's upsetting me, or expect them not to do anything with that other than just to listen and to take that in. To me a real friend is one that you can call up and would not be a surprise to call up and talk to you about anything at all. It has nothing to do with the purpose of the

call. It has nothing to do with, you know, why you're there. I don't have very many of what I would call really, true, close, close friends. A lot of acquaintances.

I can think of one that's probably grown to the point where he and I are really good friends and when we're together, we share personal concerns and personal frustrations and those sorts of things. Um, and he potentially could be my best friend. But we don't see each other very often, and when we do, we're very good friends, and when we're not together, we don't even think very much about each other. But it takes a professional reason or excuse to get together.

Several persons referred to "social friends" as personal ties transcending the work setting and involving some talking as well as doing things together (often in couples); "you consider them friends," although "to a lesser degree" than your close friends.

Though similar in their expectations of close friends for confidential discussion and dependable assistance, these men and women noticeably varied in describing their inner circles of friends. Resembling extant research, 7 of the 11 married men considered their wives to be their best friends because of their shared intimacy and their wives' understanding of them. When asked who his closest friend was, Robert, a 39-year-old professor gave a typical response:

Probably my wife, I can say more to her and have more discussions. The nature of the relationship; we share so much and have so many close dealings. If a marriage is going to work, that friendship's got to be there. If you're not close friends, and you can't confide in each other—that's a trite phrase, "My wife is my best friend," but it ought to be. There's nobody else you're going to be closer to or have to share more emotional things with, than a husband or wife.

In contrast, only 3 of the 10 married women referred to their husbands as best friends. Instead, many of the women were more inclined to discuss personal concerns with their best female friends than their husbands. Donna, a 28-year-old secretary and mother of four contrasts her attachment to her husband with that of her best friend:

They surveyed a lot of women and they asked, "Who would you feel a greater loss for, your very best friend or your spouse?" And most of the women said their very best friend. And I would say that too; but I would never tell Mark. It would be a different kind of loss. Mark, I would physically lose, as far as being there, physically putting his arm around me and hugging me and telling me it's okay. But Alicia, I mean who would I tell all of my problems to? Who would I bitch to about Mark? This is awful. I don't have to bitch about her because I don't live with her, you know.

It's not that I don't love Mark or anything; I do. But when you live with somebody in this house, with this many people, tempers are bound to flare. To release that tension, I call Alicia. It's not that I love Alicia more than Mark. I don't know how to explain it. I would feel very lonely without Mark. And I wouldn't feel lonely without Alicia; I would feel lost. Does that make sense? Mark's like, "Yea, yea, I've heard this before. I don't want to hear it anymore." Where Alicia, no matter how many times I say it, she still listens. She says, "Why don't you get another job?" But she still listens.

Interestingly, several of these men divided their close friends into the one or two persons with whom they presently had "meaningful conversations" and trusted to share their inner thoughts and feelings with, and friends from prior eras of their lives. They discussed these "friends I've grown up with," "friends from school days," and "long-standing friends" as retaining considerable present significance and emotional value, though many of them had only been seen occasionally if at all for a number of years. These primarily memorial friendships seemed to symbolize periods of active, familiar friendships and to compensate for the meager time these men currently spend in cultivating close friendships with anyone other than their wives. In contrast, this category was virtually absent from the women's descriptions, apparently because they insisted on regular contact, activities, and lengthy conversations with their friends, including remote ones from prior residences in some cases, interweaving their present lives.

Though 11 of 15 of both the men and women said that cross-sex friendships (other than spouses) were possible, only two males and one female discussed an opposite-sex friend as being their closest, with each of these relationships formed and sustained in professional contexts. Moreover, reflecting prior research in characterizing their more general cross-sex friendships maintained at work or through spouses in couple encounters, two-thirds of the men stated they could trust and talk more freely with these women friends than their male ones. Meanwhile, roughly half of the women volunteered that "you can't be as open with men as with women." With a few clear exceptions, cross-sex friendships pursued for their own sake were incidental and contingent relationships in these persons' overall social matrices.

Talking and Judging with Close Friends in Adulthood

As we have noticed about friendship since adolescence, these persons' foremost expectations of close friends were "somebody to talk to and confide in" and "to be there when you need them." Although these primary and interrelated benefits of friendship are consistent across mature adulthood, the sheer practical and emotional scope and stakes involved in managing adult life magnify both the salience of a true friend's dialogue and help during a time of need, and the constraints on his or her availability. When these interviewees celebrate their opportunities to converse with close friends, it is not surprising to hear ongoing preoccupations with work, marriage, and family life permeating their accounts. Consider Donna's expectations of friendship:

> Well, to listen. I don't expect anybody just to drop everything when I call and sometimes with friends, you have to take what you can get because you don't share a life, actually. You share bits and pieces. If I'm really, really depressed and I need somebody to talk to, she will listen. And the same way for her, if she's really depressed, even though there are 25 other things I should be doing, I will take the time for her. The funny thing about it is, we hardly ever get to go out, just because of the kids. She's single, not married, and here I am trapped; I'm married with four kids. She loves the kids and everything, but because of that there's a lot of things we can't do as friends.

Despite the stringent limitations on their shared activities, this friendship fulfills Donna's ongoing needs for a trusted conversational partner:

> I can talk to her about anything—how I hate Mark today, sex, what I did when I was 16—that I wouldn't tell anybody else in the whole wide world, things like that, personal. She could write a book and put me to shame if she wanted to. She's the only person in the whole wide world that I would be that indepth about my life with. I don't even do that with Mark. But she can relate to me.

Similarly, Caroline, a married, 41-year-old housekeeper with two children, describes her closest friendship where caring, sharing, and conversation connect the friends and help them deal with the realities of their adult lives. For Caroline that includes her ongoing cancer treatments:

> Theresa, she's my closest friend. She was off work before I worked in May, and I still see her at least once a week. Or I call her or she calls me. She's someone I want to keep in contact with. Other friends I may not call them or you know we write each other letters or little notes, little postcards or little cheer-you-ups. If she's down on the phone, I'll send her a card, or if she knows I've had a treatment, she won't wake me up because she knows I'm sleeping. She'll send me a card or she'll call my kids and ask how I feel.
> We like each other. We're concerned about each other. I want her to be happy and she wants me to be happy. I guess what I like best is that I can tell her anything and it'll stay with her. She won't tell somebody else. I like that about her. And she's just a very sharing person. There is nothing selfish about her. She's got a sense of humor. I guess I like that, that's the

most important thing. She can laugh and cry at the same thing, about something bad, you know. And I guess laugh to keep from crying, but she looks at the good side of things, "It'll get better, you know. Well it can't get any worse, you know?" I think she's my best friend.

Like many adult friends, especially women's, Caroline's talk with Theresa is both personal and encompassing, and often occurs over the telephone:

Our families, our kids, our gripes about work. (laughter) You know when you talk on the phone with your girl friend, my husband will say—me and Theresa will sometimes talk an hour and a half and he'll say, "Good Lord, what did you talk about?" I say, "Oh, I don't know, nothing." He'll say, "Nothing?" And I'll say, "Well everything and anything: school, uh, our kids, things that happen at work, you know, things that we have in common—her husband, my husband, you know, girltalk." That's all I can tell him—girltalk. Because men aren't like that. Men are short and sweet. They say what they have to say and they're done, unless they're talking with a girlfriend or something. But they're more businesslike on the phone. They really don't associate—they don't really like talking on a phone.

The personal significance of her phone conversations with Theresa and her husband's quizzical reactions to them are readily apparent in Caroline's remarks. Her observations about males' telephone use, while somewhat consistent with Aries and Johnson's (1983) findings and perhaps descriptive of her husband, were not entirely borne out in the other interviews. Overall, the men did not emphasize and refer to regular and lengthy phone conversations with friends as often as the women did (two of whose friendships were long distance, "telephone friendships"). However, talking on the telephone was still important in maintaining most of the men's close friendships. Whenever face-to-face contact between friends was significantly restricted or uncomfortable lapses in supposedly close friendships occurred, the telephone was typically the most convenient option for "keeping in touch." In addition to the frequently noted shared interests and activities characterizing male friendships, a single, 35-year-old army officer, Ted, reveals the importance of calling each other to talk in his long-term friendship:

I've known Wayne—he grew—he lived down the block from me when I/we were kids, and we've known each other since we were 3 or 4 years old, and we still do lots of things together. He is just someone that I have first off, common interest in. We both fish and hike and camp together. Uh, he's also someone that, you know, if I've got a problem—I've had a bad day at work and I need just to talk with somebody and get it off my chest, and I can give him a buzz and he can talk to me. Or if he's got a problem, he'll give me a call.

Robert also views his ability to express himself as the definitive privilege shared with his closest friend outside of his marriage:

Anything that bothered me, anything that I felt about even on a deeper emotional level, I could confide in him. I think he's done the same thing with me. Things that bother you, that you really can't talk to anybody else about, other than my wife. There have been situations there, where again, the whole thing about the male relationship versus male/female, even husband and wife, there are some things you just need to talk to somebody else about. Could be something that has to do with the other relationship. You just need another opinion, or someone who can listen and understand you well enough that they can respond with some decent advice, or at least listen and offer some sentiment in reply.

Robert's friend provides additional perspective on events in his marriage. Being able to talk like this develops over time and requires awareness of what may irritate or offend a friend, according to Robert:

At this point we're comfortable with the relationship. You can say what's on your mind. You don't have to worry about the reaction. Plus we kid each other about some of those things. You know the more you're with a friend, and the stronger the friendship becomes, the more you learn personalities, what you can say and how much you kid a person and how far you can push with the sarcasm and the teasing before you're pushing too far. You learn that and the other person learns that. And so the give and take is there and you're comfortable with it.

Thus, for *expressiveness* to be viable in a friendship trust must be established in each other's *protective* communicative practices such as confidence, discretion, and demonstrated sensitivity to the other's vulnerabilities. Although friends range freely and widely in talking together, they may simultaneously withhold incompletely formed ideas or reactions to preserve the privacy of their own thoughts, and avoid saying what they are thinking to protect the other's feelings. Donna observes that even with Alicia:

I have this thing where I won't talk about something until I'm thoroughly sure what it is I'm feeling, because a lot of times I'll be depressed and not know why. . . . I make sure I know exactly what I want to say and what was troubling me. So in that respect, I don't always tell her what's on my mind. There'll be times when she'll be talking and I'll want to get off of the phone and go to bed. I won't tell her to shut up so I can go to bed. I would never do that.

Likewise, Kathleen, a married, 36-year-old, high school teacher and mother describes her reasoning and respect for her friend's feelings that restricts openness in their friendship:

> There are times when I think that it's inappropriate and she doesn't need my feedback at that point. There have been lots of times when something is on her mind or something is worrying her or bothering her. I don't make a comment about that. I ask myself, "Why do you want to say this? What purpose is it going to serve?" And if it is only to serve me, then what's the point if it's not necessary? So there are lots of times when I don't say something because I think it would hurt her, and it would be stupid and unnecessary. It wouldn't serve any purpose; I just don't.

Continuing dialectical tensions between expressiveness and protectiveness are closely aligned with the contradictory expectations for shared judgment and acceptance in adult friendships. Individuals often want and need to feel accepted, valued, and confirmed as worthwhile people, both in their role-related capacities and for their intrinsic qualities transcending specific social functions. Feeling constantly scrutinized and evaluated, these adults, and the men in particular, expected their friendships to be "comfortable" and to offer minimal anxiety and critical assessment. Meanwhile, their responses evidence considerable need for someone they trusted to honestly appraise and perceptively counsel them about various matters, including work-related problems and decisions, relationships with spouses, and doubts and frustrations in raising children. These are crucial areas where others pervasively evaluate and rate persons on an ongoing basis and where adults simultaneously measure their own successes and failures. Since these are principal contexts shaping and displaying one's sense of self as a competent and compassionate human being during adulthood, a person sometimes needs to "step outside of them" to view his or her comportment and decisions in a more disinterested manner. But how does one transcend these domains to reflect autonomously on notions like: How is one presently living and behaving? How clear or justifiable are one's priorities? Does one's commitment to work and community activities misguidedly limit one's devotion to family, or vice versa? Is one really acting in self's and others' best interests in these various areas, or unconsciously kidding oneself? For these persons, close friendship offered someone with whom to examine similar questions and to judge with who cared and fundamentally accepted them as people.

Since most issues requiring such discussion make men and women vulnerable and potentially resentful of others' judgment or interference, it takes time and tenderness to establish the necessary joint assumptions of benevolence, as described by Robert:

You tread that ground very softly at first. It starts at the level of, "Well, do you mind if I tell you this?" or "I happened to notice this," or "Did you ever think about this?" You ease into that and you find out that the other individual is comfortable hearing those types of criticisms. And I think it maybe happens with one individual, and then you can say, "Well, if you ever notice anything you want to tell me the same way, feel free." And I suppose initially you put up a little bit of a defense mechanism, but I think when you find out there's no attempt to inflict any emotional pain, then you tend to be more open with it in the future.

Donna stated that mutual acceptance comprised the foremost reason why she and Alicia had remained close friends:

I think, this is going to sound really corny but I really think that it's the truth, because we *accept* each other the way we are. She doesn't try to change me, and I would never try to change her, and I think that's why. Most people want, don't like this about you, or don't like that about you. There may be things she doesn't like about me, but she accepts them.

I could do something totally awful and she would still like me. I can be totally myself with Alicia, and she's really the only person that I feel like that. It's really hard, because I don't get to go out and meet new people and make new friends. My lifestyle is really limited, extremely limited.

Donna further remarked that while she and Alicia can criticize each other, they "don't do it very often" because of their sensitivity to one another's vulnerable moments. The caring thing to do at such times is to hold one's tongue, "Right now, Alicia is so busy criticizing herself that she doesn't need any help. Even if I did find things at fault in her, I wouldn't tell her now. I feel like she's being so hard on herself, why should anybody else pitch in and help?"

As in many friendships, their shared tendency to accept and "baby" each other in facing daily ups and downs cultivates the trust necessary for discussing and, if necessary, mutually critiquing their private and public actions. Donna observes:

We talk a lot about work. That's my way of getting rid of the tension. She does know Patty [Donna's boss] and she understands, and that really helps. A lot of my stress is Patty, not the work load, but simply because of her immaturity. Alicia can relate to that. Mark doesn't want to hear it, he's heard it, you know, he's tired of it. But it's the only way I can get it out of my system is to talk about it. I can talk to Alicia about it. If I'm being unfair, or if I'm just being a bitch, she'll tell me. You know, "God, Donna, you're really being a bitch today." That makes me slow down and think about it; "Well yeah, I was being unreasonable. I am a bitch too, just like Patty, so we're even." And the same way with her. Sometimes she totally floors me with the things she's done at work.

These friends talk through and explore their personal frustrations as well as the social implications of their conduct. Although fundamentally concerned with each other's feelings and well-being, they also challenge actions that seem irrational and/or "unfair" to others, reflect poorly on either friend, or jeopardize their jobs or relationships. In this manner their friendship serves as a "double agency," weaving in and out of their public and private lives, serving both societal and individual integration (Rawlins, 1989b).

Terry, a 44-year-old husband, father, and college career counselor, spoke extensively about the tensions between judgment and acceptance in his long-time friendship with Mike as well. Though acceptance defines close friendship for Terry, it coexists with compassionate objectivity:

> I think it's somebody I can really be myself with. Everybody has different facets, and, uh, with a close friend I can reflect all those, and uh, I know that when they may not particularly like the side that they're seeing right now, it's still me and that it may be generated by something that caused me great pain or great anger, and they will help me work through it. Or they might tell me, "We think you're off base," you know. And I'll value that judgment, because it will probably be very objective, with a little bit of subjectiveness though.

A pivotal event in the development of their friendship involved the perceptive and empathetic discussion of extremely sensitive matters during a difficult period in Mike's life, according to Terry:

> Mike, uh, he's a regional salesman for a computer company, and he was from out of state and he would come through this area, and he would come in for a cup of coffee or meal or whatever and head out. And a couple of times I sensed that he wanted to talk about something, and it would just, it would almost get to the end of his tongue, but he just couldn't quite, you know, bite it off. And I just told him this one time, I said, "Mike you really seem stressed out, uh, why don't you tell me what's going on?" And I don't really know the exact, but I think that was what he was waiting for, is that somebody to say to him, that he trusted, that trusted the friendship or was compassionate enough to say, "You look like you're hurting guy, do you want to get it off your chest?"
>
> And we just must have caught him at a good time, because he told me about his family, you know he was having problems with his oldest son and his wife and all these things. And that really brought us together. Because he really laid his soul out there, and he knew that he was going to be judged, uh, possibly as an unfit father, uh, and he really bared it out there and it really brought us together.

Troubled relations with spouses and children are delicate matters for anyone, especially a midlife male, to reveal to others, even though they may deeply affect one's daily life. This situation was saturated with risks to Mike's self-image and Terry's good opinion of him and his family. Early on, Terry suspected Mike's desire to "talk about something" but refrained from pressing him, presumably communicating his acceptance of Mike as the proverbial "man who can take care of himself and who will tell others if he needs anything." Finally, he judged Mike as sufficiently "stressed out" and "hurting" to require extensive, though still risky, talk with his interested and indulgent friend. The apparent acceptance and comfort occurring during the ensuing conversation significantly deepened Terry and Mike's friendship.

Presuming their joint acceptance and affection, Terry states that each man continues to rely on the other for "concerned discussion, about what is happening to that person or how they're doing something or not doing something, and how that person, this other, how the friend thinks it is hurting them." In short, they care enough to monitor closely one another's actions. Reflecting the recurring tensions between judgment and acceptance regarding key concerns in many adult friendships, Terry indicates that proper parenting remains a highly salient issue of mutual appraisal in this friendship:

> There's been some times when, when Mike has said, "You know I really think you're too hard on your family; you're actually—what you want your son to do." It's hard to hear that, you know; it's really hard to hear that. Uh, but I value that because I know *he's* saying that and he's probably right to some degree. Because if he can see it, then somebody else can, and so there must be some merit to it somewhere along the line. Whether it's a large amount or a small amount, to me it doesn't matter. He has brought it to my attention; and I really should do something about that if I want to.

The issue of father–son interaction that once memorably warranted Terry's tender treatment of Mike occasionally provokes Mike's direct evaluation of Terry. Despite the acknowledged difficulty of hearing judgment of his parenting, Terry would rather receive it from his friend, because he assumes "there must be some merit to it" or Mike would not mention it. It gives him the opportunity to reexamine and perhaps improve his actions as a father. All things considered, he appreciates the compassionate objectivity of his friend.

Fondness for a friend's candid judgment persists as a testy, continuous, and jointly negotiated achievement, given the contrary expectations for an uncritical ear at moments in many adult friendships. For example, Kathleen recounts how changes in family and work arrangements, diminished contact, and too much criticism interacted in dissolving one of her friendships:

I had this one particular friend at work, and I was married and hadn't had a child yet, and she was not married at the time, and mostly we spent time at school, but occasionally after school we would do something—go for a Coke or something. And in the course of the friendship she got married, I got pregnant, and I had Ginny. And then she got pregnant, and very soon after that she moved to another school. And so I wasn't physically close to her all the time, so I didn't see her quite as much.

    And I noticed that ever since I had Ginny that she seemed to become a lot more critical of everything I said or did. When I would talk about something and really all I wanted her to do was listen, I got like an analysis of that—and I wasn't asking for analysis. I didn't say, "Don't give me an analysis, all I want you to do is listen." But I resented, I think, the fact that she seemed to be critical, and I could see the friendship disintegrate.

Perceiving and meeting the expectations of talking, listening, and judging with friends and of communicating penetrating appraisals and approvals of them across the disparate moments and circumstances of adulthood constitute hallmarks of robust friendship. In some instances, friends do not judge by tolerating faults and accepting limitations; in other situations, friends render judgments to keep people honest with themselves. But caring for a friend may justify both impulses at once. Overall, these adults disliked the word "criticism," which cannoted superiority and one-sided, gratuitous chiding. Accordingly, they stressed reciprocal listening between friends and expressing judgments primarily when they were requested, and/or when an assessment involved areas where a person possessed clear expertise. In such cases, they usually attempted to word their evaluations carefully and make their observations as constructive as possible, conveying affection for and confidence in their friends along with their suggestions. David, a divorced, 52-year-old executive with four children, summarizes:

I think there's a kind of criticism with grace that friends have; with grace or with love, whatever you want to call it. It's more like critique than criticism. And if you feel that someone cares about you and someone is truly interested in what's best for you, it's not difficult to accept a critique from someone.

. . . But I really feel that the powerful ingredients of friendship are when you realize that you can sit down and you can talk about yourself, about your feelings, with someone else and they will listen. They will listen with caring and they will listen without judgment. And I think those are the things; that kind of dynamic is what bonds people together.

Being There for Friends

When things are on an "even keel" with family and at work, it is easy to take friends for granted, but when things go poorly or well in life, people want their friends to "be there" to talk to and to help or to celebrate. Reflecting the folk wisdom, "a friend in need is a friend indeed," and "a friend is someone who mutiplies our joys and divides our sorrows," being there when needed was the measure of true friendship for these adults. Lamentably, this gift of presence, so vital for friendship, is typically metered within a larger social problematic of coordinating life structures. One's closer friends are persons that one "makes the effort" to contact regularly; one "goes out of one's way" to see them and to "stay in touch"; and they do the same. One pursues other types of friendships largely in conjunction with the common schedules, activities, and role requirements of work, neighboring or in the larger community. Network researchers have called the former type, relationships of commitment, and the latter, convenience (Feld, 1984).

But what is the nature of the commitment of close friends in adulthood? How is it communicatively and behaviorally accomplished, given two friends' concurrent involvement in their respective, multiple, social realms and their often conflicting needs for independence from and dependence on each other in managing their lives? With some overlap, differing commitment practices composed and expressed agentic or communal tendencies even in these adults' close friendships. And, with a few clear exceptions, the males' accounts of committed and close friendships exhibited agentic themes and the females' communal ones. Whereas both men and women expected close friends to be there to help and talk to them, by and large, they etched these needs differently in time and tangible encounters.

Mutual needs for assistance and discussion are routine matters in communal friendships. "Regular contact" means habitual as well as conscientious attempts to spend face-to-face time together as often as possible, weekly if not more frequently. In the interim, phone calls and sometimes notes or cards keep the friends abreast of evolving day-to-day concerns, moments of self-doubt, and minor or major triumphs or challenges at work or with one's children. Friends' daily lives are always sufficient grist for conversation, and whether a person "just" wants to talk or needs ready advice or relief, a close friend will "be there" for her or him. Commitment in these bonds is special precisely because it reflects a mundane and relatively continuous interweaving of lives.

Although also important in communal bonds, commitment in agentic close friendships is expressed by someone actually or potentially "coming through" when it is "really" needed, "in a pinch," "when the chips are down." Though "regular contact" is also part of such agentic commitment, the words mean something different as the time between interactions specifically devoted to the friendship may vary widely according to its circumstances. Individuals may see each other quite frequently at work, for example, yet have difficulty scheduling "quality time" or discretionary opportunities to speak or spend time together "as friends." The basic independence and separation of lives maintained in agentic friendships usually mean that "regular contact" is more drawn out in time than in communal ones and less organized around everyday concerns. Consequently, the commitment described in close agentic friendships evinces a "heroic" flavor. One feels or learns that one can count on a friend for counsel or help in moments of need, and tacitly indicates reciprocal availability. But these moments are typically conceived as transcending ordinary problems and requiring special effort on the friend's part. Ironically, this very conception may make friends less inclined to seek each other out because they may not want to admit to having such problems or to trouble the friend. Meanwhile, both friends may feel they can count on each other should a "real" need arise.

The differences between communal and agentic senses of commitment are amplified by their usual emphases on the contradictory motives of affection versus instrumentality. Communal friends envision their joint availability and obligations as growing out of caring for each other as intrinsically valued human beings within a shared relationship that comprises a worthwhile end-in-itself. Although both friends benefit from their involvement and efforts on each other's behalf, these actions do not fundamentally derive from a calculation of reciprocal return. Rather, each person views their friendship as a basic existential condition of their ongoing individually yet interdependently conducted lives such that the friend's happiness or sadness directly affects self's well-being.

The allegiance of agentic friends stems more from instrumental needs and reciprocated capacities for practical and emotional relief. Continuing affection and involvement with each other are important, but remain primarily contingent on personal availability and other priorities. Emphasizing individual freedom and rights, agentic friends dislike the concept of obligation in the sense of mutual responsibility applied to friendship. They want to avoid feeling dependent on one another, and they are not comfortable "owing" others, including friends, anything. Ironically, although this mutual stance seems to inhibit sustained integration and interconnection of lives, the intermittent quality of such friendships invokes instrumental assistance at important junctures or "out of the blue" phone calls or letters to attest to their continuity.

Despite variations in agentic and communal emphases in their practices, all of these adults' friendships required time together, either face-to-face or over the phone. Consequently, being there for one's friend usually demanded "making" or "taking the time" for him or her.

Time constraints were cited throughout the interviews as causing problems between friends. Kathleen's remarks are typical:

> The most trouble? I suppose that it might be time. I would have to say that ever since I had Ginny, having to share time with her and with my husband and with my job, that I find lesser and lesser time to develop or spend time with other people. And so that's probably why I find I spend more time with people like at work and stuff, because they are there, you know, and I can talk to them during the day.

Time limitations compel persons to revise their conceptions or expectations of friendship and/or combine them with work affiliations. But unavailability due to lack of time can find friends adversely interpreting each other's actions according to James:

> When we're in a bad mood, it's easy to think that if the other person doesn't have the time or take the time to listen, then that means we're of less value as a friend. And that snowballs to the point where you think this person isn't interested in you.
>
> Um, the biggest problem I have, I guess, in friendly relationships is making the time away from everything else that we do to, to cultivate it, to make sure the person understands that I care, and that I'm willing to listen. Sometimes you have to schedule that, you know, just like everything else. And if you approach it as an effort and as, I don't want to say as work, but it takes a lot of effort, I think, to make sure that you're maintaining a friendship.

The adult time crunch can make developing or cultivating friendships resemble another job, requiring scheduling and effort to make them "work." Even when one's basic premise is caring, as James implies above, the pressures of larger social configurations convert the words describing friendships into instrumental and cost effective predicates. Consider David's comments:

> Probably competition for time certainly strains commitments, even though I think friends have to understand. I don't think friends demand the time, but I think when you're caught up and getting on with your lives and all the other things that go on around you that take time, the time that you don't have available for your friends I think can eventually become a strain. It's an investment of time.

David's references to "competition for" and "investment of time," coupled with James's previous allusions to a friend's "interest" and "valuing" call to mind a principle of economics that, "The rate of interest is the price of time" (Hicks, quoted in Brown, 1959, p. 273). How much time can someone afford to "invest" in a friend? Might that time be better "spent" elsewhere, in effect, yielding a better return on one's investment? How does one justify "interest" in another person for his or her own sake within such a dominant utilitarian calculus? The prevalence of such language in "accounting for" problems among friends reveals how thoroughly economic assumptions permeate these persons' thinking about friendship, even when attempting communal ones, and ultimately how little control they have over their schedules as enactments of the values of their surrounding social systems.

Consequently, friends must understand their constricted availability to each other throughout adulthood. But resentments persist and dissolve attachments when supposedly close friends "let me down when I needed help," or could not "be there" or "show up" for weddings, anniversaries, reunions, or parties. They also begrudge friends who do not understand why they cannot "make it" to specific activities, events, or functions. People end up judging their friends' availability according to a combination of negotiated expectations, relational precedents, and the priorities and associated schedules of their respective life structures. Even so, because of the definitive anticipations and instances of close friends either being there or not during distressing or joyous moments, crucial events in one's adult life usually involve one's "true" friends and pivotal events affecting friends will rearrange one's own endeavors.

Turning Points in Adult Friendships

One's actions, difficulties, and decisions acquire expanded personal significance during adulthood due to the increasingly unfavorable ratio between time lived and time left to live and a growing awareness of one's own and loved ones' vulnerability and mortality (Neugarten, 1968). Meanwhile, people realize the often irreversible and cumulative effects of prior choices and commitments, their reliance on others in so many areas of life, and the multiple social consequences of their own conduct. Moments with friends help constitute and are viewed against this emerging backdrop of living-life-for-keeps with its intensifying sense of sadness and potential for tragedy. Adults describe the positive and negative turning points in their friendships as emerging with little fanfare on some occasions and with conspicuous urgency on others from the practical circumstances of their everyday lives.

Predicaments of Work-Based Friendships

Because of its centrality in organizing adults' lives, many dilemmas of friendship develop in the workplace. A recurring problem is identifying one's real friends, given the contradictions between competitive social systems and the favored social style of friendliness (May, 1967). James believes this ambiguity is worsened in his service-oriented occupation as a professor of biology:

> You know a lot of acquaintances, and (pause) I think that within the professional area they probably think of me as doing my job. You know, and I don't know—it's hard for me in my job, which is very service-oriented, to, to distinguish between um, being someone's friend and providing a service that they need, you know, at the time. That's why I'm calling most of those acquaintances. Because most of the time I'm giving what they need then or they ask for, and I'm doing it because I'm considering it to be part of my job. And I want to do that. So it's—most of my people that I consider my really close friends, I once knew from circles, but I have no reason to owe. And I have no need to provide them with anything or need to work with them anymore, or want to work with them anymore.

Though he tends to consider his co-workers, "acquaintances," James clearly articulates his workaday difficulties in discriminating between "being someone's friend" and "providing a service." Apparently, these activities blur because his job often requires him to give someone "what they need" or request, which closely resembles the instrumental reciprocity and periodic responsiveness to needs characterizing agentic friendships. These similarities are probably compounded when the "emotion work" of his job includes maintaining an ongoing, personalized, and positive relationship with his colleagues (Hochschild, 1979).

The telling difference for James is that his profession *compels* him to meet other persons' needs, whereas he *chooses* to share with his friends, having "no reason to owe" them. For him, the edifying feature of his friendships is the voluntary giving involved and the absence of institutional obligations and requirements. His willing assistance apart from professional "circles" symbolizes his person-qua-person regard for his "really close friends" (Suttles, 1970).

But many friendships begin or persist on the job, which repeatedly presents quandaries of deciding when given work situations or relationships primarily involve friendship or professionalism. Consequently, when James approached a presumed friend at work for consultation about personal worries directly involving his own career commitments, he was also inviting confirmation of their friendship as transcending

their vocational roles. However, as James described above, his associate
was in turn free to view the request as a matter of work or friendship:

> When I was feeling a lot of guilt about my family and having a lot of
> problems relating to my responsibility to my family and my wife because
> of work, um, there was one person that basically blew that off and said,
> "That's one problem you're going to have to deal with, and that's your job
> and just go on." And I did. And at that point I lost a lot of ability to relate
> to that person. I still have a lot of respect for him professionally. But I don't
> think he was willing to try to take the risk to understand what I was saying
> at that time.

James wanted another's opinions on a seminal anxiety of working
adults, namely, the proper balance of duty to family and to career.
Anticipating (perhaps naively) the expansive insights and concern of a
friend, James encountered the narrow injunctions and indifference of a
bureaucrat, which nullified James's former personal regard while retaining his professional respect for him. But the segmented conception of
assistance defining agentic, occupational friendships, confused with the
beguiling ethic of friendliness in work affiliations, sets up many people
for similar disappointments.

While such seemingly arbitrary choices between personal and professional responses frequently cause problems in loosely tied work friendships, too much enmeshment causes difficulties as well. Kathleen
recounts how her affiliation with Heather unfortunately entangled work
and friendship:

> My relationship with Heather began professionally and we went to things
> professionally. Then I mean she would call me a lot; I mean I liked her, she
> was nice. The problem with Heather for me was that Heather is a
> smothering person to be a friend with, and Heather likes to possess you
> and Heather wants to control you, and Heather is—she's not rude about
> it you understand, but she wants you to do it her way, and she wants it to
> be her idea, and she wants that in a friendship, not just professionally and
> not just in a classroom. And I guess I didn't realize how intensely awful I
> resented that until we were finally in the same building together and I felt
> like she was running my life.
>
>   And I think I resented her a lot because on the one hand, I liked her as
> a person, but I hated working with her, just hated it. I couldn't come to
> terms with liking her as a person and hating to work with her.

Kathleen deeply resented Heather's overall control in this tightly overlapping personal and professional relationship, with its "smothering"
spillover from work into private life. Although their friendship's extensive contact constricted her independence in and out of work, she
seemed to resent most deeply how her personal affection for Heather

muddled legitimate reservations about despising to work with her. In her eyes, both the friendship and the professional relationship were unsatisfactory due to their intermingling. Eventually, she chose to ease off her emotional ties and redefine their affiliation as a professional acquaintanceship or "work-based friendship" (Laumann, 1973):

> It's not the kind of friendship I want to have, and I think that is why I ultimately rejected Heather and what went with it, and literally I distanced myself. And so now I can be an acquaintance, professional-type friend. And occasionally I might go shopping or something with her, but I don't want to talk to her every night on the phone. Sometimes I don't even talk to her at school, and that's okay, too. That's just—I think that at sometime, surely if you're of sound mind, you have to resent the control.

Despite the justifiable, agentic calculation of interpersonal distance Kathleen portrays above, she also developed another, more communal friendship at work with Mandy. After working together and doing things in couples for a few years, she and Mandy became close friends. She narrates key changes in their personal bond:

> One of the things that brought us closer together was when John lost his job—before he had his current job—and she was going through a bigtime crisis. Bigtime, because he was, she felt he was not doing everything he should do to get another job. And it was driving her crazy, and I think a lot of pressures with money, and having to defend John all the time was where that came from. And I really think that was a turning point because I was there for her and listened a lot, just listened a lot, held her while she cried, and I think that was real hard.
>
> That was a really hard year until like John like kind of fell into this job and got started, and she saw it was going to be okay. I mean I think she had contemplated divorce, and that was hard too, because she really felt like she loved him. But she didn't feel she could live with him the way things were.
>
> This year we're kind of at a pivotal place. I would have to say Mandy is having a very bad year professionally, and she hates teaching this year. And she is the most disorganized she has ever been in her life. . . . It's like she is feeling bad about herself and so I have become her organizer. It's like I have picked up; where she normally would do things, I have just done it for her and said, "It's okay, it's okay." And I've been there to reassure her and said, "It's going to be okay." She has been thinking of going back to school and picking up classes so that she can do something other than teach. And I have said though I would miss her terribly, and I would miss her encouragement, I think she needs to go and do something else. If I had $3,000, I would give it to her and say, "Here, go to school this summer."

Though these women work together, activities of caring primarily constitute this friendship. Kathleen views as especially crucial for their bond the "really hard year" when she "was there" for Mandy, spending considerable time listening to and embracing her during her husband's unemployment and their related financial and marital difficulties. Clearly, these were acts of committed generosity, not merely episodic, instrumental assistance. During the present school year, Mandy's bad feelings about teaching and herself have occasioned extra work and comforting by Kathleen. Again, such aid and bolstering, while work-related, plainly reflect Kathleen's personal concern for Mandy. Even though she would deeply miss Mandy's presence and encouragement at work, she does not possessively insist on her dependence. Rather, she reports strongly encouraging her to pursue a career change, maintaining she would finance her friend's further schooling if she could.

However two co-workers manage the internal dialectics of their friendship, being known as friends shapes how others perceive their autonomous and jointly produced actions in and out of the work setting. As Paine observes, "For it *is* true that one is judged, in may ways, by the kinds of friends one has. This view recognises as a fact that friends, at least, are persons of one's own choosing; that they are one's own responsibility, and eventually become a part of one's social person" (1969, p. 511). Acknowledging its repeated occurrences during his career as a business executive, David describes in detail the rhetorical exigencies and conversational management of a double-edged predicament posed by one of his friendships:

> In work situations what typically happens and what has happened to me several times throughout my career is that I've found myself in a position of having to support a friend through some kind of crisis or problem or conflict and in my support of that friend, I placed my own career in jeopardy. That's happened to me several times. It's a very tough decision to make—it came to "Am I going to honor my friendship or am I going to cover my own butt?" Most likely people choose to cover themselves.
>
> I can think of an occasion that occurred recently in which a friend of mine was involved in a project, which was a very critical project, and I had recommended and supported him for that project, and on many occasions I had gone out of my way to talk the project up and talk about what a good job I thought this person could do. And as the project neared its completion date, it became apparent to everybody, including myself, that this guy had blown it! Absolutely blew the project. So here I am in a position as an executive with the company of having to make a resolve of how do I deal with the fact that I have personally aligned myself with someone who has failed to meet their obligations.
>
> What I did—I tried very hard to own up to this and I was aware of the fact that it came down to a my career versus my do-I-support-my-friend? type deal. and I decided that I would be honest about it. I confronted my friend and I said, "Look, I've supported you. This is what I've invested into it—I think you've blown the deal and I have no way to cover for you."

He thanked me for that and said, "I know you're right." And he said, "I appreciate your support. I appreciate your being honest with me now, and I'd appreciate anything you can do to help me get out of this mess."

And so what happened is that he and I talked together about how best to recover from the situation. We talked it through; we put together a plan, and it worked real well. People remembered more of how he recovered from his problems than they did about the fact that he blew off the original deal. So we came away both feeling much better about it.

This narrative presents generic features of a relational dilemma that occurs in many guises throughout life when the actions and commitments of friends are caught between public and private standards and scrutiny. Thus it exemplifies moral dilemmas occasioned by and managed through friendship practices.

David observes that supporting friends during problematic circumstances has often jeopardized his own career. In such cases the ethical question arises of doing what is right or what is expedient, "Am I going to honor my friendship or am I going to cover my own butt?" He conceives these situations morally, while suggesting that people will typically act in a self-serving manner.

He describes a case where he strongly recommended and publicly supported a friend for "a very critical project." Of course, vigorously "talking up" and promoting this person conspicuously associated David with his handling of the job. Consequently, both David and his friend's corporate humiliation loomed as the man's mismanagement of the project with little time for repair became common knowledge. Interestingly, David formulates the quandary at this point in self-centered, administrative terms with no mention of friendship, "So here I am in a position as an executive with the company of having to make a resolve of how do I deal with the fact that I have personally aligned myself with someone who has failed to meet their obligations." Rendered in this way, a steely eyed, self-protective solution seems in the offing.

But David tried diligently "to own up" to the multiple obligations composing the situation. On the one hand, David's friend did not fulfil his obligations to the company or to David. The shared expectations of their work-based friendship probably prescribe each man's competent organizational performance, especially in matters directly affecting each other's well-being. On the other hand, while David must meet the company's requirements as well, what are his obligations to his friend? Their friendship's conditions probably also include the concerned personal treatment of each other as human beings. Sometimes, however, "when push comes to shove" on the job or in other public situations, individuals renege on such private and often tacit accords of friendship. But David reasserts the "fact" that it constituted an encompassing ethical dilemma, not merely a one-sided instrumental choice, "it came down to a my career versus my do-I-support-my-friend? type deal." He decided to "be honest about it."

I describe David's confrontation with his friend below as a "reckoning," for two reasons: they settle their accounts of the unfolding problem as friends; and they determine together a direction to go in handling the problem, which simultaneously keeps their friendship on course. I want to annotate David's representation of their conversation as reflecting a candid, mutually, articulated vision of their predicament:

David speaking:

> "Look, I've supported you." (I have been a friend to you in this matter so far.)
>
> "This is what I've invested into it." (But my good judgment is now publicly at risk.)
>
> "I think you've blown the deal." (You have let down the company and me as a friend.)
>
> "I have no way to cover for you." (Your imminent failure is clear to everyone, and I cannot accept or deflect the responsibility for your actions.)

His friend speaking:

> "I know you're right." (I have let down the company and our friendship.)
>
> "I appreciate your support." (I thank you for having been a friend to me so far in this situation.)
>
> "I appreciate your being honest with me now." (You have given me a chance to discuss with you privately as friends the realities of this situation.)
>
> "I'd appreciate anything you can do to help me out of this mess." (I acknowledge it is not your responsibility, but I would value your assistance as a friend in helping me to address the likely consequences of my actions.)

Following that exchange the two men talked and judged together and designed a plan that successfully resolved the substantial challenges of the project, achieving lasting public recognition of David's friend's recovery. I read this as a heroic narrative of loyalty in friendship and of two friends conversationally clarifying and then sharing the responsibility for addressing primarily one individual's problems in a high risk setting. It depicts the counsel of friends as a practical activity with positive moral value. As presented, mutually edifying practices resulted in a right answer that addressed several exigencies: (1) it relationally confirmed the two friends' humanity; (2) it fostered continuing good will in their friendship; (3) it rescued their public images in the organization; (4) it resolved the pragmatic problems at hand; and (5) it benefited the encompassing social order.

How persons enact availability, caring, assistance, and judgment in workplace friendships affects their nature and viability both as friendships and as occupational arrangements. Such friendships are dissolved, jeopardized, and enhanced by their relational practices for handling the inevitable contradictions among chosen versus compulsory independence and dependence, and highly interrelated versus opportunistically contingent affection and instrumentality. To complicate matters, friends also incur rhetorical significance as public reflections of each other's personal and professional judgment. Since individuals are judged by the company they keep, friendships may be tested when one friend's public or professional credibility is threatened by the other's conduct or performance.

Friendship and Tragedy

During midlife adults typically assume a position between generations where they are the children of aging parents and the parents of growing children. Their cares and responsibilities for both generations supplement their involvement with age peers in forming increasingly consequential life structures with manifold potential for experiencing both the joys and tragedies of mature adulthood. These adults described various poignant instances when the presence of friends during sad moments eased their pain, helped with coping, and above all, let them know that somebody cared. Jeffrey, a 40-year-old father of three and an industrial arts teacher, pensively recalled:

> When our last child was born, she was born with a birth defect, and you know, my friends, uh, were there and said that if they could do anything, uh, you know, that they would do whatever, pray for me or whatever. Uh, some of my acquaintances ignored the situation. You know, didn't know what to say so totally ignored it. And uh, my wife and I were going through a rough time, and we needed comfort from our friends because we didn't know how to deal with that situation. And it was nice to know that we had people that cared enough to uh, approach the unapproachable, you know, try to say what can't be said.

Few people are prepared to face such an unpredictable occasion for deep sorrow and anguish in their lives. Even so, friends can offer confirmation, comfort, and the gift of their presence. Jeffrey's remarks reveal his appreciation of the dignity and compassion in their friends' struggles to find the right words of solace in a situation where ultimately they may

not exist. Susan, now remarried, a 45-year-old mother of four and a
floral designer, also viewed her friends' continuing visits and attempts
to address the ineffable in comforting her as distinguishing their
genuine affection for her:

> Probably when my husband was killed, I found out who my, you know
> you find out who keeps, who are the ones who keep coming around after
> the funeral, and really care abut you, and put up with your grieving. Then
> there's the ones who just, you know, I did my duty, went to the funeral
> home, went to the funeral. Now I'm, I don't know what to say to her now.
> So they don't come and see you or phone you or anything.

Susan views the earnest and particularized caring of her friends as
meaningfully transcending social duty. Their persistent indulgence and
contact helped relieve the lingering moments of her grief. And not
knowing what to say did not prevent their repeated visits from composing reassuring statements.

There are also times when the active practical assistance of friends
nonverbally expresses their profound concern and affection for someone
struck by tragedy. Terry will never forget his friends' unsolicited and
comprehensive efforts and attention following the sudden deaths of his
mother and his father. His heartfelt gratitude for their actions is still
apparent in his recollection:

> Both my parents died within less than two weeks of each other. Totally
> unexpected and this was three years ago. And I had three of my high
> school friends, one was my best man, one was his brother and one was
> this guy I was telling you about [Mike]. None of them live in this state.
> They all live outside of this state and this happened so quick, and with
> such suddenness, it was such a total devastation to us, and we have a very
> small family. I was emotionally drained and trying to care for my sister
> who was making the pain even worse because of her attitude and tearing
> me apart because we were not friends. I was a lost man.
>
> And these three showed up on the day of the funeral, totally unan-
> nounced, they called each other, and from that point on handled every-
> thing. I mean they came to the house and virtually handled everything
> and sort of protected me. I mean they made sure I was taken care of; they
> knew I needed some kind of, of shell. They knew I needed some kind of
> help and they provided that for several days. And if it wasn't for that, I
> don't know what I would have done. I mean, I mean to this day it means
> so much to me.
>
> I mean it was the first time I broke, um, when they came in it was, if
> you've ever had a death in the family, uh, you cry when you see loved
> ones in your own family. But when these people showed up, I knew they
> didn't come because they were family, pure-blood-type family, but be-
> cause they cared. Nothing was expected of them. I didn't call them; I
> didn't think about it. They showed up because they felt they could do
> something for me with the understanding there's nothing asked in return,

there was no payback. . . . And that really to me was the embodiment of friendship. They just flat out dropped what they were doing and they all came with their families.

Terry's narrative celebrates the special caring of his devoted friends during this deeply trying and affecting ordeal. He emphasizes their sympathetic understanding and responsiveness to his multiple subjective and utilitarian needs, and the fact that they voluntarily traveled considerable distance to be there for him without being called or expecting recompense. Noticeably, their sensitivity and generosity of spirit contrast with his frustrations in dealing with his sister, whom he did not view as a friend. The tears he shed for "the first time" when they arrived exemplified his willingness to express and share his grief with "loved ones," comparable in trust and emotional resonance to family, but there solely "because they cared." Reflecting on these events, he praises their actions as "the embodiment of friendship."

Conclusion

Throughout adulthood friendships are negotiated within continuously evolving configurations of social roles and affiliations. Seldom purely dyadic endeavors, they typically develop as part of the friends' embracing activities of work, marriage, parenthood, family, neighborhood, and community life. In this milieu of socially sanctioned adult responsibilities, friends often assume auxiliary roles, adapting to the exigencies of the other domains while ideally supporting and helping an individual to manage and experience them favorably. The potentially idiosyncratic, highly contextual, affectively based, and mutually negotiated practices of friendship allow it to operate as a "double agency," coursing in and out of private and public situations, facilitating both personal and social adjustment, integration, and goals (Hess, 1972; Rawlins, 1991). Nevertheless, the contingent status and unclear expectations of friendships in diverse settings also can produce anxiety and uncertainty about who one's friends really are.

In the face of busy schedules, physical separation, and friendship's voluntary and conditional standing in their role clusters, many adults' bonds persist because of the flexibility afforded by their jointly enacted freedoms to live independently yet also to depend on each other when necessary (Rawlins, 1983a). But dialectical tensions abound. How available can friends be for each other during adulthood, especially when they are dispersed geographically? Some dyads develop patterns of frequent, even daily, contact; others "touch base" monthly, seasonally, or even less often. What constitutes regular and satisfactory contact sustaining the emotional commitment between active (as opposed to dormant or recollected) friends is mutually negotiated on an ongoing basis, and usually recognizes developments and demands in other spheres of their lives. Yet if individuals cannot reconcile the tugs and pulls of their everyday schedules with the requirements of their friendship, a single incident or extended neglect may weaken or eventually dissolve their attachment.

Friends' expectations are rarely stated explicitly. And the tacitly negotiated privileges of independence and dependence, while permitting flexibility, can also generate uncertainty and ambiguity regarding the actual extent of their shared availability and obligations (Wiseman, 1986). Strictly speaking, friends are not compelled to "be there" for friends but choose to make the effort out of caring for each other. Significantly, this volitional basis heightens both the positive and negative connotations of friends' actions. Their presence at key junctures symbolizes personal regard, while their absence can imply indifference or pointed rejection. Anger, hurt feelings, unspoken resentment, and breaches occur when persons thought of as friends do not come through when they are expected to or needed; and joy, confirmation, and strengthened ties result from their making the effort.

Friendships can be strained by contradictory demands within the relationship for affection and instrumental assistance, judgment and acceptance, and expressiveness and protectiveness. Such tensions may be amplified and complicated when friendship overlaps with other adult roles and responsibilities. Accordingly, in pursuing friendships within their role repertoires, adults often formulate particularized and contextually determined expectations for their various friends. Distinct types of friends are associated with separate domains and moments of adults' private and public lives, serve fairly specialized functions, and may be excused from emotional or practical demands in a specific social arena (Weiss & Lowenthal, 1975). A "work friend" may not be expected to assist with a domestic crisis and a "neighborhood buddy" may never even realize one's needs in handling a career-related problem. By comparison, close friendships spanning diverse social roles and reflecting more emotional interdependence also increase possible obligations, conflicting priorities, and evaluative standards in handling given situations, and the resulting potential for both appreciation and irritation.

The vitality and problematics of friendship's "double agency" derive from its dialectical capacities both to reinforce and to unsettle personal and social worlds during adulthood. Most individuals' lives include positive and negative aspects, which are generally taken for granted in pursuing their everyday activities. However, emerging circumstances, for example, at home or work, may highlight formerly overlooked, disturbing, or changing features of the status quo. When this situation occurs, people like to talk to someone close enough to the situation to understand its particulars and to care about and support them, but also sufficiently detached to view and judge it reasonably objectively. Close friends usually fulfill this need (although it can be difficult to find others transcending these realms since one's spouse and work associates are often primary sources of friendship).

Judging together, friends may decide that an individual should maintain or adjust certain attitudes and/or actions in accepting things as they are, or that noticeable changes in one's personal orientation, behaviors, and/or circumstances are necessary. By rendering such opinions, however, a person risks being too intrusive and angering or hurting the friend and related individuals. Nonetheless, in favorable cases, talking and judging with trusted friends gets the weighty matters of adulthood off of a person's chest and into the rejuvenating play of absorbing conversation, helps articulate the meaning and implications of actions and choices, jointly establishes what is important to self and affected others, and provides nurturance, laughter, and enjoyment to keep life's challenges and tragic inevitabilities in perspective.

Two interviewees' words aptly close this chapter. Peter, a 58-year-old, married, father of four, and a business executive, observes:

> I think the older you get, number one, your situation in life changes; and number two, I think with maturity I think you learn how important friendships are. And although they are supposed to be everlasting, they can also be very, very fragile. They get bent edges and stuffed here and there.

And Kathleen reflects:

> Sometimes I think friendship is hard for lots of different reasons. But, after having gone through periods of my life that I can see when I really and truly didn't have any friends—and they are important too. And I guess I would pity someone who had never really experienced that special feeling when you have a really good friend, because I can't imagine being that alone, I guess. And I look at my mother and people her age and they begin to lose their friends, a lot of them. And I wonder what that would be like for me, to be that old and to lose my friends to death. And while that could happen, like Mandy and John are coming back from Fort Blades today and they could get killed in a car crash and I would lose my friend. But I know there will be a point in my life when lots of my friends will die, and I guess I cannot imagine what that will be like. It is kind of a scary thought.

Chapter 10

Friendships During Later Adulthood

The Legacy of Middle Adult Friendships

Due to occupational and geographic mobility, middle-class persons typically experience an assortment of friends and acquaintances across adulthood associated with different residences and periods in careers and family life cycles. Through mutual efforts at regular contact, some of these friendships remain active and important parts of people's lives. Others are maintained through sporadic interaction or correspondence, lapse into dormant connections with each other's past, or become memories.

Many older adults report that their closest friendships developed when they were younger and now live considerable distance away (Adams, 1985–86). These "old" friends are often "best" friends from a prior era who have invested the time and effort to sustain their bond over the years. Their separation in space and time has likely prevented them from routinely burdening each other or jeopardizing their jointly held favorable images (Hess, 1972). Such friends easily "pick up right where they left off" across the years, heartily enjoying their occasions of spending time together, exchanging letters and gifts, or talking on the phone. These lasting friendships reflect continual thoughts about each other as well as attempts to sustain actual contact (Harré, 1977). The meaning-giving work includes ongoing assumptions of benevolence about the friend's actions, combined with assumptions of continuity in their importance to each other, sometimes despite contrary evidence. These friends receive the benefit of the doubt and/or excuses are made for them if they have not been heard from for months or sometimes years. When they do write, call, or visit, these actions are often assigned more significance than analogous ones by relatives or other friends.

Thus, various blends of the actual and the imaginary underwrite the continuation of friendships across the expanses of adulthood. Especially

217

when concrete interactions are decisively curtailed, treasured old friendships persist partly as vital (and hopefully mutual) fantasies. In Laing's (1972) sense, while behavioral connections and observable exchanges preserve *friendships* as reciprocal and objective relationships, positive memories and personally meaningful associations sustain *"friendships"* as subjective (and possibly one-sided) fantasies. The luxury of sharing the "vivid present" with a friend in "growing old together" allows outward behaviors and inward experiences to intermingle and enrichen each other and the friendship (Schutz, 1970; Laing, 1972). Yet even when contact is stifled, particular "friendships" thrive due to either or both partners' ruminations and meaning-work.

However, in the words of a 64-year-old woman, "Time and distance take their measure." The long run of adulthood involves ongoing intentional and unintentional trials and impediments, with friends being tested, falling by the wayside, drifting away, and losing touch. Consciously and unconsciously, friends are sorted out, with social calendars, role commitments, and career moves functioning both as facilitators and disqualifiers of friendships. Friends who have stood these "tests of time" and circumstances assume special status, and close friendships increase in stability across the life course (Brown, 1981).

As the years pass, the continuity of specific friendships *documents* the persistence of selves and/or images of selves, as well as the concrete (or now imagined) social settings in which these persons were viable participants. These enduring friendships connect adults with still meaningful versions of their possibilities as human beings and rejected alternatives, transcending the finitude of "real time." As reservoirs of common histories and shared experiences, old friends are narrators and curators of the long-term coherence and significance of each other's lives. It is not surprising that well over three quarters of one sample of widows aged 50 or more years stated that no amount of effort could replace old friends (Lopata, 1973). In contrast, throughout life, new friends foster and reflect change and adaptation to altered conditions, though one implicitly compares them with one's "populated biography" of past relationships (Matthews, 1986b).

The Social and Personal Contexts of Aging

Being "elderly" in any culture means undergoing biological aging processes in conjunction with perceptions by self and others that one is "old." But since persons vary in their pace and evidence of biological aging and their ability and/or willingness to view themselves as elderly—and cultures fluctuate in their conceptions and treatments of old age—its onset and expectations reflect continuous negotiations among individuals, age cohorts, and their social orders (Blau, 1973). Societies using functional definitions view old age as beginning when biological decline affects one's capacities to do work, thereby limiting one's endeavors and indicating "the end of active adult status" (Clark & Anderson, 1967, p. 6). By comparison, formal definitions arise from arbitrary assignments of symbolic import to specific events. This latter approach has prevailed in American culture, which defines old age temporally. Legislation stipulating initial eligibility for Social Security benefits (age 62) and the Age Discrimination Act regulating mandatory retirement (age 70 for most types of jobs) legally characterize old age as commencing sometime during and surely by the end of a person's seventh decade (Clark & Anderson, 1976; Blau, 1973).

As throughout life, what is allowed and expected of older people is socially constructed and sanctioned. Until rather recently, it has been commonplace to assume that simply because a person is old, he or she is unwell, fragile, and in need of special attention and care (Matthews, 1986a). According to Mitchell and Acuff (1982), pervasive stereotypes such as "the elderly are generally sick, boring, lacking in sexual interest, mentally slower, withdrawn, unproductive, and so on" constitute "the stigma of old age" (p. 369). Actions reflecting such attitudes toward many elderly individuals strikingly recontextualize their experiences of self and others, with energetic and mentally astute older persons perceived and treated as deviants (Michell & Acuff, 1982). Such formal definitions and age-based preconceptions of older persons decreasingly correspond with functional realities in our culture due to medical advances and widespread improvements in life-style, diet, and exercise that extend physical and mental vitality. When these developments are coupled with retirement plans and health insurance policies that assure continued financial well-being, the possibilities of prolonged and active later lives multiply for these fortunately endowed persons. For example, some people may choose to work at gratifying jobs or to participate in professional or civic associations indefinitely, while others elect early retirement and vigorous travel and leisure. Thus, age norms are becoming highly flexible as a set of parameters, recognizing that images and actualities of aging are closely tied to historical moments and conditions as well as the health practices and financial wherewithal of social cohorts.

Whereas cultural contexts shape the experiences of entire cohorts of older people in various ways, the concrete contingencies of physical health and financial assets interact with habitual patterns of intimacy and sociability and others' availability in fostering the individual's degree of personal well-being and social participation during later life. Continued good health is essential for contentment as one ages. Reviewing 30 years of relevant research, Larson concluded, "Among all the elements of an older person's life situation, health is the most strongly related to subjective well-being" (1978, p. 112). Peters and Kaiser (1985) note two effects of health status on relationships with friends and neighbors. First, a person's physical and mental condition affects his or her capacity to do things with friends. As long as individuals and their friends are in good health, they are likely to continue many of the same patterns of contact and activities they have enjoyed throughout their adult years. But, as strength and mobility wane, the elderly individual must increasingly rely on healthy and dedicated friends and nearby neighbors to initiate activities and maintain affiliations. When this occurs, the mutual process of defining friendships begins to change, with jointly offered comfort and assistance progressively giving way to unilateral help from concerned others (Peters & Kaiser, 1985).

Sadly, persons with chronic health problems experience constricted choices regarding their activities and greater social isolation (Stephens & Bernstein, 1984). Diminished abilities to reciprocate may wither their pool of former friends; negative outlooks brought on by nagging illnesses may drive less devoted others away; and fading lucidity, speech, and vision may undermine the basic communication skills necessary for sustaining satisfactory face-to-face interactions with others (Stephens & Bernstein, 1984; Adams, 1988; Retsinas & Garrity, 1985). Such enforced solitude is especially disturbing since the support of friends positively affects a person's physical and psychological well-being, which recursively facilitate engagement in friendships in the first place (Ferraro et al., 1984). With this simultaneous cause and effect association of friendship and health status, the negative spiral linking health problems and inhibited social life is indeed a gloomy prospect for some aging individuals. Meanwhile, the poignant and unique destiny of the old is that eventually "the entire age cohort becomes physically frail" (Dono et al., 1979, p. 409), and markedly increasing numbers of friends are lost due to their deaths (Clark & Anderson, 1967; Hochschild, 1973; Matthews, 1986a).

Next to good health, adequate financial resources are crucial for dealing with the changing social circumstances and exigencies of aging (Larson, 1978). Persons of higher socioeconomic status maintain larger collections of close friends and confidants (Babchuk, 1978–79), more functional friends (Cantor, 1979), and more friendship support (Ferraro et al., 1984). Overall, affluent older people can afford to yield their institutional roles and make the transition to the ranks of the retired without seriously harming their morale (Lowenthal & Boler, 1965). In contrast, considerable research documents the stifled subjective well-being of the elderly of lower socioeconomic status, which heightens their vulnerability to negative conditions such as poor health and isolation (Larson, 1978; Lopata, 1979).

Despite the unavoidable biological changes and likely limitations on sociality of extreme old age, many stereotypes of later life do not correspond with many people's ongoing management of its realities. In summarizing their study of financially secure and healthy 60 to 82 year olds, Maas and Kuypers (1974) state:

> Whether one considers women or men, and whether one examines their psychological capacities and orientations or their styles of living, most of these aging parents give no evidence of traveling a downhill course. By far most of these parents in their old age are involved in rewarding and diversely patterned lives. Most of them manifest high levels of coping capacities. (p. 215)

Babchuk et al. (1979) also describe considerable involvement of the aged, including persons over 80, in voluntary organizations.

Recognizing persistent competencies and interests, scholars argue that the final period of the life course should be viewed as a career in itself, a conception that emphasizes older persons' active and conscious decisions and practices in purposefully shaping and adapting to their concrete exigencies and circumstances (Matthews, 1986a; Myerhoff & Simic 1978). Conceived in this way, old age, like the rest of life, continually involves both constraints and opportunities that individuals create and must respond to as they enact various patterns of solitude, intimacy, and sociability.

People sustain customary and satisfying social participation as they revise and relinquish various social roles and responsibilities of middle adulthood. Some persons highlight their remaining options for involvement and cultivate other possibilities, notably friendships, by selectively investing their time and energy; other individuals are content with less active or gregarious life-styles (Blau, 1973; Chown, 1981). In short, individuals typically establish practices and styles of friendship earlier in their lives (Tesch et al., 1981; Matthews, 1986a), though increased freedom and altered living arrangements during old age can also transform friendship patterns (Adams, 1985–86, 1987; Hochschild, 1973).

Ongoing, Gender-Linked Friendship Patterns and Changing Social Configurations in Later Adulthood

By and large, as their commitments to the parental responsibilities, occupational pressures, and civic obligations of middle adulthood diminish, the stage is set for healthy and financially secure older adults to engage in friendship as a primary endeavor (Brown, 1981). In gradually enacting this transition, individuals carry over various friendships as well as habits and patterns of friendship from midlife into their later years (Clark & Anderson, 1967; Matthews, 1986a). Based on recollections obtained from over 60 interviews with elderly persons, Matthews (1986a, b) describes in depth three primary friendship styles. Older persons exhibiting the "Independent" style refer more to circumstances than to specific individuals in describing friendships throughout their lives. Often resembling convenient, agentic friendships, their relationships are developed and maintained when situations allow them. As life structures change, so do these persons' main friends. Since the adults exhibiting this style primarily depend on the circumstantial availability of a pool of suitable others and not particular individuals to befriend, they are less susceptible to extreme grief over the loss of a given friend, which becomes commonplace during later life.

In contrast, the "Discerning" style reflects deep attachment to specific individuals, regardless of changing circumstances (Matthews, 1986a, b). Often, such friends were made in and/or recalled from earlier periods in the life course and do not always survive into old age. Similar to committed, communal friendships and the old friends discussed above, adults remember developing few of these friendships in their lifetimes and view each as irreplaceable, becoming vulnerable to much sadness and loneliness if they lose any one of them (Matthews, 1983).

Finally, the "Acquisitives" preserve bonds with friends from their pasts *and* remain open to forming new friendships as situations permit (Matthews, 1986a, b). As a result, they are likely to experience the personal integration and sense of continuity derived from enduring bonds, and the social integration and connectedness with present circumstances realized through developing what might be called "secondary friendships" (Adams, 1986) or "friendly relations" (Kurth, 1970). Matthews (1986b) does not discuss characteristic gender alignments in these styles, indicating through interview excerpts that both older women and men may exhibit them in recollecting their personal backgrounds and life experiences of friendship.

Whereas habitual styles of friendship remain salient, specific friendships continue to be negotiated within and contingent on each person's total configuration of social relations. If individuals have lived all or most of their lives in the same vicinity, they are likely to have a lifetime's array of friends and associates nearby to socialize with during later life. However, the prevailing middle-class pattern in our culture finds older adults retiring in the community where their occupational careers stabilized, often several relocations away in time and space from where they were born and raised (Bellah et al., 1985). Still others make a "final move" to a retirement community and/or warmer climates, requiring them once more to develop relationships with friends and neighbors. To the extent that married couples or individuals are accustomed to the interpersonal exigencies and routines of either staying put or relocating, granting good health and sufficient income, they are more likely to be practiced and reasonably satisfied with the social conditions their choices have produced.

Moreover, persons sustain and rearrange their life commitments differently depending on their preferred engagements in personal and social relationships. Overall, if individuals have been satisfied with limited social participation, preferring solitary pursuits and interaction with a small group of friends and family, they will probably strive contentedly to organize their interpersonal endeavors in later years accordingly, at least until they lose these favored others due to their relocations, disabilities, and/or deaths (Matthews, 1986b; Tesch et al., 1981). By comparison, persons who have always enjoyed considerable social participation in both sociable relations and close friendships are likely to configure their lives in ways fostering the continuation of these practices as long as they are able (Matthews, 1986b; Zborowski & Eyde, 1962).

The elderly tend to be friends with age contemporaries with similar life-styles, values, and experiences, the same gender and marital status, and residence in the same vicinity long enough for an attachment to develop (Heinemann, 1985; Peters & Kaiser, 1985; Rosow, 1970). In short, their probable friends differ minimally from the ones persons form at various points in the life cycle. Even so, age similarity is defined more broadly in later life than at earlier points because the period potentially encompasses several decades. Thus, being an age peer has more to do with sharing similar functional capacities and restrictions, cohort membership, and generational experiences, and relationship to the larger society than age per se (Peters & Kaiser, 1985; Rosow, 1970). Comparable age also increasingly involves a common sense of time, with the present shaped by an extensive past, limited future, and preparation for impending death (Marshall, 1975). However, as age peers die and available others noticeably decline in number during "old–old" age (75 years old and above), the elderly report more intergenerational friends (Brown, 1981; Usui, 1984).

Although many elderly people maintain some of their oldest and dearest friendships that are widely dispersed geographically and stem from both partners' changing addresses throughout their lives, practical restrictions foster more frequent interaction with and attachment to friends in their "immediate residential environment" (Adams, 1985–86; Peters & Kaiser, 1985, p. 136). Spakes (1979) observes, "With increasing age, the respondents tended to report an increasing number of their friends they feel closest to living in the same community" (pp. 283–284). The heightened likelihood of older people with longer time in residence making friends and neighboring with nearby elderly, led Rosow (1970) among others to advocate age-segregated housing and retirement communities to facilitate their social activity and integration. Even so, a given individual's orientation toward sociablility, lifelong patterns of friendship, and degree of choice in living situation are likely to mediate his or her satisfaction with and inclination to form friendships in any housing arrangement (Rosow, 1970; Sherman, 1975).

As we have noticed since young adulthood, the elderly primarily develop same-sex friendships; free standing cross-sex friendships are uncommon in old age. The extent of their occurrence is rather consistently documented with only one-fifth of the women in an unmarried sample (Adams, 1985) and a similar ratio of married and widowed women (Babchuk & Anderson, 1989) reporting a male friend. By comparison, Powers and Bultena (1976) indicate less then one-tenth of the women's and one-third of the men's friends in their study as being cross-sex bonds. Clearly, the pronounced statistical minority of elderly males would seemingly make these friendships an important option for them. However, social suspicions and norms as well as personal attributions of latent romantic or courtship interests persist in later life and inhibit involvement in cross-sex friendships (Adams, 1985; Rawlins, 1982). For the most part, cross-sex friendships are mediated by shared participation in an organization or club, friendship with a third party, or couple friendships (Adams, 1985; Lopata, 1979).

Friendship and Retirement

Keeping in mind the above issues, the effects of retirement on persons' social configurations depend on the centrality of work in arranging their earlier lives and therefore their friendships, their degree of liking for their occupations and/or co-workers, the timing of their retirement vis-à-vis their favorite associates, their ability to sustain contact with admired co-workers after retirement, their other interests and opportunities for sociality, their preferred style of friendship, and the existence and character of their marital bond. I discuss below certain modal patterns and sources of variation associated with men and women.

As a statistical group, middle-class men derive a sense of continuity and identity from the limited contextual changes linked with well-ordered careers up until retirement (Bott, 1955; Hess, 1979; Maas & Kuypers, 1974; Wilensky, 1968). Typically, their wide networks of instrumental acquaintances and agentic friendships associated in midlife with enhancing careers and assuming positions of responsibility in their communities dwindle in later adulthood with stabilized occupational and civic accomplishments. By the time they retire, they usually have a shrinking network of work-based acquaintances, a few closer friends developed during their middle years, and their wives as their best friends (Fischer & Oliker, 1983). In this scenario, retirement separates men from their primary arena of social participation and most of their daily interaction with friends, and increases their dependence on their wives for friendship (Blau, 1973).

Although this pattern coheres with many findings regarding retirement-age males, a few matters modify the picture in given cases. First, the issue of "retirement-age" is becoming progressively unclear. Even though money-making work is a fundamental organizer of most adult males' lives, men who dislike their occupations or co-workers increasingly have the option to retire early and configure their lives around part-time jobs, civic groups, personal interests, hobbies, or people that stimulate them more than working for their livelihood ever did. Thus, the statistically evident drop in the quantity of their relationships may be more than compensated for by their improved quality. Conversely, men in intrinsically satisfying occupations or with strong civic inclinations may continue to work or participate indefinitely, thereby retaining a pool of social contacts and friends. In either case, the timing of one's retirement relative to cherished work associates may facilitate or undermine continued association with them (Blau, 1961). Even if one remains working while others retire or vice versa, persons can always choose to devote the necessary time and effort to sustain mutual contact, just as they have with less available others throughout adulthood. Despite these possibilities, the modal tendencies of males across life suggest that many men practice friendships of convenience with their work associates. When they retire from work and give up public endeavors, these unrehearsed breaches in their accustomed social routines greatly reduce their social encounters and confer special significance (and demands) on their families and lifelong patterns of close friendship with their wives (Blau, 1973; Powers & Bultena, 1976).

By comparison, women, especially working mothers, experience segmented, tentative, and frequently interrupted careers across adulthood, which some authors argue prepare them to adapt to changing circumstances in later life (Hess, 1979; Maas & Kuypers, 1974). As the hampering of their friendship activities linked with the period of primary parenting responsibilities tapers off, women develop more acquaintances and friends than men do (Fischer & Oliker, 1983). It appears that the discontinuities and multiple contexts of their adult occupations can encourage them to make contacts and establish friendships with a variety of people in child-, community-, school-, church-, and work-related settings. In addition to friendships with their husbands, women continue to cultivate other close friends and acquaintances (Fischer & Oliker, 1983). In Roberto and Kimboko's (1989, p. 16) recent study of people aged 60 years and older, though a majority of both genders reported "having close friends throughout their lives," the women demonstrated a greater tendency to maintain particular friendships over the entire life course than the men, who had begun their ongoing friendships during midlife. In short, women seem more inclined than men to make and maintain both communal and agentic friendships across public and private contexts in later adulthood (Fischer & Oliker, 1983).

Obviously, whether or not a particular woman demonstrates this modal pattern depends on her friendship style and practices as well as how central money-making work and single-minded careerism have been in organizing her life. To the extent that her adult endeavors resemble the modal female pattern of combining and juggling work, marriage, children, voluntary associations, and friendship, her retirement does not produce especially significant changes in her social activities (although her husband's may). She approaches later life with interactional habits and types of friendship that foster ongoing intimacy as well as sociability. However, to the degree that a woman has emphatically organized her adult life around a profession or money-making career in the manner of the traditional male model, the gratifications of her occupation and co-workers, the timing of her retirement, her ability to stay in touch with appreciated associates, her avocations and chances for social interaction, her typical friendship style, and the presence and nature of her marital relationship become relevant concerns shaping her decisions about continuing to work or not. In summary, whereas retirement reduces the number of both men's and women's overall social contacts, the impact of this transition on their enjoyment and adjustment in later life depends on their customary interpersonal patterns both before and after they retire.

Friendship and Marriage

Key features of marriage viewed as a friendship and noted during middle adulthood also endure into later life. First, men need their wives to confide in more than vice versa (Babchuk, 1978–79; Chappell, 1983; Keith et al., 1984). Whereas husbands mentioned their wives most, wives cited their husbands least as confidants in a sample of persons 60 years old or more (Lowenthal & Haven, 1968). In another study, women's intimate friends accounted for almost as much of their overall interaction tallies as their husbands (Powers & Bultena, 1976). Next, wives also serve as their husbands' principal links with neighbors, relatives, and other friends (Chappell, 1983). Reflecting our discussion of patterns of sociality above, married elderly women do not consistently curtail their interactions with persons other than their husbands (Atchley et al., 1979) and are more inclined to speak with relatives and close friends than married older men are (Kohen, 1983). They tend to remain connected with a variety of persons outside of their marriage. Finally, women assume the caregiving role with their aging husbands more than the reverse (Chappell, 1983). Stoller reports, "Married women are institutionalized more frequently than married men, however, so husbands may not be quite as dependable as wives in providing long-term care" (1990, p. 229).

In view of these conditions, it is not surprising that older married women more often complain of loneliness than elderly married men, perhaps when they are overburdened and/or prevented from interacting outside the marriage (Blau, 1973). Men are considerably more liable than women to marry in old age (Chown, 1981). They continue to view their wives as their best friends in later adulthood and to limit other close ties. Yet as Hess (1979) observes, "While marriage is a mental and physical preservative for men, it is also an 'all the eggs in one basket' proposition, so that bereft of the one relationship, men have little else upon which to fall back except money and other material resources" (p. 505).

Although the marital friendship retains characteristic inequities and risks, it involves ongoing mutual benefits as well. Married persons report higher well-being than separated, divorced, or widowed individuals, though the ever-single exhibit comparable scores (providing further evidence for the satisfactions of continuous life-styles) (Larson, 1978). The married elderly require less formal support and overall do not seem to lack companionship (Johnson, 1983; Kohen, 1983; Larson et al.,

1985), even in "old–old" age (Babchuk & Anderson 1989). Finally and significantly, like other adult friendship patterns, couple friendships persist as a key basis for forming and maintaining interpersonal bonds with others (Babchuk, 1978–79; Kohen, 1983).

Friendship and Widowhood

Older women are especially likely to lose their spouses to death in later life; after the age of 75, 70% of women are widows and 30% of men are widowers (Chown, 1981). Though researchers have reported lower rates of interaction with friends following widowhood (Blau, 1961; Lopata, 1973, 1979), recent studies emphasize the continuity in the close friendship patterns of older married women and widows. It includes their rates of interaction with friends and relatives (Atchley et al., 1979; Ferraro & Barresi, 1982; Petrowsky, 1976), number of intimate friends (Babchuk & Anderson, 1989; Roberto & Scott, 1984–85), early formation and long duration of confidential close friendships, increased primary ties from work, stability of friendship network, and paucity of cross-sex friends (Babchuk & Anderson, 1989).

Although neither gender appears to be more socially isolated during widowhood than their married counterparts (Petrowsky, 1976; Ferraro & Barresi, 1982), men lose their foremost confidantes when their wives die. In contrast, widows are considerably more apt to mention at least one confidante (Lowenthal & Haven, 1968; Strain & Chappell, 1982). Lowenthal and Haven (1968) remark, "Despite the fact that there were about twice as many widows as widowers in this sample, women were more likely to have a confidant than were men (69 percent, compared with 57 percent)" (p. 398). Based solely on this probable, reduced intimate dialogue with a caring other, it is easy to see why widowers complain of loneliness more than widows do (Blau, 1973).

Nevertheless, several changes in widows' friendship patterns are evident. Overall, contact with former couple friends diminishes markedly with the death of one's husband, initially reducing their total pool of friends (Heinemann, 1985; Lopata, 1979). Meanwhile, widows progressively cultivate friendships with other single women (Arling, 1976; Heinemann, 1985), increase their daily contact with and receive more help from their close friends (Roberto & Scott, 1984–85), confide more in their trusted friends (Babchuk & Anderson, 1989), and participate more in pleasurable and socially supportive activities with friends (Lopata, 1979). The composition of their friendship networks gradually alters in reflecting their marital status (as well as potential cohort effects). In one sample, nearly two-thirds of the older widows's close friends were also widowed, with one-third married; the opposite ratio characterized the friendships of married women (Roberto & Scott, 1984–85).

Clearly, these heartening overall trends regarding widows' friendships are contingent on various factors. First, older women who retreat from society and center their lives around their husbands are at risk (Maas & Kuypers, 1974). As Lopata concludes, "In general, the greater a woman's dependence on the husband, or interdependence, the more every aspect of her life is disorganized when he dies" (1988, p. 115). Next, resembling all elderly persons' capacities to adjust, husbands' deaths disrupt women's lives and friendship networks considerably more when they have less education and financial resources to help them cope and sustain voluntary bonds (Atchley, 1975; Atchley et al., 1979; Heinemann, 1985; Hess, 1979). Third, once again, an individual's initiative, self-confidence, and prevailing orientation toward friendships affect her chances of developing them (Heinemann, 1985; Lopata, 1979). Finally, limitations linked with chronic aging reduce the size of older widows' (age 75 and older) friendship networks, though not those of comparably aged married women (Babchuk & Anderson, 1989).

Functions and Tensions of Friendship in Later Life

Friendships serve important and relatively specialized functions for elderly people for as long as they are able to actively engage in them in ways preserving their singular features. Thus, in considering its functional contributions to older persons' well-being, as well as possible tensions, it is useful to review friendship's ideal-typical attributes. First, friendship is a voluntary attachment that cannot be forced on anyone. Throughout life people choose who they will treat *and* who they will allow to treat them as friends. Next, friendship involves a person-qua-person regard for the other (Suttles, 1970). Friends care about each other as specific individuals and not as members of a particular category or role. Third, friends view and deal with each other as equals. Accordingly, they seldom patronize or play up to each other, respecting the integrity and validity of their individual experiences and situations. Fourth and relatedly, friendships include mutual trust, support, and help. Over time there are fairly symmetrical inputs into the relationship and to each other's welfare. Finally, friends feel and express shared and abiding affection. This set of features typically distinguishes friendships from other relationships, including those with most kin, in old age. But with constricted mobility and other incapacities, the elderly may have difficulty sustaining some of these qualities in their friendships, while also finding them lacking their family ties.

Socializing, Talking, and Judging with Friends

Friendships persist as primary sources of enjoyment and pleasure for older people. Friends provide day-to-day companionship as well as opportunities to talk, laugh, and have fun (Crohan & Antonucci, 1989; Gamer et al., 1975; Mancini, 1980; Peters & Kaiser, 1985). Moreover, they link the elderly person to the larger community by encouraging participation in a variety of social activities (Arling, 1976; Peters & Kaiser, 1985; Sherman, 1975). Nussbaum and his colleagues (1989) observe, "Friends are likely to go shopping, to take a walk, to go to a ball game, or just to visit one another. These activities integrate the elderly individual into society" (p. 151). Noting married couples' self-sufficiency that approached "dysfunctional isolation" as they retreated from other social interaction and into their marital relationship, Johnson (1983) observed friends acting as intermediaries, drawing the spouses out and connecting them with various social agencies and collectivities. In conjunction with enjoyment and social integration, friends are also vital for relieving loneliness (Cantor, 1979; Heinemann, 1985; Perlman, 1988).

Elderly friends spend many of their moments together engaged in pleasurable and meaningful conversation. Moreover, sharing similar positions in the life cycle and perspectives on time, they often reminisce about periods when they both were younger or memorable events involving their spouses, careers, and children. Vivifying the past in this manner enriches the present, and longtime friends are especially liable to have helped create and to enjoy recalling such memories (Chown, 1981). Increasingly over the life course, talking with close friends confirms individuals in ways sensitive to the persistence of their valued personal characteristics and self-conceptions, despite unforeseen or unavoidable changes in circumstances, physical appearance, or actual capabilities. Moreover, this intimate acknowledgment comes from someone who responds voluntarily to the friend as a whole person, recognized and admired across time and a variety of social roles and predicaments. Consequently, their remarks bespeak a continuity, quality, and depth of relationship that few persons can emulate (Lemon et al., 1972).

This affectionate affirmation is a significant provision of friendship. Nearly one-third of one sample of elderly women emphasized acceptance as a primary aspect of feeling close to someone (Adams, 1985–86). Friends shield the older person from others' negative appraisals of his or her capabilities or worth as a person, which may be based on fair criteria or unwarranted prejudices (Heinemann, 1985). Likewise, friends help prevent negative self-evaluations (Mancini, 1980), warding off debilitating statements and thoughts about oneself as "old" (Bell, 1967), deterring identification with "age-related shortcomings" (Mitchell & Acuff, 1982), providing "status" (Candy et al., 1981), and overall, encouraging positive self-perceptions (Mancini, 1980; Mitchell & Acuff, 1982). As persons relinquish public opportunities to define themselves and demonstrate their competencies, they increasingly look to friends to validate them and to help formulate their self-evaluations (Atchley, 1977; Johnson, 1983; Shea et al., 1988; Sukosky, 1977).

Consequently, the valued support and acceptance communicated by trusted close friends dialectically coexist with a reliance on them for frank judgments. Friends help "maintain objectivity" about one's abilities, decisions, and dealings with others (Sukosky, 1977) and to provide models of age-appropriate behaviors (Mitchell & Acuff, 1982). Candid exchanges help establish new standards, meanings, and interpretations of daily exigencies and problems. According to Francis (1981), difficulties with children are especially salient matters for discussion:

> Informants still discuss family problems with old friends who know their children well. They are able to assess their own status and the behavior of their children in comparison with that of their friends. They learn what is reasonable to expect from adult children, and they can adjust their expectations to conform to reality, rather than to an unrealistic ideal. This adjustment of expectations helps them to adapt their own behavior and to accept their changed status in their relations with children. (p. 93)

The counsel of friends conveys both judgment and acceptance by addressing the objective and possibly detrimental features of actions and situations, while still confirming and supporting each other's appropriate choices and inherent value as individuals. These practices of judging together and sharing advice distinguish old friends from new ones among the elderly (Shea et al., 1988).

In sensitively managing the dialectical tensions of expressiveness and protectiveness and judgment and acceptance in their ongoing interactions, many close friendships comprise relationships of confidence during old age, though women are more likely than men to reveal and discuss their concerns (Roberto & Kimboko, 1989; Kohen, 1983). In fact, three-fifths of Adams' sample of older women considered "confiding behavior as a measure of closeness" in their friendships (1985–86, p. 59). Evidence repeatedly demonstrates that elderly persons' psychological well-being and morale are significantly associated with the quality of interaction characterizing their stable confidant relationships, not the overall quantity of their social encounters (Conner et al. 1979; Lowenthal & Haven, 1968; Strain & Chappell, 1982). Enjoying a relationship of confidence with at least one close friend may be enough to inhibit demoralization and prolong the elderly person's good mental health (Lowenthal & Haven, 1968; Blau, 1973).

Negotiating Independence and Assistance with Friends and Family

Most noninstitutionalized older people are self-sufficient and value their independence and privacy (Peters & Kaiser, 1985; Stoller & Earl, 1983; Wentowski, 1981). Reflecting our culture's preoccupation with individualism and self-reliance and its simultaneous tendency to underestimate and denigrate the capabilities and initiative of the elderly, many older persons are sensitive about their autonomy and reluctant to rely on others. Preserving their freedom to choose with whom, when, and whether or not they will be sociable is a key issue for them (Chown, 1981). Even married persons spend 40% of their time in solitude (Larson et al., 1985). Yet when persons must adjust to declining abilities to care for themselves, their lifelong patterns of independence, dependence, or interdependence influence the extent of others' availability to them, and how comfortable they feel about depending on and assisting others (Jonas, 1979; Wentowski, 1981).

When a voluntaristic ethic predominates, the limited obligations and flexible demands of friendship derive from and work to preserve both parties' freedom to be independent and their freedom to depend on each other (Rawlins, 1983a). Though friends remain able to call on each other for help and support in later life, they typically do so only in emergencies or for sporadic and limited assistance (Cantor, 1979). Enacting this policy accomplishes several individual and relational aims. First, by avoiding excessive dependence on their friends, they register their own continuing autonomy. Further, by not burdening their friends, they acknowledge their corresponding needs for independence, escape testing instrumentally the extent of affection and commitment upholding the friendship, and avoid setting precedents for assistance that they may not want or be able to deliver (Johnson, 1983). Meanwhile, occasionally relying on friends for necessary and appropriate help implicitly recognizes their caring, competence, and ability to assist. Such carefully managed participation enhances all parties' self-esteem and cultivates the voluntary, equal, mutual, and affective qualities of friendships (Conner et al., 1979; Heinemann, 1985).

However, dialectical tensions may develop in friendships due to one person providing too much assistance to the other or, conversely, making undue demands. Crohan and Antonucci remark that, "Feeling needed is crucial to the elderly person's well-being. When older people define themselves as important to the welfare of a peer, their own ability to adapt to old age is enhanced" (1989, p. 139). And Hochschild (1973) describes nurturant relationships where more capable persons care for clearly less fortunate others in mutually beneficial arrangements. Even so, both individuals must be reconciled to this form of relating; such complementarity can diminish friendships because it highlights a lack of parity in the partners' personal resources and abilities, and one person's dependence on the other. In a sample of noninstitutionalized men and women aged 65 to 91 years old, Roberto and Scott (1986a) discovered that both equitably benefited and underbenefited individuals reported higher morale than did the overbenefited ones. In explaining why persons obtaining the same or less advantages than they offered friends felt better than those receiving more, the authors argue:

> This inability to reciprocate undermines the older adult's sense of independence and self-worth, which may explain the greater anger expressed by those individuals who perceive themselves as receiving more from their friends than they were giving. The realization that one is less capable than in previous years to do for oneself is a stressful experience for older adults. (1986a, p. 246)

While recognizing the enhanced self-esteem derived from helping less fortunate others, elderly persons are also well aware of the imposition and effort involved. They are often careful about how much they will inconvenience their friends, not wanting to incur obligations that they in turn may be unable to fulfil, or to redefine the relationship as fundamentally instrumental in nature (Johnson, 1983). In most cases they will turn to family members for long-range assistance or when they are more seriously or chronically ill (Cantor, 1979). Johnson (1983) reports that many elderly men and women recently discharged from a hospital orchestrated their encounters with friends, avoiding face-to-face contact until marked improvement in their health occurred, maintaining communication through letters and phone calls, and preventing them from feeling pressured to do anything beyond the normal definition and expectations of their friendship (Johnson, 1983). Even so, in Johnson's (1983) study friendships tended to dissolve when illnesses were too extended. Meanwhile, family members remained steadfast in their attention for as long as the former patient required it. The author states:

> Nine months after hospitalization, the older people, who experienced an improvement in health and functional status, reported a decrease in

contact with relatives and an increase in contact with friends. In contrast, those who remained highly impaired reported little change in contact and support from family members and a decline in support from friends (Johnson & Catalano, 1983). This finding suggests that friendships have difficulty in standing the test of time if the relationship is also tested by illness and dependency. One can also conclude that friendships are quite specialized in the emotional or expressive domain, and in view of this voluntaristic character, are likely to break down when tested by the illness of one partner. (Johnson, 1983, p. 113)

But several factors mediate who is liable to assist older persons in given circumstances. Dono et al. (1979) argue that potentially supportive others vary in terms of their proximity, sheer number, length and nature of commitment, physical capabilities, financial resources, and degree of caring. As long as older persons have able relatives nearby to rely on for aid, their friends are used minimally; yet when the elderly are unmarried or lack available family members, friends and neighbors are likely to furnish support (Heinemann, 1985; Johnson, 1983; Stoller & Earl, 1983). Emotionally close friends who live nearby are particularly apt to help with a variety of tasks (Adams, 1985–86). The potential strains of unbalanced reciprocity noted above in general friendships do not affect older persons' satisfaction with their best friends (Roberto & Scott, 1986b). As in communal friendships throughout life, the elderly are apparently more inclined to help and to receive help from their best friends without feeling burdened or uncomfortable; instrumental assistance emerges from and expresses affection. They usually view periods of inordinate demands as embedded in a long-term relationship of mutual reliance, while less close relationships involve more attention to fair exchange (Roberto & Scott, 1986b).

By and large, however, friendships are valued for companionship and family members for instrumental help in later life (Rook, 1989; Stoller & Earl, 1983). Although relationships with specific friends and relatives may share overlapping features and fulfill similar functions for elderly persons, they typically vary in important ways (Dono et al., 1979). Family relationships involve culturally sanctioned obligations (Brain, 1976); their ongoing enactment may be rooted in a sense of duty and responsibility for the elderly relative, not in the inherent pleasure of seeing him or her (Arling, 1976; Blau, 1973). Helpful kin usually are not peers (Lopata, 1988; Stoller & Earl, 1983). They differ in age and orientations toward life stages (Heinemann, 1985), with asymmetries in health status and personal resources generating lopsided capacities to reciprocate goods and services (Arling, 1976; Chappell, 1983). Since family members' perceived responsibilities may primarily dictate their sustained attention and regular visits, they may display positive concern but not necessarily liking or feeling close to the older person (Babchuk, 1978–79; Heinemann, 1985). As a result, their patterns of contact may be neither mutually desired nor jointly fulfilling.

In contrast, friendships arise from voluntary attachments based on personal regard for another person and intrinsic enjoyment of his or her company. Friends are usually peers, sharing equivalent status based on their common membership in an age cohort, similar experiences of life course transitions, and comparable ability to assist each other (Arling, 1976; Heinemann, 1985; Jonas, 1979). The relationship rests on mutual choice and mutual need and continues as long as the partners feel shared affection. Even though they are more liable to dissolve than family bonds if circumstances, declining health, mobility, or financial resources restrict interaction, either friend makes excessive demands, or they cannot preserve equal inputs over time, ongoing friendships are extremely important for older persons' self-esteem and continued enjoyment of life (Arling, 1976; Johnson, 1983). Across numerous studies, participating in friendships is more closely associated than family activity with high morale and psychological well-being (Arling, 1976; Johnson, 1983; Larson, 1978; Wood & Robertson, 1978) and life satisfaction (Chappell, 1983; Edwards & Klemmack, 1973; Lemon et al., 1972; Pihlblad & Adams, 1972; Spakes, 1979). Despite their potential tensions and vulnerability to changes beyond either person's control, friendships help people feel good in later life.

Conclusion

In many ways the patterns of solitude, intimacy, and sociability that persons negotiate within their evolving social configurations during mature adulthood continue into later life. Further, the boundaries marking individuals' transitions to old age itself are mutable and subject to the cultural constructions of older people prevailing at given historical moments interacting with their specific physical and mental capacities and financial resources. Accordingly, this chapter views later life as a career in itself, an extension of adult interpersonal and social practices involving active and conscious decisions by older people in shaping and managing their situated opportunities and impediments.

Nonetheless, friendships among the elderly exhibit normative contours evident across the life course. Friends are close enough in age to share analogous generational experiences; and they are usually alike in gender, and marital and occupational status, all of which promote comparable life-styles and values. Patterns of friendship related to activity in the workplace, participation in neighborhood, civic and professional associations, and recreation in groups of couples persist as long as these collectivities remain viable options. As persons voluntarily or involuntarily reduce or conclude their efforts as workers, association members, parents, or spouses, they may choose to change or sustain their degree of involvement in their other social endeavors. Conceivably, friendships endure as significant alternatives to pursue independently of diminished institutional activity and responsibilities throughout this period (Brown, 1981). Yet, once again, most persons' ongoing engagement in friendships reflects their previous practices and inclinations, given adequate health and finances.

For example, modal gender differences in friendship activity remain clearly evident in later life. Men's social friends from professional and community settings taper off when they retire from these pursuits, yet they still depend on their wives for close friendship. They tend not to maintain their friends from youth and are less likely than women to have close friends or to replace ones made in adulthood as they are lost (Powers & Bultena, 1976). Though they report more frequent interpersonal contact than women do, it is confined to family and established friends (Powers & Bultena, 1976). In contrast, elderly women have more extensive ties with other people and are also liable to be more intimately concerned with and dependent on their friends than men; theirs is a diverse social landscape with enduring community involvement and amiable ties expanding their group of close friends (Babchuk, 1978–79; Clark & Anderson, 1967; Roberto & Scott, 1986b; Spakes, 1979). They tend to preserve friendships from various points in their lives, losing their cherished friends only to death, and continue to acquire new close friends and sociable companions in later life (Zborowski & Eyde, 1962).

By and large, friendship appears to be a protected and privileged relationship during old age, reflecting both its vulnerable, voluntary basis and its specialized functions. Except for their time-tested and closest bonds, the elderly are reluctant to ask for too much instrumental assistance from friends. Family members, usually adult daughters, tend to provide material and service supports instead. However, friends are uniquely valued to talk, reminisce, and judge with, and to keep confidences. They relieve loneliness, help with incidental needs, connect individuals to larger communities, and foster their ongoing enjoyment of life. Let us now turn to older persons' descriptions and some literary depictions of experiences of friendship during later adulthood.

Chapter 11

Illustrative Analysis: Patterns of Friendship in Later Life

Talking with older adults about their friendships reveals both continuities and discontinuities with earlier patterns for individuals and the group as a whole. Friendship profiles remain diverse across this developmental period for many reasons. First, the period potentially spans 40 or more years of human endeavor. People also enact disparate personal styles, decisions, and initiatives in conducting their social lives. As well, areas of diminishing or minimal individual control, such as persons' social capabilities, health, and mobility as well as their friends' proximity, abilities to interact, or mortality, become salient at varying junctures. To a great extent, continuities in friendship practices are linked with stability in the participants' capacities for interpersonal contact and enabling situational variables, whereas discontinuities stem from changes in these conditions, which often transcend individual choice.

Key notions, expectations, and dialectical tensions of friendship evident since at least middle adolescence characterize the comments of the older persons we interviewed, though some themes received distinctive emphasis. They include friends as primary sources of enjoyment and relievers of loneliness, and the attrition of friends and loved ones. Generally speaking, a friend in later life is someone to talk to and to depend on, but equally important, someone to enjoy and to have fun with. We interviewed 13 women and 10 men, ranging in age from 64 to 100 years old and living in the midwestern United States, who described good times visiting, eating, playing cards, chatting and reminiscing with their friends, and traveling and playing golf and tennis together for as long as they were able.

These older adults still distinguish their close friends from other types according to a greater ability to confide in them and in many cases more willingness to depend on them. For example, Edward, an 84-year-old retired baker who lives alone, describes the meaning of friendship to him:

> Well, it means uh a whole lot. I've got friends that I depend on, they
> depend on me uh for going to the doctor, just call me and tell me to come
> over, we need you to play cards. And we go to breakfast together and uh
> we talk about the topics of the day and just have a good time.

Although this general category of friends is important to him, he is more
restrictive in considering someone a close friend, "Close friend, I can
depend on completely is a close friend. Number one, you can say things
that can't go no farther. That's a close friend. . . . I have a lot of
friends, but I would say I got about three that I really can depend on."

Helen, an 83-year-old retired school teacher who also lives independently, defines friendship similarly, "It means togetherness, enjoying
each other. When you think of some ways to, think of this friend or
whoever you're together with, having good times." Having a good time
together is a crucial aspect of Helen's generic conception of friendship.
However, she stipulates confidence as essential to close friendship and
indicates that she has lost and apparently not replaced her former
intimate confidante. What is a close friend to her?

> One that you would, I guess, tell everything to. I don't have one of those
> now, cause I don't tell everything. . . . I just don't. My closest friend
> passed away about ten years ago. And I have friends, but I don't—I just
> keep things to myself. I don't tell much.

The shared conversation, dependence, and enjoyment experienced with
friends alleviate loneliness, especially for individuals living alone. Since
Edward's wife went to reside in a nursing home 5 years ago, he misses her
companionship and feels the financial pressures of paying for her care. In
his current situation the advantages of friendship are clear to him:

> Well, it takes a, it really helps you in a lot of ways, especially if you're
> lonesome. If you've got a lot of friends, there's always somebody calling
> you or you've got somebody to call. And there's some friends that are
> close enough that you can tell them your troubles, and usually they're the
> ones that are sympathetic.

Notice again that Edward values both having "a lot of friends" to
interact with to ease his feelings of loneliness and a subset of more
intimate ones with whom to confide his worries. At 81, Sarah discusses
how the meaning of friendship has altered for her since the loss of her
husband 3 years earlier:

> Well I guess it means quite a bit more to me than it would to some people;
> some people don't value their friends like I do mine. I guess after you live
> alone and are alone, you value your friends quite a bit, cause when you're

there at night alone, somebody calls you and talks to you, it just makes you feel, perks you up, you feel more like uh going on. And that's kinda the way I feel about being by myself.

Friendships and Changing Social Configurations

People continue to initiate and react to various changes in their social configurations during later adulthood. Predictably, some of the most common and consequential events affecting interpersonal networks mentioned in our interviews included retiring from work, losing one's spouse, friends, and relatives due to their deaths, and the relocation of oneself or one's friends.

As discussed in Chapter 10, a number of personal and professional contingencies mediate a given individual's timing and experience of retirement. Reflecting this diversity, we spoke with a woman who retired from paid work at age 27 to raise children and another who owned and ran her own retail business until she was 82 years old. One 71-year-old man enthusiastically recounted his retirement from the military at age 46, while an 88-year-old farmer stated that he retired at 84 but still "kept a hand in things." Kurt, a married, 65-year-old caterer, expressed his reluctance to retire:

> It's not for everybody. How do I feel? You know I looked forward to being sixty-five, I don't know why, when I was younger. And now I'm sixty-five, and I don't want to retire now. So as long as I'm having fun and my health's halfway decent, and I meet a lot of friends. I mean, during, through the business, like in weddings and family groups and stuff like that, I meet a lot of people and it's just interesting to me to know a lot of people.

At another point Kurt, remarked, "I don't require a lot of my friends, I just like to be around them. And I hope they're around me a little bit, and that's what my friends are all about." Basically, his friendly relations with suppliers, clients, and their families fulfill his general expectations of friendship (though he also described his wife as his closest friend and confidante, as discussed below), and continuing to work provides his principal opportunities for such contact.

For the most part, when the people we talked with or their work-oriented friends retired and left the vicinity of their jobs, retirement limited their continued contact. Yet when people stayed in the same locale and wanted to remain friends, leaving work had minimal impact on their established patterns of mutual visitation. For others, retirement provided a chance to renew old friendships from prior periods or to make different friends through traveling and participating in new activities or voluntary organizations. A 70-year-old widow and retired department store employee, Paula, depicts the combination of personal volition, persistent patterns, and altered circumstances affecting her conduct of friendships after retirement:

> You don't keep in contact with everybody like you do everyday when you go to work. But then there were a few that you always kept in contact with and ran around with and had a good time with. . . . Now a girl I worked with in the store, Fleetwood's, we keep in touch with each other, but she moved to Florida, but we keep in touch with each other. When she comes to Indiana, she comes to see me. We go out and have a good time.

Irene's discussion of selling her business, retiring at 82, and moving into a nursing home also indicates several key issues and decisions involved in managing relationships with friends and kin in reconfiguring her social world. Now 88 years old, she relates:

> In 1982 or 1983 I kinda quit. Before that I went to the store to see about things every day, and then I came up here to Lafayette, I think it was 1983. I'm not sure because my son lived here and he is all I had and I was there by myself and I felt like, I do him—He wanted me to come here, they did, and I felt like he had to check on me and see about me, and it was too much for him to run down there 200 and some miles and called and talked every day. But I thought, well, that I had my life and I wanted him to have his. That was why I wanted to go to a home, not to go to his home. He had room. He has a wonderful wife, and I could go there but I don't want to. I am too independent, I know, but that's the way I am.
>   . . . When I came here I made new friends. I didn't know anybody and I made new friends when I came here. I think I have made several new friends since I've been here at the home, maybe some enemies but I think more friends. I feel like I've made, I've always tried to help them and because you can make friends or you can lose friends. Being insulting to them for one thing. You want to be a friend, talk to them like you would like for them to talk to you. And if you try to do something for someone and they want you to do it for them, and they kind of slur you, say something back to you, "Well I knew that," or something, then I am through with it.

Irene articulates a clear rationale for deciding to move into a nursing home on retirement that demonstrates both independent spirit and consideration of the imposition of living with her obviously devoted son and his wife. Further, she celebrates her success at making friends since moving to the nursing home. Even so, Irene suggests the risks of an active social life, her ongoing attempts to help others, and the crucial reciprocal importance of protecting feelings and rhetorically managing how to speak to friends, especially concerning the potentially touchy matter of assistance.

Many persons spoke of the continuous effort required to preserve friendships as active parts of their lives during later adulthood. The challenges include maintaining contact with friends in spite of changing residences and one-sided or joint constraints on mobility. And there were extensive references to friends who had died. Since she is unable to write or visit them anymore, Irene stays in touch with friends outside of the nursing home by telephoning them, receiving occasional letters and cards, and enjoying the infrequent visits of those friends who still can accomplish them:

> Now I see them when they come here to see me. And that is not very often because they are like I am, not able to go. But a close friend here, no I don't have one I don't think. Here in the home I got some friends, yes every day I mean we speak, and one of them just died I'd seen, it shocked me. She was buried I think yesterday. She was younger, a lot younger but she was here in the home. Set there at that table and eat.

In describing her limited face-to-face encounters with her older friends, Irene does not consider new friends in the home to be close. Even so, she talks with them "every day," and the recent death of one of them palpably affected her.

Meanwhile, she tries to remain informed of friends from previous circumstances by asking family members for news:

> I hear about them through their children. I've got one, I told my son I've got to find out about Joyce. She is the same age I am, her birthday is the 7th of November and she has a son who lives here in Lafayette. And they said she was coming here last fall, and that she would come and see me. But she is like me, but she can't see. She can't see anything hardly. She is the same age and has a big family. Through all of these years, I think we met when we was in the fourth or fifth grade of school and we have been friends ever since. So I think that's keeping it. And she is one of the few that has—I know has been as long as I have. Most of my friends are dead and gone.

Even an energetic person like Irene eventually faces constraints on her abilities to reach old friends as well as their attrition. Nevertheless, she still reports actively seeking, thinking about, and cherishing a lifelong friend, in addition to making other friends in her present residence.

While living independently, Helen describes the continuity in her old friendships ironically juxtaposed with their marked attrition, and the consequent ageless importance of making new friends:

> It seems like my friends I had years ago I still have, course, they are less and less. Cause where I came from, we had sixteen people who belonged to a little club—men and women. And we'd get together and play cards and have suppers together and go to New Harmony and various places.

But there is only two of us left, Darlene Messick and myself, out of that group. So, see, I have to make new friends. Every day you've got to make some new friends.

Her strategies for developing new friendships resemble those of other moments in the life cycle, striking up conversation, showing interest in others, and inviting them to share activities. She states:

Well, you have to talk to people. You have to find something that they're interested in, and you cooperate and be interested too. And sometimes you can make some friends, "We're going to play cards tonight, we need another person. Would you like to come and fill in for us?" Or something like that.

Helen both develops and maintains contact with friends through regularly scheduled card playing at their local senior citizens' center:

Like tonight I'm going to play bridge down here. There's two ladies that pick me up, and I wouldn't have known either of these ladies very well had I not been playing cards. There was the contact there. And they brought me down to bridge now, let me see, for at least five years. And before that, I had a friend who passed away that picked me up too for bridge. So I will have to say that bridge kinda brought us together.

When asked how often she sees her friends, Helen laughs and replies, "About twice a week. At least twice a week. I play on Tuesday and I play on Friday. I did play on Thursday, and my partner passed away—so that table has been silent since then." This answer expresses the ongoing rhythm of her friendship activities and eloquently implies a collective tribute to her former friend.

As occurs throughout adulthood, the loss of their spouses noticeably affected many of these individuals' friendships with other married couples. Cliff, an 88-year-old retired factory foreman and nursing home resident, wistfully recalls, "When my wife was living, we had all kinds of friends. We would go here and visit here and visit there. But since she is gone, I am all alone, and she is gone six years ago already." Despite other factors possibly contributing to Cliff's current isolation, he clearly associates a pronounced decline in his friendships and visiting patterns with his wife's death. Likewise, Edward, whose wife currently lives apart from him in a nursing home, asserts:

I don't have the company comes like they did when she was there. Families that, you know, we'd know as man and wife, they don't— whenever one of the spouses is gone, you don't have the company that you used to have. You don't have man and wife coming to your house see. And that's true for everybody.

Similarly, in Elizabeth Taylor's novel about relationships among the elderly, Laura Palfrey, an Englishwoman able to afford to live out her days at a residential hotel in Great Britain, expresses these sentiments about the retreat of couples from widows as well as the widespread demise of friends:

> Of course, I found it easier to make friends when Arthur was alive—other couples, you know. We dined at one another's houses. Widows aren't quite the same thing: they get asked only to large parties where odd numbers don't matter, and are really only seldom asked to *them*. And then, as one gets older, people die, or drop out of one's life for other reasons. One is left with very little. (Taylor, 1975, p. 98)

Helen concurs with this account, but has been able to stay involved socially after her husband's death by pairing off with another widow in their circle of friends. She observes somewhat tartly:

> You are what you would call a fifth wheel in anything. But I was fortunate enough that when Jack passed away, another gentleman in the group had passed away. So they put Julie and I together as a couple. That is the biggest thing that I can think of about friendship. It does break a friendship. Well, you're only one, you see, you're only one. "Well, we'd have invited you, but we needed four," you see.

She clearly understands the encompassing constraints on friendships presented by this social pattern of excluding widow(er)s, mentioning she was "fortunate enough" that another gentleman in their group of couple friends died at the same time as her husband. Indignantly, she reenacts the attribution of being "only one" in this context and the seeming necessity for symmetricality in couple gatherings, emphasizing, "That is the biggest thing that I can think of about friendship. It does break a friendship."

Notably, the loss of their husbands leaves women without their long-term partners and commonly isolates widows from previous friendship groups comprised of couples. Meanwhile, this event often provides on a dyadic level the impetus for forming and/or strengthening intimate friendships with other women. Betty, a 64-year-old widow and dormitory director, relates the extensive conversations, comforting, and interdependence that bonded her friendship with Mary after the deaths of their husbands within a year of each other:

> Her husband committed suicide about a year after my husband died a natural death. And Mary went through a very guilt-ridden period where she felt that she might have done more to prevent his suicide. Instead of going into therapy, I made it a point to talk to her for two to three hours

every evening. And after about three months, I could see that she was going to be fine. But during that time, I think that really cemented our friendship both on her part and on mine, and she was grateful. But I was grateful to her because it was a form of therapy for me too, having just gotten over the death of my husband.

A 66-year-old secretary, Emily, recounts a comparable process of deepening mutual commitment and confidence in her friendship with Marcia as they talked through the deaths of their husbands. Noting that she had lost her own husband the previous year, Emily recalls:

Marcia came about the time my husband passed away—Julia has always been there—but the friendship grew deeper after she [Marcia] lost her husband. There's, there's being a widow, I think, uh, I think you, you're kind of attracted to each other. Not attracted, I mean uh, drawn closer—yes, that's a better word—because of your experience. But, but we don't talk about that experience any more than we have to, because that's a personal thing. We talked about it, they know all about my feelings at the time, and everything like that. And they know like family, how the family is reacting to this change in my life, you know. And how my friends have reacted to this change in my life. There is differences, you know, so this is what we talk about. We all are in the same position, sharing the same type of experiences. And sometimes it gets, you know, we can see how it uh, how maybe to deal with it in another light, from their experience.

The common exigencies of dealing with widowhood drew Emily and Marcia closer together. Notice as well the dialectical process of discussing their respective situations. Emily has talked "all about" her feelings and her family and friends' reactions with Marcia and Julia, suggesting they have described kindred concerns. Further, they have compared their predicaments' similarities and differences to increase their options for handling them. However, Emily notes that this extensive expressiveness has simultaneously given rise to protective practices and sensitivity to each other's privacy regarding the loss of her husband, "We don't talk about that experience any more than we have to, because it's a personal thing." Thus, the openness shared among these friends simultaneously establishes communal conditions for their respectful closedness.

Dialectics of Later Adult Friendships

As individuals shape and face constancies and changes in their social configurations occasioned by retirement, relocation, and attrition, basic dialectical tendencies of friendships require continual communicative management. In their discussions our interviewees highlighted contradictory inclinations toward independence and dependence, judgment and acceptance, and expressiveness and protectiveness in conducting their friendships.

The Dialectic of the Freedom to Be Independent and the Freedom to Be Dependent

Most people want respect for their dignity and autonomy even when they need to count on others for assistance. In old age these concerns are especially salient in the face of declining personal capabilities and condescending reactions by other persons. We have already witnessed Irene's independent spirit in spite of current restrictions in her ability to visit former friends. It is not surprising that she admires personal autonomy and gumption in her relationships with others:

> I say the friendships I like are the ones that try to do something for theirselves; but these that sit back and want you to do it all, they're off of my register. I am very independent that way. I have always been independent myself and I don't like for someone to sit down and wait on someone to feed them. The birds don't feed me fast enough. Maybe that's wrong; but I am a very—things like that, if people I see are down, I'll go all the way out for someone who is trying to help theirselves. But someone that wants you to notice them, to be, have sympathy on them are out with me. I don't want to be petted and I don't want to pet anybody.

Irene's insistence on her own and her friends' self-reliance has influenced her lifelong practices of reciprocity in conducting her friendships. This orientation apparently worked well in managing her own business, where she retained appreciative employees and customers as friends for decades, and that still seems viable for her. She narrates how she negotiates balanced contributions in her relationships with others:

> I made cut out work that's, and I've got a lot of quilts that I made. I give them away; I never sold a quilt in my life. I give one, the last one I give was after I came here. I know it was after I came here. It was my daughter-in-law's mother, my daughter-in-law's sister this was. I told her, I said, "Barbara, I want to give you a quilt." And I asked Shirley, I said—Shirley's my daughter-in-law—which one she thought Barbara would like. She said any of them; she wouldn't care. So I gave her a quilt, and she says she really likes them and thought it was nice of me. I said, well I didn't know who I wanted to give it to anymore than I did her because she does things for me. When she has them over—she lives at Bridgeville—and one day she asked them would they take me over to her house, she gives me a Christmas gift and her mother gets a thing for me when she is able. Of course, her mother is about 18 or 20 years younger than I am.

This woman, whose career was merchandising, attaches special meaning to having "never sold" her handmade quilts. They have always been tokens of friendship. Like numerous elderly persons, Irene maintains her independence, dignity, and self-esteem in depending on others through giving what she can in friendly exchange.

Delving further into Emily and Marcia's friendship following their husbands' deaths reveals that their heightened interdependence at that time also included tensions. In recalling difficulties with her friendships, Emily refers to a "bit of hesitancy" that she began to feel towards Marcia. She explains:

> She more or less wanted to possess me, you know. Wherever I was or we went, you know, she was real close. And if I would decide to do something with somebody else, that would upset her, you know—so that, and that's the only ah thing that I had. But we're still very very good friends.

Asked if she had talked with Marcia about the situation, she says, "Mm-hmm, she learned from it. Yes, I did." Even so, Emily acknowledges that Marcia may not have realized her excessive dependence and that she herself may have instigated their mutually enacted patterns. She reflects:

> I don't really think that she was aware of what she was doing. Because that's kind of the way that her life had been prior to me. See I lost my husband the year before she did. So we started our relationship right then, which has been 8 years, and I, some of it could have been on my part, because I had been through it, and still was going through it. But the initial, ah, part of it, why, I was trying to help her. You know, and I stayed close to her, what during that time. And then she just kind of leaned on me, you know, from then on. So it could have been me reaching out a little too far, too hard; I don't know, but I felt that that was the thing to do at that time.

In this quotation Emily exhibits admirable insight, sensitivity, and willingness to assume partial responsibility for their problematic joint dependence when they were first widowed. She mentions the possibility of "reaching out a little too far, too hard" at that time. This admission also implies the essential communality of their experiences as friends in "going through" these circumstances. Her account enacts Robert Paine's conceptual insight that "The emphasis in anthropological writings seems to be on friendship as the act of proffering the outstretched hand; I suggest that we also look at the matter in reverse; namely, as the act of finding a hand which will clasp one's own" (1974, p. 119). Despite her earlier period of reluctance, the women are "still very, very good friends," and Emily concludes that reaching out and helping was the right action.

Likewise, the intimate dialogue and interdependence characterizing Betty and Mary's relationship after their husbands' deaths persist as an overarching ethic shaping their friendship even though the emotional intensity of those times has subsided. Betty refers to Mary and seemingly, herself, in relating what a close friend is:

> A close friend, again, would be someone that anytime of the day or night I could call her with either a problem and, even more difficult, to share happiness with. I think the mark of a true friend is: How many people would be happy because you are? I think human nature being what it is, people have a tendency almost to be jealous or even resent the good fortune that might come into your life. But a good friend would be as happy as you are and, conversely, they would be as sad as you are if you had a tragedy.

Evidently, Mary's possible remarriage may limit the two women's freedom to depend on each other in the future. Yet Betty graciously grants precedence to her friend's potential marital commitment, honoring the freedom to be independent negotiated between these close friends (Rawlins, 1983a). She relates, "She is now dating a man that I think could cause our friendship to lessen because the third party would be sharing her. And I think that naturally that if she does marry him, then her first allegiance would be to him." But despite the perceived necessity of relinquishing exclusive rights to her friend should the marriage occur, she still registers their mutually offered freedom to depend on each other as an unspoken and enduring privilege of their friendship:

> Well, I'd like to think that she could call on me. She knows that if it were a real problem that she was having, I would probably come to her and see what I could do to help her, even though we're some distance away. There is ninety miles between us now. She knows, just as I do, that if there were the need for the presence of the other, they would be there.

The Dialectic of Judgment and Acceptance

Friendship is first and foremost a relationship of mutual enjoyment and personal validation in later life; people look to their friends for pleasant conversation, relaxation, and opportunities to feel good about themselves. This benevolent interpersonal climate is facilitated by friends' tendencies to accept, if not understand, each other's idiosyncrasies and perceived shortcomings. Even so, at any age people may see actions or events differently, and disagreements may arise momentarily or persist. Such discrepancies, in turn, challenge friends to reconcile their contrasting judgments of each other's ideas or actions with their customary mutual acceptance.

Lester, an 88-year-old retired farmer, knows almost everyone in the small community where he has lived all of his life and considers many of them friends. In this milieu blending long-term friendly relations and friendships, he describes how he handles disagreements:

> Well, I just accept their viewpoint whatever it might be, and that's their business, and I just accept it, whatever it might be. As long as it don't interfere with me or my thinking. It's, oh I don't know what I'd do in my old age if I didn't have friends. . . . Now we don't always agree. Even the best of friends I think don't. But I'm not one to try to change 'em. So if they have got a different viewpoint on something than I have, why, that's their prerogative and hard luck if it has to be that way. . . . So even though I don't agree with them—well maybe they're right and maybe I'm wrong—but that don't necessarily have to interfere with friendship.

Lester emphasizes a few principles here. First, each person has a right to his or her opinion or judgment. As long as his friends' views do not "interfere with" his thinking, he will accept their right to a different outlook. Second, he values and seeks to preserve his present friendships, observing, "I don't know what I'd do in my old age if I didn't have friends." Accordingly, though he might disagree about a matter, he is unlikely to express it if it could "interfere with friendship." Basically, he compares the degree of interference with his own thinking occasioned by another's views with the potential of asserting his own judgments for undermining their friendship. Ironically, he accepts others' opinions and does not state his own to preserve his friendships, meanwhile acknowledging and accepting that other persons may or may not be that broad-minded. Thus, he opts for tolerance and avoids disagreeing, saying:

> Well, that's sometimes a good way to destroy a friendship. And not all the time, there's a lot of people who would take, are broad-minded enough to accept someone else's views. But there's some that not, aren't too. So that's human life, nature.

Nancy, a 100-year-old widow and former housewife, describes a similar source of problems and rationale for accepting differences among her group of friends in the nursing home; "Problems, well, sometimes I don't agree with what they say (small laugh), but I do in order not to destroy our friendship."

Despite the harmony preserved by accepting incongruities in general friendships, the practices of close friendship commonly include the injunction to judge the other person when one has strong convictions. In doing so, one creates the possibility of airing differences and judging together as friends potentially divisive concerns. For Roger, a 71-year-old widower and retired military officer, such judgments compose one of the distinct advantages of friendship:

> Well, they kind of give you a stableness in life that if you don't have friends, you, because you can go to them and talk, talk about various things. And if they are real friends, which I've, mine have been, why they will say, "Hey you better back off and take another look at this, because it's ridiculous." That's the kind of friend I like to have. If it's ridiculous, I'd like to know it.

The candid judgments of "real friends" help an individual maintain an objective outlook and avoid being "ridiculous." Even so, Roger observes that this privilege comes through learning to accept and overlook insignificant vagaries, "But there again you learn, I think with friends more than you do with other people, to kind of overlook certain things. And then you can also bring their attention to those, to some of those things." Demonstrated sensitivity in disregarding certain matters dialectically earns a friend the right to comment on these issues at another, perhaps more auspicious, time.

Betty depicts an identical process in managing the contradictory requirements of judgment and acceptance in her friendship with Mary. On the one hand, she says, "I tend to overlook negative feelings that might come up from time to time and say the good things my friend has done and is. These certainly overcome whatever petty negative things I may find in her." Such tolerance shapes and reflects an assumption of benevolence within this friendship, allowing for substantive mutual evaluations. Betty maintains:

> Our criticisms would be taken in the manner they were intended. I'm trying to think of where I might criticize her. Probably, I think she is too generous with her son, who is thirty-five and who certainly does not need a mother for help. But if this is what she wants to do, then it's her money and she could do what she wants with it. But I do let her know that maybe she should spend some of it on herself, rather than give it constantly.

In later life many friends confer about their relationships with their adult children, rehashing predicaments and seeking opinions on appropriate conduct. Ultimately, Betty will accept her friend's decisions in relating with her son. But since their appraisals ignore trivial issues, emphasize acceptance and the friend's positive qualities, and reflect sustained caring, the friendship also provides a forum for communicating judgments and challenging observations that neither friend will hear in the same way from anyone else.

The Dialectic of Expressiveness and Protectiveness

Someone to talk to and to depend on are defining attributes of friendships and involve dialectical practices throughout life. Moreover,

mutual confidence repeatedly distinguishes close friendship. In identifying Mary as her closest friend, Betty views this ability as criterial,
"Again, I go back to confidentiality. I have told her the past ten years,
she has shared many of my darkest secrets. I have never heard them
revealed to anyone else. We both share tragedy. We both share joy."
Similarly, Nancy asserts about her close friends, "You can tell them if
you have any trouble of any kind. You can tell them about it, and they
can console you and help make you feel better." Finally, perhaps
reflecting the somewhat subdued intimacy associated with male friendships across the life course, Victor discriminates his close friends as
"some of the fellows that you kinda let your hair down to a certain
extent and discuss some of your problems and things that some of
which are more or less of a personal nature that you just don't pass all
around."

As I have observed in other contexts and at various points in the life
course, the expressiveness and confidence characterizing close friendships develop in conjunction with both friends' demonstrated protectiveness and trustworthiness. That is, at the same time persons feel free
to confide in and talk openly with their friends, they still protect their
own privacy, and avoid burdening the other too much or speaking about
tender issues.

Julia, a 66-year-old widow, displays these contrasting tendencies of
expressiveness and protectiveness in defining close friendship as
"Somebody that you confide in and tell your things that you wouldn't
tell anybody else, or tell your troubles to, and those are close friends."
But in receiving such confidences, she learns of and must be sensitive to
topics that potentially hurt her friends. She observes, "If I know
something that has particularly hurt them, which one of them has a
grandson that committed suicide, I never mention it unless she does.
And just things that hurt, we don't mention what we know hurts each
other." Openness with intimate friends, then, includes ongoing and
careful monitoring and rhetorically informed practices regarding matters
that are closed to discussion. Doris concludes that respecting a friend's
vulnerabilities may protect oneself as well, "I think you should always
be alert that the other person has feelings as well as yourself, and you
shouldn't always speak out what you feel and hurt their feelings.
Because they can come back at you. And I don't do that because I try to
be very careful what I say."

Styles of Friendship during Later Adulthood

Matthews' (1986b) conception of friendship styles presents a useful
way of organizing these interviewees' diverse descriptions of conducting

and classifying their friendships across varying adult social configurations in conjunction with communicatively managing the dialectical exigencies of friendship in our culture. I employ five persons' recollections below to illustrate various styles of friendship evident in later life. They are derived from the individuals' patterned emphases on particular persons, changing circumstances or some combination thereof in composing their friendships as they grow older.

The Discerning Style

Grace is 82 years old, widowed, and has lived in a nursing home for 3 years. In defining what friendship means to her, she highlights private conversation and enjoyment, typically reported attributes of close friendship across the life course, "Well, it really means somebody that you can talk to confidentially and know that uh it won't go any further, uh somebody that oh is congenial and you can have fun with." She immediately qualifies these commonly valued features, noting their lifelong association with primarily one person:

> I really don't have a lot of friends. I've had a lot of acquaintances, but I think I only have one friend, one and I really and truly love her. We've been friends since we were tots, tiny tots. But I like people, I like people very much. But I'm pretty much a loner; when I want to be alone, I don't want anyone else around me. . . . I think I'm a friendly person, as I said before. I like people and I like to talk with them uh, but I don't really go out of my way to really make friends.

Grace clearly exhibits the "discerning" style of friendship identified by Matthews (1986b). Although she is "a friendly person" and well disposed toward many acquaintances, when Grace speaks of friendships, she describes ongoing contact and recollects shared moments with her cherished friend, Sadie.

Her account resembles a primer on communal friendship, sustained across life's joyful and painful spells:

> We have been friends since we were school age. We went all through school together and we always palled around together. And then we both worked over at the university, and we always helped one another if we could, teen-aged, with our little teen-aged problems and things like that. And we both married local boys and uh we married within a couple of months of one another and our husbands died within two months of one another. And we just, our lives have been similar all through the years; but she lives in Middletown now, and is not well. But whenever there was any problems like a death in the family or something, always she was the first

one there to help. And if she couldn't come she would always call, and weddings and things like that, she was always right there.

This narrative highlights the combination of happenstance, caring, and mutual effort necessary for such a friendship to flourish throughout the life course. These women lived in close proximity for most of their lives, enabling them to share primary school days and adolescent quandaries, work together, and marry "local boys." Key events such as their marriages and husbands' deaths have also coincided, synchronizing the two friends' encounters with a variety of seminal life transitions from young to later adulthood. Finally, reflecting each woman's personal initiative, Grace reports a lifetime of active mutual assistance and concern. She emphasizes that during especially sad or happy times, her friend was "always right there" for her in person or through phone calls.

In recalling the early days of their bond, themes of ready availability, tentatively growing affection, and joint help are evident even as Grace fondly remarks on their personal contrasts:

> I guess we were just kids together and just more or less liked one another. And we both ran around in the same crowd and we mostly, she was a very popular girl, very popular. I wasn't quite so popular so I could help her out of a lot of difficulties. She was the type that would make a couple of dates for the same night, you know (laugh), and I'd get a call, "Oh please help me out!" just things like that, you know. We were not the same personalities, we were different personalities altogether. She was, nothing bothered her and she could always find a solution to any problem, so I think that's why we became so well-acquainted.

Grace vividly relates an event from their younger days that made strawberries a mutually significant symbol of their many good times. Listening to her tell it, you can almost hear young people laughing and carrying on, and see her close friend amiably bearing the brunt of a humorous accident:

> Well, one occasion I laughed so hard and yet it was nothing to laugh at. We had been to a dance and we both dated the boys from the same fraternity. And we stopped at the old Deer Park, it was a real famous eating place for younger people in those days. She had, Sadie always had beautiful clothes, she was the only child you know, and she, well, she was all dressed in white. She had a white sweater and a white pleated skirt. So we stopped at the Deer Park and we all had strawberry shortcake. So, and this one, there were about four couples, and this one boy, he was the clown of the crowd, so he was going to get it for us and serve it. So he did, and when he came back, he was carrying a tray and he went to turn it and slide it off onto the table. Instead, it all slid over on Sadie; she was strawberries—and her beautiful dress was ruined. We laughed and that's

one thing we remember. She said, "I never look at a strawberry that I don't think of that." And I said, "Well the same with me." I just uh, but those were good times.

Illustrating a similar evocation of previously shared experiences, Robert Drake's (1987) short story, "1975 Has Come and Gone" depicts a fleeting encounter between two lifelong friends, Anne Louise and Martha Alice, who grew up together, are "both old enough to start having grandchildren" (p. 188), and now seldom see each other. Transcending the constraints of a public situation inhibiting intimate contact, Ann Louise manages a loud quip, puzzling everyone but Martha Alice:

> "The year 1975 has come and gone, and we're not wearing hoopskirts!" was what Ann Louise Parker—who had married Johnny Emerson—hollered to her old friend, Martha Alice Craig—whom she hadn't seen for a long time and whose husband, Don Phillips—was a big cardiologist in Memphis—when they happened to be seated near each other at a Kenny Rogers concert. Martha Alice had promptly snorted with pleasure, but there was no time to pursue the matter right then because the music—or rather, the sound—was getting under way. And afterwards the two couples had time for only the briefest of greetings, since the crowd was so large and the next day was Monday. (p. 182)

As often occurs with long-term friends' expressions, Ann Louise's remark alludes to one of many past interchanges, implying connected earlier lives, enjoyed activities, habitual styles of interaction, and open-ended issues of mutual interest:

> What the "1975" and "hoopskirts" was about, as Ann Louise explained to her husband as they were driving home, was all to do with when she and Martha Alice were growing up in Woodville and playing with their *Gone With the Wind* paper dolls, shortly after the movie had just come out and everybody was going to Memphis on Saturdays and taking their children to see it. Martha Alice had seen fit to hold forth then on fashion and style: how things came and went and were the height of fashion today but out of date tomorrow; and she had proclaimed that it was all perfectly clear to her that hoopskirts, which they both just adored, would certainly be back in by 1975. She would brook no argument, either, not that Ann Louise was disposed to give her much of one. (Drake, 1987, pp. 182–183)

Like Grace and Sadie's "strawberries," Ann Louise's utterance presupposes, tacitly registers, and succinctly celebrates the rich mutual history and ongoing significance of their bond.

During young adulthood, Grace and Sadie arranged to walk together to and from work, enjoying one another's company and enacting the small and often quirky events that compose the mutually created stories and memories of enduring friendship:

We used to have more fun when we worked over at the university; that's when we really had our fun, the old Memorial Hall. You don't remember that, is it still there? I doubt if they ever tear that down because I think that was probably one of the first ones built. Well, she worked there and I worked over in the Armory and we walked back and forth. We both lived on this side but we'd walk; we'd meet after hours and walk home and uh walk to work in the morning. She lived about two blocks from where I lived and we used to stop and we had a bakery and a meat market right close together. And that's one thing that I used to criticize her for. She loved oysters, and she'd stop at this meat market and buy one of those little tiny half pint ice cream buckets of oysters. And she'd eat those on the way home and I said "Ugh," I said, "One of these days one of those things are going to choke you." Ooo, I couldn't stand it. But it was little things like that that you remember you know.

Grace quit working at the university in her late twenties in order to raise three daughters. In keeping with her discerning style of social participation, leaving the work force minimally affected her overall pattern of activities. She observes, "I was pretty much involved with family and I was never much of a club person, never played cards, or I would rather be by myself and do my crafts and sewing. I did a lot of sewing; I have three girls and I did all of their work. But I just didn't seem to have time to run around a lot and uh I wasn't much of a club woman" (laughter). However, she and Sadie still spent time together, doing things for and with their children.

After living many of their adult years in close proximity raising their families, 20 years ago Sadie moved to Middletown, 65 miles away. Even so, Grace reports practices for maintaining contact that they still employ today:

We write to one another and if we should happen to see a pretty card, friendship card or something that we think we would like, we send it, or something that would remind us of our youth we would send it, or something in the newspaper that we would both be interested in, letters mostly we would write.

Moreover, phone conversations currently allow for the spoken expressiveness and mutual confidence that has always characterized their face-to-face dialogues about their families and their activities. These chats often include shared reminiscences as well:

Oh, we talk about our children now and she has a couple of great grandchildren and so do I and we talk about them. We talk about our girls when they were in high school and uh we used to get together and make their costumes for their little plays and things like that, and just ordinary things that we used to have fun doing. . . . I would talk about anything with her because I know that it wouldn't go any further. I have that confidence in her and I think she feels the same.

The mutual trust and assumption of benevolence composing their indepth discussions are apparent in Grace's description of their ability to judge and criticize each other:

> Maybe she'd have a dress or something that she didn't look a bit well in it and she liked it, but I'd say, "Well, you don't look good in it." And she'd say, "Well, would you want it?" you know and just kid around. No, we could really criticize one another and not get mad, just criticize one another in a friendly way.

Seven years ago when the two women's husbands died within 2 months of each other, they drew upon their practiced ability to talk, empathize, and judge with each other in formulating their living arrangements as widows. Despite their similar predicaments and proven ability to depend on each other, they also felt free to pursue independent adjustments to life alone. Grace recalls:

> Her husband died two months before mine did, so we both had that in common. We were both undecided what to do. And we talked that over but she finally decided to stay in her home. But I didn't. My house was too big and I couldn't do the work and I couldn't afford to have it done. So I sold my house and bought a mobile home. And then I lived in that four years and then I came out here.

Both women's limited mobility in recent years has virtually eliminated their face-to-face interaction, "I haven't seen her since, bout five maybe six years ago; her brother died and he was a local person, so I met her at the funeral home. But I hadn't seen her; she doesn't get around well and I don't either so we just don't come in contact with each other much." Yet she still experiences their relationship as a significant part of her everyday life. When asked whether anything might cause their friendship to end, she laughs and responds, "No, no, not at this point—course we're both getting up there in years. Lot of things are changing and different, but you have to accept those changes." She reflectively observes that photographs and memories of this emotionally vibrant friendship periodically cheer her up just as Sadie's presence always has:

> Sometimes it gets lonely at times, but I try not to concentrate on it. And all I have to do is get out my album and look at my pictures and think, "Oh, what a wonderful time we had that day and how much fun it was!"—and then I would laugh and feel real good again. And that's the way it would

be when we'd be with Sadie. We'd first be crying and then we'd be laughing.

Another interviewee, Frank, 64 years old and married, will retire in one year as a university administrator and professor. Throughout his adult life, Frank has interacted socially and professionally with large numbers of persons in a variety of settings, remarking, "I obviously know a lot of people, hundreds of people." However, like Grace, his definition of friendship reflects a consistently discerning style (Matthews, 1986b). He states:

When I think of the word friendship, I think of specific people, and two people come to mind, my wife and my dearest friend, now departed, James Wilson. And these are the two closest friends I've had as an adult. And that doesn't mean I don't have many, many acquaintances. But as far as close friends—them.

In describing the people he knows, he makes clear distinctions between friends and acquaintances. For Frank, a close friend must fulfill his high expectations regarding both quantity and quality of contact:

I'm not classifying acquaintances as friends. And of course I have some people that I've known since I was maybe in fourth grade in school that I still keep in contact with. And we might see one another every couple of years, but uh, and while I might call them friends, they're not the kind of people I'm describing as my dearest friends. And um of course the difference is one of being near one another. Most of the friends of childhood of course are many many miles distant and I don't see them very frequently. So distance is extremely important here, the time one spends with people they call friends is what makes the difference. . . . I think that the quality of this time is extremely important too. It's a give and take proposition, and I think that if the person you call a friend didn't get something from the relationship with you, just as you're getting something from your relationship with them, I think it would not last.

Frank's requirements limit those eligible for close friendship with him. An intimate friend must reside nearby so he can see that person often. Even though he has maintained contact with and occasionally encounters childhood friends who live far away, he does not consider them his "dearest friends." Moreover, Frank wants his frequent interaction with close friends to involve considerable reciprocity, "It's a give and take proposition," and common interests. He asserts, "Anyone that's a close friend of mine has got to be knowledgeable about what's going on in the the world, well-read, and have some mutual interest, and the same kind of interests I have. I hardly have time for anyone that doesn't have similar interests." For him, friendships cannot endure without common concerns and jointly beneficial exchange. He describes how such mutual assistance and stimulation were preserved in the close friendship developed during adulthood with his former teacher, despite the fact that he was 18 years older than Frank:

> As our friend James Wilson got older, I would in the winter time clean off his walks and driveway and things like that, or do, you know, the heavy work around the house that might need doing, cleaning gutters and all this kind of stuff that you have to do. And that doesn't mean that he didn't know how to do this, but his physical capabilities waned as he got older, so I did a lot of that for him. But I think the major difference is you seek out these friendships because of your interest in a particular field. And you want to get as much, you want to stimulate one another as much as possible in this common interest area. That's a major difference. But with James Wilson of course he was *so* versatile. He was a great cook, he loved music, good music, he traveled everywhere in the world. So, as a result, he guided us in our travels, we've traveled many, many places too, and he had a wide knowledge about woodworking and carpentry and things like that I have an interest in so, a very good commonality.

Despite the reciprocally instrumental flavor of Frank's comments, his affection for his deceased friend and his pride in being the intimate companion of a similarly selective person are evident throughout his discussions. He states:

> I think love is the most important thing in the world of course. And finding someone that you can love and respect is extremely important. But again I don't expect these kinds of friends to develop daily. In the case of James Wilson, he was not a person—he had many acquaintances—but he was not a person to develop close friends. So the fact, and he knew everybody, but the fact that we knew him so well, and in every condition and circumstance is something that none of other his students ever attained. . . . I have no idea why he took such a shine to us, but he did. We felt very fortunate.

Expressing the spirit of a communal attachment, he describes the intrinsic pleasure of their friendship's shared advantages as rooted in their deep regard for each other, "I think the bulk of this is benefit, and is mutual benefit, and the joy of doing something for someone else, the opportunity to have that joy is very important. And the converse, their joy in doing something for you. It's a mutual love and respect; it's very important." Frank cherishes the memory of his friend, remarking, "There isn't a day that goes by that Louise and I don't miss him," and he poignantly relates the hazards in later life of a discerning style of friendship:

> Friendship can cause disappointments too. And the stronger your friendship, of course, the more, the more emotionally upset you are when you

lose it. . . . In the case of James Wilson . . . that was only four years ago, we had to settle his estate and do all those things, but the fact that you were very, very close to him and saw him every day, and now you don't see him is a very, very big shock. So to the degree that you have a close friendship, the closer the friendship, the more the disappointment when it's over. One has to—but on the other hand, that's the risk you take. And if you don't take that risk you wouldn't have the joys of friendship. So one must understand that. It doesn't mean that new friends can't be developed. But you can't have a whole raft of friends when you're busy as I am . . . You can only have a few.

The Independent Style

Raymond is 69 years old, married, and will retire in 8 months from university teaching and public relations. He has resided in the same vicinity for the past 20 years and, like Frank, speaks of his wife as his closest friend. But he has developed and maintained an "independent" style of friendship due to frequent moves throughout his adult years (Matthews, 1986b):

> I've lived in, let's see, Florida, um Florida, Pennsylvania, Washington, D.C., New York, back to Washington, D.C., Colorado, Minnesota, Illinois, California, um back to Illinois, and down to Indiana, so this is the longest I've stayed anywhere. I've been here about twenty years now. . . . So every time you have a change of life, you have a whole change of friendships you have to create all over again. . . . I'm a total stranger in the city I was born in. But that doesn't bother me see 'cause my friends are, you know, some of the people I work with, so on and so forth, and I make friends wherever I go.

Promotions and career changes have resulted in a number of relocations for Raymond. Although this pattern of multiple moves has limited his close friendships, he has become practiced at forming casual ones, which complement his personal preference for avoiding routinized social activities. He relates:

> See, I don't have close friends as such, but that's mainly because of my background. I have traveled extensively across the nation here and so on. And so it's because of having moved all over the place, I haven't developed a group of friends as one would coming up into the same city and staying in the same city for the whole of your life. So my friends are very varied, actually. They're telephone friendships; I'm not much to going out and sitting in every Friday night, let's play cards with a couple of people. That would be very boring for me because I think life has to be more exciting than just going out with the same people and doing the same thing and talking about the same thing, Mrs. Jones's baby and who cares about Mrs. Jones's baby, you know? So the friends I have are casual; they're not lifetime friends.

Like persons exhibiting the discerning style of friendship, Raymond clearly distinguishes between casual and close friends, but values them differently. Whereas Grace and Frank both praise the mutual assistance and emotional interdependence of a specific intimate friendship, Raymond prefers the freedom and flexibility of less involved affiliations. When asked what problems or difficulties he associates with friendship, he replies:

> Curtailment. You get to the point—and this is one of the reasons why I haven't pursued this—it's because I don't wanna be dependent on anybody. You get such a close friendship and then you go to their house once a week and then you do something with them once a week and so on and so forth, and eventually it gets to be such a habit you don't want to do it. And all of a sudden this big guilt problem comes along, "How am I going to tell Harry?" you know. I don't want, I don't want that limitation. I wanna be me; I wanna be free to do what I want, where I want and when I want and with whom I want.

Raymond's autonomous stance toward friendship fits with his overall self-confident, youth-oriented, and somewhat restless attitude toward life. Having succeeded at several different lines of work, often without appropriate initial qualifications, he forbids the students he advises to utter the words, "I can't." When he retires from his present positions, he plans to "divorce" himself from current work associates but to continue his active participation with university student organizations. Additionally, he is contemplating "going into the public school system and teaching junior high school as a substitute teacher. I think I would enjoy that thoroughly." He argues, "I would like to leave myself a little bit of elasticity in there so that if I decide that I want to go away for a month, I can go away for a month. And as a substitute teacher, you can do that." Thus, he would avoid the obligations of a full-time job, even though he still loves "getting up and going to work in the morning."

Aware of the drawbacks of his lifelong independent style of friendship, Raymond occasionally reflects on the absence of close friends in his life. Nonetheless, he speculates about continuing his social practices as he grows older:

> The casual friend is the one I have now. The close friend would be the one that um that you would be visiting in their home and you would be having dinner together and they would come to your house, you'd go to their house, almost part of a family type of thing, the one that you have an arrangement that every Friday night you go and play cards at their house, or they come to your house. You go on trips together and things like that. I don't have that type of friendship. Now I have thought about it. I've thought about the consequences of not having someone like that as one grows older and more feeble and then you don't have anybody. Who's

gonna visit me in a nursing home if I go to a nursing home? Nobody, because everybody is just a casual friend of mine. But I suspect that I may make friends in a nursing home, you know. So this is not really a problem for me, but I have given it thought. The value of friendship, I've given it a thought. But, it doesn't concern me enough that I'm gonna go out now and say, "I want to find a bond with someone that I can say this is a real true friendship." Uh, I don't have that need.

He summarizes his lifelong stance toward friendships as, "I'm never lost for friends; I don't have a strange city; I don't have a strange town. Wherever I go, I can make friends very easily; that's not a problem for me. But they're not lifetime friends as my family had. And I credit this to just moving around."

The Acquisitive Style

Margaret, a 73-year-old retired secretary and widow, lives alone in her lakeside home in the country, where she enjoys nature and her neighbors. After working throughout early adulthood, she quit and married at age 40. When her husband became ill 5 years later, she resumed fulltime employment until her retirement 13 years ago at age 60. Since retiring, she remains busy, actively maintaining a diverse collection of old and new friends and doing volunteer work at the local senior center once a week. When asked how her retirement affected her friendships, her reply displays her acquisitive style of managing friendships (Matthews, 1986b):

> I just made different friends. I kept some of the old ones, of course; I worked in Dayton—I'm originally from Dayton—and I keep up with them a lot—some of them. Some of them, you know it's just like when you marry too, you sort of drift away from other people. But I've made lots of new friends here. And I've been here permanently for 20 years. So I'm half Hoosier and half Buckeye.

Margaret's present assortment of friends developed in Indiana coupled with those sustained from her working days in Dayton, Ohio support relationally her self-identification as "half Hoosier and half Buckeye." She feels meaningfully connected to both locales through her friends.

One of Margaret's current close friends is her next door neighbor, a "fairly new" person in her life. She describes their complementary features and upbeat first encounter with great enthusiasm:

> My close friend is my neighbor next door. She's fairly new; she's only been there about four years, but I don't know, she's like I am; she's a little bit younger than I am—about four or five years. She's short like me; I'm dark,

she's blonde—perfect contrast. . . . We just hit it off right away. In fact, she bought the house from another couple that lived next to me. And they drove up that day and they got out of the car, and I said, "I'm sorry, but they're not at home." And the lady turned around and she said to me, "Well, we're going to be your new neighbors." And I said, "Oh, how nice!" And that's how we met, and we just hit it off just like that. And I think that's been four years now.

Although residential proximity, positive first impressions, and appreciation for another's personal appearance are important in beginning friendships throughout life, Margaret and June also seem to have negotiated relational practices for suitably handling inherent contradictions of ongoing close friendships. In offering reasons why their intimate bond has lasted, Margaret describes their able management of the cross-pressures of judgment and acceptance, and independence and dependence. She emphasizes that they are not overbearing or judgmental in their interactions while relying on each other for honest appraisals of their appearance:

We don't, we are not *bossy* with each other, more or less, you know. But we are truthful with each other, let's put it that way. If something doesn't look right for me, she'll tell me and the same way with her. . . . It is constructive criticism. In fact, I've put on weight, and she said, "Margaret, you're going to have to spend a little money and get some bigger clothes, and then when you get back down to the others you can leave them sit there." I mean like this weekend when I went to put on jeans and I couldn't even get them together, I thought, "Oh my gosh, I've got to do something."

June was straightforward, yet tactful, in remarking on the fit of Margaret's clothing since she has gained weight. Because of their trust in each other's ability to keep confidences, objective judgment, and good will, Margaret observes, "We discuss everything. And she tells me things she knows won't go any further, and I tell her things like that—I mean you need a sounding board like that. You do. I can't think of anything that we can't handle between the two of us."

In describing their ongoing involvement, Margaret recounts that June "has just had surgery a couple of times, and I was there to help her when she needed me." Being there for friends at such moments is usually deeply appreciated. Even so, she emphasizes their respect for each other's autonomy and freedom to depend on one another. Accordingly, they do not impose on the other and compromise privacy or independence, even to provide assistance:

We don't run in on each other, but we know they're there when you need help. And a case in point. I had been working in the yard a couple of years ago; it was Labor Day weekend. And I went to sleep, and I slept. In the meantime my mother passed away at Heritage Home; and they called me and I didn't hear the phone. I wear a hearing aid, but at night you take them out. So finally they called my brother in Richmond, Virginia and he couldn't get me. And they called my son, and he called and I didn't hear it. And finally they called my cousin in Middletown; it went all around the country. Finally, they said, well, I have her next door neighbor's phone number, which they called her, and they came to my window and had to yell. And we have keys to each other's house in case we need any help, and her husband was ready to walk in when they finally woke me up. I said, "Oh my gosh." But I can, that to me is a neighbor. And my mother had this philosophy of saying that really your neighbors are your best friends even more so than your relatives, because if you need help they are right there. Your relatives like in my case are miles away from me, so that is what my friend is. I have friends on both sides of me out at the lake.

Ironically, the social network involved in notifying Margaret about her mother's death confirms the latter woman's philosophy about the importance of having neighbors as friends and their easier accessibility than relatives. It appears that none of Margaret's mother's kin were nearby when she died. Predictably, the nursing home personnel then tried to contact her closest living family member, her daughter residing in the same county. Unable to reach Margaret directly, they "finally" called her brother, who lives several states away. After calling Margaret's son, cousin, and going "all around the country," they finally resorted to the number Margaret presumably provided of someone outside their immediate family and called June. The assumption played out by this pattern of calls was that Margaret's kin would be in closer touch with her than her next door neighbor. This premise may be valid for persons with accessible relatives and who are less outgoing and actively integrated within their neighborhood and local community than Margaret.

It is interesting to note the steps June and her husband took to avoid "running in" on Margaret even though they have keys to her house. After several tries they succeeded in waking her up from outside her window, thereby protecting her privacy. The practices of friendship illustrated by Margaret's narrative suggest her neighbor and close friend's caring and availability, but also her respect for Margaret's independence and solitary moments. With her relatives "miles away," Margaret has neighbors she has befriended to depend on to be there in times of need.

Due to her acquisitive style, Margaret mentions four people as her closest friends, developed at different points and places in her life. She met her next door neighbor 4 years ago and her close friend of 35 years while working in Dayton. Her male friend, John (discussed below regarding cross-sex friendships), she met while traveling 6 years ago. Finally, she and her cousin Lucille "adopted each other as sisters" and have been intimate friends since childhood. She puts considerable effort into maintaining her friendships, telephoning, visiting, and traveling with them:

> I visit them; I've got a lot of miles on my car. . . . There's a group that has breakfast the third Wednesday in Dayton. I go in the night before so I won't have to get up early in the morning. And then once a month I have lunch with the former people that I worked with. So I keep in contact that way.

Her final comment epitomizes the acquisitive friendship style and her spirited engagement in preserving long-lived and developing new friendships:

> I just like to meet new people; I like old people, they're fine too. I mean I like new people and my old friends I hang on to. And in fact, I met one on a farm tour and she lives in Seaford, Indiana, and boy, I kept thinking today, I ought to take a trip and visit her. She went on a cruise with us one time out of Big Meadows. I had her come down and stay with me so we could go to the airport together. And well I have a friend that lives in Prescott, which is very close, and I met her through Senior Dances. And we got very close. She's another friend that I consider a friend friend. And I don't know, I think that's it. As I said, I like people and the more I know the better I like it.

Victor is an 82-year-old retired engineer and widower who lives alone in his own home. Like Margaret, his discussions reveal an "acquisitive" style of friendship in organizing the social activities of later adulthood (Matthews, 1986a). Although he retired 16 years ago, Victor keeps up connections with former work associates and develops new friends through volunteer work in his community:

> I've maintained a fairly close relationship and contact with the people in the department where I retired. Some of the men that worked for me and with me are still working, aren't up to retirement age yet, and we get together, oh, 'bout 2 or 3 times a month for coffee and just hash over old times and current problems and so on. And just keep abreast of what's going on, because I was in the construction department so I'm still interested. And then I have other friends; I work as a volunteer as a Red Coat over at Nanticoke Hospital. So I've got acquainted with an entirely different group of people which I've some fairly close friends there and I enjoy that very much.

In enacting his acquisitive style of making friends, Victor combines an overall attitude of friendliness with a tendency to avoid interacting with persons whom he finds unappealing. When asked about how he makes friends, he answers:

> Oh I don't have too much trouble. I can meet people and get along. I have a, maybe it's a fault, if uh I don't particularly like a person, I don't want to

have anything to do with them, so that may be a fault. But, uh, I don't have any particular problem in getting acquainted and being friendly with people generally.

Victor estimates the present number of his close friends as "8 or 10" who are "still living," reflecting both his extensive social network and the characteristic attrition in friendships due to death in the later adult years. He observes, "Most of 'em are what I've had in working and go through church and the civic organizations and so on. . . . I see some of them every week, not the same one every week, but generally I got uh 1 or 2 different ones practically every week." Since he sustains such an array of friendships with customary interaction, it is not easy for him to name his closest one. However, he feels that his current closest friend is a former co-worker now similarly retired. Because of this shared status, Victor states, "We probably get together more often than most of the others on a regular basis." He recounts the work environment within which this friendship was established:

> See, I was construction superintendent and our duties were to inspect and monitor the construction projects for the company's contract work we had, so that uh we were doing inspection. And when I got men to come into the department, I picked men from the personality standpoint, ability, because we had all of the working trades—we had carpenters, electricians, plumbers and all the different trades. And when we brought a man into the department, he was a man that had the respect of the tradesmen on the job and showed them how to do their work. And that I thought was important. And as I say the friendships were developed on that type of basis. It was mutual respect to start with, and then it gradually developed.

Working together is a primary basis for forming friendships during adulthood. Such bonding is facilitated to the extent that both persons engage in gratifying work that emphasizes their cooperation. Clearly, Victor's interest in his department 16 years after retiring indicates his ongoing regard for his former profession. Moreover, he describes how, as a supervisor, he hired people on the basis of their personal qualities and ability to work with others and earn their respect through demonstrating competence. These conditions composed the basis of an initial "mutual respect" between himself and his former co-worker that "gradually developed" into the close friendship lasting into their retirement years.

According to Victor, there are distinct advantages for his well-being in having friends in his circumstances. Especially during his late wife's illness, he grew to appreciate the friends and acquaintances who continued to visit and help him during those troubled times:

Well, being alone, like I am, it would be a pretty dismal life if you didn't have friends that you could call on the telephone or visit back and forth. I don't, I've never had any, see my wife's been dead five years. And she had Alzheimer's disease, so she was uh, we were pretty well isolated for a certain period of time, although some of our longtime friends and acquaintances would still come in and visit with you. But, uh, some of them were a little embarrassed. They weren't, uh I tried to explain what the situation was, but they don't, ten years ago people never heard of Alzheimer's disease. So they weren't too comfortable with it. It was a little hard to explain, but uh that's one of those things that happens. But as I say, some of those friendships are what helped me through that period also.

In speaking of those times, Victor implies certain of the tensions between independence and dependence among friends. Apparently uncomfortable in witnessing Elsie's deteriorating condition, many of their friends abandoned Victor and his wife during her illness, making them feel "pretty well isolated." He is clearly thankful for the "longtime friends and acquaintances" who cared enough to continue visiting. Meanwhile, reflecting his simultaneous desire for independence, Victor mentioned some problems with friends during this time because, in his words, "I think sometimes you get to a point where you may lean on some people a little bit that you wouldn't otherwise do." However, overall, his gratitude for their presence outweighs his reduced autonomy when he recalls this period.

Like many of the older persons we spoke with, Victor's siblings and children are spread across the country. Consequently, he considers his persistent style of vigorously preserving old and developing new friendships a prudent activity to limit his isolation. He explains:

The friends I have are most of 'em located here locally and I see them more often than I see my relatives. . . . My family is so widely scattered that uh I have to keep up the relationships here and friendships maintain them here or I'd be sitting here staring at the wall part of the time.

Cross-Sex Friendship among Older Adults

Except for friendships between spouses, attachments mediated by couple relationships, or by publicly conducted group activities like card-playing, our interviewees described few close free-standing cross-sex friendships. However, persons exhibiting an overall acquisitive or independent style of friendship were more likely than the discerning to describe one or more cross-sex friends. Margaret, in describing her various friends, says:

Oh, I have young friends; I have middle aged, I have older people, I have male, I have female. I have one in Ashford, Ohio. I met him on a trip to Greece. And that was about six years ago. And we travel a lot together; we go on a lot of trips together. This man was just 81 and doesn't look it. And he is very active and about four years ago, he had a six bypass and has survived. And, in fact, when he knew he had to have it, he said, "Oh there goes our trip to Australia." And I said, "Well that's six months away. Let's wait until the time comes and we'll see." We went on our trip. It was 21 days and lovely. And then I have lady friends too. If he doesn't like to go, I say, "Okay, you stay home, I'll go." I have lady friends that I travel with a lot.

Likewise, asked if he has female friends, Victor replies:

Sure, I have several; I have two particularly, friends, widows that uh, one is the widow of a man that I worked with, and the other is uh, well he's not exactly a casual acquaintance, he worked in a different department so I knew him. But I'd never met his wife until after he died. And uh, I got acquainted with her through some mutual friends. And we go out to dinner occasionally and things of that nature. But I'm not interested and those ladies are not interested in any permanent type—it's just a friend-ship type of thing—and no, no uh permanent commitments or anything of that nature. . . . I enjoy very much getting together with them occasion-ally just the same as I do getting together with the men.

Many of Victor's comments qualify his relationships as "just a friend-ship type of thing," involving "no permanent commitments." In fact, most of these individuals tended to address and negate the possibility of romantic overtones in their cross-sex friendships, stating things like: "I was married for 59 years with my former wife, and I'm not looking for another one," or "He is a friend to me of that kind, see, not a love affair or anything. . . . He's good to all of us—all we old ladies" (laughter). Similar to Adams's (1985) findings, by and large our interviewees felt their cross-sex friendships had to be structurally beyond reproach or verbally accounted for due to actual or perceived social judgments and attributions.

Interestingly, every married male except Edward, whose wife has been in a nursing home for 5 years, designated his wife as his best friend. Regardless of their overall pattern or style of friendships across their adult years, these males, save one, uniformly singled out their spouse's friendship. While our female interviewees were all widows, none of them mentioned their deceased husbands as friends, as some widowers did, despite frequent allusions to departed female friends.

For instance, Frank, my male exemplar of the discerning style, states:

Well, I'm without any close friend other than my wife now, and I think mutual respect is probably one of the major aspects of the friendship.

Again, helping the other person wherever possible and vice versa. So it's a mutual helping thing and sharing of ideas, talking about common observations and things we have read and what have you. At the present time other than my wife I don't have any what I call very close friends.

Frank attributes the persistence of their marital friendship to its growth over the years in sharing their lives:

I think because we've both grown in our friendship. We've both gone from callow youth to old age with education and new knowledge being very, very important. We've had a lot of common experiences in travel and you name it. We have common friends, common experiences, and you build it.

Not only is his wife Louise Frank's closest friend, but as commonly occurs, she maintains the connections with the couple's other "acquaintances." He states decisively and appreciatively:

Well, if it weren't for my wife, I wouldn't have any contact with acquaintances, probably because I don't tend to write personal letters. But she's a very very good correspondent, so she's writing all the time to our mutual acquaintances and relatives. So this kind of link is being carried on all the time.

Frank summarizes a view of cross-sex friendship widely shared by other males throughout adulthood, "One ought to marry their best friend if they're the opposite sex. It's extremely important to have your wife as your best friend." His friendship with Louise has been vivifying, as he remarks, "I don't think marriages are very exciting if that isn't true. We have never run out of conversation. We always have great fun together. We've been together for forty years, so that tells you something."

By comparison, my exemplar of the independent friendship style, Raymond, gives a personally consistent response when asked about his closet or best friend, "I don't have one. My wife is my closest friend; she is, she's the only one that I have." He explains this bond:

Because we're so close, we're just one. We do everything together, we go places together. We do, I incorporate her into all the things that I do, all the social things, she goes to all the weddings with me and so on. And so she is part of the whole deal. And, in turn, the things that she's involved in, I become involved in, if she wishes. But we're just extremely close, which is perhaps why we don't need to search for friendship.

If the availability and willingness of participants allowed it, I would always prefer to interview both participants in researching relationships. Unfortunately, practical limitations often prevent this practice. These men's remarks about their relationships with their wives are a case in point. I wonder how their wives perceive these friendships, especially since the older women we interviewed did not mention husbands as friends. Clearly, Raymond's statement contradicts his prior repeated claims about having no close friends. When encouraged by an interview to look his interpersonal world "in the eye," he recognizes his intimate friendship with his wife.

Finally, Kurt, who early in the chapter describes minimal expectations of his largely community and professional friendships, specifies his wife as his close friend for typical reasons:

> Cause I can open up to her more than I could anybody else. I mean tell her how I feel on different things. And I wouldn't tell other people what I tell her. So that's why I call her my closest friend. Well more personal there and everything.

He elaborates further at another point:

> The more personal you get, the more closeness you get, to a degree. But then that degree hits with me, I cut it off, I won't tell you any more. So you're probably my top friend, more or less, friendship friend. But that's as far as you're gonna go with me. Now Janice [his wife] has gone over that period, see, that's why she's my best friend.

These men's statements reflect the frequent finding that the marital relationship is the primary domain of intimate friendship for adult males in later life.

Conclusion

The words of these older people reveal persistent functions, strains, and assortments of friendships in later life. As long as personal capacities and situational factors allow, people look to their friends to talk about a wide range of topics, confide in and relate to, have a good time with, and rely on for assistance and moral support. Further, contacting and being contacted by friends alleviates loneliness, particularly for individuals living alone. As a result, interaction with friends plays a central role in composing these persons' enduring patterns of intimacy and sociability as well as adjusting to changing social configurations in later life.

Nonetheless, maintaining friendships still involves communicatively managing inherent contradictions. Each person's freedoms to be independent and to depend on the other must be reconciled. Moreover, friends must manage recurring needs for frank counsel and judgment versus desires for ongoing acceptance and confirmation. And the expressiveness and confidence associated with close friendship contrasted with the sensitivity and respect for self's and other's privacy and vulnerabilities also must be addressed. How relational partners handle these tensions continues to shape and reflect the trajectories of specific friendships across the concrete circumstances of their later lives.

These individuals depict their experiences of friendship in later adulthood using narratives that variously express sustained involvement with select individuals, consecutive sets of friends associated with changing residences and social circumstances, or a pattern of preserving certain longterm friendships as well as developing new ones as personal situations alter. Thus, their accounts resemble the friendship styles identified by Matthews (1986b) as "discerning," "independent," and "acquisitive."

Regardless of their personal styles, these persons valued the past and present moments of friendship in their lives. Despite the sometimes bittersweet recollections of bygone days, or deceased or now minimally available friends and loved ones, overall, speaking of their relationships seemed uplifting for them; it touched a vital nerve. Several individuals spontaneously expressed almost identical summary thoughts about friendship. Art, a 79-year-old farmer and recent widow said, "I don't know how anyone would ever live without friends. Because to me, they're next to good health, and all your life depends on friendship." Irene echoed, "I don't see how anyone could live without friends." Helen concurred, "Well, honey, I don't think we could hardly live a normal life without having friends. I think that is one of the first requirements: Make yourself a friend to somebody." Emily stressed the need for close friends:

> Well, I don't know, I don't know how anyone could ever live, live a full life, a happy life, and not have good friends, and have friendships, and special friendships especially. It's a necessary thing. And I just don't know how people can live without being close to somebody, and several people, not just one or two, but several people that it just makes for a fuller life.

Finally, Lester observed at one point, "Life wouldn't be worth living if I didn't have friends." He concluded his interview with an observation that also comprises the coda for this chapter, "So I've had a good life. And I've had a, I think that my friends had a lot to do with it. Probably miss many of them more than I realize."

Conclusion

Vistas of Friendship: Individuation, Intimacy, and Community

As a cultural category and source of imagery about ideal human relationships and social being, the term "friendship" usually evokes positive connotations. Its ideal-typical characteristics include the freedom to choose and maintain one's bonds with others voluntarily, the personalized recognition of and response to particular individuals' intrinsic worth as human beings, the pursuit of equality based on the corresponding validity of friends' subjective experiences, a shared orientation of mutual good will, understanding, trust, support, and acceptance, and heartfelt feelings of platonic affection and concern.

In actuality, only specific close or best friendships seem to achieve fully this ideal collection of traits and practices. Even they remain vulnerable to multiple strains arising between friends as they try to manage the private and public involvements and contingencies shaping their lives. Moreover, people develop numerous affiliations with widely varying attributes that they refer to as friendships, and they incorporate assorted activities and orientations of friendship into their relationships with spouses, parents, siblings, children, relatives, neighbors, coworkers, and fellow citizens. Consequently, the friendships described throughout this book assume various forms, gradations of intimacy and sociability, and interpretations of ideal practices depending on their circumstances, interaction patterns, and participants' inclinations.

In studies using diverse approaches to gathering and analyzing data, adolescents to older adults repeatedly describe three expectations of close friendship consistent with its cultural ideals. A close friend is somebody to talk to, to depend on and rely on for help, support, and caring, and to have fun and enjoy doing things with. Though these general expectations of close friendship endure throughout life, the existential, relational and social circumstances in which they are realized change over time. Our vistas of friendship are strongly rooted in life's finitude, the constraints and opportunities of given moments.

Except for those maintained as memories, friendships persist only to the extent that individuals treat each other in mutually fulfilling ways, according to how they define their required contact, evaluative standards, and appropriate actions. Because of its voluntary basis, either friend can abruptly "walk away" or let the friendship gradually lapse if treated in a manner he or she deems improper. As a result, the interaction of friends is of particular interest for understanding inherently valued communicative practices as well as how and why people negotiate optional allegiances with others throughout their lives. Of related concern is the satisfactory enactment and communication of a "friendship component" in diverse personal and social bonds.

This book has emphasized the utility and richness of viewing the ongoing communicative achievement of friendship from a dialectical perspective. I have examined four interactional dialectics forming and reflecting the communicative challenges and contradictory demands of friendship throughout life. The *dialectic of the freedom to be independent and the freedom to be dependent* describes the patterns of availability, obligation, absence, and copresence characterizing friendships in light of the voluntaristic ethic underlying friendships in American culture. From the time that children understand the possibility of and threats to enduring voluntary attachments, sustaining friendships requires coming to grips with the boundaries and interdependence of self and other within specific relationships, and the demands that friends are able to make on each other within embracing social configurations.

The *dialectic of affection and instrumentality* articulates the tensions arising in friendship between caring for a friend as an end-in-itself or as a means-to-an-end. All friends periodically rely on each other for a range of emotional and practical assistance. Yet distinctive meanings of friendship are implied when persons feel befriended primarily because of what they can do for each other, as opposed to relationships where the parties' utilitarian capabilities are incidental or stem from a more fundamental mutual regard.

The *dialectic of judgment and acceptance* formulates the recurring dilemmas in friendship between providing objective appraisals of a friend's actions and ideas versus giving unconditional endorsement and support. What do friends really need or want to hear in specific situations? When persons view each other with compassionate objectivity, they often synthesize the contrasting reactions of evaluation and support in these friendships as constructive criticism. Friends acknowledge the existence of faults and limitations, yet still communicate overall acceptance of the other as a worthy person. In short, they are judicious, not judgmental, providing evaluation carefully in ways that the other can handle, with a gentle manner, using discretion.

Although relying on a friend's opinions and judging together in this manner are clearly vital and valued activities of friendship, one risk is that friends may tolerate detrimental tendencies or interpret vices as virtues. In doing so, friends may create private cultures with views and behaviors that are antithetical or oblivious to objective accomplishments, the larger community, or the common good. Even so, sometimes risking the friendship itself, trusted friends will strongly object to a person's ideas and actions if they judge their likely consequences as serious enough. Accepting or chiding, friends are a salient moral presence in our lives.

Finally, *the dialectic of expressiveness and protectiveness* addresses the opposing tendencies to speak openly with a friend and relate private thoughts and feelings, and the simultaneous need to restrain one's disclosures to preserve privacy and avoid burdening one's friend. Interestingly, once they develop a mature capacity for friendship, people of all ages view the ability to confide as a privilege distinguishing their closest friendships. But the personal vulnerability occasioned by revealing sensitive information, and the corresponding responsibilities imposed on others not to misuse intimate knowledge of self, make confidence and trust problematic achievements throughout many individuals' lives and find many people, notably males, without friends to confide in when they need to talk about weighty matters.

A dialectical perspective calls for investigating and situating enactments of friendship in their concrete social conditions over time. In considering their nature, functions, dialectical exigencies, and communicative management, I have described how friendships participate in the challenges, satisfactions, and dramas of characteristic social configurations during each stage in the life course. I have also depicted how each period reflects and contributes to a lifelong narrative of friendship. Robust friendships take time to develop and maintain, and the moments available for friends wax and wane at various points in the life course depending on the simultaneous demands of other normatively sanctioned relationships and commitments—such as school, family, and extracurricular activities during youth, and career, family, and community ventures during adulthood. Whereas such endeavors may promote or constrain friendships, pursuing friendships may in turn either foster or undermine one's commitment to them. At any juncture, we can celebrate or critique friendship for its role in shaping an individual's immediate experiences of self, others, and society in living life's configured and interpenetrated moments to their fullest. We can also evaluate friendships according to how adequately they reflect prior interpersonal lessons or facilitate future well-being for self and others.

Despite their fundamental reliance on private negotiation for continued existence and viability, friendships are highly patterned culturally and contextually. The normative patterns of friendships evident across the life course reveal their undeniable contingency and finitude and their ties to enveloping social conditions and practices. Whereas the ideals of friendship include free choice, personalized responsiveness to others' intrinsic qualities, and equality, mutuality, and affection, actual patterns of friendship reflect social stratification and economic disparities. Empirical studies repeatedly report the pronounced likelihood of friends being similar in age, gender, race, educational attainment, marital and career status, and socioeconomic level. Consequently, friendships are statistically more likely to reinforce and reproduce macrolevel and palpable social differences than to challenge or transcend them. The prevailing friendship practices of the American middle class constitute marginal forces in presenting alternatives to the status quo or pursuing comprehensive social justice.

The modal patterns of *communal* and *agentic* friendships portrayed in this book noticeably reflect "traditional" gender-linked differences throughout life. Communal friendship addresses an individual's needs for intimate communication, caring, subjective validation, and personal involvement with particular others. These friendships seem especially suited to private life, where persons can try to avoid struggles for power and competition for resources. Here they can negotiate norms of mutual assistance, enjoyment and sustained affection, rendering excessive self-seeking inappropriate and inimical to common well-being.

In contrast, agentic friendship reflects a person's needs for sociable communication, interpersonal harmony, objective validation, and social involvement with a variety of others. Such friendships are highly conducive to public and business life, where competition for power and resources is inevitable and public norms and community implications encourage and regulate individual gains and favors. Depending on the contexts in which they occur, both styles of friendship can contribute positively to reconciling selves, others, and social worlds. But how well versed are typical males and females in the two modes?

By and large, females learn and practice communal friendship at a younger age than males and are more likely to describe sustained involvement with close same-sex friends throughout their lives, even when married and working. In contrast, males typically first describe intimate friendships somewhat later than females. Across life, fewer males mention close same-sex bonds, and available evidence suggests that their reported close male friendships are usually not as disclosive, emotionally involving, or affectionate as similar female dyads. Instead, the agentic features of autonomy and activity-orientation typify male bonds, with married men frequently relying chiefly on their wives for intimacy and close friendship.

These patterns apparently reflect stereotypical sex-role training and persistent practices linking females with nurturance and the private sphere and males with competition and the public domain. However, there are indications that these gender alignments in friendship practices are changing, with women's patterns of friendship exhibiting the most vivid shifts. Basically, as greater numbers of women enter the work force, pursuing fulltime careers and participating in politics, the "traditional" separation of predominantly female private and male public realms and their associated patterns of friendship decreasingly comprises a tenable comprehensive description. Facing multiple tasks in coordinating their personal, family, and work lives, some women are developing primarily agentic friendships, allowing for good feelings, camaraderie, and easy rapport but avoiding the demands and tensions of more intimate bonds. Others try to maintain their customary communal friendships, transcending the boundaries of their public and private lives. Though these bonds often prove difficult to manage due to contradictory requirements of affiliation and achievement, the deeper affection, trust, and personal fulfillment they offer seem to justify the effort required. Finally, some women segment their social activities around agentic friendships in their public endeavors and communal ones in their personal realms.

Across life the borders between private and public relationships are frequently blurred for males and females, and specific friendships can thoroughly transcend modal practices, blending the attributes of communal and agentic friendships in various ways according to the participants' stages in the life course and personal circumstances. Overall, however, males do not demonstrate females' flexibility or range of jointly negotiated possibilities in their friendships. They are hampered by negligible early training and reinforcement in matters of communal interpersonal relationships and insufficient lifelong practice in developing same-sex intimacy. Moreover, cultural proscriptions against male vulnerability, persistent overdependence on women for emotional confirmation, and continued confinement to competitive, career-oriented arenas and achievements for their foremost validations of self-conceptions as worthwhile human beings limit their interpersonal options. Although prevailing cultural arrangements statistically link males and females with the patterns described here, I consider the continual social construction of genderized relational practices in concrete circumstances to be the critical concern, not biological gender per se. Given the limits of time and energy in specific periods and overall life spans, tracking types and modes of friendship reveals subjective priorities, negotiated practices, and moral visions enacted within all-too-tangible systemic constraints.

Even though the normative contours of middle-class American life comprehensively pattern most of the possibilities for friendship, every single case develops through the voluntary interaction of particular persons. Each union offers a forum for both upholding and transcending cultural injunctions. People employ specific standards in choosing friends, which they expect each other to live up to, consciously or not. As their friendship evolves, they negotiate mutual commitments and further expectations, resulting in a distinguishable moral order of acceptable practices and common standards of evaluation. How partners manage ongoing dialectical tensions in their private and public moments yields shared friendship practices variously emphasizing individuation, intimacy, and/or a larger community. What I have called the "double agency" of friendship refers to its unique capacity to facilitate personal integration and/or social participation in given cases. This pivotal quality constitutes a definitive flexibility and problematic of ongoing friendships; it is their potential redemption and moral risk.

Many of life's most poignant quandaries concern questions of personal and social responsibility. One of the most vital activities of friendship is judging together, consulting with a trusted friend about questions of right and wrong, prudent and imprudent action. Where does my personal responsibility leave off and selfishness begin? Am I being fair to myself in this situation or am I asking for more than I deserve? Conversely, where does my social responsibility stop and selflessness start? Am I treating the other(s) fairly in making this decision or am I meekly accommodating? In situations where much is at stake and choices are not clearcut, people often turn to their friends for empathic counsel. Because of close friendship's double-agency and compassionate objectivity, caring friends do not necessarily indulge or endorse personal whims in a kneejerk fashion, but neither do they invoke social pieties. Ideally, concerned friends respond in a manner sensitive to the particulars of an individual's situation while mindful of its broader social consequences.

The conversation of friendship simultaneously transcends individualism and reduces susceptibility to conformism when friends earnestly appraise together the emotional and practical meanings of their predicaments—enacting an enterprise I call "significance testing." The pun is intentional as questioners seek to avoid two analogous types of error, but the examination's conclusions are based on dialogically established insights, not statistical magnitudes. Type I error is the perception of the individual self as significantly different than other human beings and/or removed from the encompassing implications of one's actions, when such conceptions threaten worthwhile social arrangements. It is the error of excessive inner-directedness, self-service, and individualism. A friend's insights and critique can broaden one's conscience in situations where a person is too focused on his or her own costs or gains. Cutting through apartness and dissolving isolation, friends can summon each other to community consideration and involvement.

Type II error is the failure to register significant differences between one's thoughts, feelings, and values and dominant social tendencies, when it would be in self's and others' best interests to do so. This indifference facilitates and reproduces false consciousness on both individual and social levels. It is the error of extreme other-directedness and unreflective conformism. A friend's acceptance and support may be exactly what is needed to strengthen one's commitment to "deviant" perceptions that could potentially serve widespread and just but understated needs and interests. Challenging docility and praising convictions, friends can encourage each other to stand and be counted. The discourse of friendship can sometimes help people distinguish principled, creative individuation from myopic, alienating individuality, and mindful social participation from mindless conformity.

Pursuing friendship is not necessarily or merely a subjectivist retreat from the world-shaping activities of politics and public life. Self and community are enacted in public and private contexts; and there are both political and existential expressions of character. Whereas given friends can turn inward, reinforcing similar world views and their own egocentricity, other friendships open outward and foster broader human connections. Further, robust friendship is not merely a convenient technique for self-confirmation, but an exacting interpersonal relationship, a responsible coordination of actual and possible worlds. Viable intimate and social friendships enact moral stances and orientations toward the participants' well-being and potential as members of common social orders.

As such, friendships constitute intersubjective though particularized sites for cultivating and practicing ethical sensibilities as well as appraising character. They function this way developmentally—as children develop practices of cooperation, caring, good will, commitment, and loyalty that enhance their abilities to get along with others later in life. During other periods of the life course, trusted friends also offer a place where persons can "step back" from the press of daily activities, cross-examine decisions and actions, and enjoy and help each other. Despite the potential virtues and satisfactions of friendships, however, they remain problematic endeavors throughout the life cycle. Just as they are sites for learning prosocial practices during childhood, they also foster selectivity, coalitions, and bitter rejections. Whereas friends may help us transcend difficulties, gain favors, and relax during adolescence and adulthood, they also can draw us into volatile predicaments, create unspoken obligations, and burden us with things we wish we did not know. For all their fulfillments, friendships can be hard to accomplish, harder yet to sustain, fragile, vulnerable, and, quite often, tragic.

Individual lives embody disparate and complex replies to questions about how, why, and for whom friendship matters. Friendships teeter on the borders of self and other(s), dyads and social systems, and idealized and realized pasts, presents, and futures. Like their authors' life stories, friendship narratives are not the works of single voices but are inherently shared and social compositions. So too are texts like this one about them. In attempting to describe the communicative management of friendships across the life course from a dialectical perspective, I have compared, contrasted, and synthesized insights from a variety of authors, ranging from everyday actors to professional social scientists and writers of "fiction." Clearly, all these persons' contributions were constrained and facilitated in multiple ways by the conventions regulating the production of their discourse as well as by my rendering. Even so, I am convinced of the value of collecting and bringing to bear as diverse an array of cultural texts as possible when investigating the communicative construction of social lives and worlds. Certainly as we enact our relationships with others, the cultural resources and images of social being we draw on and reproduce are not limited to specified or narrowly authoritative genres. Rather, as Kenneth Burke reminds us, we use and continue to create whatever there is in the symbolic realm of human action.

I am struck by the pronounced cleavage between the rich detail and absorbing character of the lived accounts of friendship presented here and the too often stereotyped and bleached descriptions offered in the modal work in social science. Further, like so much meaningful social activity, the discourse of friendship is largely moral, making it necessary to cross the borders separating humanistic and scientific discourses. I hope that juxtaposing the ostensibly neutral descriptions of modal social science with the lived experience of interpretive human and literary studies in this book illustrates the value of bridging these different ways of knowing.

As I reflect on this manuscript, I notice omissions and ways of improving it, granting my admittedly restricted focus on the American middle class. In gathering data, I strongly recommend interviewing both parties in studying interpersonal relationships, like the case studies in Chapter 7. Because relational worlds are co-created, both persons' perspectives bring us much closer than one individual's comments can to their shared realities and intersubjective concepts. I also believe that displaying and analyzing more of the actual discourse of friends better represents the negotiated character of their time together. Perhaps willing pairs of friends would let a tape recorder run during their outings or conversations. More extensive oral histories will enrich our understanding of how thoroughly the practices and possibilities of friendship interact with individuals' biographies and ongoing social configurations. For this reason, such histories are quite useful in studying any juncture in the life course, not just later life. Unquestionably, longitudinal studies contribute invaluable information about the ebb and flow of relationships, though they are quite costly. Probably more intimidating to researchers, they bring the calendrical and life cycle time constraints of the persons being studied into sobering alignment with those of the investigator.

Substantively, this book enacts limitations of rational and analytical social inquiry. Consequently, it overlooks or underplays much of the emotionality, happenstance, and impulsiveness of friendship as well as the dialectical dynamics of desire, sexuality, and the erotic. The importance of these issues cannot be denied, and one can trace their scholarly recognition back to ancient Greek thinkers. As well, scholars can further explore the nature and practices of friendships among family members, especially siblings.

I hope this book raises more questions than it answers. If that is the case, it does some justice to its subject. As a timeless cultural category, resourceful and edifying array of practices, and bounded human relationship, friendship poses endless riddles. Yet in doing so, it continually offers hopeful and benevolent occasions to respond.

References

Abbey, A. (1982). Sex differences in attributions for friendly behavior: Do males misperceive females' friendliness? *Journal of Personality and Social Psychology, 42,* 830–838.

Acker, J., Barry, K., & Esseveld, J. (1981). Feminism, female friends, and the reconstruction of intimacy. In H. Z. Lopata & D. Maines (Eds.), *Research in the interweave of social roles: Friendship* (Vol. 2, pp. 75–108). Greenwich, CT: JAI Press.

Adams, A. (1979). What should I have done? In *Beautiful Girl* (pp. 221-230). New York: Alfred A. Knopf.

Adams, G. R., & Gullotta, T. (1983). *Adolescent life experiences.* Monterey, CA: Brooks/Cole.

Adams, R. G. (1985). People would talk: Normative barriers to cross-sex friendships for elderly women. *The Gerontologist, 25,* 605–610.

Adams, R. G. (1985–86). Emotional closeness and physical distance between friends: Implications for elderly women living in age-segregated and age-integrated settings. *International Journal of Aging and Human Development, 22,* 55–76.

Adams, R. G. (1986). Secondary friendship networks and psychological well-being among elderly women. *Activities, Adaptation and Aging, 8,* 59–72.

Adams, R. G. (1987) Patterns of network change: A longitudinal study of friendships of elderly women. *The Gerontologist, 27,* 222–227.

Adams, R. G. (1988). Which comes first: Poor psychological well-being or decreased friendship activity? *Activities, Adaptation and Aging, 12,* 27–41.

Adler, T. F., & Furman, W. (1988). A model for children's relationships and relationship dysfunctions. In S. W. Duck (Ed.), *Handbook of personal relationships* (pp. 211–229). New York: John Wiley.

Allan, G. A. (1979) *A sociology of friendship and kinship.* London: Allen and Unwin.

Annas, J. (1977). Plato and Aristotle on friendship and altruism. *Mind, 86,* 532–554.

Aries, E. J., & Johnson, F. L. (1983). Close friendship in adulthood: Conversational content between same-sex friends. *Sex Roles, 9,* 1183–1196.

Aristotle. (1980). *The Nichomachean ethics* (D. Ross, Trans.). Oxford: Oxford University Press.

Arling, G. (1976). The elderly widow and her family, neighbors and friends. *Journal of Marriage and the Family, 38,* 757–768.

281

Ashton, N. L. (1980). Exploratory investigation of perceptions of influences on best-friend relationships. *Perceptual and Motor Skills, 50,* 379–386.

Askham, J. (1976). Identity and stability within the marriage relationship. *Journal of Marriage and the Family, 38,* 535–547.

Atchley, R. C. (1975). Dimensions of widowhood in later life. *The Gerontologist, 15,* 176–178.

Atchley, R. C. (1977). *The social forces in later life,* 2nd ed. Belmont, CA: Wadsworth.

Atchley, R. C. (1982). The life course, age grading, and age-linked demands for decision making. In K. W. Schaie & J. Geiwitz (Eds.), *Adult development and aging* (pp. 145–153). Boston: Little, Brown & Co.

Atchley, R. C., Pignatiello, L., & Shaw, E. C. (1979). Interactions with family and friends: Marital status and occupational differences among older women. *Research on Aging, 1,* 83–95.

Austin, M. C., & Thompson, G. C. (1948). Children's friendships: A study of the bases on which children select and reject their best friends. *The Journal of Educational Psychology, 39,* 101–116.

Babchuk, N. (1965). Primary friends and kin: A study of the associations of middle class couples. *Social Forces, 43,* 483–493.

Babchuk, N. (1978-79). Aging and primary relations. *International Journal of Aging and Human Development, 9,* 137-151.

Babchuk, N., & Anderson, T. B. (1989). Older widows and married women: Their intimates and confidants. *International Journal of Aging and Human Development, 28,* 21–35.

Babchuk, N., & Bates, A. P. (1963). The primary relations of middle-class couples: A study in male dominance. *American Sociological Review, 28,* 377–384.

Babchuk, N., Peters, G. R., Hoyt, D. R., & Kaiser, M. A. (1979). The voluntary associations of the aged. *Journal of Gerontology, 34,* 579–587.

Bakan, D. (1966). *The duality of human existence.* Boston: Beacon.

Ball, R. A. (1979). The dialectical method: Its application to social theory. *Social Forces, 57,* 785–798.

Ball, S. J. (1981). *Beachside comprehensive.* Cambridge, MA: Cambridge University Press.

Banta, T. J., & Heatherington, M. (1963). Relations between needs of friends and fiances. *Journal of Abnormal and Social Psychology, 66,* 401–404.

Basseches, M. (1984). *Dialectical theory and adult development.* Norwood, NJ: Ablex.

Bateson, G. (1958). *Naven.* Stanford: Stanford University Press.

Baxter, L. A. (1984). Trajectories of relationship disengagement. *Journal of Social and Personal Relationships, 1,* 29–48.

Beim, L., & Beim, J. (1945). *Two is a team.* New York: Harcourt Brace, & World.

Beiner, R. (1983). *Political judgment.* Chicago: The University of Chicago Press.

Bell, R. (1975). Swinging: Separating the sexual from friendship. In N. Glazer-Malbin (Ed.), *Old family/new family* (pp. 150–168). New York: D. Van Nostrand.

Bell, R. R. (1981). *Worlds of friendship*. Beverly Hills: Sage.

Bell, T. (1967). The relationship between social involvement and feeling old among residents in homes for the aged. *Journal of Gerontology, 22*, 17–22.

Bellah, R. N., Madsen, R., Sullivan, W. M., Swidler, A., & Tipton, S. M. (1985). *Habits of the heart: Individualism and commitment in American life*. Berkeley: University of California Press.

Bensman, J., & Lilienfeld, R. (1979). *Between public and private: The lost boundaries of the self*. New York: Free Press.

Berger, P., & Kellner, H. (1964). Marriage and the construction of reality. *Diogenes, XXXVI*, 1–24.

Berger, P., & Luckman, T. (1966). *The social construction of reality*. Garden City, NY: Doubleday.

Berger, T. (1981). *Friends*. New York: Julian Messner.

Bernard, J. (1972). *The future of marriage*. New York: World Publishing Co.

Bernard, J. (1981). *The female world*. New York: Free Press.

Berndt, T. J. (1981a). Effects of friendship on prosocial intentions and behavior. *Child Development, 52*, 636–643.

Berndt, T. J. (1981b). Relations between social cognition, nonsocial cognition, and social behavior: The case of friendship. In J. H. Flavell & L. Ross (Eds.), *Social cognitive development: Frontiers and possible futures* (pp. 176–199). Cambridge: Cambridge University Press.

Berndt, T. J. (1982a). The features and effects of friendship in early adolescence. *Child Development, 53*, 1447–1460.

Berndt, T. J. (1982b). Fairness and friendship. In K. H. Rubin & H. S. Ross (Eds.), *Peer relationships and social skills in childhood* (pp. 253–278). New York: Springer-Verlag.

Berndt, T. J. (1985). Prosocial behavior between friends in middle childhood and early adolescence. *Journal of Early Adolescence, 3*, 307–317.

Berndt, T. J. (1986). Sharing between friends: Contexts and consequences. In E. C. Mueller & C. R. Cooper (Eds.), *Processes and outcomes in peer relationships* (pp. 105–127). New York: Academic Press.

Berndt, T. J., & Das, R. (1987). Effects of popularity and friendship choice on perceptions of the personality and social behavior of peers. *Journal of Early Adolescence, 7*, 429–439.

Bigelow, B. J. (1977). Children's friendship expectations: A cognitive-developmental study. *Child Development, 48*, 246–253.

Bigelow, B. J., & La Gaipa, J. J. (1975). Children's written descriptions of friendship: A multidimensional analysis. *Developmental Psychology, 11*, 857–858.

Bigelow, B. J., & La Gaipa, J. J. (1980). The development of friendship values and choice. In H. C. Foot, A. J. Chapman & J. R. Smith (Eds.), *Friendship and social relations in children* (pp. 15–44). New York: John Wiley.

Blau, Z. S. (1961). Structural constraints on friendships in old age. *American Sociological Review, 26*, 429–439.

Blau, Z. S. (1973). *Aging in a changing society*. New York: Franklin Watts.

Bloch, M. (1971). The moral and tactical meaning of kinship terms. *Man, 6,* 79–87.

Bloom, M. V. (1980). *Adolescent–parental separation.* New York: Gardner Press.

Bochner, A. P. (1978). On taking ourselves seriously: An analysis of some persistent problems and promising directions in interpersonal research. *Human Communication Research, 2,* 381–397.

Bochner, A. P. (1984). Functions of communication in interpersonal bonding. In C. Arnold & J. Bowers (Eds.), *Handbook of rhetoric and communication theory* (pp. 544–621). Boston: Allyn & Bacon.

Booth, A. (1972). Sex and social participation. *American Sociological Review, 37,* 183–192.

Booth, A., & Hess, E. (1974). Cross-sex friendship. *Journal of Marriage and the Family, 36,* 38–47.

Bott, E. (1955). Urban families: Conjugal roles and social networks. *Human Relations, 8,* 345–384.

Bott, E. (1971). *Family and social networks.* New York: Free Press.

Brain, R. (1976). *Friends and lovers.* New York: Basic Books.

Brown, B. B. (1981). A life-span approach to friendship: Age-related dimensions of an ageless relationship. In H. Z. Lopata & D. Maines (Eds.), *Research in the interweave of social roles: Friendship* (Vol. 2, pp. 23–50). Greenwich, CT: JAI Press.

Brown, N. O. (1959). *Life against death.* Middletown: Wesleyan University Press.

Buhrke, R. A., and Fuqua, D. R. (1987). Sex differences in same- and cross-sex supportive relationships. *Sex Roles, 17,* 339–352.

Buhrmester, D., & Furman, W. (1986). The changing functions of friends in childhood: A neo-Sullivanian perspective. In V. J. Derlega & B. A. Winstead (Eds.), *Friendship and social interaction* (pp. 41–62). New York: Springer-Verlag.

Buhrmester, D., & Furman, W. (1987). The development of companionship and intimacy. *Child Development, 58,* 1101–1113.

Bukowski, W. M., & Kramer, T. L. (1986). Judgments of the features of friendship among early adolescent boys and girls. *Journal of Early Adolescence, 6,* 331–338.

Bukowski, W. M., Nappi, B. J, & Hoza, B. (1987). A test of Aristotle's model of friendship for young adults' same-sex and opposite-sex relationships. *The Journal of Social Psychology, 127,* 595–603.

Bukowski, W. M., Newcomb, A. F., & Hoza, B. (1987). Friendship conceptions among early adolescents: A longitudinal study of stability and change. *Journal of Early Adolescence, 7,* 143–152.

Burleson, B., (1986). Communication skills and childhood peer relationships: An overview. In M. L. McLaughlin (Ed.), *Communication Yearbook* (Vol. 9, pp. 143–180). Beverly Hills, CA: Sage.

Burt, R. S. (1983). Distinguishing relational contents. In R. S. Burt & M. J. Minor (Eds.), *Applied network analysis* (pp. 35–74). Beverly Hills: Sage.

Button, L. (1979). Friendship patterns. *Journal of Adolescence, 2,* 187–199.

Caldwell, M. A., & Peplau, L. A. (1982). Sex differences in same-sex friendship. *Sex Roles, 8,* 721–732.

Campbell, E. Q. (1969). Adolescent socialization. In. D. A. Goslin (Ed.), *Handbook of socialization theory and research* (pp. 821–859). Chicago: Rand McNally.

Candy, S. G., Troll, L. E., & Levy, S. G. (1981). A developmental exploration of friendship functions in women. *Psychology of Women Quarterly, 5,* 456–472.

Cantor, M. H. (1979). Neighbors and friends: An overlooked resource in the informal support system. *Research on Aging, 1,* 434–463.

Carroll, J. (1984). *Prince of peace.* Toronto: Little, Brown and Company.

Chafetz, J. S. (1974). *Masculine/feminine or human?* Itasca, IL: Peacock.

Chappell, N. L. (1983). Informal support networks among the elderly. *Research on Aging, 5,* 77–99.

Chodorow, N. (1976). Oedipal asymmetries and heterosexual knots. *Social Problems, 23,* 454–468.

Chown, S. M. (1981). Friendship in old age. In S. Duck & R. Gilmour (Eds.), *Personal Relationships 2: Developing Personal Relationships* (pp. 231–246). London: Academic Press.

Clark, M., & Anderson, B. G. (1967). *Culture and Aging.* Springfield, IL: Charles C. Thomas.

Cohen, J. J., D'Heurle, A., & Widmark-Petersson, V. (1980). Cross-sex friendship in children: Gender patterns and cultural perspectives. *Psychology in the Schools, 17,* 523–529.

Cohen, M. (1973). *Best friends.* New York: Macmillan.

Coleman, J. C. (1980). Friendship and the peer group in adolescence. In J. Adelson (Ed.), *Handbook of adolescent psychology* (pp. 408–431). New York: John Wiley.

Colman, H. C. (1978). *The secret life of Harold the bird watcher.* New York: Harper & Row.

Conger, J. (1979). *Adolescence: Generation under pressure.* New York: Harper & Row.

Conner, K. A., Powers, E. A., & Bultena, G. L. (1979). Social interpretation and life satisfaction: An empirical assessment of late-life patterns. *Journal of Gerontology, 34,* 116–121.

Corsaro, W. A. (1981). Friendship in the nursery school: Social organization in a peer group environment. In S. R. Asher & J. M. Gottman (Eds.), *The development of children's friendships* (pp. 207–241). Cambridge: Cambridge University Press.

Corwin, R., Taves, M. J., & Haas, E. J. (1960). Social requirements for occupational success: Internalized norms and friendship. *Social Forces, 39,* 135–140.

Costanzo, P. R., & Shaw, M. E. (1966). Conformity as function of age level. *Child Development, 37,* 967–975.

Cottle, T., (1976). *Perceiving time: A psychological investigation with men and women.* New York: John Wiley.

Crohan, S. E., & Antonucci, T. C. (1989). Friends as a source of social support in old age. In R. G. Adams & R. Blieszner (Eds.), *Older Adult Friendship* (pp. 129–146). Newbury Park: Sage.

Cutrona, C. E. (1982). Transition to college: Loneliness and the process of social adjustment. In L. A. Peplau & D. Perlman (Eds.), *Loneliness: A sourcebook of current theory, research and therapy* (pp. 291–309). New York: John Wiley.

Damon, W. (1977). *The social world of the child*. San Francisco: Jossey-Bass.

Davidson, L. R., & Duberman, L. (1982). Friendship: Communication and interactional patterns in same-sex dyads. *Sex Roles, 8,* 809–826.

Davidson, S., & Packard, T. (1981). The therapeutic value of friendship between women. *Psychology of Women Quarterly, 5,* 495–510.

Davis, K. E., & Todd, M. J. (1982). Friendship and love relationships. In K. E. Davis & T. Mitchell (Eds.), *Advances in descriptive psychology* (Vol. 2, pp. 79–122). Greenwich, CT: JAI.

Diaz, R. M., & Berndt, T. J. (1982). Children's knowledge of a best friend: Fact or fancy? *Developmental Psychology, 18,* 787–794.

Dickson-Markman, F., & Markman, H. J. (1988). The effects of others on marriage: Do they help or hurt? In P. Noller & M. A. Fitzpatrick (Eds.), *Perspectives on marital interaction* (pp. 294–322). Philadelphia: Multilingual Matters.

Dono, J. E., Falbe, C. M., Kail, B. L., Litwak, R., Sherman, R. H., & Siegel, D. (1979). Primary groups in old age. *Research on Aging, 1,* 403–433.

Douvan, E. (1983). Commentary: Theoretical perspectives on peer association. In J. L. Epstein & N. Karweit (Eds.), *Friends in school: Patterns of selection and influence in secondary schools* (pp. 63–69). New York: Academic Press.

Douvan, E., & Adelson, J. (1966). *The adolescent experience* New York: John Wiley.

Doyle, A. (1982). Friends, acqaintances, and strangers: The influence of familiarity and ethnolinguistic background on social interaction. In. K. H. Rubin & H. S. Ross (Eds.), *Peer relationships and social skills in childhood* (pp. 229–252). New York: Springer-Verlag.

Drake, R. (1987). "1975 has come and gone." In *Survivors and others* (pp. 182–188). Macon, GA: Mercer University Press.

Dubois, C. (1974). The gratuitous act: An introduction to the comparative study of friendship patterns. In E. Leyton (Ed.), *The compact: Selected dimensions of friendship* (pp. 15–32). St. Johns: Institute of Social and Economic Research.

Duck, S., & Gilmour, R. (1981). *Personal relationships 2: Developing personal relationships*. New York: Academic Press.

Dunphy, D. C. (1963). The social structure of urban adolescent peer groups. *Sociometry, 26,* 230–246.

Eder, D., & Hallinan, M. T. (1978). Sex differences in children's friendships. *American Sociological Review, 43,* 237–250.

Edwards, J. N., & Klemmack, D. L. (1973). Correlates of life satisfaction: A re-examination. *Journal of Gerontology, 28,* 497–502.

Eisenstadt, S. N. (1956). *From generation to generation*. Glencoe, IL: Free Press.

Eisenstadt, S. N. (1974). Friendship and the structure of trust and solidarity in society. In E. Leyton (Ed.), *The compact: Selected dimensions of friendship* (pp. 138–145). St. John's: Institute of Social and Economic Research.

Elkind, D. (1967). Egocentrism in adolescence. *Child Development, 38*, 1025–1034.

Elkind, D. (1980). Strategic interactions in early adolescence. In J. Adelson (Ed.), *Handbook of adolescent psychology* (pp. 432–444). New York: John Wiley.

Elkind, D. (1984). *All grown up and no place to go*. Reading, MA: Addison-Wesley.

Epstein, J. L. (1983). Examining theories of adolescent friendships. In J. L. Epstein & N. Karweit (Eds.), *Friends in school: Patterns of selection and influence in secondary schools* (pp. 39–61). New York: Academic Press.

Epstein, J. L., & Karweit, N. (1983). *Friends in school: Patterns of selection and influence in secondary schools*. New York: Academic Press.

Erikson, E. (1963). *Childhood and society*. New York: Norton.

Erikson, E. (1968). *Identity, youth and crisis*. New York: Norton.

Farrell, M. P., & Rosenberg, S. D. (1981). *Men at midlife*. Boston: Auburn House.

Feld, N. (1984). The structured use of personal associates. *Social Forces, 62*, 640–652.

Ferraro, K. F., & Barresi, C. M. (1982). The impact of widowhood on the social relations of older persons. *Research on Aging, 4*, 227-247.

Ferraro, K. F., Mutran, E., & Barresi, C. M. (1984). Widowhood, health, and friendship support in later life. *Journal of Health and Social Behavior, 25*, 245–259.

Feshback, N., & Sones, G. (1971). Sex differences in adolescent reactions toward newcomers. *Developmental Psychology, 4*, 381–386.

Fiebert, M. S., & Fiebert, P. B. (1969). A conceptual guide to friendship formation. *Perceptual and Motor Skills, 28*, 383–390.

Fine, G. A. (1980). The natural history of preadolescent male friendship groups. In H. C. Foot, A. J. Chapman, & J. R. Smith (Eds.), *Friendship and social relations in children* (pp. 293–320). New York: John Wiley.

Fine, G. A. (1981). Friends, impression management, and preadeolescent behavior. In S. R. Asher & J. M. Gottman (Eds.), *The development of children's friendships* (pp 29–52). Cambridge: Cambridge University Press.

Fine, G. A. (1986). Friendships in the work place. In ·V. J. Derlega & B. A. Winstead (Eds.), *Friendship and social interaction* (pp. 185–206). New York: Springer-Verlag.

Fischer, C. S., & Oliker, S. J. (1983). A research note on friendship, gender, and the life cycle. *Social Forces, 62*, 124–133.

Fischer, J. L. (1981). Transitions in relationship style from adolescence to young adulthood. *Journal of Youth and Adolescence, 10*, 11–23.

Fischer, J. L., & Narus, L. R., Jr. (1981). Sex roles and intimacy in same sex and other sex relationships. *Psychology of Women Quarterly, 5*, 444–455.

Fiske, M. (1980). Changing hierarchies of commitment in adulthood. In N. J. Smelser & E. H. Erikson (Eds.), *Themes of work and love in adulthood* (pp. 238–264). Cambridge, MA: Harvard University Press.

Foot, H. C., Chapman, A. J., & Smith, J.R. (1977). Friendship and social responsiveness in boys and girls. *Journal of Personality and Social Psychology, 35*, 401–411.

Foot, H. C., Chapman,, A. J., & Smith, J. R. (1980). Patterns of interaction in children's friendships. In. H. C. Foot, A. J. Chapman, & J. R. Smith (Eds.),

Friendship and social relations in children (pp. 267–289). New York: John Wiley.

Fox, M., Gibbs, M., & Auerback, D. (1985). Age and gender dimensions of friendship. *Psychology of Women Quarterly, 9,* 489–502.

Francis, D. G. (1981). Adaptive strategies of the elderly in England and Ohio. In C. L. Fry (Ed.), *Dimensions: Aging, culture and health* (pp. 85–107). New York: Praeger.

Furman, W., & Bierman, K. L. (1983). Developmental changes in young children's conceptions of friendship. *Child Development, 54,* 549–556.

Furman, W., & Buhrmester, D. (1985). Children's perceptions of their personal relationships in their social networks. *Developmental Psychology, 21,* 1016–1024.

Gamer, E., Thomas, J., & Kendall, D. (1975). Determinants of friendship across the life span. In F. Rebelsky (Ed.), *Life: The continuous process* (pp. 336–345). New York: Alfred Knopf.

Geertz, C. (1976). 'From the native's point of view': On the nature of anthropological understanding. In K. H. Basso & H. A. Selby (Eds.), *Meaning in anthropology* (pp. 221–237). Albuquerque: University of New Mexico Press.

Gerstel, N. (1987). Divorce and stigma. *Social Problems, 34,* 172–186.

Gerstel, N. (1988). Divorce, gender, and social integration. *Gender and Society, 2,* 343-363.

Giele, J. Z. (1980). Adulthood as transcendence of age and sex. In N. J. Smelser & E. H. Erikson (Eds.), *Themes of love and work in adulthood* (pp. 151–173). Cambridge, MA: Harvard University Press.

Gilbert, L. A. (1988). *Sharing it all: The rewards and struggles of two-career families.* New York: Plenum Press.

Gilligan, C. (1982). *In a different voice.* Cambridge: Harvard University Press.

Ginsberg, D., & Gottman, J. (1986). Conversations of college roommates: Similarities and differences in male and female friendship. In J. M. Gottman & J. G. Parker (Eds.), *Conversations of friends* (pp. 241–291). Cambridge: Cambridge Univ. Press.

Goldman, J. A., Cooper, P. E., Ahern, K., & Corsini, D. (1981). Continuities and discontinuities in the friendship descriptions of women at six stages in the life cycle. *Genetic Psychology Monographs, 103,* 153–167.

Goode, W. (1956). *Women in divorce.* New York: Free Press.

Gordon, S. (1978). *Crystal is my friend.* New York: Harper.

Gottman, J. M. (1982) Emotional responsiveness in marital conversations. *Journal of Communication, 32,* 108–120.

Gottman, J. M. (1986). The world of coordinated play: Same- and cross-sex friendship in young children. In J. M. Gottman & J. G. Parker (Eds.), *Conversations of friends: Speculations on affective development* (pp. 139–191). Cambridge: Cambridge University Press.

Gottman, J. M., & Parkhurst, J. T. (1980). A developmental theory of friendship and acquaintanceship processes. In W. A. Collins (Ed.), *Development of cognition, affect, and social relations* (pp. 197–253). The Minnesota Symposia on Child Psychology, Volume 13. Hillsdale, NJ: Lawrence Erlbaum.

Gould, R. L. (1972). The phases of adult life: A study in developmental psychology. *The American Journal of Psychiatry, 129,* 521–531.

Gould, R. L. (1980). Transformations during early and middle adult years, In N. J. Smelser & E. H. Erikson (Eds.), *Themes of love and work in adulthood,* (pp. 213-237). Cambridge, MA: Harvard University Press.

Gouldner, H., & Strong, M. S. (1987). *Speaking of friendship: Middle-class women and their friends.* New York: Greenwood Press.

Granovetter, M. S. (1974). *Getting a job.* Cambridge, MA: Harvard University Press.

Green, E. H. (1933). Friendship and quarrels among preschool children. *Child Development, 4,* 237–252.

Green, S. K., & Sandos, P. (1983). Perceptions of male and female initiators of relationships. *Sex Roles, 9,* 849–852.

Greenberg, M. T., Siegel, J. M., & Leitch, C. J. (1983). The nature and importance of attachment relationships to parents and peers during adolescence. *Journal of Youth and Adolescence, 12,* 373–386.

Greene, C. C. (1981). *Your old pal, Al.* New York: Dell.

Grotevant, H. D., & Cooper, C. R. (1985). Patterns of interaction in family relationships and the development of identity exploration in adolescence. *Child Development, 56,* 415–428.

Hacker, H. M. (1981). Blabbermouths and clams: Sex differences in self-disclosure in same-sex and cross-sex friendship dyads. *Psychology of Women Quarterly, 5,* 385–401.

Haley, J. (1963). *Strategies of psychotherapy.* New York: Grune & Stratton.

Hallinan, M. T. (1978/79). The process of friendship formation. *Social Networks, 1,* 192–210.

Hallinan, M. T. (1979). Structural effects on children's friendships and cliques. *Social Psychology Quarterly, 42,* 43–54.

Harré, R. (1977). Friendship as an accomplishment: An ethogenic approach to social relationships. In S. Duck (Ed.), *Theory and practice in interpersonal attraction* (pp. 339–354). London: Academic Press.

Harry, J. (1976). Evolving sources of happiness for men over the life cycle: A structural analysis. *Journal of Marriage and the Family, 38,* 289–296.

Hartup, W. W. (1975). The origins of friendships. In M. Lewis & L. A. Rosenblum (Eds.), *Friendship and peer relations* (pp. 11–26). New York: John Wiley.

Hays, R. B. (1984). The development and maintenance of friendship. *Journal of Social and Personal Relationships, 1,* 75–98.

Hays, R. B. (1985). A longitudinal study of friendship development. *Journal of Personality and Social Psychology, 46,* 909–924.

Hays, R. B. (1988). Friendship. In S. W. Duck (Ed.), *Handbook of personal relationships* (pp. 391–408). New York: John Wiley.

Heinemann, G. D. (1985). Interdependence in informal support systems: The case of elderly, urban widows. In W. A. Peterson & J. Quadagno (Eds.), *Social bonds in later life: Aging and interdependence,* (pp. 165–186). Beverly Hills, CA: Sage.

Helgeson, V. S., Shaver, P., & Dyer, M. (1987). Prototypes of intimacy and distance in same-sex and opposite-sex relationships. *Journal of Social and Personal Relationships, 4,* 195–233.

Hellman, L. (1973). *Pentimento.* New York: Signet.

Henry, J. (1971). *Pathways to madness.* New York: Vintage Books.

Henry, W. E. (1971). The role of work in structuring the life cycle. *Human Development, 14,* 125–131.

Hess, B. (1972). Friendship. In M. W. Riley, M. Johnson, & A. Foner (Eds.), *Aging and society: A sociology of age stratification* (Vol. 3, pp. 357–393). New York: Russell Sage Foundation.

Hess, B. B. (1979). Sex roles, friendships, and the life course. *Research on Aging, 1,* 494–515.

Hill, C. T., & Stull, D. E. (1981). Sex differences in effects of social and value similarity in same-sex friendship. *Journal of Personality and Social Psychology, 41,* 488–502.

Hoban, R. C. (1969). *Best friends for frances.* New York: Harper & Row.

Hobfoll, S. E., & Stokes, J. P. (1988). The process and mechanics of social support. In S. W. Duck (Ed.), *Handbook of personal relationships* (pp. 497–517). New York: John Wiley.

Hochschild, A. R. (1973). *The Unexpected community: Portrait of an old age subculture.* Berkeley: Univ. of California Press.

Hochschild, A. R. (1979). Emotion work, feeling rules, and social structure. *American Journal of Sociology, 85,* 551–575.

Hodgson, J. W. & Fischer, J. L. (1979). Sex differences in identity and intimacy development in college youth. *Journal of Youth and Adolescence, 8,* 37–50.

Horrocks, J. E., & Benimoff, M. (1966). Stability of adolescents' nominee status, over a one-year period, as a friend by their peers. *Adolescence, 1,* 224–229.

Horrocks, J. E., & Buker, M. E. (1951). A study of friendship fluctuations of preadolescents. *Journal of Genetic Psychology, 78,* 131–144.

Howes, C. (1983). Patterns of friendship. *Child Development, 54,* 1041–1053.

Hunter, F. T. (1985). Individual adolescents' perceptions of interactions with friends and parents. *Journal of Early Adolescence, 5,* 295–305.

Hunter, F. T. & Youniss, J. (1982). Changes in functions of three relations during adolescence. *Developmental Psychology, 18,* 806–811.

Hutter, H. (1978). *Politics as friendship.* Waterloo, Ontario: Wilfrid Laurier University Press.

Jackson, R. M. (1977). Social structure and process in friendship choice. In C. S. Fischer, R. M. Jackson, C. A. Stueve, K. Gerson, L. M. Jones, & M. Baldassare (Eds.), *Networks and places: Social relations in the urban setting* (pp. 59–78). New York: Free Press.

Jackson, R. M., Fischer, C. S., & Jones, L. M. (1977). The dimensions of social networks. In C. S. Fischer et al. (Eds.), *Networks and places: Social relations in the urban setting* (pp. 39–58). New York: Free Press.

Jacobson, D. (1976). Fair weather friend: Label and context in middle class friendships. In W. Arens & S. P. Montague (Eds.), *The American dimension* (pp. 149–160). New York: Alfred Publishing Co.

Jaynes, R. (1967). *Friends! friends! friends!* North Hollywood, CA: Bowmar.

Jessor, R., & Jessor, S. L. (1975). Adolescent development and the onset of drinking. *Journal of Studies on Alcohol, 36,* 27–51.

Johnson, C. L. (1983). Fairweather friends and rainy day kin: An anthropological analysis of old age friendships in the United States. *Urban Anthropology, 12,* 103–123.

Johnson, C., & Catalano, D. (1983). A longitudinal study of family supports. *The Gerontologist, 23,* 612–618.

Johnson, F. L., & Aries, E. J. (1983). Conversational patterns among same-sex pairs of late-adolescent close friends. *The Journal of Genetic Psychology, 142,* 225-238.

Jonas, K. (1979). Factors in development of community among elderly persons in age-segregated housing: Relationships between involvement in friendship roles within the community and external social roles. *Anthropological Quarterly, 52,* 29–38.

Kacerguis, M. A., & Adams, G. R. (1980). Erikson stage resolution: The relationship between identity and intimacy. *Journal of Youth and Adolescence, 9,* 117–126.

Kandel, D. B. (1978a). Homophily, selection, and socialization in adolescent friendships. *American Journal of Sociology, 84,* 427–436.

Kandel, D. B. (1978b). Similarity in real-life adolescent friendship pairs. *Journal of Personality and Social Psychology, 36,* 306–312.

Karweit, N., & Hansell, S. (1983). Sex differences in adolescent relationships: Friendship and status. In J. L. Epstein & N. Karweit (Eds.), *Friends in school* (pp. 115–130). New York: Academic Press.

Keith, P. M., Hill, K., Goudy, W. J., & Powers, E. A. (1984). Confidants and well-being: A note on male friendship in old age. *The Gerontologist, 24,* 318-320.

Kelvin, P. (1977). Predictability, power and vulnerability in interpersonal attraction. In S. Duck (Ed.), *Theory and practice in interpersonal attraction* (pp. 339–354). London: Academic Press.

Knapp, M. L. (1978). *Social intercourse: From greeting to goodbye.* Boston: Allyn and Bacon.

Knapp, M. L., Ellis, D. G., and Williams, B.A. (1980). Perceptions of communication behavior associated with relationship terms. *Communication Monographs, 47,* 262–278.

Knowles, J. (1959). *A separate peace.* New York: Bantam Books.

Kohen, J. A. (1983). Old but not alone: Informal social supports among the elderly by marital status and sex. *The Gerontologist, 23,* 57–63.

Komarovsky, M. (1974). Patterns of self-disclosure of male undergraduates. *Journal of Marriage and the Family, 36,* 677–686.

Komarovsky, M. (1976). *Dilemmas of masculinity: A study of college youth.* New York: Norton.

Kon, I. (1981). Adolescent friendship: Some unanswered questions for future research. In S. Duck and R. Gilmour (Eds.), *Personal relationships 2: Developing personal relationships* (pp. 187-204). New York: Academic Press.

Kon, I., & Losenkov, V. A. (1978). Friendship in adolescence: Values and behavior. *Journal of Marriage and the Family, 40*, 143–55.

Kurth, S. B. (1970). Friendships and friendly relations. In G. J. McCall, M. M. McCall, N. K. Denzin, G. D. Suttles, & S. Kurth (Eds.), *Social relationships* (pp. 136–170). Chicago: Aldine.

La Gaipa, J. J. (1979). A developmental study of the meaning of friendship in adolescence. *Journal of Adolescence, 2*, 201–213.

La Gaipa, J. J. (1981a). A systems approach to personal relationships. In S. Duck & R. Gilmour (Eds.), *Personal relationships: Developing personal relationships 1* (pp. 67–89). New York: Academic Press.

La Gaipa, J. J. (1981b). Children's friendships. In S. Duck & R. Gilmour (Eds.), *Personal relationships 2: Developing personal relationships* (pp. 161–185). New York: Academic Press.

La Gaipa, J. J. (1987). Friendship expectations. In. R. Burnett, P. McGhee, & D. Clarke (Eds.), *Accounting for relationships: Explanation, representation, and knowledge* (pp. 134–157). London: Methuen.

Laing, R. D. (1971). *Self and others*. Middlesex: Penguin.

Laing, R. D. (1972). *The politics of the family*. New York: Vintage.

Larson, R. (1978). Thirty years of research on the subjective well-being of older Americans. *Journal of Gerontology, 33*, 109–125.

Larson, R. W. (1983). Adolescents' daily experience with family and friends: Contrasting opportunity systems. *Journal of Marriage and the Family, 44*, 739–750.

Larson, R. W., & Bradney, N. (1988). Precious moments with family members and friends. In R. M. Milardo (Ed.), *Families and social networks* (pp. 107–126). Newbury Park: Sage.

Larson, R., Zuzanek, J., & Mannelli, R. (1985). Being alone versus being with people: Disengagement in the daily experience of older adults. *Journal of Gerontology, 40*, 375–381.

Laumann, E. O. (1973). *Bond of pluralism: The form and substance of urban social networks*. New York: John Wiley.

Le Guin, U. (1966). *Very far away from anywhere else*. New York: Atheneum.

Lemon, B. W., Bengtson, V. L. & Peterson, J. A. (1972). An exploration of the activity theory of aging: Activity types and life satisfaction among in-movers to a retirement community. *Journal of Gerontology, 27*, 511–523.

Lepp, I. (1966). *The ways of friendship*. New York: Macmillan.

Lever, J. (1976). Sex differences in the games children play. *Social problems, 23*, 478–487.

Levinson, D. J., Darrow, C. N., Klein, E. B., Levinson, M. H., & McKee, B. (1979). *The seasons of a man's life*. New York: Alfred A. Knopf.

Lewis, M., Young, G., Brooks, J., & Michalson, L. (1975). The beginning of friendship. In M. Lewis & L. A. Rosenblum (Eds.), *Friendship and peer relations* (pp. 27–66). New York: John Wiley.

Lewis, R. A. (1978). Emotional intimacy among men. *Journal of Social Issues, 34*, 108–121.

Liebow, E. (1967). *Tally's corner*. Boston: Little & Brown.

Lincoln, J. R., & Miller, J. (1979). Work and friendship ties in organizations: A comparative analysis of relational networks. *Administrative Science Quarterly, 24*, 181–199.

Litwak, E., & Szelenyi, I. (1969). Primary group structures and their functions: Kin, neighbors, and friends. *American Sociological Review, 34, 465–481*.

Lopata, H. Z. (1971). *Occupation: Housewife*. New York: Oxford.

Lopata, H. Z. (1973). Social relations of black and white widowed women in a northern metropolis. *American Journal of Sociology, 78*, 1003–1010.

Lopata, H. Z. (1975). Couple-companionate relationships in marriage and widowhood. In N. Glazer-Malbin (Ed.), *Old family/new family* (pp. 119–149). New York: D. van Nostrand.

Lopata, H. Z. (1979). *Women as widows: Support systems*. New York: Elsevier.

Lopata, H. Z. (1981). Friendship: Historical and theoretical introduction. In H. Z. Lopata & D. Maines (Eds.), *Research in the interweave of social roles: Friendship* (Vol. 2, pp. 1–19). Greenwich, CT: JAI.

Lopata, H. Z. (1988). Support systems of American urban widowhood. *Journal of Social Issues, 44*, 113–128.

Lowenthal, M. F., & Boler, D. (1965). Voluntary vs. involuntary social withdrawal. *Journal of Gerontology, 20*, 363–371.

Lowenthal, M. F., & Haven, C. (1968). Interaction and adaptation: Intimacy as a critical variable. In B. L. Neugarten (Ed.), *Middle age and aging* (pp. 390–400). Chicago: Univ. of Chicago Press.

Maas, H. S., & Kuypers, J. A. (1974). *From thirty to seventy*. San Francisco: Jossey-Bass.

Madden, T. R. (1987). *Women vs. women*. New York: Amacom.

Maines, D. R. (1978). Bodies and selves: Notes on a fundamental dilemma in demography. In N. Denzin (Ed.), *Studies in symbolic interaction* (Vol. 1, pp. 241–265). Greenwich, CT: JAI.

Maines, D. R. (1981). The organizational and career contexts of friendship among postdoctoral students. In H. Z. Lopata & D. Maines (Eds.), *Research in the interweave of social roles: Friendship* (Vol. 2, pp. 171–195). Greenwich, CT: JAI.

Maines, D. R. & Hardesty, M. J. (1987). Temporality and gender: Young adults' career and family plans. *Social Forces 66*, 102–120.

Mancini, J. A. (1980). Friend interaction, competence, and morale in old age. *Research on Aging, 2*, 416–431.

Mannarino, A. P. (1980). The development of children's friendships. In H. C. Foot, A. J. Chapman, & J. R. Smith (Eds.), *Friendship and social relations in children* (pp. 45–63). New York: John Wiley.

Marcia, J. E. (1980). Identity in adolescence. In J. Adelson (Ed.), *Handbook of adolescent psychology* (pp. 159–187). New York: John Wiley.

Margolies, E. (1985). *The best of friends, the worst of enemies*. Garden City, NY: Doubleday.

Marshall, V. W. (1975). Socialization for impending death in a retirement village. *American Journal of Sociology, 8*, 1124–1144.

Matthews, S. H. (1983). Definitions of friendship and their consequences in old age. *Aging and Society, 3,* 141–155.

Matthews, S. H. (1986a). Friendships in old age: Biography and circumstance. In V. W. Marshall (Ed.), *Later Life: The social psychology of aging* (pp. 233–269). Beverly Hills, CA.

Matthews, S. H. (1986b). *Friendships through the life course: Oral biographies in old age.* Beverly Hills, CA: Sage.

Matthis, S. B. (1971). *Sidewalk story.* New York: Viking Press.

May, W. F. (1967). The sin against the friend: Betrayal. *Cross Currents, 17,* 158–170.

Mayer, J. E. (1957). The self-restraint of friends: A mechanism in family transition. *Social Forces, 35,* 230–238.

McAdams, D. P. (1985). Motivation and friendship. In S. Duck & D. Perlman (Eds.), *Understanding Personal Relationships: An Interdisciplinary Program* (pp. 85-105). London: Sage.

McAdams, D. P., & Losoff, M. (1984). Friendship motivation in fourth and sixth grades: A thematic analysis. *Journal of Social and Personal Relationships, 1,* 11–27.

McGuire, K. D., & Weisz, J. R. (1982). Social cognition and behavior correlates of preadolescent chumship. *Child Development, 53,* 1478–1484.

Mead, G. H. (1934). *Mind, self and society.* Chicago: University of Chicago Press.

Mettetal, G. (1983). Fantasy, gossip, and self-disclosure: Children's conversations with friends. In R. N. Bostrom (Ed.), *Communication yearbook 7* (pp. 717–736). Beverly Hills: Sage.

Metts, S., Cupach, W. R., & Bejlovec, R. A. (1989). "I love you too much to ever start liking you": Redefining romantic relationships. *Journal of Social and Personal Relationships 6,* 259–274.

Milardo, R. M., Johnson, M. P., & Huston, T. L. (1983). Developing close relationships: Changing patterns of interaction between pair members and social networks. *Journal of Personality and Social Psychology, 44,* 964–976.

Miles, B. (1958). *Having a friend.* New York: Knopf.

Miller, A. A. (1971). Reactions of friends to divorce. In P. Bohannan (Ed.), *Divorce and after* (pp. 63–86). Garden City, NY: Anchor Books.

Mills, J., & Clark, M. S. (1982). Exchange and communal relationships. In L. Wheeler (Ed.), *Review of personality and social psychology* (Vol. 3, pp. 121–144). Beverly Hills, CA: Sage.

Mitchell, J. J. (1976). Adolescent intimacy. *Adolescence, 11,* 275–280.

Mitchell, J., & Acuff, G. (1982). Family versus friends: Their relative importance as referent others to an aged population. *Sociological Spectrum, 2,* 367–385.

Moncure, J. B. (1976). *A new boy in kindergarten.* Elgin, IL: Child's World.

Montemayor, R., & Van Komen, R. (1985). The development of sex differences in friendship patterns and peer group structure during adolescence. *Journal of Early Adolescence, 5,* 285–294.

Morin, S., & Garfinkle, E. M. (1978). Male homophobia. *Journal of Social Issues, 34,* 29–47.

Myerhoff, B., and Simic, A. (1978). *Life's career—aging: Cultural variations on growing old*. Beverly Hills, CA: Sage.

Naegele, K. D. (1958). Friendship and acquaintances: An exploration of some social distinctions. *Harvard Educational Review, 28*, 232–252.

Neugarten, B. L. (Ed.) (1968). *Middle age and aging: A reader in social psychology*. Chicago: University of Chicago Press.

Neugarten, B. L., and associates. (1964). *Personality in middle and late life*. New York: Atherton.

Newcomb, A. F., & Brady, J. E. (1982). Mutuality in boys' friendship relations. *Child Development, 53*, 392–395.

Newman, B. M., & Newman, P. R. (1975). *Development through life: A psychological approach*. Homewood, IL: Dorsey Press.

Nussbaum, J. F., Thompson, T., & Robinson, J. D. (1989). *Communication and Aging*, New York: Harper & Row.

O'Donnell, W. J. (1976). Adolescent self-esteem related to feelings toward parents and friends. *Journal of Youth and Adolescence, 5*, 179–185.

Olstad, K. (1975). Brave new man: A basis for discussion. In J. Petras (Ed.), *Sex: Male/gender: Masculine*. Port Washington, NY: Alfred.

Oliker, S. J. (1989). *Best friends and marriage: Exchange among women*. Berkeley: University of California Press.

Paine, R. (1969). In search of friendship: An exploratory analysis in "middle-class" culture. *Man, 4*, 505–524.

Paine, R. (1970). Anthropological approaches to friendship. *Humanitas, 6*, 139–159.

Paine, R. (1974). An exploratory analysis in "middle-class" culture. In E. Leyton (Ed.), *The compact: Selected dimensions of friendship* (pp. 117–137). St. John's: Institute of Social and Economic Research.

Parker, S. R. (1964). Type of work, friendship patterns, and leisure. *Human Relations, 17*, 215–220.

Parsons, E. C. (1915). Friendship, a social category. *American Journal of Sociology, 21*, 230–233.

Pearlin, L. I. (1980). Life strains and psychological distress among adults. In N. J. Smelser & E. H. Erikson (Eds.), *Themes of work and love in adulthood* (pp. 174–192). Cambridge, MA: Harvard University Press.

Peevers, B. H., & Secord, P. F. (1973). Developmental changes in attribution of descriptive concepts to persons. *Journal of Personality and Social Psychology, 27*, 120–128.

Perlman, D. (1988). Loneliness: A life-span, family perspective. In R. M. Milardo (Ed.), *Families and Social Networks* (pp. 190–220). Newbury Park: Sage.

Peters, G. R., & Kaiser, M. A. (1985). The role of friends and neighbors in providing social support. In W. J. Sauer & R. T. Coward (Eds.), *Social support networks and the care of the elderly* (pp. 123–158). New York: Springer.

Peters, G. R., & Kennedy, C. A. (1970). Close friendships in the college community. *The Journal of College Student Personnel, 11*, 449–456.

Petrowsky, M. (1976). Marital status, sex, and the social networks of the elderly. *Journal of Marriage and the Family, 5*, 749–756.

Piaget, J. (1932). *The moral judgement of the child*. New York: Harcourt Press.

Pihlblad, C., & Adams, D. L. (1972). Widowhood, social participation and life satisfaction. *International Journal of Aging and Human Development, 3,* 323–330.

Pleck, J. H. (1975). Man to man: Is brotherhood possible? In N. Glazer-Malbin (Ed.), *Old family/new family* (pp. 229–244). New York: D. Van Nostrand.

Powers, E. A., & Bultena, G. L. (1976). Sex differences in intimate friendships of old age. *Journal of Marriage and the Family, 38,* 739–749.

Putallaz, M., & Gottman, J. M. (1981). Social skills and group acceptance. In S. R. Asher & J. M. Gottman (Eds.), *The development of children's friendships* (pp. 116–149). Cambridge: Cambridge University Press.

Rake, J. M. (1970). Friendship: A fundamental description of its subjective dimension. *Humanitas, 6,* 161–176.

Rangell, L. (1963). On friendship. *Journal of the American Psychoanalytic Association, 11,* 3–54.

Rawlins, W. K. (1982). Cross-sex friendship and the communicative management of sex-role expectations. *Communication Quarterly, 30,* 343–352.

Rawlins, W. K. (1983a). Negotiating close friendships: The dialectic of conjunctive freedoms. *Human Communication Research, 9,* 255–266.

Rawlins, W. K. (1983b). Openness as problematic in ongoing friendships: Two conversational dilemmas. *Communication Monographs, 50,* 1–13.

Rawlins, W. K. (1985). Stalking interpersonal communication effectiveness: Social, individual or situational intergration? In T. W. Benson (Ed.), *Speech communication in the twentieth century* (pp. 109–129). Carbondale: Southern Illinois University Press.

Rawlins, W. K. (1989a). A dialectical analysis of the tensions, functions and strategic challenges of communication in young adult friendships. In J. A. Anderson (Ed.), *Communication yearbook 12* (pp. 157–189). Newbury, CA: Sage.

Rawlins, W. K. (1989b). Cultural double agency and the pursuit of friendship. *Cultural Dynamics, 2,* 28–40.

Rawlins, W. K. (1989c). *Boys and girls as friends versus boyfriends and girlfriends: Adolescents' conceptions of cross-sex relationships*. Paper presented at the meeting of the Speech Communication Association, San Francisco.

Rawlins, W. K. (1991). On enacting friendship and interrogating discourse. In K. Tracy (Ed.), *Understanding face-to-face interaction: Issues linking goals and discourse* (pp. 101–115). New York: Lawrence Erlbaum.

Rawlins, W. K., & Holl, M. (1987). The communicative achievement of friendship during adolescence: Predicaments of trust and violation. *The Western Journal of Speech Communication, 51,* 345–363.

Rawlins, W. K., & Holl, M. (1988). Adolescents' interactions with parents and friends: Dialectics of temporal perspective and evaluation. *Journal of Social and Personal Relationships, 5,* 27–46.

Rawlins, W. K., Leibowitz, K., & Bochner, A. P. (1986). Affective and instrumental dimensions of best, equal, and unequal friendships. *Central States Speech Journal, 37,* 90–101.

Reisman, J. M. (1981). Adult friendships. In S. Duck & R. Gilmour (Eds.),

Personal relationships 2: Developing personal relationships (pp. 205–230). London: Academic Press.

Retsinas, J., & Garrity, P. (1985). Nursing home friendships. *The Gerontologist, 25,* 376–381.

Richey, M. H., & Richey, H. W. (1980). The significance of best-friend relationships in adolescence. *Psychology in the Schools, 17,* 536–540.

Ricoeur, P. (1970). *Freud and philosophy: An essay on interpretation* (D. Savage, Trans.). New Haven: Yale University Press.

Riegel, K. F. (1976). The dialectics of human development. *American Psychologist, 31,* 689–700.

Rieger-Shlonsky, H. (1969). The conceptualization of the roles of a relative, a friend, and a neighbour. *Human Relations, 22,* 355-369.

Riesman, D. (1961). *The lonely crowd.* New Haven & London: Yale University Press.

Roberto, K. A., & Kimboko, P. J. (1989). Friendships in later life: Definitions and maintenance patterns. *International Journal of Aging and Human Development, 28,* 9–19.

Roberto, K. A., & Scott, J. P. (1984-85). Friendship patterns among older women. *International Journal of Aging and Human Development, 19,* 1–10.

Roberto, K. A., & Scott, J. P. (1986a). Equity considerations in the friendships of older adults. *Journal of Gerontology, 41,* 241–274.

Roberto, K. A., & Scott, J. P. (1986b). Friendships of older men and women: Exchange patterns and satisfaction. *Psychology and Aging, 1,* 103–109.

Rook, K. S. (1989). Strains in older adults' friendships. In R. G. Adams & R. Blieszner (Eds.), *Older adult friendship* (pp. 166–194). Newbury Park: Sage.

Rose, S. M. (1984). How friendships end: Patterns among young adults. *Journal of Social and Personal Relationships, 1,* 267–277.

Rose, S. M. (1985). Same- and cross-sex friendships and the psychology of homosociality. *Sex Roles, 12,* 63–74.

Rose, S., & Serafica, F. C. (1986). Keeping and ending casual, close and best friendships. *Journal of Social and Personal Relationships, 3,* 275–288.

Rosow, I. (1970). Old people: Their friends and neighbors. *American Behavioral Scientist, 14,* 59–69.

Rossi, I. (1983). *From the sociology of symbols to the sociology of signs.* New York: Columbia University Press.

Rotenberg, K. J. (1986). Same-sex patterns and sex differences in the trust-value basis of children's friendship. *Sex Roles, 15,* 613–626.

Rubenstein, C., & Rubin, C. (1984). Children's fantasies of interaction with same and opposite sex peers. In T. Field, J. L. Roopnarine, & M. Segal (Eds.), *Friendships in normal and handicapped children* (pp. 99-124). Norwood, NJ: Ablex.

Rubenstein, C., Shaver, P., & Peplau, L. A. (1979). Loneliness. *Human Nature* (February), 58–65.

Rubin, L. B. (1975). *Just friends: The role of friendship in our lives.* New York: Harper & Row.

Rubin, Z. (1980). *Children's friendships*. Cambridge, MA: Harvard University Press.

Rubin, Z., Peplau, L. A., & Hill, C. T. (1980). Loving and leaving: Sex differences in romantic attachments. *Sex Roles, 6*, 821–835.

Ryder, R. G., Kafka, J. S., & Olson, D. H. (1971). Separating and joining influences in courtship and early marriage. *American Journal of Orthopsychiatry, 41*, 450–464.

Sampson, E. E. (1977). Psychology and the American ideal. *Journal of Personality and Social Psychology, 35*, 767–782.

Sants, H. (1984). Conceptions of friendship, social behaviour and school achievement in six-year-old children. *Journal of Social and Personal Relationships, 1*, 293–309.

Sapadin, L. A. (1988). Friendship and gender: Perspectives of professional men and women. *Journal of Social and Personal Relationships, 5*, 387–403.

Schofield, J. W. (1981). Complementary and conflicting identities: Images and interaction in an interracial school. In S. R. Asher & J. M. Gottman (Eds.), *The development of children's friendships* (pp. 53–90). Cambridge: Cambridge University Press.

Schutz, A. (1970). Interactional relationships. In H. R. Wagner (Ed.), *Alfred Schutz on phenomenology and social relations* (pp. 163-199). Chicago: University of Chicago Press.

Seiden, A. M., & Bart, P. B. (1975). Woman to woman: Is sisterhood powerful? In N. Glazer-Malbin (Ed.), *Old family/new family* (pp. 189–228). New York: D. Van Nostrand.

Selman, R. L. (1976). Toward a structural analysis of developing interpersonal relations concepts: Research with normal and disturbed preadolescent boys. In A. D. Pick (Ed.), *Minnesota Symposia on Child Psychology* (Vol. 10, pp. 156–200). Minneapolis: University of Minnesota Press.

Selman, R. L. (1981). The child as a friendship philosopher. In S. R. Asher & J. M. Gottman (Eds.), *The development of children's friendships* (pp. 242–272). Cambridge: Cambridge University Press.

Sennett, R. (1978). *The fall of public man*. New York: Vintage.

Shantz, C. U. (1975). The development of social cognition. In E. M. Hetherington (Ed.), *Review of child development research* (Vol. 5). Chicago: University of Chicago Press.

Sharabany, R., Gershoni, R., & Hofman, J. E. (1981). Girlfriend, boyfriend: Age and sex differences in intimate friendship. *Developmental Psychology, 17*, 800–808.

Shaver, P., Furman, W., & Buhrmester, D. (1985). Transition to college: Network changes, social skills, and loneliness. In S. Duck & D. Perlman (Eds.), *Understanding personal relationships: An interdisciplinary approach* (pp. 193–219). London: Sage.

Shea, L., Thompson, L., & Blieszner, R. (1988). Resources in older adults' old and new friendships. *Journal of Social and Personal Relationships, 5*, 83–96.

Sheehy, G. (1974). *Passages: Predictable crises of adult life*. New York: Dutton.

Sherman, S. R. (1975). Patterns of contacts for residents of age-segregated and age-integrated housing. *Journal of Gerontology, 30,* 103–107.

Shulman, N. (1975). Life-cycle variations in patterns of close relationships. *Journal of Marriage and the Family, 37,* 813–820.

Smollar, J., & Youniss, J. (1982). Social development through friendship. In K. H. Rubin & H. S. Ross (Eds.), *Peer relationships and social skills in childhood* (pp. 279–298). New York: Springer-Verlag.

Snyder, M., & Smith, D. (1986). Personality and friendship: The friendship worlds of self-monitoring. In V. J. Derlega & B. A. Winstead (Eds.), *Friendship and social interaction* (pp. 63–80). New York: Springer-Verlag.

Spakes, P. R. (1979). Family, friendship, and community interaction as related to life satisfaction of the elderly. *Journal of Gerontological Social Work, 1,* 279–293.

Spanier, G. B., & Thompson, L. (1984). *Parting: The aftermath of separation and divorce.* Beverly Hills: Sage.

Stephens, M. A. P., & Bernstein, M. D. (1984). Social support and well-being among residents of planned housing. *The Gerontologist, 24,* 144–148.

Stoller, E. P. (1990). Males as helpers: The role of sons, relatives, and friends. *The Gerontologist, 30,* 228–235.

Stoller, E. P., & Earl, L. L. (1983). Help with activities of everyday life: Sources of support for the noninstitutionalized elderly. *The Gerontologist, 23,* 64–70.

Stolz, M. S. (1980a). *Cider days.* New York: Harper & Row.

Stolz, M. S. (1980b). *Ferris wheel.* New York: Harper & Row.

Strain, L. A., & Chappell, N. L. (1982). Confidants: Do they make a difference in quality of life? *Research on Aging, 4,* 479–502.

Stueve, C. A., & Gerson, K. (1977). Personal relations across the life-cycle. In C. S. Fischer, R. M. Jackson, C. A. Stueve, K. Gerson, L. M. Jones, & M. Baldassare (Eds.), *Networks and places* (pp. 79–98). New York: Free Press.

Sukosky, D. G. (1977). Sociological factors of friendship: Relevance for the aged. *Journal of Gerontological Nursing, 3,* 25–29.

Sullivan, H. S. (1953). *The interpersonal theory of psychiatry.* New York: Norton.

Sullivan, H. S. (1965). *Personal psychopathology.* New York: Norton.

Suttles, G. D. (1970). Friendship as a social institution. In G. J. McCall, M. McCall, N. K. Denzin, G. D. Suttles, & S. Kurth (Eds.), *Social relationships* (pp. 95–135). Chicago: Aldine.

Swidler, A. (1980). Love and adulthood in American culture. In N. J. Smelser & E. H. Erikson (Eds.), *Themes of work and love in adulthood* (pp. 120–147). Cambridge, MA: Harvard University Press.

Szwed, J. F. (1969). The mask of friendship: Mumming as a ritual of social relations. In H. Halpert & G. M. Story (Eds.), *Christmas mumming in Newfoundland* (pp. 105–118). Toronto: University of Toronto Press.

Taylor, E. (1975). *Mrs. Palfrey at the claremont.* New York: The Dial Press.

Tesch, S. A., & Martin, R. R. (1983). Friendship concepts of young adults in two age groups. *The Journal of Psychology, 115,* 7–12.

Tesch, S., Whitbourne, S. K., & Nehrke, M. F. (1981). Friendship, social interaction, and subjective well-being of older men in an institutional setting. *International Journal of Aging and Human Development, 13,* 317–327.

Thorne, B. (1986). Girls and boys together . . . but mostly apart: Gender arrangements in elementary schools. In W. W. Hartup & Z. Rubin (Eds.), *Relationships and development* (pp. 167–184). Hillsdale, NJ: Lawrence Erlbaum.

Tognoli, J. (1980). Male friendship and intimacy across the life span. *Family Relations, 29*, 273–279.

Tokuno, K. A. (1983). Friendship and transition in early adulthood. *The Journal of Genetic Psychology, 143*, 207–216.

Tokuno, K. A. (1986). The early adult transition and friendships: Mechanisms of support. *Adolescence, 21*, 593–606.

Townsend, M. A., McCracken, H. E., & Wilton, K. M. (1988). Popularity and intimacy as determinants of psychological well-being in adolescent friendships. *Journal of Early Adolescence, 8*, 421–436.

Udry, J. M. (1961). *Let's be enemies*. New York: Harper & Row.

Usui, W. M. (1984). Homogeneity of friendship networks of elderly blacks and whites. *Journal of Gerontology, 39*, 350–356.

Vaillant, G. E. (1977). *Adaptation to life*. Boston: Little, Brown & Company.

Van Vlissingen, J. F. (1970). Friendship in history. *Humanitas, 6*, 225–238.

Verbrugge, L. M. (1979). Multiplexity in adult friendships. *Social Forces, 57*, 1286–1309.

Verbrugge, L. M. (1983). A research note on adult friendship contact: A dyadic perspective. *Social Forces, 62*, 78–83.

Wallerstein, J. S., & Kelly, J. B. (1980). *Surviving the breakup: How children and parents cope with divorce*. New York: Basic Books.

Weiss, L., & Lowenthal, M. F. (1973). Perceptions and complexities of friendship in four stages of the adult life cycle. *Proceedings of the 81st annual convention of the American psychological association*, Vol. 8 (pp. 773–774).

Weiss, L., & Lowenthal, M. F. (1975). Life-course perspectives on friendship. In M. F. Lowenthal et al. (Eds.), *Four stages of life* (pp. 48–61). San Francisco: Jossey-Bass.

Wells, S. (1985). *The dialectics of representation*. Baltimore: Johns Hopkins University Press.

Wentowski, G. J. (1981). Reciprocity and the coping strategies of older people: Cultural dimensions of network building. *The Gerontologist, 21*, 600–609.

Werebe, M. J. G. (1987). Friendship and dating relationships among French adolescents. *Journal of Adolescence, 10*, 269–289.

Wheeler, L., Reis, H., & Nezlek, J. (1983). Loneliness, social interaction, and sex roles. *Journal of Personality and Social Psychology, 45*, 943–953.

Whyte, W. H., Jr. (1956). *The organization man*. New York: Simon & Schuster.

Wilensky, H. L. (1961). Life cycle, work situation, and participation in formal associations. In R. Kleemeier (Ed.), *Aging and leisure* (pp. 215–241). New York: Oxford.

Wilensky, H. L. (1968). Orderly careers and social participation: The impact of work history on social integration in the middle mass. In B. L. Neugarten (Ed.), *Middle age and aging: A reader in social psychology* (pp. 321–340). Chicago & London: University of Chicago Press.

Williams, D. G. (1985). Gender, masculinity-femininity, and emotional intimacy in same-sex friendship. *Sex Roles, 12*, 587–600.

Williams, J. H. (1958). Close friendship relations of housewives residing in an urban community. *Social Forces, 36*, 358–362.

Williams, R. M., Jr., (1959). Friendship and social values in a suburban community: An exploratory study. *The Pacific Sociological Review, 2*, 3–10.

Wiseman, J. P. (1986). Friendship: Bonds and binds in a voluntary relationship. *Journal of Social and Personal Relationships, 3*, 191–211.

Wood, V., & Robertson, J. F. (1978). Friendship and kinship interaction: Differential effect on the morale of the elderly. *Journal of Marriage and the Family, 40*, 367–375.

Wright, P. H. (1982). Men's friendships, women's friendships, and the alleged inferiority of the latter. *Sex Roles, 8*, 1–20.

Wright, P. H. (1984). Self-referent motivation and the intrinsic quality of friendship. *Journal of Social and Personal Relationships, 1*, 115–130.

Wright, P. H. (1985). The acquaintance description form. In S. Duck & D. Perlman (Eds.), *Understanding personal relationships: An interdisciplinary approach* (pp. 39–62). London: Sage.

Wright, P. (1989). Gender differences in adults' same- and cross-gender friendships. In R. G. Adams & R. Blieszner (Eds.), *Older adult friendship* (pp. 197–221). Newbury Park: Sage.

Wright, P. H., & Keple, T. W. (1981). Friends and parents of a sample of high school juniors: An exploratory study of relationship intensity and interpersonal rewards. *Journal of Marriage and the Family, 43*, 559–570.

Youniss, J. (1978). Dialectical theory and Piaget on social knowledge. *Human Development, 21*, 234–247.

Youniss, J. (1980). *Parents and peers in social development.* Chicago: University of Chicago Press.

Youniss, J., & Smollar, J. (1985). *Adolescent relations with mothers, fathers, and friends.* Chicago: University of Chicago Press.

Youniss, J., & Volpe, J. (1978). A relational analysis of children's friendship. In W. Damon (Ed.), *New directions for child development 1* (pp. 1–22). San Francisco: Jossey-Bass.

Yuan, Y. (1975). Affectivity and instrumentality in friendship patterns among American women. In D. Raphael (Ed.), *Being female* (pp. 87–98). Hague & Paris: Mouton.

Zborowski, M., & Eyde, L. D. (1962). Aging and social participation. *Journal of Geronotology, 17*, 424–430.

Index